AF880985

GLOBAL DRUGS LAW

GLOBAL DRUGS LAW

Selected papers presented at
the Indian Law Institute/UNDCP/
International Law Association, Regional Branch, India
International Conference on Global Drugs Law,
New Delhi, 28 February – 3 March 1997

Editors

D. C. JAYASURIYA
R. K. NAYAK
A. WELLS

HAR-ANAND
PUBLICATIONS PVT LTD

Har-Anand Publications Pvt Ltd
364-A, Chirag Delhi, New Delhi-110017

Copyright © Indian Law Institute and UNDCP, 1997

All rights reserved. No part of this publication may be reproduced in any form without the prior written permission of the publishers.

PRINTED IN INDIA

Published by Ashok Gosain & Ashish Gosain for Har-Anand Publications Pvt Ltd.
Typeset at S.S. Computers and printed at Nice Printing Press, New Delhi.

FOREWORD

Hon'ble Justice J.S. Verma
Chief Justice of India

Drug abuse has assumed frightening proportions and has become a global menace. It has a deleterious effect on society and contributes to depravity on a large scale. On the one hand, there is growing awareness of human dignity and the need for improving the human stock while, on the other, drug abuse poses a serious threat to its very existence. This is a major challenge of the times. Drug addiction adversely affects all-round development and reduces the efficacy of the efforts being made to secure social and economic development. No time can be lost in finding lasting solutions to check the menace of drug abuse.

In addition to curative measures to meet the challenge of drug abuse, effort is needed to devise effective measures to prevent its growth. An effective preventive measure is to check the availability of illicit drugs for which stringent measures to curb drug trafficking are essential. Like illegal activities, illegal drug trafficking promotes criminalisation which, in turn, results in the criminalisation of society. Deterrent action is called for to meet the challenge.

Drug abuse being a global phenomenon, it is necessary for the international community to develop a coordinated action plan. Illicit drug trafficking transcends national barriers and requires greater emphasis on the UN drug control conventions and international co-operation. This alone can have a lasting impact.

The New Delhi Charter on Global Drugs Law emphasizes the need for evolving suitable strategies and revamping the criminal justice systems to meet the challenge of drug abuse, encouraging the development of proper mechanisms for mutual legal assistance and other forms of international co-operation, so as to make the law an instrument of social change. We must strive towards a drug free society. The International Conference held in New Delhi was an attempt in that direction.

Let us hope that the International Conference papers contained in the book will serve as a guide to the governments and international organisations the world over in meeting the challenge of this global menace to modern society.

I offer my best wishes for the success of this endeavour.

New Delhi
31 July 1997

EDITORIAL ADVISORY BOARD

PRESIDENT

Hon'ble Mr. Justice. J. S. Verma
Chief Justice of India
and
President, The Indian Law Institute

VICE PRESIDENT

Mr. R. K. Anand
Senior Advocate
Vice President, The Indian Law Institute

MEMBERS

Hon'ble Mr. Justice Ashok Desai
Judge
Bombay High Court

Mr. P.H. Parekh
Advocate/Organizing Secretary,
International Law Association,
Regional Branch, India

Mr. Koli Kouame
Director a. i.
UNDCP Regional Office
for South Asia
New Delhi

Mr. Rakesh Munjal
Advocate
Supreme Court of India

EDITORS

Dr. D .C. Jayasuriya
Regional Project Coordinator
Precursor Control Project
UNDCP Regional Office
for South Asia
New Delhi

Professor R. K. Nayak
Secretary General,
International Conference
on Global Drugs Law and
Member, Governing Council
The Indian Law Institute
New Delhi

Mr. Andrew Wells
Senior Legal Adviser
UNDCP
Vienna

PREFACE

This volume is a collection of the papers presented at the International Conference on Global Drugs Law, jointly organized by the Indian Law Institute (ILI), the United Nations International Drug Control Programme (UNDCP) and the International Law Association (India Regional Branch). The Conference was held in New Delhi from 28 February - 3 March 1997, and was attended by a large number of foreign and Indian participants and observers. It was the first of its kind to look at the following issues from a world-wide perspective:

a) Upgrading justice systems to meet the drug challenge beyond the year 2000;
b) Overcoming inter-legal system obstacles to international legal co-operation;
c) Increasing the use and effectiveness of mutual legal assistance and other forms of international legal co-operation; and
d) Improving national justice system impact.

In addition to the papers, the volume also contains the text of the speeches made at the Opening Ceremony and the text of the Valedictory Address. Among these are the speeches of the then Vice President of India, Hon'ble Mr.K.R. Narayanan; the then Prime Minister of India, Hon'ble Mr. H.D. Deve Gowda; the then Chief Justice of India and the President of the ILI, Hon'ble Mr. A.M. Ahmadi and the Executive Director of UNDCP, Mr. Giorgio Giacomelli.

The deliberations of the Conference culminated in the adoption of the *New Delhi Charter on Global Drugs Law*, the text of which is also reproduced.

The Conference preceded two important events—the release of the inaugural issue of the *World Drug Report* on 26 June 1997 (the International Day Against Drug Abuse and Illicit Trafficking) and the preparatory meetings leading up to the United Nations General Assembly Special Session on Drugs scheduled for June 1998.

In order to enable the papers presented at the Conference and the New Delhi Charter to receive due consideration in the context of the forthcoming Special Session of the United Nations General Assembly, it was decided by ILI and UNDCP to accord priority to the publication of selected papers in the form of this volume. In order not to delay publication, the selected papers are reproduced here substantially in the form in which they were originally submitted, or revised after the Conference, without the references and citations being edited to maintain uniformity.

Due to space limitations, not all the papers presented at the Conference are included in this volume, in their entirety or in abstract form. Some papers that were published in the Conference Souvenir are also not reproduced.

Needless to add, the papers in this volume reflect the views of the individual authors and not those of the ILI or UNDCP.

The editors wish to acknowledge, with thanks, the assistance provided by Mr. Pramod Singh of the ILI in compiling the index and by Ms. Maureen Sachdev of UNDCP and Ms. Neena Bhatia of the ILI in typing the manuscript.

UNDCP, New Delhi, India — D.C. Jayasuriya
ILI, New Delhi, India — R.K. Nayak
UNDCP, Vienna, Austria — Andrew Wells

CONTENTS

Foreword 5

Preface 7

PART I
TEXT OF SPEECHES AT OPENING CEREMONY AND VALEDICTORY ADDRESS

Welcome Speech Delivered by the Executive Chairman 17
R. K. Anand

Presidential Speech Delivered by the Hon'ble Chief Justice of India 21
A. M. Ahmadi

Statement on behalf of UNDCP 26
Mr. Francesco Bastagli, Director, Treaty Implementation and Policy Development Division, UNDCP on behalf of Mr. Giorgio Giacomelli, Executive Director of UNDCP

Inaugural Speech Delivered by the Hon'ble Vice-President of India 30
K.R. Narayanan

Speech on the Agenda Delivered by Conference Secretary-General 34
R. K. Nayak

Vote of Thanks 37
P.H. Parekh

Valedictory Address Delivered by the Hon'ble Prime Minister of India 40
H.D. Deve Gowda

PART II
OVERVIEW: INTERNATIONAL

International Drug Control: Recent Developments, Patterns and Trends 45
Andrew Wells

International Legal and Policy Framework for Drug Control 53
Andrew Wells

Evolving Global Drugs Law for the 21st Century 69
R. K. Nayak

International Effort to Combat Illicit Drugs: The British View 82
Derek Plumbly

International Legal Co-operation against Serious Crime 88
Dianne Stafford

Breaking Down the Barriers: International Co-operation in Combating Transnational Crime 99
Kimberly Prost

International Mutual Legal Assistance and Other Forms of International Legal Co-operation 114
Jan d'Oliveira

Counter-Narcotics Law Enforcement Co-operation: A Necessity 131
Michael E. Fredericks

Establishing Priorities and Policies to Enable the Criminal Justice System to Respond Most Effectively to the Requirement of Drug Control 136
Herman Woltring

PART III
OVERVIEW: NATIONAL

Criminal Justicing in India to Control the Drug Menace 145
Ashok A. Desai

India's Drug Laws - A Survey 147
A. Abdul Hadi

Drugs Scenario: Overview 152
Rakesh Munjal

Possession and Trafficking of Drugs and the Indian Judiciary 154
Raghunath Patnaik and B.B. Panda

Drugs, the Saviour Versus Drugs, the Killer: Arena - Life and Law 155
Susanta Chatterji

Convictions for Drug-Related Offences: A Socio-Legal Study 157
Daljeet Singh and Subhash Sharma

Drug Addiction and Adolescents 162
Meena H. Rao

Legislative and Administrative Measures for Prevention of Drug Abuse in Pakistan 163
Sajjad Ali Shah

American Drug Courts: A Common Sense Approach to the Drug-using Offender 168
Jeffrey Tauber

Confiscation and Money Laundering in the U.K. 180
Kennedy Talbot

Canada's Proceeds of Crime Legislation: An Overview 191
D.D. Graham Reynolds

Drug Abuse Laws of Botswana 205
P.T.C. Skelemani

M.D.M.A. ('ECSTASY') in Italy: Epidemiology, Policy and Legal Aspects 209
Angelo Zaglio

Drug Policy and Drug Culture: National Experiences from the United States and Micronesia 211
Marke E. Wojcik

PART IV
SPECIFIC ISSUES

The Criminal Justice System and the Treatment of Drug Misuse 229
Hamid Ghodse

Accessibility to Pain Killers and International Drug Control Treaties 235
D.C. Jayasuriya

The Second Objective of Drug Control Laws 241
Tokuo Yoshida

WHO's Role in International Harmonization of Pharmaceutical Legislation and Regulations 243
Agathe Wehrli

Money Laundering: International Efforts and Recent Developments in the Movement of Drug-Related Money 245
Nara Srinivasan and Roderic Underwood

Black Hawala, Financial Crimes and the World Drug Trade 261
Patrick Jost

The Forty Recommendations of the Financial Action Task Force on Money Laundering 281

An Overview of the Global Money Laundering Problem, International Anti-Money Laundering Standards and the Work of the Financial Action Task Force 291
Rick McDonell

Drug Trafficking: Confiscation, Forfeiture of Assets and Money Laundering 305
M. Zakaria Siddiqi

Money Laundering 321
Bishwajit Bhattacharyya

Controlled Delivery 326
Nihal Jayasinghe

The Drug Trade and Police Corruption 329
B.S.J. O'Keefe

The Scourge of Drugs 345
Frank Elbe

Drug Use and Human Rights 348
Norbert Gilmore

Harm Minimization - Engaging Police 370
Steve Allsop and Roger Nicholas

Promoting Harm Minimization: The Ongoing Antipodean Debate about Drug Law Reform 380
Duncan Chappell

Towards Prosecuting the Illicit Drug Traffickers Before the Proposed International Criminal Court - A Challenge Beyond 2000 395
Narayana Rao Rampilla

Prevention and Control of Drug Abuse Among Children 404
Hira Singh

Drugs-Related Crime and Criminal Justice System - A Gender Analysis 412
Mala Kapur Shankardass

Adolescents at Risk: Low Socioeconomic Status and Early Onset Drug Use in the U.S. 414
Geoffrey M. Curran and Helene R. White

PART V

NEW DELHI CHARTER ON GLOBAL DRUGS LAW

PART VI

ANNEXURES

Annexure 1 - International Advisory Conmittee 441
Annexure 2 - Organizing Conmittee 442
Annexure 3 - Agenda 444
Annexure 4 - List of Delegates 447

Index 465

PART I

TEXT OF SPEECHES AT OPENING CEREMONY AND VALEDICTORY ADDRESS

WELCOME SPEECH DELIVERED BY THE EXECUTIVE CHAIRMAN

R.K. Anand

In the next few days, we shall embark upon to deliberate on what, I am sure, all of us perceive, as perhaps one of the most serious threats to society. I am, of course, referring to "Drugs." There are primarily two dimensions, which come to my mind relating to the issue in question. Firstly, "Drug Trafficking" and secondly, "Drug Abuse and Drug Addiction." Together these two have acquired proportions which may well make them perhaps the most lethal socio-economic malaise to affect mankind in the century that awaits us. I am certainly not over emphasizing when I say that all nations, including us here in India, do see drug abuse and drug trafficking as a major threat to the socio-economic fibre of our society.

India, by the very nature of its location on the global map is surrounded on at least three sides by illegal drug production areas namely, the Golden Crescent on the west and the Golden Triangle on the east and finally, the extensive border that India shares with Nepal, an area also used extensively for the cultivation of cannabis. Although, initially, the importance of India with respect to its geographical location was primarily to the extent of it being a transit point for the products generated by both the Golden Crescent and the Golden Triangle for the movement of the drugs, by the 1980's India had developed into a fairly big base for providing a domestic market for narcotics, specially heroin and morphine, which, by now, has assumed alarming proportions, not only crippling those who are dependent upon it, thus laying bare the social fabric, but also posing a serious threat to the economy owing to the fact that immense profits are derived from this illicit drug trafficking which has a direct effect on making the economy dependent on the trade and thus eventually endangering the political stability of the nation itself.

I must confess that I carry with me only a peripheral knowledge of the social and cultural aspects relating to drug abuse especially in the presence of eminent academicians, social scientists and other experts who, I am sure, will enlighten us in the coming days with respect to the devastating effects that the abuse and trafficking of drugs have caused to our social system and strata within our society and with respect to preventive and curative measures like de-addiction and rehabilitation.

As far as the role of law regarding illegal drug trafficking and consumption is concerned, suffice it to say that drug trafficking is most certainly not a national phenomenon. It transcends the boundaries of national laws, international conventions and comprises a horde of other criminal offences such as banking law violations, tax evasions and illegal money transfers. Consequently, it requires international participation in terms of legislation, enforcement, coordination and sharing of information, particularly with specialist agencies like the UNDCP, in order to curb this menace.

India has always been responsive to the problems of drug abuse and trafficking and we have had legislation as early as the Opium Act of 1857 and the Opium Act of 1878 to prove the same. The Dangerous Drugs Act, 1930 was introduced to tackle the menace of narcotics etc. However, as happens with old legislation, they lost significance and teeth with the passage of time as new forms of drug abuse emerged on the national scenario coupled with the most ingenious methodology used by the drug traffickers. The law-makers sensing the need to introduce new legislation in this arena to combat the growing menace of narcotics, passed the NDPS Act, 1985 which was also a result of India's participation in various international conventions in this area and its commitment to enforce the guidelines agreed upon in the said conventions.

The NDPS Act consolidated and repealed the two Opium Acts and the Dangerous Drugs Act. A bare perusal of the various sections of this Act is an indication of the national government's commitment and firm decision to eradicate and prevent the illegal drug trafficking and increasing abuse of drugs in India. This Act imposes a blanket ban on the cultivation of coca plant, opium, poppy or cannabis plant or of production, manufacturing, possession, sale, purchase, transport, using and consumption etc. of any narcotic drugs or psychotropic substances except for medical or scientific purposes. The penalty for violating the same is a minimum of ten years' imprisonment and a fine of Rs. 1 lakh which can be extended upto thirty years and a fine of Rs. 3 lakhs and even the death penalty.

As a follow up action, the Narcotics Control Bureau was set up in May, 1986 as the primary enforcement agency to deal exclusively with drug related offences. This high powered body is headed by a Director General having direct liaison with the United Nations Narcotic Control Board and other international agencies working against drug trafficking.

Apart from establishing the Narcotics Control Bureau, a number of other enforcement agencies have been providing effective support with the Narcotics Control Bureau acting as the nodal agency to enforce the law namely, the Central Excise, Customs, Border Security Force, CBI, Directorate of Revenue Intelligence and Food and Drug Control Officers.

We also have legislation such as the Prevention of Illegal Trafficking in Narcotic Drugs and Psychotropic Substances Act, 1988 which provides for preventive detention of persons involved in drug trafficking in order to prevent them from illicit trafficking in narcotic drugs and psychotropic substances.

The amended Drugs and Cosmetics Act, 1940 and Rules, 1945 *inter alia* provide for deterrent punishment and more stringent control over the manufacture, sale, distribution, etc. of psychotropic substances. The Government of India has banned the import, manufacture and sale of all methaqualone as far back as 1984. The provisions of the Conservation of Foreign Exchange and Prevention of Smuggling Activities Act 1974 are also applied to the detention of narcotic smugglers wherever justified.

As I have mentioned earlier, drug trafficking offences and other drug related crimes generate huge illicit funds which are used to support other criminal activities such as smuggling of foreign currency, illicit arms trading etc. To curb the utilisation of ill-gotten profits from the drug trade and to provide an effective deterrent to the drug traffickers, in 1976 India enacted specific legislation providing for the forfeiture of property and assets of smugglers including traffickers and foreign exchange manipulators. Smugglers and Foreign Exchange Manipulators (Forfeiture of Property) Act provides for the forfeiture of illegally acquired property and assets of smugglers and drug traffickers.

The provisions of the Foreign Exchange Regulation Act, 1973 also deserve a special mention as they not only control payment in foreign exchange but most importantly payment in Indian currencies as well. This latter payment is intended to counter what we call compensatory payments i.e. what is locally known as *Hawala*.

I feel these laws are essential because as long as the funds generated by drug trafficking are allowed to be laundered and put back into economy, the trade will flourish, the economy will weaken and the political stability of the nation will suffer. It is a well-known fact that money laundering is not a new activity. However, the ominously growing drug trafficking trade and the laundering of its proceeds in the last few years have seen an enormous increase in national and international efforts to combat this problem. In order to combat the laundering of the finances generated from illicit drug trafficking, we require a continuous global effort and internation action as it is one of the most well-organized crimes in existence extremely responsive to counter measures by the Government and limited only by the imagination and abilities of the networks of the launderers themselves. So long as we are unable to put a hold on the laundering of the monies generated from drug trafficking, the drug trade will keep flourishing and along with it will flourish those who were involved in this ghastly trade.

The above legislation, which I have briefly touched upon till now, has been reasonably successful in curbing the menace of drug trafficking. However, there are two points which I wish to highlight; firstly the legislation has to undergo constant change because I have already pointed out that the drug trafficking trade is extremely responsive to legislation curbing their activities and hence traffickers are constantly changing their methodology of operation; and secondly, I personally feel that the laws which the country has in force, to deal with drug trafficking and abuse are more punitive in nature, and are not substantially equipped to deal with the aspect of de-addiction and rehabilitation of those caught in the vicious web of drug abuse. There is also the problem of strict procedural requirements which must be scrupulously followed in respect of search, seizure, arrest etc. The procedures are often deviated from by the enforcement personnel which lead to acquittals in a large number of cases. Corruption in the ranks of enforcement agencies and the very fact that inspite of one central agency, there are several agencies dealing with this problem are drawbacks which hamper the effectiveness of legislation intended at curbing the menace of drug trafficking. Most importantly, we know by experience that laws after all will remain as good as what they intend to achieve and how well they are enforced and obeyed.

To sum up, I can say that for the moment, we have the requisite legislation and agencies fully geared and ready to interact with their international counterparts to combat the menace of drugs and I have every reason to repose my faith in the law-makers and the enforcement officials not only to devise new and more effective counter measures but also to enforce them in the most optimal manner.

However, we must not forget that this is one vital area where we cannot remain complacent, resting on our laurels and feeling proud of what we have achieved if we are to root out this evil from our system. It will require active interaction and cooperation not only from the law-makers and enforcers, but from every individual organization and all the agencies connected with the problem of drugs, ranging from the very genesis of addiction to enforcement, de-addiction and rehabilitation.

I am certain that the next three days of deliberation will yield concrete ideas, guidelines, and a viable action plan, which, I am sure, will be most useful in better understanding the problem of drug addiction, drug abuse and drug trafficking and making us better equipped in curbing and preventing it efficaciously.

PRESIDENTIAL SPEECH DELIVERED BY THE HON'BLE CHIEF JUSTICE OF INDIA

A.M.Ahmadi

The danger that drug abuse poses to humanity was realized by the international community in the 1980s, when the U.N. General Assembly, at its meeting held in December 1984, addressed itself to the ever-growing threat it posed to world peace, and adopted a resolution recognizing that trafficking in narcotic drugs had become 'an international criminal activity' which called for an all-out war against the menace. Realizing the magnitude and seriousness of the problem, the U.N. body emphasized the need to take urgent measures to curb the production of these harmful drugs since it impeded social and economic growth. The international body said that eradication of trafficking in narcotic drugs should be the responsibility of the international community, and called upon member-states to intensify efforts and coordinate strategies to control and eradicate the menace. The anxiety of the United Nations was based on the fact that, though it was difficult to correctly estimate the extent of business in drug trafficking because of its clandestine nature, rough estimates varied from 300 to 500 billion dollars a year. Even if the conservative estimate was taken to be reasonably accurate, there was sufficient cause to feel worried because of its potential to disturb international peace, apart from posing a grave danger to the health of the international community. This anxiety was reflected in the statement made by the U.N. Secretary-General, Javier Perez de Cuellar, in 1990, when he described drug abuse as a 'time-bomb' which was ticking away and warned that, before it exploded and destroyed us, it was necessary for the international community to act fast and decisively. As to the extent of the menace, he observed that 'the monetary value of drug trafficking has recently surpassed that of international trade in oil and is second only to arms trade'. Despite this warning, the business in drug trafficking continued unabated and, while speaking on the occasion of the observance of the International Day Against Drug Abuse and Illicit Trafficking on 26 June 1991, he reiterated his deep concern since the production was increasing and consequently the drug trafficking trade was seen to be growing, notwithstanding the war declared against it by the international community. The U.N. Secretary-General rightly lamented the fact that, despite the resolution adopted at the Vienna Conference (1988), the same had not been ratified by all nations till then. How can the international community tolerate this apathy towards the world's most threatening war against humanity? Its magnitude can be discerned from the figures released by the World Health Organization which had by then estimated that over 200 million persons the world over were addicted to drugs. India's rough estimates revealed that more than 15 to 20 million persons had become victims of drug abuse. It is the international character of the problem and the enormity of the effects of drug abuse that we refer to when we talk of Global Drugs Law. When narcotic drugs or psychotropic substances are produced in one country and transported to another, the recipient country not only imports drugs but also the problems associated with drugs. While the impact of drugs on physical and psychological health is patent, its impact on economic, human or social development is not so openly visible. However, it is now universally recognized that over the past decade illicit drug production, trafficking and consumption have spread throughout the world, breaking new ground in countries and communities once thought safe from such activities. Drug-related activities may appear lucrative for the unemployed and for those who have money to invest and seek to multiply the investment. It should not, however, be forgotten that such activities require a shift of limited resources from those sectors needing the capital and labour for overall national growth to the sector of drugs which has only a negative impact on development. The economic gains of the illicit drug industry must also be weighed against opportunity cost. While neither the developed countries nor the developing ones can afford the social and economic burden of drug trafficking, the problem is particularly severe for the developing ones. The money that is generated by the drug industry is tainted. The resources in the hands of the profiteers in the trade are therefore used in their clandestine business. In the compilation of statistics 'Crime in India 1994' published by the Ministry of Home Affairs, Government of India, the following remark about the drug trade is of immense significance:

> The drug trade has a thriving market and is well run as a business and the money generated from the trafficking is capitalized through various money laundering processes. Recent incidents show drug money has created a number of neo-rich class of people who could sit on empires in legitimate business and control real-estates, film production, airlines, corporate houses, including manufacturing sectors. Their role in anti-national

smuggling, terrorist activities and clandestine trading in arms and ammunition have since recently surfaced.

Illicit drug trade has resulted in the globalization of the money market and products which move internationally from producer countries that are usually more developed. Products in some areas are transported to and sold in other countries after enormous price increases along the way providing high profit and risk incentives to traffickers. The ultimate users of drugs are generally the poor and the impoverished who buy drugs while ignoring the necessities of life.

Drug delinquency and crime are related in many ways. In some cases, drug abuse may lead to crime and in others, criminal behaviour precedes drug abuse. Drug-related crimes and terrorism cause instability and overloads police, courts and prisons. Drug problems may marginalize governments and institutions as well as people. In extreme cases these problems may create parallel governments where drug mafias or drug lords exercise enormous personal and financial powers. It is a challenge and a challenge of vast dimensions which has neither a single cause nor a simple straight cure, and drug-abuse and its many related problems continue to increase in many regions of the world. Disease, accidents, deaths, crime, lowered productivity and many other problems are frequently reported. If drug-abuse goes unchecked or unmonitored, it will continue to act as a brake on human and social development and cannot be separated from endemic problems of disease, poverty, unemployment and violence in all perceivable forms. Illicit drug use has powerful effects on the brain and behaviour, influencing a wide range of human activities.

AIDS is an added dimension of the drug scenario. Injectable drugs like Bupernorphine are used by addicts in groups who share the same needles and thereby spread AIDS. This abuse is predominant in Nepal, India and Bangladesh.

The major enactment on narcotics in India is the Narcotic Drugs & Psychotropic Substances Act, 1985. The scheme of the Act envisages long-term prison sentences and heavy fines for the offenders. The jails are overcrowded with undertrial offenders under the Act. The cultivator, the seller as well as the consumer of drugs are offenders and have to suffer minimum prison sentences which in most cases is ten years. Yet crime is on the rise.

The present Act is widely criticized for treating the drug user and drug trafficker on par. Possession for personal use in small quantity is also an offence (where a user is in possession of a small quantity, the sentence may go upto six months or one year, depending upon the nature of the drug). But the small quantity fixed by the Government is so small that it may barely suffice for one single use. The basis for arriving at these quantities is not known. Such provisions make it difficult for the drug addicts who have, wittingly or unwittingly, become victims of the drug trade, to come out in the open and seek medical attention and rehabilitation. Another strong criticism is that the Act does not distinguish between soft drugs and hard ones, and such failure is said to be responsible for the promotion of hard drugs compared to soft ones. Much can be said about the policy of the Act prescribing the minimum sentence of ten years. Harsh minimum sentences result in a low conviction ratio. We may think of suitable amendments to the Act to produce the desired result.

When we talk in terms of Global Drugs Law, we have to first think of minimum common norms. Despite the conventions, the laws in different countries remain different. Uniformity in laws will ensure that drug trafficking is not more attractive in one country than another. If the countries of the world can think alike, we may evolve simpler methods of dealing with the matters relating to investigations into international offences, arrest, detention and extradition of persons from one country for offences committed in another, speedy trials and punishments. Money laundering is another important aspect of the drug trade which needs a global solution.

When the NDPS Act was enacted, perhaps the strength of the extant infrastructure was not sufficiently examined. Perhaps no proper study was made as to the required capacity of the police force and other investigating agencies, the criminal courts, the prosecuting agencies and the jails, so that a larger number of offenders got arrested, the criminal courts became overloaded with cases and the jails were suddenly over-crowded. Limited capacity of forensic laboratories added to the prolonged litigations. (The minimum sentence of ten years prevents even the petty offenders from confessing their guilt. Once in jail, the convicts and undertrials have almost a permanent settlement. Keeping this situation in mind, we had to make a judicial order for grant of bail according to a scheme evolved therein. All such situations will have to be averted whenever we think afresh.)

Along with Global Drugs Law, we also need to strengthen regional and international cooperation and coordination for dealing with the issue. Here, we may recall the United Nations International Drug Control Programme, 'UNDCP' for short, in developing a regional strategy for a drug-free future. UNDCP has been playing a key role in exchanging information and skills relevant to controlling drug trafficking. The Programme has extended support to the NGOs who are working in drug demand reduction and in related programmes such as community development in health, youth, education and HIV/AIDS.

Evolving a Global Drugs Law will depend upon the eagerness and cooperation of all the nations of the world. The problem should be looked upon as a global one, rising above narrow interests, as it is the worst menace facing humanity today. I hope the conference will be able to cull out valuable suggestions from the discussions and offer an effective solution for the consideration of the policy-makers at the national and international level.

STATEMENT ON BEHALF OF UNDCP

Mr. Francesco Bastagli, Director, Treaty Implementation and Policy Development Division, UNDCP on behalf of Mr. Giorgio Giacomelli, Executive Director, UNDCP

On the drug control side, the reality is that problems continue to grow worldwide for both governments and the communities they serve. To deal with those problems we have placed a whole network of national and international legal frameworks and instruments for drug control. However, licit regulatory measures, criminal justice measures and other preventive and corrective measures are having less of an impact than they might, both against drug trafficking and drug abuse.

On the criminal justice side, serious drug-related offences by national and transnational organized crime contribute significantly to the damage caused to governance, institutions and society in a growing number of countries. Investigators, prosecutors and courts are facing higher and higher caseloads, often dominated by relatively minor cases having a limited—even marginal—positive impact if successful. Many judges and magistrates have little case disposal options and flexibility under the law, particularly in relation to drug abusers. This can lead to prison overcrowding, with disproportionately high numbers of minor offenders and few, if any, major criminals—those criminals who do most damage to the fabric of our societies.

The ancients spoke of justice dawning like the morning star—as surely as the sunrise they said—and of justice coming like showers of spring rain upon the dry expanses of the earth. Justice in that ideal sense hasn't come yet. Indeed, it will not come as long as resources remain so scarce, other political and economic priorities crowd justice out, and everyone involved is increasingly requested to do more with less. Everywhere, the delicate balance between the quantity and quality of justice is under strain.

This Conference presents an important opportunity to try and change all that. We can and must do better—not necessarily more, but definitely better. Doing better requires us to take a fresh look at the way we do things—within baseline legal limits such as those set by the international drug control conventions. Major change is not easy—particularly if it unsettles customs or traditions. The original reasons which led to things being done in a certain way may have changed fundamentally. They must all be tested rigorously and dispassionately to ensure that we are still acting in the most effective and appropriate manner.

And so it's quite valid, indeed necessary, for this Conference to assess both what is working well and needs to be kept and affirmed, and what is not and needs to be discarded or changed—again within those baseline legal limits. Many of the issues to be dealt with in Plenary 2, Plenary 5 and their associated panels lend themselves to this kind of rigorous assessment.

If Impact is to be Improved, Governments Must Bridge the Gap Between Pledge and Action

Whatever recommendations or action plan this Conference may produce, it will take political will and financial resources to implement them.

Governments in the United Nations and other international fora have expressed at the highest levels the view that drugs and crime are a top priority. However, such concern is often not embodied in concrete national policies and programmes, and—more importantly—in effective implementation. Resources are not proportionate to the recognized scale and gravity of the problem. In fact, some governments, rather than increasing their commitment have seriously curtailed the national budgets allocated for the fight against drugs. Similarly they have reduced their support for international drug control, including contributions to the UNDCP fund.

Sometimes one hears that we are losing the so-called 'war on drugs' or that measures to counter drug trafficking 'do not work.' In reality too many have not yet really joined the battle in the field. The threat to national security and public safety posed by drug trafficking and abuse has too often been underestimated or has received too little attention. For example, the 1988 Convention, the main instrument targeting illicit drug trafficking, although ratified or acceded to by 138 states, has been fully implemented by only a handful of them.

Governments must seriously address implementation if we are to make collective progress. Any ambiguous position taken by a government with regard to its treaty obligations sends the wrong signal, particularly to young people, and undermines the credibility of the international drug control system.

To deal successfully with drug barons and protect our youth from drug abuse, the state and its institutions must remain a credible force. Accordingly, any serious discrepancy between proclaimed intentions and action to put them into practice should be eliminated. For us to make real progress, 'drugs' has to be a priority for action at both the national and international levels—reflected as such in budget allocations and demonstrated through political will at all levels of government.

The criminal justice and health care communities are key actors in implementing drug control legislation and contributing to the reduction of drug abuse and serious drug-related crime. So they in particular must have the necessary resources to carry out their functions effectively. It goes without saying that modern, workable national legislation, infrastructure, strategies and programmes also need to be in place if impact is to be optimal. To help in this process, the international community has undertaken to assist countries in need through technical cooperation and other means, including the drafting or amending of legislation and the development of integrated national strategies and programmes. Thus, the United Nations provides a wide range of 'hands-on' services and support whether the need is strictly related to drug control matters or concerns the criminal justice system in general.

This Conference and the 1998 Special Session of the UN General Assembly on Drugs

I would like to draw your attention to the forthcoming high-level Special Session of the General Assembly on drugs, because what you do over the next few days and the recommendations you draw up at the end of the Conference are likely to be of considerable interest to it.

This Special Session is to be convened in 1998. Its mandate is to consider the fight against the illicit production, sale, demand, traffic and distribution of narcotic drugs and psychotropic substances and related activities. The General Assembly is to propose new strategies, methods, practical activities and special measures to strengthen international cooperation in addressing the problem of illicit drugs.

— In pursuit of its mandate, we expect the Special Session will, *inter alia:*
— make an assessment of the existing situation within the framework of a comprehensive and balanced approach;
— review the international drug control instruments, particularly the 1988 Convention;
— adopt and promote drug abuse control policies and other measures to reduce illicit demand for drugs, including at the international level;
— further adherence to and full implementation by all States of the drug control conventions.

The Special Session is also likely to review progress made in implementing the Global Programme of Action on Drugs adopted by the General Assembly in 1990, and the Naples Political Declaration and Global Action Plan Against Organized Transnational Crime which were approved in 1994.

The 1990 Global Programme against Drugs represents the most comprehensive statement of the actions that should be taken by countries, both individually and collectively, through the system of international organizations. It provides a framework for the international community, and offers wide-ranging guidance to governments facing drug-related problems.

The 1994 Action Plan against Crime is similar, but in the criminal field, it extends to all serious organized transnational crime. It outlines ways and means to strengthen and improve national capabilities, and lays the foundations for concerted and effective global action against such crime and to prevent its further expansion. The Plan addresses current problems and dangers, national legislation issues and guidelines, international cooperation at the investigative, prosecutorial and judicial levels, regional and international cooperation, feasibility of international legal instruments against organized transnational crime, prevention and control of money laundering, and the control of the proceeds of crime.

The issues you will address over the next three days directly relate to the implementation of the drug control conventions, the Programme of Action on Drugs and the Action Plan on Organized Crime. Hence, you will cover some of the main concerns of the Special Session of the General Assembly. This is particularly so for the subjects to be dealt with in the two key plenary sessions on International Cooperation against Serious Crime and Justice System Impact on Drug Problems, and their associated panel discussions. From an international perspective, this adds a special flavour and interest to your deliberations.

Concluding Remarks

To conclude, I reiterate the main task of the conference as finding ways to

- improve the impact of the justice system on serious drug-related crime;
- improve international legal cooperation to that end; and
- better deal with cases involving drug abusers.

The agenda before you covers all the key issues. The renowned panelists assembled here will contribute considerable and diverse experiences when the substantive work starts tomorrow morning. Thus, there are all the promises for success.

This is vital work, and that is why the UNDCP has agreed to co-sponsor and help support this important event. We now look forward to assisting you in your endeavours and to benefitting, along with the entire international community, from the results of your deliberations.

INAUGURAL SPEECH DELIVERED THE BY HON'BLE VICE-PRESIDENT OF INDIA

K.R. Narayanan

Governmental policies and world opinion are clear in regard to the menace of drugs. But the production, supply, trafficking and consumption of this noxious substance is on the increase. As early as 1917, Mahatma Gandhi, addressing the All India Social Service Conference in Calcutta, had said prophetically: 'The cocaine habit was sapping the nation's manhood, and that like the drink habit, it was on the increase in its effect more deadly than drink.'

Historically, this Global Drugs Law Conference marks a revolutionary change in the attitude of international opinion to the question on the use and the abuse of drugs. It was in 1800 A.D. that the then Government of China issued an edict prohibiting the import of opium as it constituted a threat to the health of the Chinese people. The story is well-known; how the European powers organized massive smuggling of this substance into China, and how, when the Chinese resisted, it sparked off the infamous Opium War in the name of the right of free trade. In sharp contrast today, the world is united in fighting illicit trade and trafficking in drugs as it is posing a deadly menace to the health of people and to the cohesion of civilized society.

Today the total narcotic drug trade in the world is estimated at $ 500 billion. It is more than the GDP of all but the seven richest countries of the world. The global value of the drug trade is many times more than the $ 62 billion spent on official development assistance in 1992. In today's world, every major gang engaged in criminal or terrorist activities gets handsome amounts from this drug fund, most of which comes from the affluent cities of U.S.A. and Europe. It is said that 50 per cent of the world's illicit drugs are sold in the U.S.A. and Europe. An OECD Financial Action Task Force reported in 1990 that, while the producing countries consume important quantities of the drug, a sizeble portion of it is consumed in industrialized countries. The Task Force also noted that psychotropic substances like amphetamines and LSD are produced in clandestine laboratories including some in OECD countries. These facts establish two conclusions. Firstly, this enormous trade cannot take place without the connivance and collusion of at least some sections of the authorities in various countries, even though the policies of the governments are opposed to it. In fact, in every insurgency and terrorist situation, especially in developing countries, drug money is an important source of funding and one knows that governments are involved in some way or another. Secondly, the demand side of the drug problem is as important, if not more important, than the problem of the production and supply side. I am not ignoring or minimizing the fact that drug-producing countries, mostly developing countries, are guilty, and indeed the problem of danger to the health of people in developing countries by the use of drugs is even greater because of the vulnerability of the people due to general health and environment conditions in these countries. But what I am driving at is that the control of production and supply of drugs would not be the sole or the main remedy to this deadly problem facing humanity. It has been said that measures to control the supply side constitute only a short-term approach and that measures to control the reduction of demand for the drugs would be the long-term solution.

Richard Clutterbuck, in his book, *Drugs, Crime and Corruption*, has emphatically stated that 'the cure must lie in the main consumer countries, the USA and Europe, rather than the drug-producing countries in Latin America and Asia.' He further says, 'Crop eradication and crop substitution will never be more than half-hearted, at best, so long as the citizens of affluent Western countries continue to pay highly inflated prices for drugs on their streets.' 'It is up to the Western countries,' he says, 'either to cut the demand or, in other ways, to cut the massive flow of money to the criminals who organize the supply and distribution.' I am sure that the conference will deliberate on this issue of consumption and make recommendations with regard to changing and enforcing the law to curb the habit of drug abuse among increasing sections of people.

Whatever be the origin of drug abuse, this dangerous practice has gravely affected the youth all over the globe. The World Bank has estimated that average users typically fall within the age-group of 15-40 and most of them are in their mid-twenties. Therefore, through drug-abuse the most productive and dynamic section of our society gets affected, causing inestimable loss to the social, economic and cultural life of the people. Drugs also play a part in the spread of diseases like AIDS.

Another aspect of the drug problem is its deleterious impact on the environment. As the Third World countries face the problem of falling commodity prices, some of the farmers resort to coca farming, which gets huge returns in the market. Massive use of pesticides and herbicides, and the clearing of forests for the cultivation of drug-related crops, have degraded soils, destroyed bio-diversity and fostered dependence on drug money. It is astounding to know that in Peru the coca cultivation has resulted in deforestation of 700,000 hectares in the Amazon region. Similarly, in Bolivia vast tracts of forest land have been cleared. As one expert put it, 'unlike indigenous farmers, cultivators of drug crops have fewer ties to the land and are less respectful of it.'

The deforestation, soil degradation and water pollution are the consequences of these new drug crops.

In fact, drug problems cannot be looked at separately; these are part of the larger problems of disease, poverty, joblessness, violence, economic disparities and the styles of living, especially in affluent societies. We have to follow sustainable development and promote health and education for all and rehabilitate the addicts and integrate them to the mainstream of society. We have to control population, respect human rights and finally resort to good governance. These are the goals which have to be incorporated in the programme of drug control as well as economic development. It is said that education is the principal means of preventing drug abuse. It is through education and awakening consciousness of the people through the use of mass media that we can bring them back to the right path.

Global Drugs Law must incorporate all these aspects of the problem. We have the U.N. Single Convention in Narcotic Drugs, 1961 as amended by the protocol of 1972 and the Convention of Psychotropic Substances, 1971. The implementation of such instruments of law greatly depends on cooperation among the contracting parties and harmonization of their legislative enactments. It is said that 'the control of drug-abuse—like the control of contagious disease and promotion of clear air—cannot be denied as a public good.' The courts in India have amplified these concepts of jurisprudence in pronouncements on the right to life, right to health and right to environment. I am sure that this Conference will also give a new dimension to drug laws by tackling the many-sided problems that are bedeviling the existence of mankind. Mahatma Gandhi once said:

> the world has been suffering a great deal from evils such as drinking, smoking, addiction to opium, ganja, hemp and so on. All of us are caught in this snare and so we cannot truly measure the magnitude of its unhappy consequences.

Today one understands that in some countries of Latin America drug cartels have grown, having at their disposal tens of billions of dollars, huge arsenals of weapons, sophisticated communication systems, aeroplanes and executive jets and a whole web of connections with governmental authorities that enable them to operate with impunity. In other countries also this phenomenon is growing. Therefore, the world is literally caught in a snare, as Gandhiji had said.

I am sure that the jurists, lawyers and social and political thinkers assembled in the Conference will deliberate the many facets of the drug problem and evolve a comprehensive legal framework to fight this growing menace to mankind. I wish their deliberations every success.

SPEECH ON THE AGENDA DELIVERED BY CONFERENCE SECRETARY-GENERAL

R.K. Nayak

The Indian Law Institute, a national and international centre, has been leading the move for constructive reform of legal education through legal creativity and research. This great institution is the host of this international conference on Global Drugs Law. It has been endeavouring to set new trends through its advisory role to the governmental agencies for three and a half decades and holding international conferences on the contemporary problems facing developing societies the world over. Once the great philosopher Socrates was asked about his nationality and instantly the great thinker said: 'I am not a citizen of Athens or Greece but the citizen of the World.' In the same way the legal creativity of the Indian Law Institute is not confined only to the geographical boundaries of India but this institution belongs to the whole world in serving the greater cause of suffering humanity. The Conference on Drugs Law is another concerted and serious attempt to wage war against consumers of drugs. Inspite of unprecedented material prosperity which this century has brought globally, millions of people are suffering under the heavy weight of poverty, disease and squalor throughout the world. There are numerous problems which come to the surface such as alcoholism, family conflicts, drug addiction, heart ailment, cancer and lately the monster of human civilization—AIDS. All these diseases are linked with human behaviour. Drug abuse is on the increase everyday leaving behind deep scars, affecting the physical and economic health of the countries and threatening the very foundation of their politico-legal fibre. Machiavelli once said 'that wisdom consists of in being able to distinguish among other dangers and make a choice of the least harmful.'

This Conference is not only unique in nature and approach but will also provide an excellent opportunity to the cross-section of eminent drug experts who have come from different parts of the world to exchange their ideas and philosophies and apply their best creative minds for human good.

It serves as an international forum in close cooperation with the UNDCP and ILI for evolving the long awaited and much needed global drugs law for the new century. ILI under the institutional leadership of the Hon'ble Chief Justice of India has spent many days in carving out an agenda for this Conference in which the role of Mr. Andrew Wells, Mr. Koli Koume and Dr. D.C. Jayasuriya, all high officials of the UNDCP, has been constructive towards the preparation of a pragmatic agenda. The treasurer of the conference, Rakesh Munjal, has spent many restless days and nights in preparing the Agenda along with me and the Executive Chairman.

This Conference in various plenary sessions and panel discussions will make an articulated effort to evolve the socio-legal strategy to march speedily towards a drug free human race based on a new *dharma* to destroy the drug sub-culture and deal effectively with drug multi-nationals and drug cartels. We will also ponder over the humanitarian aspects of the proposed world law of drugs in which education, health and human rights aspects will be given due consideration. An Arabian proverb says 'he who has health has hope, and he who has hope has everything.' To deal with the drug abuse problem, the highest human good will be the sole criteria. Rousseau said 'man is born free but he is always in chains.' The eminent jurists, drug experts and policy makers from about twenty-five countries of Asia, Africa and America will make a serious attempt to break the chains of drug abusers to make them free and decent citizens of human civilization for which the ILI, in close cooperation with the UNDCP and ILA India Regional Branch will not leave any stone unturned. We are in an age in which we are closely and keenly perceiving the process of globalization of markets, products, industries and even education everywhere except our minds and hearts. Is this globalization worth it when the war against drugs has not been won so far? Millions of people are in the grip of the drug menace. It is estimated that drug abuse may be costing the world $500 billion a year according to the U.N. Commission on Narcotics. Ever since the advent of civilization, drugs have been used for medication, meditation, divination and recreation. But at no time in history, has the threat to human society ever so existed as it does today. We need to bring down the per capita consumption of illicit drugs by reducing their availability through socio-legal welfare or social-welfare-oriented global drugs law. In this gigantic task reform-minded thinkers, judges, lawyers, academics, physicians, legislators and policy makers should join hands together and come forward with determination to eradicate the miseries of millions of drug addicts around the globe. Efforts should be made to control illicit cultivation, production and distribution of drugs. The criminal justice system has to be humane in dealing with drug addicts. Any strategy for the twenty-first century in relation to global drugs law has to have a balanced approach to battle the worldwide drug menace in all its pervasive forms. The proposed law should promote human dignity and legitimate aspirations of humankind for which a decent life is imperatively essential with moral, humanitarian and spiritual values in a healthy, safe and advanced environment. Every nation around the globe should unequivocally commit itself to vigorous international action against drug abuse and illicit trafficking as an important goal of the international drugs law.

The Conference will concentrate on the issues relating to the drug scene as it exists today and approaches the twenty-first century; international legal cooperation against serious crime; upgrading the justice system and improving international cooperation, in implementing drug-related laws; impact of the justice system on drug problems etc. The eminent experts of the Conference will work unitedly to evolve an agreeable recommendation in the end which will be called 'New Delhi Charter on Global Drugs Law' for serving the cause of humanity and saving mankind from the scourge of drugs.

Thomas Jefferson the great constitutionalist said that law and institutions must go hand in hand with the progress of the human mind. The minds of drug specialists and jurists will give the best to make a drug-free world.

In the gigantic task of evolving a Global Drugs Law I would draw the inspiration, knowledge and strength from the *Holy Geeta* which has been a perennial reservoir of the strength of the human mind for ages. I quote:

> Daring intellects, bravely pushing ahead in the quest to understand and comprehend the law of the life and the meaning and purpose of the universe, cannot but accept that the existence of an individual in its present embodiment is but a single pearl in the necklace of infinite Beauty, adorning the bosom of truth. The present is the product of the past, and thought by thought, action by action, knowledge by knowledge, we are creating for ourselves in the present the blueprint of the future.

VOTE OF THANKS

P.H. Parekh

Our Vice-President, the Hon'ble K.R. Narayanan, is a scholar right from his school days. He did his M.A. in English literature, securing a first class degree from Travancore University. He then did his B.Sc. (Economics) and secured a first class honours degree from the London School of Economics.

After returning to India, he joined the Indian Foreign Service. He served in Indian missions in all the continents and was High Commissioner to the United Kingdom in London. He was later appointed as Secretary of the External Affairs Ministry. He has also been the Indian Ambassador to the United States of America. He was elected to the House of People after retirement from the Foreign Service for three successive terms 1984, 1989 and 1991. He served the country as Minister and held various portfolios, including that of External Affairs.

The Hon'ble K.R. Narayanan as Cabinet Minister has represented India at the United Nations Organisation on various occasions. He is a member of the Universal Academy of Cultures, Paris, and Honorary Fellow of the London School of Economics. When he was elected Vice-President of India, he secured more than ninety-nine percent of votes cast by all members of Parliament. In fact, all parties, cutting across their differences, voted for him to make him the Vice-President. He is, of course, the *ex-officio* Chairman of the Upper House of our Parliament. He has visited various countries as Vice President and during his recent visit to London, a London newspaper reported that the British Government treated the visit of our Vice-President with a high profile similar to that accorded to the visit of Dr. S. Radhakrishnan when he was a state guest in 1963.

The Chief Justice of India, Justice Ahmadi, is the President of both the Indian Law Institute as well as the International Law Association (Indian Branch) which is a co-sponsor of this Conference. He is the President of the Organising Committee. The Chief justice has directed me not to thank him and I do not propose to commit contempt of court, certainly not in the presence of the Vice-President of India. But 1 would like to tell that whenever we wanted any help or guidance, inspite of being so busy, he has been always available to us and has guided us very well.

Justice Verma, the Chief Justice-designate, is the Chairperson of the Organising Committee. Justice Verma is a man of few words and a man of action. Justice Verma feels embarrassed if anyone thanks him and 1, therefore, do not propose to thank him, except to say that he has guided us at all times in order to make the International Conference a success.

We are thankful to the contributors of papers and to all the delegates. More than two hundred delegates are with us from all over the world and we are very happy to welcome them. We hope they will enjoy the Conference and thereafter visit different parts of India. We will be pleased to be of assistance to them.

We are extremely thankful and delighted to have the Chief Justices of Pakistan and Kyrgyzstan with us and we welcome them to this Conference.

I would particularly like to thank our Supreme Court judges who have come here after a hard day's work, each dealing with fifty to sixty matters. I would like to thank Justice Punchhi, Justice K. Ramaswami, Justice Agrawal (who is going to chair a Plenary Session), Justice Jeevan Reddy, Justice A.S. Anand, Justice Sujata Manohar, Justice B.N. Kirpal, Justice Patnaik, Justice Kurdukar and Justice Thomas for their guidance, support and participation.

I would like to thank the Attorney-General, Mr. Ashok Desai, and the Solicitor General, Mr. Tempton Andhyarulina, who are Vice-Chairmen of the Organising Committee of this Conference, for their help.

I would like to especially thank Justice Saikia, Justice Ranaganathan and Justice K.J. Reddy, former judges of the Supreme Court, who are present with us. We are thankful to the Chief Justices and judges of the High Courts, past and present. We are also thankful to the members of the Governing Council who have helped us.

We are thankful to the Government of India for providing air tickets from both Air India and Indian Airlines for some of our overseas delegates.

The United Nations Drug Control Programme is the co-sponsor of this Conference and its staff have worked very hard to get the right participants from all over the globe. In fact, we have participants from all the continents in the world and we are thankful to the Executive Director, Mr. Georgio Giacomelli, who has been helping us. We are very happy that Mr. Francesco Bastagli, Director, Division for Treaty Implementation and Policy Development, has come all the way from Vienna on behalf of the Executive Director. I am particularly thankful to Mr. Andrew Wells, who helped us a great deal in structuring the working sessions. Mr. Koli Kouame and Dr. D.C. Jayasuriya of UNDCP (Delhi) have been very helpful to us and we are thankful to the entire UNDCP.

We are thankful to the officials of the Indian Law Institute, in particular to Mr. K.S. Bhati (the Registrar), Mr. Pramod Singh, Mr. P.L. Batra, Mr. S.N.K. Anand and Mr. A.K. Jain, who have worked tirelessly all the time. Last, but not least, I would like to thank Mr. R.K. Anand (Executive Chairman), Prof. R.K. Nayak, (Secretary General) Mr. Rakesh Munjal (Treasurer) and Mr. Vishvajit Bhattacharya for their ceaseless efforts to make this Conference a success.

VALEDICTORY ADDRESS DELIVERED BY THE HON'BLE PRIME MINISTER OF INDIA

H.D. Deve Gowda

Measuring the magnitude of the menace of drug-abuse is really difficult because its causes and effects are highly complex. Nevertheless, it will be a truism to say that drug abuse is one of the worst curses that is afflicting societies the world over, a curse that threatens the very survival of humanity. It blows its ways into the portals of society targetting as it does the most vulnerable sections, namely our youth. It is a matter of great concern that the majority of the drug addicts are in the age-group of 19 to 25 years. These young men and women are not born addicts. They acquire the habit from the society they live in. Drug abuse sheds the vitality and vigour of our youth in their most productive years and drives them towards a life of delinquency and crime. The problem in our country is all the more acute, sandwiched as we are geographically between the Golden Cresent and the Golden Triangle. Drugs have become an illegal currency financing criminal activities in many countries. In this way drugs harm human society in more than one manner. International conventions on the subject namely, the Single Convention on Narcotic Drugs in 1961, the Convention on Psychotropic Substances in 1971 and the United Nations Convention Against Illicit Traffic in Narcotic Drugs and Psychotropic Substances of 1988, provided for the various ways to prevent drug trafficking. In order to make the international conventions more effective, we have adopted the SAARC Convention on Narcotic Drugs and Psychotropic Substances in 1990. India has ratified all these conventions and our legislation on the subject is presently contained mainly in the Narcotic Drugs and Psychotropic Substances Act 1985, supplemented by the Prevention of Illicit Traffic in Narcotic Drugs and Psychotropic Substances Act 1988, and the Drugs and Cosmetics Act, 1940. Our laws, *inter alia*, contain stringent penal provisions and procedures for the investigation and trial of drug offences and streamlined procedures for the licensing and authorization for illicit production and use of drugs for medical and scientific purposes. Measures for reduction of demand by prevention and treatment of drug addiction and education after cure, rehabilitation and social reintegration of addicts along with the implementation of obligations under the international conventions relating to the narcotic drugs and psychotropic traffic substances, the statutory controlling of production of steroids, transportation, the export, import, sale, purchase, possession and use of narcotic drugs and psychotropic substances have been exercised in India for a long time through a number of Central and State enactments. The Government of India in recognition of the need and importance of taking further stringent and effective action against drug abuse and illicit drug trafficking set up in August 1993, a high-level committee under the chairmanship of the Minister of State for Finance to undertake a comprehensive review of the arrangements for dealing with the various aspects of the problem and for the development of a centrally coordinated multidimensional strategy to tackle it.

Our concern and responsibility are still more important because India is the only country in the world authorized to cultivate opium and supply it to all the countries demanding it for manufacture of vital medicines. Our Government has decided to introduce in the current session of Parliament a Bill for amending the Narcotic Drugs and Psychotropic Substances Act, 1985 with a view to incorporating most of the provisions of the United Nations Convention of 1988, besides other changes based on our experience of working with the said Act. Provisions will be incorporated, *inter alia*, to provide for the exercise of jurisdiction for offences committed by any citizen of India in places beyond India or any ship or aircraft registered in India wherever it may be, graded punishment for graded countries, leading to rationalization of the sentence structure and for allowing the use of controlled delivery with a view to identifying the real persons involved in the commission of drug offences. Permitting the use of the National Fund for controlling drug abuse, for combating illicit traffic, allowing tracing, identification, seizure and freezing of illegally acquired property held by a drug offender will also be provided for. Acquisition, possession, use, conversion, transfer or concealment of the property derived from a drug offence will also be made punishable. The plea of political offences as a defence in the proceedings for extradition of the persons accused in drug offence will not be available. International cooperation in the suppression of illicit traffic is extremely important. Eradication of illicit trafficking is a collective responsibility of all the nations. And the Government of India would not in any way lag behind in implementing the global programme of actions, this being the United Nations Decade against Drug Abuse. The Government will accord top priority to the consideration of the recommendations of the Conference and implement without delay the relevant suggestions, if need be, by further amendments to the laws. I would like to add only one word about the suggestion made by the Honourable Chief Justice with regard to the disposal of the cases. He made some valuable suggestions regarding the present rate of disposal not being satisfactory for the way in which the accused persons were going to be unnecessarily detained for a number of years and their subsequent uncertain outcome. The Government of India will certainly take these points into consideration and if need be, the number of special courts will be increased.

I must compliment the organizers of this three-day Conference. This is one of the most important issues concerning the entire human society. I don't think I am crossing my limits in saying that the drug addict problem is mostly in the affluent sections, mostly in the advanced countries. The problem of drug addiction in the advanced countries is much more than in the developing countries or underdeveloped countries. On behalf of myself and my country, I would like to convey my thanks to you, Mr. Andrew Wells for your assurance that the United Nations, one of the sister organizations, and your country are going to extend full cooperation to put an end to this menace. This is going to be one of the major problems in the coming years. When the wealth of nations grows the menace will also automatically grow. It is the concern of every nation to see that the human race should not be affected by this drug menace. As our Honourable Chief Justice has mentioned, if all the countries are prepared to extend cooperation, resource mobilization may not be a major problem. On behalf of my country, I would assure you that we are prepared to extend our full cooperation by bringing suitable amendments on the basis of the recommendations of this international conference. I will ask the Ministry of Law and Justice to examine the recommendations and see that in the current session itself if need be, we will bring suitable changes in the existing law. And as far as the share of the Indian government for resource mobilization is concerned, we are prepared to cooperate with the international organizations from our side.

PART II

OVERVIEW: INTERNATIONAL

INTERNATIONAL DRUG CONTROL: RECENT DEVELOPMENTS, PATTERNS AND TRENDS

Andrew Wells

20th Century—The First Century of International Drug Control

International drug control began only this century. At the beginning of the 20th century, there was no drug problem in any global sense, no global framework of legal obligations to deal with drug problems, and no network of states with domestic controls in place. At the end, there are all three.

That is not to say there was no drug abuse in the early 1900s. There was, particularly in east Asia. Opium production had existed for millennia in the region comprising modern Turkey, Iran and Afghanistan, with later growth further east into China and north into the region around the Black Sea. Demand for opium, especially in smokable form, had been growing in east Asia since the 17th century. Demand in China grew rapidly in the 19th century.

Concerns over the opium trade to China and growing addiction problems in both the Far East and the then colonial powers led to the United States convening a special commission in Shanghai in 1909. 13 world powers participated.

The 1909 conference led directly to the first ever international drug control treaty, the 1912 Hague Opium Convention. The Convention set the guiding principles for all subsequent international drug control treaties—namely, regulating production and trade of mind and mood-altering drugs to ensure they would be available for exclusively medical and scientific purposes, and not diverted for drug abuse. In particular, it placed under global control opium, morphine and its derivatives, heroin, as well as cocaine and its derivatives.

Towards 2000-Global Factors Affecting International Drug Control

The major reason for the intractability of the drug problem worldwide is the strength and diversity of the political, economic and social forces driving both supply and demand for mind-altering or mood-altering drugs.

Changes in the global economy and in technology over the past 30 years have stimulated investment and financial flows, and significantly enhanced market competition and economic growth at both domestic and international levels. For example:

* goods, services and people move more frequently and with greater ease across international borders than ever before;
* world trade has grown at unusually robust rates—the amount of goods and money changing hands across national borders has never been greater;
* trade liberalization, privatization and across-the-board de-regulation have been encouraged by the international community all over the world for the past decade, and have become for many, economic and political imperatives,
* rapid technology changes have led to the present reality of instantaneous global communications and, instantaneous international transfer of currency—including international data exchange networks such as the Internet

Paradoxically, these benefits have also come at an unexpected price- they have provided unprecedented opportunities for organized criminal networks to expand their operations, and with it their economic and political power . They can now transfer and conceal their illicit funds more easily. With their systematically accumulated criminal proceeds, they can now buy and sell institutions—even governments. Often this is done behind a convincing facade of legitimacy and integrity, pretending to be a lawful corporate citizen—but in reality seriously distorting and damaging the market, through criminal intimidation, extortion, corruption and violence.

An important warning to sound in the last years of the 20th century is that organized crime is rapidly moving beyond the laundering of the proceeds of particular crimes to the laundering of their entire criminal operations. We may well soon be passing a point of no return. In one sense, it was inevitable that organized crime would increasingly seek to infiltrate legitimate business, because it has the same economic objectives—namely, to maximize long-run profitability and growth, while minimizing all associated risk. Hence, organized crime will seek to:

* strategically invest in licit assets promising strong capital growth or future net income stream, particularly assets which facilitate money laundering;

* strategically invest to secure future 'leverage' (eg. bribery, corruption, political power);
* infiltrate the legitimate economy through takeovers or mergers (eg. start/buy a bank), or use of market power.

The past decade has seen a vast growth in banking de-regulation and in the privatization of state-owned businesses in countries where the regulatory capability was still in an embryonic state. While these actions were intended to encourage investment and economic development as well as improve efficiency for local consumers and investors, the lack of effective regulation left these financial systems vulnerable to criminal exploitation.

Significant social factors have also emerged over the last 30 years which have an impact on the future of effective drug abuse control, particularly on the demand side of the drug-market in developed countries. I include in these some purely personal views:

* rise in consumerism (eg. If I have a problem, there is a 'thing' I can buy or consume to fix it);
* declining traditional values and standards without an adequate replacement (eg. 'nothing I do is wrong, unless I'm caught'), and for the institutions that set them ('they are a nuisance, but needed mainly by others who can't help themselves');
* a tendency towards greater self-centredness ('me first'), and increasing preoccupation with personal rights, privacy and the short term ('I have a right to consume anything I choose and to do anything. I like to own my own body');
* increasing confusion and sometimes apathy over non-medical drug-use, leading to a very vocal advocacy of varying degrees of legalization;
* an almost universal lack of awareness of how widespread and deeply ingrained in society 'dependency' is, in its widest, and most fundamental 'non-technical' sense—namely, our giving away to some person or thing the power to influence or even determine our personal well-being, or happiness.

I believe there is considerable preventive and remedial potential to reverse a growing pro-drug culture through well-targetted 'wake-up' type education (eg. I don't need a 'Walkman' to be happy).

Recent Trends and Developments in Cultivation, Production, Trafficking and Consumption

Turning to global and regional trends towards the turn of the century—but first, a word of caution. UNDCP gains much of its data on the supply and demand for illicit drugs from member states through annual questionnaires sent to both parties and non-parties to the conventions. For various reasons such as the 'hidden' nature of the illicit drug industry, it is difficult to isolate the various patterns and trends which define it with a high level of certainty. However, some broadly indicative trends can be discerned:

(a) *Illicit Cultivation of Drugs*: Global hectarage devoted to illicit opium poppy cultivation expanded to about 260,000 hectares in the mid-to late 1980's, then, after a drop in 1990-91, increased gradually to about 280,000 in 1994:

* almost 90% of the world's illicitly produced opiates originate from the two main production areas the Golden Crescent (Afghanistan, Iran, Pakistan) and the Golden Triangle (Lao PDR, Myanmar, Thailand);
* overall, Afghanistan and Myanmar are the two main countries of illicit opium poppy cultivation; to a much lesser extent illicit cultivation takes place in Colombia, Lao PDR, Vietnam, Pakistan, Mexico, India, Thailand, China and the Middle East;
* emerging and potentially important producers include the Central Asian Republics of Uzbekistan, Kyrgyzstan, Tajikistan, Kazakstan, and Turkmenistan.

Estimates suggest that global illicit production of opium has almost tripled over the 1985-94 period (UNDCP, 1996). The illicit production of opium gum was estimated to have reached 5,000 tonnes in 1995. About 40% of the total is consumed as opium which historically is used almost exclusively in Asia. In illicit laboratories, the remainder is converted into heroin, most of which is exported.

Most of the world's illicit cocaine is grown in the Andean countries—Peru, Colombia, and Bolivia, which together account for more than 98% of world cocaine supplies. Estimates of global illicit production of coca leaves suggest a doubling of production over the 1985 to 1994 period, although production seems to be down from the 1991/1992 level (UNDCP, 1996).

Cannabis is cultivated in almost all regions of the world. Significant cultivation has been reported by South Africa, Morocco, Mexico, Colombia, Jamaica, the USA, and the Central Asian Republics. Cannabis also grows wild in many parts of the world and is used for licit hemp cultivation:

* similar to the large-scale illicit cultivation of coca bush and the opium poppy, most cannabis cultivation still takes place in areas remote from law enforcement;
* the detection of indoor cultivation of cannabis, however, has been increasingly reported from regions with a large local market, such as North America and Europe.

Illicit markets for synthetic drugs have developed rapidly in recent years. The principal synthetic and semi-synthetic drugs produced clandestinely are amphetamines and lysergic acid diethylamide (LSD):

* in addition, a number of other synthetic drugs have recently become popular, including methylenedioxymethamphetamine (MDMA), known as ecstasy, and methcathinone;
* if worldwide seizures are taken as an indicator, the use of methaqualone and other depressants is also increasing, with seizures increasing markedly in the period 1985-1994.

In general, the manufacture of illicit synthetic drugs is expected to increase owing to their relatively low production costs and high profit margins. Synthetic drugs can be produced near the consumer market and therefore those responsible for illicit distribution can economize on normally high trafficking costs, increasing their profit at the retail level. Also, the makeshift nature of most illicit laboratories producing synthetic drugs facilitates the rapid movement of production when the controls are tightened.

(b) *Detection of Illicit Laboratories*: One of the most important trends in laboratory production is the shift of production sites from the vicinity of chemical substances to the immediate neighbourhood of growing areas in the case of heroin and cocaine, which implies significant implications for law enforcement and for prices (UNDCP, 1996).

Detections of amphetamine-type stimulant (ATS) laboratories worldwide exceeded those of both heroin and cocaine laboratories from 1991 to 1994. There has been a notable increase in ecstasy group laboratory detections in Europe, accounting for about 55% of the globally detected laboratories since 1990, compared to the late 1980's, when the illicit manufacture of ecstasy was virtually confined to North America.

(c) *Drug Seizures*: Seizures of illicit drugs by law enforcement agencies are one of the main indicators used to assess the level of illicit drug trafficking, although these data must be used cautiously, since the evidence they provide can only be considered as an indirect indication of drug trafficking. The data are corroborated by cultivation, price and demand estimates.

The three countries with highest seizure levels—USA, Colombia and Mexico—accounted for almost half of the global amount.

Indices for global drug seizures during the 1990-1995 period demonstrate an average rate of increase for all drugs seized with the highest rate of increase in the 1990's occurring among hallucinogens, depressants and opiates. Stimulant seizures have been rising, while cocaine and heroin seizures, though consistently higher than those of stimulants, have been stable.

The bulk of precursors seized globally are used in cocaine production During 1990-1994, three-quarters of global precursor seizures converted into potential dosage units* took place in Colombia. In 1990-1994, around 4 billion potential dosage units of precursors were seized annually.

The most significant trend in the 1990-1994 period was the growth in ephedrine seizures which ran parallel to the massive growth in the consumption of methamphetamine. In this period, the seizure of ephedrine grew from 13% of global precursor seizures in 1990, to 46% in 1994. The diversion of ephedrine is expected to continue growing, as long as demand for methamphetamine and methcathinone continues to rise.

(d) *Demand for Illicit Drugs*: Cannabis continues to be the most widespread illicit drug with all regions of the world reporting its consumption. Almost 180,000,000 persons, or 3.1% of the global population are estimated to have used cannabis (marijuana and hashish) within the past 12 months, according to UNDCP estimates derived from 1992-1995. Daily users are estimated to make up around 40% of the total.

The potential global consumption of heroin/morphine ranged from 285 to 310 tonnes in 1995. Asia's heroin user population represents a third of the global user population with Asian consumption of heroin amounting to around 40% of the total quantity. This, combined with opium use, makes Asia the world's largest market for opiates.

Global manufacture of cocaine has tripled since 1980 to around 900 tonnes. UNDCP estimates a past-year cocaine user population of 30-45 million persons. To be more or less consistent with supply data, this population should represent a considerable share of persons with low annual use of the drug.

Since the mid-1980's, the illicit use of amphetamine-type stimulants (ATS) has increased at an alarming rate. In contrast to the localized outbreaks of abuse in the past, ATS are now consumed in practically every region of the world. Use of ATS has surpassed that of cocaine and heroin abuse together in some countries of South America, the Far East (especially the Republic of Korea, Japan, and the Philippines) and northern Europe, mainly Denmark, Sweden, and the UK.

* Precursor seizures are presented here in 'potential dosage units' of drugs in question according to the average conversion factors calculated from the ranges given by INCB (1996). For a drug, one litre of a precursor can produce millions of doses of the drug, while in the case of the other precursors the range is in hundred of doses.

Other Global Trends in Abuse

In summary, they are:

* increasing use of amphetamine type stimulants (ATS);
* increasing polydrug abuse—this can include ingesting a cocktail of drugs to enhance the effects of each drug, taking drugs sequentially to minimize the adverse effects of the first drug taken, or varying the drug of choice which is particularly common among young people;
* decreasing age of first contact with drugs, coupled with the related lowering of the age at which drugs are injected;
* growing illicit use of drugs in regions formerly little affected by the drug problem;
* shifting patterns of use towards more dangerous drug consumption patterns, i.e. injecting.

Injecting Drug Use and AIDS

Drug injecting has been identified in more than 100 countries, of which 80 report HIV infection among injecting drug users. The Joint United Nations Programme on HIV/AIDS, UNAIDS, estimates that the global proportion of HIV infections due to contaminated injection equipment was 5-10% in 1996.

The gradual transition from opium smoking to heroin smoking, and finally to heroin injection in Thailand with rapid flow-on AIDS infection is well-known. A similar pattern of rapid spread of HIV infection among IDUs was experienced in several countries of the South-east Asian subregion between 1987 and 1990.

In Africa, especially in the countries of Sub-Saharan Africa, the HIV/AIDS situation has been dramatic although the epidemic is spread primarily by heterosexual transmission, and only rarely through IDU.

In most Western European countries, HIV transmission among IDUs peaked around the mid-1980's, and has stabilized at different levels with considerable geographic variations, and is receding in some. Although the HIV epidemic is generally more recent and the prevalence is much lower in Central and Eastern Europe than in Western Europe, HIV among IDUs has begun to emerge.

Final Remarks

International drug control is a creature of the 20th century. The legal mechanisms and infrastructures of control have evolved rapidly, as abuse has grown, particularly in the second half of the century. The causes of drug abuse are many and complex, crossing all socio-economic and political boundaries, both domestically and internationally.

At the close of the millennium, there is clear international consensus that:

* drug abuse and trafficking is a global problem;

* effective action against drug problems is a shared collective responsibility of all states—no single state can be effective against its own drug abuse or trafficking problems without the strong support and cooperation of all others;

* well coordinated international cooperation by the various national and international actors is needed for all national and international efforts to have maximum impact;

* national and international impact against drug problems will be limited unless a holistic and balanced approach is taken by governments, recognizing and addressing the social, economic, political, environmental, scientific and psychological factors which affect the nature and extent of drug abuse;

* appropriate emphasis is placed on both supply reduction and demand reduction;

* all sections of society are mobilized for the purpose, from grass roots upwards; and

* flexibility is factored into all policy frameworks at the national and international levels to ensure that control regimes are not unduly rigid—because of the pace at which new drugs are developed, and frequent changes within both the licit and illicit markets in response to shifts in market forces.

Much has been done in response to the drug problem, but clearly much more still needs to be done. The appropriate international drug control legal infrastructure is in place at the international level. Many states have now passed the necessary new and amending legislation to bring their domestic laws in line with the conventions.

What is now needed is implementation, and more implementation meaning of course, effective implementation—facing up to and working through implementation problems arising and developing concrete practical measures to do it better, within the existing framework as it stands today—certainly, the international drug control conventions are, to be realistic, at about the same level of resources available today.

INTERNATIONAL LEGAL AND POLICY FRAMEWORK FOR DRUG CONTROL

Andrew Wells

In the strict technical sense, there is no single global drugs law binding every country. In terms of international treaty law, while treaties may be self-executing for some states, most common-law tradition states still need to enact their own enabling or implementing legislation before becoming a party to treaties.

However, the international drug control treaties (conventions) do provide a framework of binding legal obligations on states party to them, and in that sense that may be called a 'Global Drugs Law.' These conventions also appear to be unique in the global sense, in that drug control legislation was one of the first generic groups of legislation to originate for most countries at the international level rather than from purely domestic initiatives.

System of Control Provided for by the UN Drug Control Conventions

The operation of the international drug control system is based on the twofold principle of national control by states and international cooperative control in accordance with the international drug control conventions. States not a party to a particular convention are encouraged to apply treaty provisions voluntarily. These conventions underpin all national drug control laws, and lie at the heart of the Conference proceedings. The three most important currently in force are:

* Single Convention on Narcotic Drugs of 1961, and that convention as amended by the 1972 Protocol ('Single Convention');

* Convention on Psychotropic Substances, 1971 ('1971 Convention'); and

* United Nations Convention Against Illicit Traffic in Narcotic Drugs and Psychotropic Substances ('1988 Convention').

As at 31 January 1997, there were 158 parties (85 per cent of all UN Member States) to the 1961 Convention or that Convention as amended, 147 parties (80 per cent) to the 1971 Convention and 138 parties (75 per cent)[1] to the 1988 Convention. There are still 27 states not yet party to the 1961 Convention or that Convention as amended, 38 not yet party to the 1971 Convention and 47 not yet party to the 1988 Convention.[2]

[1] Afghanistan, Algeria, Antigua and Barbuda, Argentina, Armenia, Australia, Azerbaijan, Bahamas, Bahrain, Bangladesh, Barbados, Belarus, Belgium, Belize, Bhutan, Bolivia, Bosnia and Herzegovina, Botswana, Brazil, Brunei Darussalam, Bulgaria, Burkina Faso, Burundi, Czech Republic, Cameroon, Canada, Cape Verde, Chad, Chile, China, Colombia, Costa Rica, Côte d'Ivoire, Croatia, Cuba, Cyprus, Denmark, Dominica, Dominican Republic, Ecuador, Egypt, EL Salvador, Ethiopia, Fiji, Finland, France, Gambia, Germany, Ghana, Greece, Grenada, Guatemala, Guinea, Guinea-Bissau, Guyana, Haiti, Honduras, Hungary, India, Iran, Ireland, Italy, Jamaica, Japan, Jordan, Kenya, Kyrgyzstan, Latvia, Lebanon, Lesotho, Libya, Luxembourg, Madagascar, Malawi, Malaysia, Mauritania, Mali, Malta, Mexico, Moldova, Monaco, Morocco, Myanmar, Nepal, Netherlands, Nicaragua, Niger, Nigeria, Norway, Oman, Pakistan, Panama, Paraguay, Peru, Philippines, Poland, Portugal, Qatar, Romania, Russian Federation, Saint Kitts and Nevis, Saint Lucia, Saint Vincent and the Grenadines, Sao Tome and Principe, Saudi Arabia, Senegal, Seychelles, Sierra Leone, Slovak Republic of Macedonia, Togo, Tonga, Trinidad and Tobago, Tunisa, Turkey, Turkemenistan, Uganda, Ukraine, United Arab Emirates, United Kingdom, United States of Amercia, Uruguay, Uzbekistan, Venezuela, Yemen, Yugoslavia, Zambia and Zimbabwe. On 31 December, 1990, the European Economic Community deposited its instrument of formal confirmation to the Convention (extent of competence: Article 12).

[2] Countries not yet party to these conventions are as follows:

Europe: Albania, Andorra and San Marino (1988, 1971 and 1961): Austria, Liechtenstein (1988 and 1971); Estonia, Holy See, Iceland, Lithuania and Switzerland (1988);

Africa: Angola, Central African Republic, Comoros, Congo, Djibouti, Equatorial Guniea; Eritrea, Mozambique and Namibia (1988, 1971 and 1961); Liberia (1988, and 1971); Gabon, Mauritius, Rwanda, Somalia, South Africa and Zaire (1988); Kenya (1971); Tanzania (1971 and 1961).

Asia: Cambodia, Georgia, Kazakhstan, Korea (DPR), Maldives and Vietnam (1988, 1971 and 1961); Laos, Mongolia (1988 and 1971); Indonesia, Iraq, Israel, Korea (RO), Kuwait, Singapore, Thailand (1988); Iran, Nepal, Oman (1971); Azerbaijan, Bhutan, Tajikistan (1971 and 1961)

Oceania: Kiribati, Nauru, Palau, Samoa, Tuvalu, Vanuatu (1988, 1971 and 1961); Solomon Islands (1988 and 1971); Marshall Islands, Micronesia, New Zealand, Papua New Guinea (1988).

Americas: Belize, El Salvador, St. Vincent and the Grenadines (1971 and 1961); Haiti, Honduras, St. Lucia (1971); Grenada, Guyana (1961).

(a) Overview of the International Instruments Prior to the 1988 Convention

There are many and complex legal instruments enacted prior to the most recent Convention.

(b) Overview of the Single Convention, 1961

The Single Convention had three objectives:

* merging all prior existing multilateral treaties in the field;
* streamlining the roles and functions of two previous international drug control bodies into one; and
* extending the existing control regime to include cultivation of plants grown as the raw material of narcotic drugs.

The overall objectives of the earlier treaties remained, namely the provision of adequate supplies of narcotic drugs and preparations for medical and scientific purposes with complementary control measures to prevent diversion into the illicit market.

The Single Convention provides for the control of some 116 narcotic drugs. They include mainly plant-based products such as opium and its derivatives (eg. morphine, codeine and heroin) but also synthetic narcotics (e.g. methadone and pethidine) as well as cannabis, coca and cocaine. The convention divides drugs into four groups or schedules to enable differentiation between the levels of strictness of controls for each group depending on the degree of medical or scientific value of the substance on the one hand, and public risk associated with its abuse on the other. Opium smoking and eating, coca leaf chewing, cannabis, resin smoking and the non-medical use of cannabis are prohibited.

(c) Overview of the 1972 Protocol to the Single Convention

Among other things, this Protocol calls for increased efforts to prevent illicit production of traffic in and use of narcotics. It also highlights the need to provide treatment and rehabilitation services to drug-abusers, stressing that treatment, education, aftercare, rehabilitation and social reintegration may be considered instead of or in addition to imprisonment or other deprivation of liberty in cases involving drug users.

(d) Overview of the 1971 Convention

Growing concern over the harmful effects of psychotropic substances such as amphetamine-type drugs, sedative-hypnotic agents and hallucinogens led to the adoption of this Convention. It extended the international drug control system to include hallucinogens such as LSD and mescaline, stimulants such as amphetamines and sedative-hypnotics such as barbiturates.

The Convention also groups the substances into four schedules much like the Single Convention—strictest controls for substances with lowest medical or scientific value and highest public detriment from abuse, through to least strict control for those with highest medical or scientific value and lowest public detriment from abuse.

Special provisions concerning abuse prevention were aimed at ensuring early identification, treatment, education, aftercare, rehabilitation and social reintegration of dependent persons. The Commission on Narcotic Drugs and INCB were given particular responsibilities relating to the control of drugs in the Convention.

(e) Overview of the 1988 Convention

The 1988 Convention complements the Single Convention and 1971 Convention, both of which were primarily directed at the control of licit activities—namely ensuring the availability of narcotic drugs and psychotropic substances for exclusively medical and scientific purposes, while seeking to ensure that they were not illicitly produced or made available or diverted from the licit system.

The 1988 Convention was formulated specifically to deal with the growing problem of international drug trafficking which had only been dealt with marginally by earlier legal instruments. It is of wide and detailed ambit. Although drug trafficking is its main focus, it equally requires states to take their demand reduction obligations seriously.

This was one of the main compromises between the negotiating parties, resulting in the inclusion of an offence relating to personal consumption, but for which demand reduction measures were available without the need to resort to penal sanctions. This is in sharp contrast to the provisions relating to trafficking offences (other than those of a minor nature), for which penal sanctions and international criminal justice system cooperation were required.

On the serious trafficking side, the 1988 Convention filled gaps in the earlier Conventions and added a package of powerful 'state of the art' international legal cooperation measures, e.g. by:

* expanding trafficking offences to reach more clearly those who enable or facilitate large-scale trafficking, such as the money launderers, planners, managers and financiers, and others who with knowledge of the criminal purpose enable the use of drug-making chemicals, equipment or facilities;

* reducing availability of extradiction 'safe havens' for traffickers and their helpers (relatively uniform extraditable offences, appropriate penal sanctions for serious offences, long statute of limitations periods, wider extraterritorial criminal jurisdiction, etc);

* removing previous legal obstacles to international cooperation, or enabling powerful new forms of such cooperation, eg. by:

— seeking to codify and advance extradition law and practice;

— requiring the widest measure of mutual legal assistance, so that parties effectively 'lend' each other their coercive investigatory and judicial powers;

— requiring measures to enable the tracing, temporary 'freezing' and eventual confiscation of proceeds of trafficking, notwithstanding bank or commercial secrecy;

— requiring international cooperation:

* over legitimate international trade in chemicals often used in the illicit manufacture of controlled drugs, materials and equipment, to prevent their diversion (suspicious trade monitoring controls also required);

* to suppress illicit traffic in free trade zones, free ports and on the high seas.

The net result of the 1988 Convention for our purposes is:

* first, drug trafficking must be made a serious offence and stringently dealt with by the criminal justice system, unless 'an appropriate case of a minor nature' (in such cases where the trafficker is also a user, demand reduction measures can be employed, with or without civil or penal sanctions);

* second, possession, purchase and cultivation for personal use must be made an offence, but criminal sanctions are not *required*—parties are free to deal with such cases exclusively on a treatment, rehabilitation, aftercare and reintegration basis, if they so choose;

* third, the powerful investigatory and international cooperation requirements of the 1988 Convention permit criminal justice authorities to focus priorities and resources (investigatory, prosecutorial and judicial) to:

— dismantle the top structure of major national and international trafficking networks, rather than just the lowest levels (couriers, or user-traffickers); and

— deprive the major criminals involved of their profits, wherever held.

(f) Summary of the Legal Effect of all the UN Drug Control Conventions

The drug control conventions are essential points of reference for all states seeking ways to more effectively deal with drug abuse and drug-related crime problems in their countries. They set the important legal limits on what States Party to them can and cannot do, and comprise the legal framework for national and international action by governments party to them. Since they are binding on the governments concerned, their obligatory effects trickle down through each level of government to community level and beyond to individuals.

To summarize their legal effect in terms of the issues at the Conference:

* first, the international drug control conventions are binding legal instruments on the parties to them. In general:

— they are created by States;

— only States can be Party to them;

— they can be amended or denounced only by such States, in accordance with procedures set out therein;

— no legal entity other than a State Party to the Conventions can change them or denounce them;

* second, the Conventions are not set in concrete, fixed for all time, unable to be changed. They are forward-looking. They anticipate that needs, problems and problem-solving strategies experience will constantly evolve. They therefore contain machinery for their amendment and updating. But the procedures for change are demanding, providing checks and balances against unconvincing proposals;

* third, they oblige or exhort parties to take particular measures to reduce drug abuse and drug-related criminality (often, but not always, detailing the outcome or result required, but leaving it to governments concerned to determine the most appropriate ways and means of achieving it);

* fourth, in general, they set minimum requirements only, leaving governments free to implement above the minimum if considered appropriate, but not below. This is a critical point to remember, because in some cases it is often wrongly assumed that certain implementation action by a particular Party above the Convention minimum is required by the Conventions when it is not;

* fifth, implementation of the Conventions cannot be looked at *in vacuo*, but in the context of policy expressed in other less formal instruments expressing international consensus, including;

— the Comprehensive Multidisciplinary Outline (CMO), which emerged from the International Conference on Drug Abuse and Illicit Trafficking, 1987 (ICDAIT);

— the Drugs Global Programme of Action adopted by the UN General Assembly, 1990.

Together, these constitute the basic policy blueprint for global efforts in drug abuse control, and to be reviewed by the 1998 Special Session of the General Assembly.

Other Multilateral and Bilateral Instruments

Considerable legal instrument developmental and implementation work has been done by a large number of interregional, regional and bilateral actors. Without being exhaustive, the following are of special importance:

(a) Commonwealth Secretariat

* the various schemes for international legal cooperation developed under the auspices of the Commonwealth Secretariat, namely:
— Commonwealth Scheme for the Rendition of Fugitive Offenders;
— Scheme relating to Mutual Assistance in Criminal Matters within the Commonwealth;
— Scheme for the Transfer of Convicted Offenders within the Commonwealth.

The Commonwealth Secretariat provides a range of helpful legal services to member states including the Commonwealth Legal Assistance News and Crime Watch publications and model legislation for small jurisdictions on money laundering (including provisions on anti-money laundering supervision, freezing and forfeiture of assets, mutual legal assistance and extradition in relation to money laundering).

(b) Financial Action Task Force (FATF)

Since it was launched in 1989, FATF has developed and refined a strategy against money laundering.

This strategy, set out in the 40 recommendations, has formed the basis of national legislation against money laundering in many countries. This has particularly been so for member states of the European Union, as the FATF recommendations form the basis of the EC Money Laundering Directive.

The FATF recommendations address a wide range of issues that are essential to any effective programme to combat money laundering. The recommendations apply to three main areas—the legal framework, the financial system, and international cooperation.

(c) Council of Europe

The Council of Europe has been particularly active in treaty development on issues relating to serious crime, including serious drug crime. These instruments include:

* European Convention on Extradition (1957);
* European Convention on Mutual Assistance in Criminal Matters (1959);
* European Convention on the Supervision of Conditionally Sentenced or Conditionally Released Offenders (1964);
* European Convention on the International Validity of Criminal Judgements (1970);
* European Convention on the Transfer of Proceedings in Criminal Matters (1972);
* European Convention on the Suppression of Terrorism (1977);
* European Convention on the Transfer of Sentenced Persons (1983);
* European Convention on the Compensation of Victims of Violent Crimes (1983);
* Agreement on Illicit Traffic by Sea, Implementing Article 17 of the United Nations Convention Against Illicit Traffic in Narcotic Drugs and Psychotropic Substances, done at Strasbourg, 31 January 1995.

Work is currently proceeding on a number of instruments including a future European Convention Against Corruption.

(d) Other Instruments

Many regional organizations have developed legal instruments and implementing guidelines on a wide range of drug-related subjects. Among these are the:

* Inter American Drug Abuse Commission (CICAD) of the Organization of American States;
* Organization of African Unity (OAU), Economic Community of Central African States (ECCAS), Economic Community of Western African States (ECOWAS) and the Southern African Development Community (SADC);
* Economic Cooperation Organization (ECO)—comprising Iran, Afghanistan, Pakistan, Turkey, Azerbaijan, Tajikistan, Kyrgyzstan, Uzbekistan, Turkmenistan and Kazakhstan, South Asian Association for Regional Cooperation (SAARC); Colombo Plan; Association of South-East Asian Nations (ASEAN) and the South Pacific Forum.

UNDCP has concluded a number of Memoranda of Understanding (MOU) to promote cross-border cooperation in drug matters on a subregional basis. At this stage, MOUs have been concluded with Golden Triangle Countries (1993), Iran and Pakistan (1994), Eastern Europe (1995), the Central Asian Republics (1995), Southern Cone (1995), Mexico and Central America (1996). They have also been concluded with OAU (1994), ECO (1996), SAARC (1995).

The International Policy Framework for Tackling Drug Problems

(a) *The 1987 Comprehensive Multidisciplinary Outline (CMO)*: National authorities and interested organizations were exhorted to use the CMO as a basis for developing and translating into action, at the national, regional and international levels, to the widest extent possible, balanced strategies aimed at combating all aspects of drug abuse and illicit trafficking, and in particular:

* prevention and reduction of drug abuse with a view to elimination of the illicit demand for narcotic drugs and psychotropic substances;

* treatment, rehabilitation, and social reintegration of drug addicts;

* control of supply of narcotic drugs and psychotropic substances:

— eradication and substitution of illicit production of narcotic drugs, and eradication of illicit processing of such drugs and of illicit production and diversion of psychotropic substances;

— licit production, manufacture and supply of narcotic drugs and psychotropic substances:

— cooperation on the multilateral level;

— monitoring and control measures.

* suppression of illicit trafficking in narcotic drugs and psychotropic substances;

— traffic;

— distribution.

* measures to be taken against the effects of money derived from, used in or intended for use in illicit drug trafficking, illegal financial flows and illegal use of the banking system;

* strengthening of judicial and legal systems, including law enforcement;

* measures to be taken against the diversion of arms and explosives and illicit traffic by vessels, aircraft and vehicles;

* resources and structure.

(b) *The Global Programme of Action on Drugs*: The Global Programme of Action[3] was adopted in 1990, by the General Assembly at its 17th Special Session. It is devoted to the question of international cooperation against illicit production, supply, demand, trafficking and distribution of narcotic drugs and psychotropic substances. It reflects the will of the international community to consider as an urgent matter the improvement of international cooperation in order to render effective and efficient the fight against illicit drugs and drug abuse.

[3] Report of the International Conference on Drug Abuse and Illicit Trafficking, Vienna, 17-26 June, 1987 (United Nations Publication, Sales No. E.87.1.18).

In the spectrum of international action plans, the Global Programme of Action represents the most comprehensive statement of the action that needs to be taken by individual countries and collectively through the system of international organizations it provides a framework and guidelines to the international community.

The Global Programme offers a wide range of guidance to governments facing drug-related problems and recommends concrete measures to address issues such as illicit cultivation and processing, trafficking, money laundering and illicit demand.

(c) *1994 Naples Political Declaration and Global Action Plan Against Organized Transnational Crime*: This Political Declaration and Global Programme of Action, like the earlier 1990 drugs one, represents the most comprehensive international statement yet of the action needed by countries individually and collectively.

Notable in the Political Declaration by the Heads of State and Government, ministers and other high-level representatives was:

* their determination to

— join forces and fight together against the expansion and diversification of organized transnational crime and terrorist crime with which it is often linked;

— protect their societies from organized crime in all its forms through strict and effective legislative measures and operational instruments, consistently with internationally recognized human rights and fundamental freedoms;

— direct particular efforts toward defeating the social and economic power of criminal organizations, plus their ability to infiltrate legitimate economies, launder criminal proceeds, and use violence and terror;

* their agreement to see the strengthening and enhancement of capability to achieve more effective international cooperation against threats posed by organized transnational crime, for example by

— closer alignment of legislative texts concerning organized crime; and

— strengthening international cooperation at the investigative, prosecutorial and judicial levels in operational matters.

The Global Programme of Action contains a number of relevant elements, namely:

* national legislation dealing with organized transnational crime and guidelines for legislative and other measures;

— shared intelligence and experience of States for useful guiding principles concerning the substantive, procedural and regulatory legislation and organizational structures needed to prevent and combat the phenomena;

— States should ensure that they possess structures and capabilities throughout their entire criminal justice system adequate to deal with complex organized criminal activities, including safeguards against corruption, intimidation and violence;

— States must overcome the code of silence and intimidation of organized crime to effectively combat it—reliable evidence-gathering techniques such as electronic surveillance, undercover operations and controlled delivery should be contemplated subject to appropriate safeguards—measures should also be considered which encourage the cooperation and testimony of members of organized crime including protection programmes for witnesses and families and subject to national law concessions recognizing collaboration provided in the prosecution process;

— money laundering, proceeds of crime, and other administrative law mechanisms to reinforce transparency and integrity in business and government should be considered preventive measures of equal importance with penal law as a means of combating organized crime;

* international cooperation at the investigative, prosecutorial and judicial levels;

— develop and improve bilateral and multilateral assistance eg. through more widespread promotion and use of model treaties and relevant regional instruments;

— implement fully existing bilateral and multilateral extradition and mutual legal assistance conventions and agreements;

— improve practical application of existing agreements through informal and operational mechanisms (eg. central authorities, exchanging manuals, focal points, joint task forces, best practice investigative techniques, sharing advanced investigative technology).

* modalities and guidelines for international cooperation at the regional and international levels;

— strengthen technical cooperation to assist developing countries and countries in transition to enhance capability of their law enforcement and judicial systems;

— coordinate bilateral and multilateral technical cooperation to avoid overlap and duplication;

— UN to provide and facilitate technical cooperation including exchange of experience and expertise, training of police and judicial staff and on the use of effective counter measures—plus legislation drafting, special training courses for police, prosecutors, judges and magistrates, and on gathering, analysing and exchanging relevant information.

* prevention and control of money laundering and control of proceeds of crime;

— strategy should be aimed at defeating the economic power of criminal organizations and include both criminal and regulatory mechanisms;

— make money laundering a criminal offence;

— adopt adequate preventive measures (clear identification of position of company owners, accurate information on acquisitions and transfers, high ethical standards in the public and private sectors including financial institutions and relevant professions, plus cooperation between financial and economic sector regulators and criminal justice authorities);

— consider adopting legislation for seizure, forfeiture and confiscation of assets and illicit proceeds, plus provisional measures—subject to appropriate safeguards;

— consider sharing forfeited assets;

— consider seizing or confiscating illicit proceeds without criminal conviction or sums higher than those relating to the crime of which the person is convicted (again subject to appropriate safeguards)—limit financial secrecy for money laundering control and international cooperation purposes—adopt other legislative or regulatory measures such as know your customer, reporting suspicious transactions, indemnities for good faith reporting—high priority to be given to measures to prevent displacement of money laundering from tightly supervised banks to non-supervised entities offering financial services—identify the likely ones and consider extending regulatory obligations to them if not a banking or financial institution;

— the UN to assist States in need of assessment, treaty development and development of criminal justice infrastructures and human resources by providing technical assistance using expertise and cooperation of all its institutes and other agencies.

Overview of Implementing Legislation of Convention Parties

Since the Conventions set only minimum standards, the Parties are free to go above them but not below. Accordingly, differences in policy approach are reflected in their implementing laws.

While most parties have relatively uniform laws against serious drug trafficking, there are wide variations of approach in terms of the nature, extent and severity of sanctions and of the extent to which they are given effect in practice;

* at one extreme, a stringent *enforcement* of prohibitions, including against personal consumption, this tends to be found in the laws of countries where, eg:

— the conduct is also proscribed under religious law, or there are strongly held community norms and standards favouring a strict approach; or

— for resources reasons, demand reduction measures are not available or not yet well-developed (eg. some least developed and developing countries);

at the other extreme, a liberal approach to the *enforcement* of laws relating to personal consumption, at least of certain drugs such as cannabis—this tends to found in a small number of countries where the much criticized view is taken that by permitting non-addict users to consume certain small quantities of drugs such as cannabis under controlled conditions, this might help prevent them from progressing to so-called 'hard' drugs.

The Main Legislative Tendencies

The following is an account of some of the more broadly indicative legislative trends and different choices of Parties in implementing their obligations under the Conventions:

(a) Legislative Approach to Drug Abusers

* First, towards a more balanced, holistic approach, involving all relevant sectors and disciplines, with:

— demand reduction, with preventive and health care measures the primary resort;

— backed by sanctions, (administrative, penal or a combination of both);

* Second, towards a combination of both voluntary and compulsory treatment regimes, usually with compulsory treatment as the fall back ('carrot and stick' approach), however:

— in some jurisdictions, treatment regimes are compulsory;

— they are probably never exclusively voluntary;

* Third, towards removing criminal justice system barriers to addicts seeking or obtaining treatment, rehabilitation or similar help:

— prior to detection by law enforcement authorities;

* by permitting addicts, who have not committed serious offences, to come forward for treatment under legally conferred confidentiality;

previously, unless confidentiality could be guaranteed, the risk of prosecution for possession or use was said to deter addicts from coming forward for help;

— after detection by law enforcement authorities;

* by diverting the case from the criminal justice system into the health care system, or by requiring reference of the case to health care authorities for treatment and rehabilitation assessment and report back;

* this can occur at any material time in the criminal justice process eg. after arrest, before trial or hearing, before pronouncement of sanction, after pronouncement of sanction or even after implementation of the sanction has begun;

— however, checks and balances are usually included in legislation, to ensure it is not abused and to maximize the incentives for abusers to voluntarily undertake and complete the programme, eg. systems of rewards, remissions or even pardons;

* Fourth, towards an expansion of administrative sanctions:

— usually administered by a multidisciplinary tribunal, or officials, including mayors of cities/towns (this is good, because it helps drive drug abuse problem-solving responsibility downwards from the top government levels to cities and community in areas where cities and communities may be in the best position to respond);

— usually backed up by resort to a judge, if coercive intervention becomes ultimately necessary;

* Fifth, in some states, towards so-called 'harm reduction,' by making lawful under controlled conditions certain activities which previously may have violated the law, for example:

— permitting needle exchanges to contain the spread of infectious transmissible diseases;

— methadone substitution programmes;

There is substantial lack of international consensus over many harm reduction measures, particularly those which may facilitate, sustain or perpetuate drug abuse.

* Sixth and finally, towards a wider range of sanctions, both administrative and civil, to avoid the need for inappropriate imprisonment, eg:

— non-institutional detention, weekend detention, community service orders, and other temporary measures of supervised short-run limitations or deprivations of liberty;

— temporary prohibition of going to or from particular places, of frequenting particular places or of associating with particular persons;

— temporary withdrawal of other valuable rights, privileges or benefits, eg passport, visa, vehicle vessel or aircraft licences;

— temporary closure, or suspension or cancellation of valuable licences of public premises, where their management permit them to be used for supplying or using drugs.

(b) Legislative Approach to Trafficking and Related Activities

* First, towards relatively harmonized legislation on offences; however differences in sanctions and enforcement policy still create practical anomalies within particular regions or subregions eg:

— about supplying/promoting/permitting the consumption of cannabis;

— there tend to be widely differing levels of severity of sanctions for trafficking, which can lead to eg:

* refusal of cooperation assistance (eg. death penalty in requesting State, but not in the requested State);

* punishment in two countries for the same offence (eg. second country regards the foreign sentence as 'inadequate');

* Second, while the general level of legislative implementation of the more 'classical' trafficking activities has been broadly satisfactory, it has been much less so with the newer offences relating to the crucial facilitating or support activities of money-laundering and illicit precursor supply:

— this can compromise attempts to dismantle trafficking networks by depriving them of criminally-tainted funds, because they simply move the funds from one State to another as one implements controls but the other does not;

— nevertheless, there has been pleasing progress, particularly the following:

* the path-breaking work both original and follow-up work of both the Financial Action Task Force and the short-lived but effective Chemical Action Task Force on practical measures to implement, give full effect to, and necessarily go beyond the strict requirements of the 1988 Convention;

* many regional and interregional initiatives on money laundering and precursor controls by, for example the Commonwealth Secretariat, Council of Europe, European Union, Commission and the Organization of American States.

Conclusion

There is now in place an unprecedented international legal and policy framework for dealing with current and foreseeable problems of drug abuse and drug-related criminality. Since the adoption of the 1988 Convention there has been a concerted effort by most States to become party, not only to that Convention, but also the 1971 and 1961 Convention. There has also been pleasing progress across most regions of the globe towards upgrading domestic laws in line with the Conventions, particularly in:

* introducing greater flexibility and interdisciplinary approach to the problems of drug users, abusers and addicts;

* expanding the package of serious drug-related offences to include money-laundering, trafficking in precursor chemicals, and appropriate preventive and regulatory mechanisms;

* putting in place the enabling provisions for modern investigatory techniques to better penetrate criminal organizations and obtain the evidence needed to secure conviction and the confiscation of criminal gains;

* enabling new forms of international co-operation, like mutual legal assistance, and improving old ones like extradition, and cooperation against maritime trafficking

* enabling confiscation of the proceeds of crime, and provisional measures pending final judicial order;

* reducing the earlier wide discrepancies between countries with regard to penalties and sanctions for serious drug crime.

Having set the international legal context for national laws implementing the drug control conventions, we can now move forward in this Conference to look at implementation. To what extent are these laws being effectively implemented? Where are the implementation problems you may be experiencing—particularly within the criminal justice system, and what can be done to reduce or remove them? So let us now begin the work of bringing important implementation problems and opportunities to light—beginning with the capacity and needs of the justice system in our various countries to deal with the drug challenge—both now, and beyond 2000.

[Editorial Note:

Copies of the following documents attached to the paper distributed at the Conference are available from the Legal Advisory Programme, UNDCP, Vienna, on request:

— History of International Drug Control;

— Description of the Key United Nations Bodies Involved in Drug Problems; and

— Penalties, Sanctions and Sentences for, or related to, Drug Trafficking in National Legislation].

EVOLVING GLOBAL DRUGS LAW FOR THE 21st CENTURY

R.K.Nayak

Introduction

The use of drugs is considered to be as old as human civilization[1]. Drugs have been used or misused by most groups in society from time immemorial for their pleasurable and relaxing effects in order to facilitate communication with the spirits of Gods for religious reasons or for simply prolonging physical exertion in the face of hunger or adversaries.[2] This reveals that in olden times, perhaps after-effects of drugs and other societal aspects were not known. Notwithstanding, with the rapidly expanding pharmaceutical industry, the number of drugs having some property attractive to misusers has increased to a great extent.[3] It is difficult at times to demarcate where the use ends and misuse begins. An Expert Committee of the W.H.O. thus defined drug addiction very appropriately:

> Drug addiction is a state of periodic or chronic intoxication, detrimental to the individual and to society, produced by repeated consumption of a drug either natural or synthetic. Its characteristics include (a) an overpowering desire or need (compulsion) to continue taking the drug and to obtain it by means, (b) a tendency to increase the dose; and (c) a psychi (psychological) and sometimes a physical dependence on the effect of drugs.[4]

According to UNDP, based on information available, at least 40 million people are abusing drugs worldwide. Notwithstanding, trafficking and drug

[1]R.K. Siegel, *Life in the Pursuit of Artificial Paradise*. 313-314 (E.P. Duton), New York 1989).

[2]J.K. Mason, *Forensic Medicine for Lawyers* 251 (1983).

[3]*Id.* at 252.

[4]K. Mitra, *Social Welfare in India* 140 (1960).

abuse have taken the shape of an epidemic and consequently a serious threat to humanity. The global drug menace relates to illicit drugs which reflect and contribute invariably international crime, tension and huge exchange of money in different parts of the world. The origin owes to some of the tensions created by rapid changes in geopolitics and new alignment of forces, reduced family and community's social and economic cohesiveness, increased unemployment and above all increased crimes. Inspite of these realities the macro economic environment has basically changed radically. World trade on investment had brought uprecedented economic benefits to both the developed and developing world. Inspite of radical changes the world over, the socio-economic scenario for billions of poor people remained the same. The macro-economic environment, which has facilitated the unprecedented and legitimate growth and development of business on a global scale has also provided enormous opportunity for drug producers and traffickers to organise drug cartels for distribution and marketing all over the world. The huge drug trade globally allowed people, goods and money to move from one country to another and provided opportunities to move money around the world through many highly sophisticated and electronic devices. In this process some national regulations and controls also permit drug producers and traffickers to launder illicit profits under the guise of legal transaction.

In the world of today, there is more awareness of the problem of drug abuse and illicit drug and drug trafficking than ever before. The three drug conventions adopted by the United Nations viz., the Single Convention on Narcotic Drugs of 1961 as amended by the 1972 Protocol, the Convention on Psychotropic Substances, 1971 and 1988 UN Drug Trafficking Convention are mainly concerned with the prevention and eradication of drug problems arising due to use and abuse of narcotic drugs and psychotropic substances. These Conventions oblige States to enact legislation criminalising drug trafficking in all forms.

Drug trafficking as a crime of international demension is the root cause of drug addiction and a major source of the worldwide menace. It is also the root cause of medico-social and socio-economic harm at the international scale. Globally people are affected, therefore, this evil cannot be eradicated by one nation or group of nations but by a comprehensive and positive Global Drugs Law. The threat of drug abuse linked with trafficking is so grave that the world community or enlightened people of the world society have to wage a serious war to combat the evil. In this regard, international cooperation is a must to develop further international rules and enforce them effectively with all seriousness to curb the trafficking based on the universal common jurisdiction which imposes responsibility on the States to prosecute offenders or give them up.[5]

The Enormous Cost

The cost of drug abuse worldwide is considered to be as high as $ 400 billion a year according to UN sources. The cost includes precious money spent on law enforcement services, on handling crime and accidents, treatment and from the loss of productivity.[6] Besides, it also involves rising social and unemployment costs and those of related illnesses including the spread of dreadful disease - HIV/AIDS.[7] Drug use rather abuse throws people out of jobs and schools and place them in hospitals, prisons and in poverty or death trap. The toll is really serious and heart-touching and dismaying. Chronic alchoholism and drug abuse are responsible for world's one sixth of disabled people out of the total disabled population.[8] In U.K. and U.S.A. industries suffer losses by billions of dollars due to alcohol misuse.

International Narcotics Control Board reports:

> Some decades ago, the abuse problem was the concern of only a limited number of countries, but today countries that are not suffering from the harmful consequences of drug abuse are the exception rather than the rule.[9]

Drug abuse is most frequent in the age group of young people between the ages of 18 and 35-a time of life when men and women should be in life-making and family raising carriers. Therefore, the health and behaviour problems linked with drug abuse have serious repercussions on family life and industrial productivity. It is aptly said by the U.N. Secretary General:

> Drug consumption is costly to society and corrodes its values. Absenteeism and erratic and unsafe behaviour at work increase production costs in industry. Billions of dollars of public money are swallowed up in the additional services society has to provide to deal with other kinds of damage. Drug consumption leads to accidents, which place national burdens on medical and social welfare programmes. The consequences of drug abuse include criminal damage, which necessitates additional deployment of law enforcement resources. Terrorists use the drug trade to purchase

[5]M. C. Bassiouni, "The International Narcotics Control Scheme" in M. C. Bassiouni (ed.) *International Criminal Law: Crimes* 507 (1986).

[6]The Times of India (New Delhi) P.21 (23 April, 1994).

[7]*Ibid.*

[8]L. Despouy, Human Rights and Disabled Persons (Study Series 6, U.N. Centre for Human Rights (Geneva, Switzerland, U.N. Publication Sale No. E 92, XIV 4) 15 (1993).

[9]*Ibid.*

arms and finance their subversive operations. The fabric of democracy is threatened by the ability of powerful criminal groups to corrupt and even assassinate public officials and undermine the rule of law.[10]

With a view to curbing the menace of drugs in the century serious efforts have been made through international legal instruments. The attempt started with the controlling of opium trade in Asia.[11] Then many countries attempted to control the ever increasing international commerce through legislation.[12] Many countries enacted laws in consonance with international drug control treaties and conventions. These laws control production, trafficking and possession of drugs without intent to sell.[13] Drug laws were the outcome of drug abuse and moulded according to perception and socio-economic needs of each society. "Drug control models seldom recognize fully the differences in the actions, effects, and consequences of drug use or the purposes for which drugs are used.[14] Resultantly, sincere legal and public policy meant for controlling harmful drug use remained a distant dream. People enslaved to drugs could not be reformed or helped due to public policy and law. Drug abuse, in one way or other, affects normal socio-economic activities, intelligent and responsible behaviour, and ability and motivation to perform tasks necessary for human development and advancement. In this regard cooperative, in comparison to coercive, measures can work better to prevent or reduce drug use and its resultant harms.

International Legal and Policy Approach Towards Drug Abuse

In the beginning of the 19th century a small number of governments advocated the need for international drug control through law and policy[15] and efforts were made to control illicit cultivation, production and distribution of drugs rather than to regulate legal commerce in opiates and cocaine. In the

[10]See Message, Boutros Boutros Ghali, on the occasion of the International Day Against Drug Abuse and Illicit Trafficking, June 26, 1996.

[11]See generally J. Beeching, *The Chinese Opium Wars* (1975).

[12]H. Abadinsky, *Drug Abuse, An Introduction*, 34-40 (Nelson-Hall, Chicago, IL, 1989).

[13]R.Fox and I. Mathews (eds.), *Drug Policy, Fact, Fiction and the Future* 69-70(1992).

[14]Norbert Gilmore, "Drug Use and Human Rights Privacy, Vulnerability, Disability and Human Rights Infringement." 12 *J. Contemporary Health Law & Policy* 335 at 392-383 (1996).

[15]G. Arnao, "Italian Refrendum Deletes Criminal Sanctions for Drug Users", 24 *J. Drug Issues* 483-497 (1994).

most industrialised countries, legal control of drugs deals mainly with production, distribution, sale and possession of prohibited drugs, the power to seize assets relating to these illicit activities, the power to prosecute and punish offenders and the power to require drug users to accept medical treatment. Besides, other powers deal with the regulation of prescription drugs and marketing and taxation of restricted drugs, for example tobacco and alchohol. Through some reform and education measures governments must make attempts to reduce the demand for drugs. Measures such as education, rehabilitation and reintegration into society have proved useful to reform the drug abusers.[16]

The scenario differs from country to country in relation to the balance between supply reduction and demand reduction for the control of drug use. For, example in the United States in 1991 federal allocations for supply and demand reduction were seventy one percent and twenty nine percent.[17] In contrast, allocations for supply and demand reduction in Canada from 1987 to 1992 were thirty percent and seventy percent, respectively.[18]

The control of drug abuse in industrialised countries is more or less based on international legal instruments and these controls differ from jurisdiction to jurisdiction but they are influenced more or less by the U.S. "War on Drugs".[19] Canadian and American approaches to drug abuse prevention are very common. Canadian laws prohibit the cultivation, production, sale and possession of prescribed drugs under two federal laws, viz. the Narcotic Control Act, 1970 and the Food and Drugs Act, 1971 which define offences and penalties and the police powers relating to entry, search, seizure and forfeiture but not procedural rules.[20] Procedural rules are covered by the Criminal Code which also includes driving under the influence of drugs, including alchohol. Attempts to curb illicit drugs use or the war against drugs have not yielded good results in some countries due to its ineffectiveness and harmfulness. Consequently these countries have strong reservations in following U.S. policies; hence they have not been following such policies.[21]

[16]B.Shahandeh. "Rehabilitation Approaches to Drug and Alcohol Dependence", Geneva, International Labour Office, (1985).

[17]A Goldstein, H. Kalant. *Drug Policy: Striking the Right Balance* 1514 (1990).

[18]Government of Canada, Action on Drug Abuse. Making a Difference [Ottawa, Min Supply and Services] 7 (1998).

[19]J. Mandel, H.W. Fieldman, *The Social History Teenage Drug Use* in H.Beschner, et. al. eds., *Teen Drug Use*, 19-42 (1996).

[20]*Ibid.*

[21]See P.J. Endicott et.al., *Panic and Indifference. The Politics of Canada's Drug Laws* (1991).

In view of the growing drug trafficking and money laundering many countries are strongly in favour of more effective and more stringent, more productive, less expensive and less harmful measures. The tough drug laws had two characteristics. Firstly explicit prohibition or restriction on people, probation or suspension of sentence in cases of violent crimes. Secondly convicted drug offenders to be sentenced to a mandatory minimum prison term.[22] The various types of laws in various countries are not able to meet the growing menace of drug abuse and therefore some new approach is needed to be evolved.

Need for Global Drugs Law

Many Heads of State and governments have realised and directed for launching offensives against the drug menace and Secretary General of the United Nations while addressing the Economic and Social Council on May 24, 1985 noted that the time had arrived for the international community to expand its efforts in a global undertaking that would be more concerted and more comprehensive. It is necessary to contain the plague of illicit drugs and thus it is absolutely urgent to evolve a global drugs law or international drugs law. The proposed world legislation may be able to meet the situation; hence counter offences are needed at the national and international levels to deal with the threat of drug abuse worldwide. The drug menace poses a threat not only to millions irrespective of population groups, societies and economies in some countries but the very foundation of the human race. Nevertheless, significant progress has been made by the international community in building up environmental defences against the production of addictive drugs and the illicit traffic in abusing drugs. In the last eighty years, substantial cooperation has been achieved on that basis; the U.N. can play a very constructive role to expand its work in the fight against illicit drug trafficking.

Notwithstanding, prevention and reduction of the illicit demand for narcotic drugs and psychotropic substances through education, checks in the workplace, programmes by civil community, special task forces, law enforcement agencies and active role of media are necessary measures to deal with.

The strengthening of the international system of control of narcotics drugs and psychotropic substances, suppression of illicit trafficking and treatment and rehabilitation of drug addicts to facilitate their reintegration into the community are equally important and relevant for both developed and developing countries. These aspects need to be given serious attention by the world community.

[22]Gilmore, *supra* note 14 at 404.

Any proposed international drugs law will have to take into consideration on the part of the international community the need for speedy and effective action to curb the disturbing situation arisen due to drug abuse and the illicit drug traffic. The U.N. General Assembly in its Resolution 40/12 directed to convene the International Conference on Drug Abuse and Illicit Trafficking in 1987. The General Assembly gave the Conference an ambitious mandate encompassing the full range of issues relevant to the fight against drug abuse, illicit trafficking and related criminal activities at the national, regional and international levels. The international drugs law has to be multidisciplinary in approach and outline. Generally, under national law as well as under the international drug control treaties, a 'narcotic drug' and psychotropic or psychoactive substance include cocaine, morphine, heroin, mescaline and diazepam (Valium). Psychotropic substances alter mood by affecting the users central nervous system and may act as sleep aids, tranquillizers or stimulants.[23]

Psychotropic drugs have a direct and significant impact on the processes of the mind that influence emotion, thinking, perception, feeling etc.[24] However, psychotropic drugs belong to a single, cohesive class and tend to be habit forming, health impairing and capable of being used recreationally or medicinally as a symptom reliever.[25] In the interest of fairness, all psychotropic drugs are essentially equivalent and they should be assigned to a single regulatory system.[26] There are five possible systems through which drug abuse can be tackled viz criminal law prohibition, medical prescription, rationing, tax licensing and the free market.[27] Out of these five which system would be preferable as a universal plan to be proposed to which international drug law can adapt and develop, is to be considered seriously. If drug consumers under the influence cause serious harm in that situation criminal law should punish that harm alone and not the drug use. Drug use should not amplify criminal penalties to be in consonance with the values of humantarian law.[28]

Social Impact of Drug Abuse

Global increases in problems of illicit drugs both reflect and contribute to international tensions. Illicit drug trafficking takes place in most countries

[23]Chester, N. Mitchell, "A Justice Based Argument for the Uniform Regulation of Psychoactive Drugs", 31 *McGill L.J.* 212 at 215 (1986).

[24]E.Goode, *Drugs in American Society*. 17 (19k34).

[25]Supra note 23 at 215.

[26]*Ibid.*

[27]*Ibid.*

[28]*Id.* at 234.

of the world. "Recognition of illegal importation and distribution-a criminal activity frequently involving foreigners — is politically less troublesome than purely domestic illicit production or consumption."[29] The organized groups or cartels deal and move in large quantities of drugs. Cocaine trafficking begins in the Andean region and spread northward through Central America, Mexico and the Caribbean region to end points in North America, Europe and elsewhere.[30] South west and South east-Asia are the major points of heroin trafficking.[31] To deal with the problem of drug abuse, however, a common conceptual structure is provided by international drug treaties.

Several treaties have obligations which require penal[32] provisions in national laws for illicit traffic offences. Crime and drugs may be related in several ways but none of them are simple in nature and straight answers cannot be expected. Illicit production, manufacture, distribution or possession of drugs may constitute a crime. Drugs may also give rise to other non drug crimes. Drugs may be used to make money with subsequent money-laundering. Drugs may be linked to other major problems, such as the illegal use of guns, various kinds of violence and terrorism.[33] Researchers have found a nexus between drug abuse, criminal behaviour and social attitudes.[34] Usually heroin addicts are part and parcel of the crime scenario. Daily opiate use increases criminality several fold and many heroin abusers are not interested in treatment of their health problems,[35] although drug treatment programmes do reduce the criminality of addicts while they are in the treatment processes.[36]

Drug abuse by children in developing countries must be prevented. In many countries there are no legal provisions to protect children and young people from drug abuse.

In Australia the control of drugs is primarily a matter of state law. However, legislation in each state prohibits the sale to and consumption of

[29]The Social Impact of Drug Abuse, UNDCP series No. 2, 6 (1996).

[30]*Ibid.*

[31]*Ibid*

[32] *Id.* at 24.

[33]*Ibid.*

[34]*Ibid.*

[35]*Ibid*

[36]*Ibid.*

[37]Poison Act, 1966 (NSW); Dangerous Drugs Act, 1980 (N. Terr.); Poisons Drugs Ordinance 1976 (Aust. Cap. Terr); Public Health (Prohibited Drugs) Ordinance, 1975 (Aust. Cap. Terr.); Narcotic and Psychotropic Drugs Act, 1934-1978 (S. Aust); Poisons Act 1962-1980 (Victoria); Poisons Act, 1964-1980 (W. Aust); Health Act 1937-1980 (Ss 130-131) (Queensland); Poisons Act 1971 (Tasmania).

drugs by young people. No legislation exists to give young addicts a legal right to treatment and rehabilitation.[37] In Colombia, although it is prohibited by law to supply alcoholic beverages to persons under 18 years of age,[38] a young person found to be a drug addict would not necessarily be considered to have committed a crime.[39] Under Cuban Penal Code it is an illegal act to induce a person under 16 years of age to take toxic or hallucinogenic drugs of any kind. It is also illegal in Cuba for guardians, either through negligence or carelessness, to allow minors under their care to use toxic or hallucinogenic drugs of any kind.[40] Greek legislation provides for punishment of those who supply drugs to places where young persons live or work in groups.[41] In Kenya, the Dangerous Drugs Act does not distinguish between adults and children, consequently children would not receive adequate protection against drug abuse. It is the main legislation of Kenya which regulates the import, export, manufacture, sale and use of opium and other dangerous drugs.[42]

The Strategy for Global Drugs Law

Any strategy for the 2lst Century in relation to Global Drugs Law must have a balanced approach to battle with the drug menace in all pervasive forms. The proposed law should promote human dignity and legitimate aspirations of humankind for which a decent life, with moral, humanitarian and spiritual values in a healthy, safe and advance looking environment, is a must. Every nation around the globe should commit itself to vigorous international actions against drug abuse and illicit trafficking as an important goal of the international drugs law. Every nation needs to express determination to strengthen action and cooperation at national, regional and international levels towards the goal of an international society free from drugs or freedom from drug abuse. Global drugs law must strive hard to keep pace with the objectives of the three international drug conventions and their strict implementation as well as any further Conventions that may be adopted.[43]

The global drugs law like public international law will safeguard the principles of the sovereignty of the State and the primacy of the fundamental principles of the law and constitution of each State. This global law of drug control has to evolve global control mechanisms to limit the

[38]Law 83, Organic Law for the Defence of the Child, 1946 article 116.
[39]Code of Police Regulations, 1970, article 178.
[40]The Cuban Penal Code, articles 370 and 371.
[41]Law No. 743 of 1970, article 14(1).
[42]Law No. 22 of 1968.
[43]*Ibid.*

availability of drugs of abuse. It was long ago realised that no single country can succeed on its own in the task of preventing drug abuse and illicit trafficking. Between 1912 and 1972 twelve multilateral drug control treaties were concluded. Under the U.N. the Single Convention on Narcotic Drugs, 1961, as amended by the 1972 Protocol, consolidated most of the earlier instruments and the 1971 Convention on Psychotropic Substances created a system of international control for a number of previously uncontrolled psychoactive substances. During this period, emphasis was on gradual devising and reinforcing of a network of administrative controls, having as its primary object the regulation of the supply and movement of drugs with a view to limiting their manufacture and imports to the quantities required for legitimate medicinal and scientific purposes. The United Nations Fund for Drug Abuse Control, in cooperation with the WHO and other international organizations, should provide assistance to States at their request in order to combat problems arising out of drug abuse.

It is also necessary to have a comprehensive system for the collection and evaluation of data on drug use and abuse which are available from many sources including the records of medical practitioners, hospitals. social insurance agencies, school administrators, police, customs authorities and courts. Medical associations and organisations worldwide should in collaboration with WHO be urged to cooperate in assembling this information while keeping them confidential. At the national level appropriate authority must facilitate collection of information about drug abuse from agencies concerned with different aspects of abuse. All information collected at the national levels should be used as a foundation for epidemiological surveys.

Global Drugs Law should provide for comprehensive and effective education programmes as a necessary part of measures for counteracting drug abuse worldwide. In many countries drug abuse has already spread to the various age and population groups. It is essential that all individuals in the formal and general education system as well as their families should be enlightened about the risk of drug abuse and grave danger to health.

Prevention through education should be considered as a continuous process and a lengthy exacting action. The objective is to seek and improve understanding of the long term and immediate causes of recourse to drugs with a view to helping young people and adults to find solutions to their drug problems in the right perspective and enabling them to lead a peaceful life with dignity

Prevention of drug abuse in the workplace is very much important to solve the problem of multiple and harmful consequences associated with the menace. Occupational activities include deterioration of productivity and performance, defective quality of products, loss of qualified employees, accidents, loss of income and professional disqualification - all of which are costly to the individual, the employees and the community at large.

The utmost achievement of the international community in controlling the supply of drugs has been the development of a system for the international control of narcotic drugs which also includes control of the cultivation, production, manufacture and use of and international trade in substances controlled under the Single Convention on Naıcotic Drugs, 1961 and that Convention as amended by the 1972 Protocol. The object of the system is to ensure a global equilibrium between demand for and supply of narcotic drugs for licit purposes and to prevent their diversion to illicit channels.

Any Global Drugs Law however has to accept the rational use of pharmaceuticals containing narcotics drugs or psychotropic substances. There is evidence that supply of essential narcotic drugs and psychotropic substances is not always adequately assured in every country. It is incompatible with the spirit and letter of international drug treaties and with the WHO's avowed goal of "Health for all by the Year 2000", to deprive ill people of the very essential and appropriate drugs and drug therapy. The Global Drugs Law has to demarcate the genuine use of drugs for human good and misuse by people at large.

Identification of illicit narcotic plant cultivation, elimination of illicit planting, redevelopment of areas formerly under illicit drug crop cultivation, suppression of illicit trafficking, timely information and speedy action on the criminal activities of traffickers are some of the crucial areas needed to be tackled by the provisions of international law on drugs. Furthermore, tightening of controls of movement through official points of entry, surveillance of land, water and air approaches to the frontier, anti smuggling measures, and control over ships on the high seas and aircraft in international air space and a humanitarian policy for treatment of drug abusers etc. are also some of highlights and crucial areas to deal with. Last but not the least, care for drug addict offenders within the criminal justice and prison system[44] is a must. A large number of drug abusers come into contact with the criminal justice system. In some countries drug related offences represent more than half of all the criminal cases dealt by the national courts. Hence, the criminal justice and constitutional system occupy prominent places in the handling of treatment and rehabilitation of

[44]Single Convention on Narcotic Drugs, 1961 in Article 36 paragraph 1(b) and article 38, paragraph 1 and the Convention on Psychotropic Substances, 1971 in article 22, paragraph 1(b) require drug abusers to be provided with measures of treatment, education, after care, rehabilitation and social reintegration in addition to punishment.

persons who have committed a criminal offence in relation to illicit drugs. These crucial aspects are the sheet anchor of a well conceived Global Drugs Law. Nevertheless, it is a great challenge as to how to prevent any further increase in consumption of illicit drugs and make a drug free world and a drug free future as envisaged by the United Nations International Drug Control Programme, the main co-sponsor of the International Conference on Global Drugs Law 1997 which the Indian Law Institute is hosting.

The illicit drug trade has resulted in the globalization of money, markets and products which move internationally from producer countries in less developed areas of the world to consumer countries that are usually more developed. Productions in rural areas are transported to and sold in other continents after an enormous price increase along the way providing high profit and risk incentives to traffickers. The ultimate user of the drug is generally poor or impoverished persons who buy drugs while ignoring the necessities of life. This is a hard reality which any international thinker on drug abuse has to deal with in the evolution of a Global Drugs Law for the good of humanity.

A Pragmatic Approach

Drug delinquency and crime are related in many ways as in some cases drug abuse may lead to crime and in others, criminal behaviour precedes drug abuse. Drug-related crimes and terrorism cause instability and overload police, courts and prisons. Drug problems may marginalize governments and institutions as well as people. In extreme cases, these problems may create parallel governments where drug mafias or drug lords exercise enormous personal and financial powers; in some cases they control the national economy. It is a challenge and a challenge of vast dimensions which neither have a single cause nor a simple straight cure; henceforth drug abuse and its related problems increase in many regions of the world. Problems related to the abuse of drugs are severe in some parts of both developing and industrialized world. Disease, accidents, deaths, crime, lowered productivity and many other problems are frequently reported. If drug abuse continues unchecked or unmonitored, it will to act as a brake on human and social development and cannot be separated from endemic problems of disease, poverty, unemployment and violence in all perceivable forms. With varying degrees illicit drug use has powerful effects on the brain and behaviour thus influencing a wide range of human activities.

The success of drug abuse prevention to a large degree depends on cooperation and dedication of the people, communities and institutions involved for which a Global Drugs Law is very much essential. In the evolution of a Global Law people should be considered as the heart of the problem and the beginning of any solution. Evolving Global Drugs Law will depend on the attitude of people, nations and the United Nations. The problem should be considered beyond narrow regional, national or, continental level and viewed as a positive instrument to deal with the worst menace of the humanity. The contribution of drug money in the hands of a small number of persons is as important as its size. Further, when people become rich from illicit drugs, how they use and reuse money are not publicly accountable. The accumulation of huge sums outside the official governmental or economic structures threatens the stability of governments, economic institutions, civil society and above all the human race. Unlawful activities in drug trade generate enormous social costs in governance, health care, crime control and integrity of public institutions and officials. The social costs of drug abuse and their related problems are greater than any benefits of the illicit fund, and basic principles of social justice require that these funds should not be considered as legitimately earned money.

The International Conference must produce a well conceived, pragmatic, executionable and world-wide acceptable Global Drugs Law, in the larger human interest which will serve as beacon light for the eradication of the menace. The Global Drugs Law must stress human dignity, legitimate aspirations of humankind and basic rights of drugs users and it must take into account moral, humanitarian and spiritual values in order to establish a healthy, safe and decent environment with a view to ameliorating the pathetic conditions of the drug abusers to the extent consistent with national socio-economic conditions and the laws. Thus, all these aspects genuinely form the sheet anchor of a Global Drugs Law for the consideration of the nation states of the United Nations in the new century about to begin.

In the gigantic task of evolving a Global Drugs Law, it is apt to quote and remember, the spiritual utility to the human mind of the present day as embodied in the *Holy Geeta*:

> that man is disciplined and happy who can prevail over the turmoil that springs from desire and anger here on earth, before he leaves his body.

[45]The Holy Geeta, Chapter, 5.23.

INTERNATIONAL EFFORT TO COMBAT ILLICIT DRUGS: THE BRITISH VIEW

Derek Plumbly

Fifty years ago there was no international drugs problem. There was, of course, illicit traffic in opium, cocaine and cannabis and there were international conventions in place to address it. But the consumption of narcotic drugs, and the criminality associated with it, was not a universal challenge threatening the young, and civil order in societies around the world.

That, however, is the nature of the threat today. The production of illicit drugs feeds on, and sustains, lawlessness and civil war—in Afghanistan, in the frontier regions of Burma, in the guerilla-controlled jungles of Colombia. The power and money of the traffickers and their cartels threatens stability and democratic institutions in producer and transit countries—island states in the Caribbean, yes, but we have seen instances of their reach also recently in Mexico, in Turkey, and in Colombia, in all of which senior officials have been brought down amidst accusations of narco-corruption. If we are frank with ourselves we will recognize that such instances are the tip of iceberg world-wide. They are also of course only one, political, manifestation of a traffic which leads to incalculable misery and human suffering around the world. The disturbing increase in heroin abuse and in the consumption of synthetic drugs in the Indian sub-continent is an example of a global trend.

In the UK too the challenge we face has grown. The volume of heroin and cocaine seizures has increased by as much as 500 per cent over the last decade, yet street prices have declined. The number of registered opiate and cocaine addicts has doubled over the past five years, and the use of heroin and a variety of synthetic drugs has grown sharply among young people. Those affected are not just the user and his or her immediate circle: a 1995 study commissioned by the Department of Health of 1,100 drugs misusers found that 664 of them had committed no less than 70,000 separate crimes in the three months before beginning treatment.

The United Kingdom is well represented at the Conference, with participants from the Home Office and Her Majesty's Customs and Excise as well as myself. They are more deeply versed in the legal aspects of the problem than I.

The United Kingdom has been active in up-dating its legislation in respect of illicit drugs and money laundering: indeed, measures on sentencing are before Parliament at this moment. We are not complacent. Our legislation is kept under constant review. It has been strengthened in the past, and will continue to be where necessary. We have however also sought to address the problem at home in a broad-based way, through accessible treatment and education as well as vigorous law enforcement. This approach was set out in the White Paper, 'Tackling Drugs Together,' issued in 1995. The White Paper recognized that there was also a direct relationship between the government's domestic strategy and efforts internationally to reduce the flow of drugs. This thought underlay my own appointment in July last year, as the British Government's first International Co-ordinator for Drugs, based in the Foreign Office but with a remit to draw together the efforts of all government departments in this area.

It is my intention to dwell, if I may, on the international aspects of the United Kingdom's drugs policy. But first a word about the wider debate. There are those in my country, as in others, who argue for some liberalization of our laws on drugs, particularly in respect of soft drugs. The parallel is drawn with the Netherlands, and its relative tolerance of cannabis. It will be no surprise to this audience that the British Government, and indeed all major political parties in Britain, reject such an approach. Quite apart from its inconsistency with our obligations under the international conventions, there is no doubt in our minds that the effect of liberalization would be to encourage the consumption of the drugs concerned, and create an atmosphere which insidiously facilitated the consumption of, and trafficking in, hard drugs too. I have to say that this has been the experience of the Netherlands' neighbours with the Netherlands.

The other red herring frequently raised is the alleged ineffectiveness of action against supply, including at the international level. It is argued that the problem is essentially one of demand, fed by youth culture and communications. Of course, that is central. But it is counter-intuitive to suppose that availability does not also effect levels of abuse. A primary objective of the effort against drugs internationally has therefore to be to achieve a reduction in supply through action against the criminals and their organizations; their assets; the drugs themselves, whether en route or at source; and the precursor chemicals used in their manufacture.

Nobody would suggest that achieving such an objective can be easy. Its difficulty is increased by the rapidity with which patterns of supply change.

The Conference programme quotes the UN's estimate of the proceeds of the trade in illicit drugs world-wide—500 billion dollars annually. An industry of this scale is able quickly to exploit weaknesses in source, transit and recipient countries—lack of training and equipment, inadequate legislation and corruption. It can also adapt quickly to law enforcement successes. Routes diversify: the trend in cocaine trafficking to the US back to the Caribbean from Mexico is an example, the increased traffic in opiates to Europe from South-West Asia through Central Asia is another. At the same time trafficking organizations diversify, and control of them becomes more diffuse.

But for all the difficulties we have seen significant advances. The increase in seizure rates world-wide doubtless reflects an increase in the quantities of drugs trafficked, but it is also a testimony to the growing expertise and professionalism of law enforcement agencies in this field in many countries. The arrest of the Cali cartel leaders in Colombia last year was a particular success: the relatively light sentences they subsequently received were therefore a major disappointment, underlining the importance of having effective legislation in place.

A country such as the United Kingdom has a particular interest in seeking to tackle the traffic from the main source areas supplying it: in our case opiates from South-West Asia, cocaine from Colombia and the Andean countries, cannabis resin from Morocco, synthetics from the Netherlands. With limited resources we obviously need to prioritize, though we also need to retain flexibility to respond to shifts in patterns of supply. But the principal lesson to be drawn from any study of the supply situation—a lesson I do not need to stress to an audience such as this—is that no single country can combat the threat alone, or expect by its own efforts to reduce the traffic in a significant or durable way. The response to it must be international partnership, bilaterally, regionally and multilaterally.

A heartening and important development recently has been precisely this—the growth, often through the agency of UNDCP—of regional co-operation against drug trafficking between governments which may have differences in many other fields but are brought together by a common goal. In our own region one thinks of the collaborative law enforcement project between Iran and Pakistan on their shared border, the MOU signed by the five Central Asian states in May 1996, and of course the agreement between India and Pakistan to co-operate in operations against drug trafficking. There has been progress too in efforts to tackle money laundering, which must be a key part of any strategy to tackle drugs. Depriving criminals of the proceeds of their crime is a powerful disincentive. Like drugs, money laundering is a truly international activity. The Financial Action Task Force has produced 40 recommendations covering the various steps countries need to take domestically. These steps include not only criminal legislation, but crucially the measures which governments need to take in co-operation with their private sector financial institutions. The FATF 40 Recommendations have been endorsed by Commonwealth members. Our policy now is to encourage their implementation at a regional level, to ensure a common international standard. Initiatives are underway in the Caribbean, Eastern Europe and among offshore centres. There is an Asian Steering Group, which met last week in Bangkok. Their work—to raise awareness, to co-ordinate training, and to implement the 40 Recommendations—is a key part of the regional fight against drugs and other international crime. It deserves the full support of all countries in the region.

Six months into my term of office as the UK International Drugs Co-ordinator is a good time to say something about my own country's approach to the drugs problem internationally. That approach rests in the first place on law enforcement co-operation. One strand in this is information exchange through INTERPOL and EUROPOL. There is an interesting debate going on in Europe at present between those who wish to see EUROPOL'S powers extended and those who take a more cautious and pragmatic approach. Our own view is that there is an important role for multilateral law enforcement co-operation. But that, given the sensitivity of the issues involved, the key to effective action internationally will remain bilateral co-operation between individual agencies. Some 47 drugs liaison officers from the police and customs services are now accredited in British diplomatic missions around the world, two of them here in India. The statistics bear witness to the achievements of this network. In 1996 the sharing of intelligence, joint operations and controlled deliveries involving UK DLOs were responsible for seizures worth £931 million world-wide, and for 834 arrests.

Another aspect of our strategy is the assistance we give to governments overseas, mainly in the principal producer and transit countries. This has totalled in excess of £30 million pounds over the past three years. The figures are likely to increase in the coming years as agencies, including the Overseas Development Administration, raise the priority they give to drugs-related assistance. Such assistance can take a variety of forms. In 1996 the British Government funded Customs training courses in 32 countries around the world. We have also funded major police training programmes, particularly in the Caribbean, and offered paramilitary training in the Caribbean and Latin America. Our resources nationally are not such as to support large alternative development schemes, but we have contributed through the EU and UNDCP in Latin America and Pakistan and now, potentially, in Afghanistan.

Such assistance needs to be placed in a wider context. To be effective, it must be co-ordinated—through mechanisms such as UNDCP and the Dublin Group—with that of other donors. And it needs to be underpinned by a drugs diplomacy with clear strategic goals—supporting law enforcement, ensuring the effective implementation of the various international instruments which are in place, curbing the flow of drugs. The threat illicit drugs pose to our societies is too great for us not to use all of the resources of the state—diplomatic; intelligence; even, on occasion military—to assist in countering it.

There is nothing new to drugs diplomacy. In the UK the Home Office have been active over the years in negotiating a network of bilateral confiscation agreements, mutual legal assistance treaties and drugs co-operation agreements. We derived particular satisfaction from the conclusion of the bilateral agreement with the Government of India which came into force in May 1995 and which enables our two countries to co-operate in the investigation and prosecution of drugs trafficking and other crimes and to assist each other in tracing, restraining and confiscating the proceeds of such crimes, including drug trafficking and terrorist funds.

But we want to raise the issue higher on the diplomatic agenda more generally. Within the EU we have sought to mobilize resources to assist on a regional basis those affected by the production of or trafficking in illicit drugs. In December 1995, Prime Minister Major and President Chirac secured EU endorsement for a Caribbean Drugs Initiative which was subsequently backed by Caribbean governments. This December they proposed a similar initiative for Central Asia: an EU mission will visit the five Central Asian Republics next month to see what assistance they require, and how the EU may be able to help.

Of course, one cannot always assume the existence of willing partnerships. International relations are rarely as simple as that. They are cases where—in the view of the British Government at least—the actions, or inaction, of foreign governments, often in key supply or transit countries, compound the problems. We are now in that season when annually, the United States goes through the decertification process provided for in the Foreign Assistance Act. It would be neither appropriate nor feasible for the UK or the EU to seek to replicate such an approach. But I do believe that we should all be frank in urging our friends in key producer or transit countries, or with banking systems which are attractive to money launderers, to go on to the offensive, whether by imposing stiffer sentences for traffickers, or permitting extradition; or by ending banking secrecy laws, which are so easily exploited by traffickers; or by establishing the necessary local legislative basis for controlled deliveries.

As this Conference has been organized in collaboration with UNDCP, it may be fitting to end by looking briefly at the UN's role in the international effort against illicit drugs. I am an old UN hand, but even prior to my arrival on the scene the British Government was in no doubt as to the centrality of UNDCP in international efforts to tackle the drugs problem. We are the third largest contributor to the Programme. We see it as playing a crucial role, not only as a source of advice and assistance to governments, but also as a catalyst which can put together coalitions of countries—regional and donor—in support of particular drugs control strategies. I have seen UNDCP staff at work in the field in Afghanistan and on the border with Pakistan and Iran, and can testify to their effectiveness. The pity is that, six years into the programme's existence and despite the sterling efforts of Mr. Giacomelli, the Programme continues to exist on a shoe-string budget. The next big multilateral event in the drugs field will be the Special Session of the United Nations General Assembly on Drugs next year. Making a success of that will be a priority for the United Kingdom. We look forward to working with other UN members on the declaration to be adopted then and hope that —as well as reaffirming the international community's commitment to the existing plan of action—it will reflect real advances in some areas, for example money laundering. But the best present the international community could give itself then would be for donors who have not to date done so to come forward in UNDCP's support, and to place its finances on a sounder footing.

INTERNATIONAL LEGAL CO-OPERATION AGAINST SERIOUS CRIME

Dianne Stafford

An essential component of the legal and policy framework to facilitate international legal co-operation against serious crime is an effective network of treaties or arrangements designed to ensure that national boundaries cannot be used by criminals to hinder or defeat lawful attempts by the authorities to combat drug trafficking and those other serious crimes which are closely related to the drug trade. These crimes include money laundering, corruption, and the growing phenomenon of organized crime.

The need for such a framework is perhaps best exemplified by the 1988 United Nations Convention Against Illicit Traffic in Narcotic Drugs and Psychotropic Substances. This landmark Convention, as at the end of January 1997, had 138 parties, making it one of the few nearly universal instruments. Article 7 of the 1988 Convention obliges parties to afford to one another the widest measure of mutual legal assistance in investigations, prosecutions and judicial proceedings in relation to the offences established by the Convention. This Convention is the first multilateral instrument to absolutely require parties to provide such assistance and it does so whether or not a party seeking assistance has a treaty or other mutual legal assistance arrangement with the party from which help is sought.

Article 7 is the main provision of the 1988 Convention dealing with international co-operation. Article 5 requires parties to adopt measures to confiscate the proceeds and instrumentalities of offences described in the Convention, and to provide assistance to other parties wishing to institute confiscation proceedings. Article 6 deals with extradition and, although it is couched in language which does not require surrender in the absence of a separate treaty, it poses an absolute obligation, where a country refuses to extradite, for that country to submit the case to its competent authorities for the purpose of prosecution. Article 8 imposes an obligation on parties to give consideration to the possibility of transferring proceedings for relevant offences and Article 9 requires parties to co-operate to enhance the effectiveness of law enforcement action to suppress the commission of convention offences.

It is over six years since the 1988 Convention entered into force and now is perhaps the time to ask whether these articles have operated to increase effective co-operation between parties to the Convention and, if not, why not.

The Elements of International Co-operation to Combat Crime

Where criminals operate across borders, national legal systems must respond by providing appropriate legal mechanisms to ensure that national borders are not barriers to effective law enforcement. Have the 1988 Convention and other multilateral efforts to combat drug trafficking and other serious crime resulted in the creation of national legal mechanisms which will facilitate effective co-operation?

In any country where treaties do not, of themselves, have the force of law it is necessary to enact legislation which will enable the country to give effect to the obligations it has assumed upon becoming a party to a treaty. For the vast majority of Commonwealth countries domestic legislation is needed. Indeed, in many civil law countries the situation is the same.

Legislation which gives effect to a country's obligations under the 1988 Convention must, as a bare minimum, enable the country to:

(i) respond to requests for assistance in the investigation and prosecution of offences by exercising, on behalf of other countries, the powers it has to investigate and prosecute domestic offences;

(ii) co-operate with other parties in the confiscation of the proceeds of drug trafficking; and

(iii) extradite for Convention offences or to prosecute in cases where it refuses extradition.

In addition to these elements, international experience is tending to suggest that legal mechanisms for the transfer of proceedings and for the transfer of convicted persons to serve their sentences are also worthy components of effective structures to combat crime.

Will the enactment of such laws, in and of itself, solve the problems of international co-operation? The answer is 'no' unless the laws take account of the need to deal with countries having different legal traditions and unless the evidence laws of the enacting country are sufficiently flexible to permit the reception by courts of evidence obtained from overseas.

The Development of Criminal Law Co-operation

Modern transport, communication and finance facilities necessarily mean that national boundaries will be crossed easily and with great speed by criminals who often deliberately use these boundaries to make the detection and investigation of their criminal activities more difficult. Where crossing a national boundary means moving into another legal system the complications for law enforcement agencies are compounded.

Until the middle of this century there was little or no formalized co-operation between countries for the purpose of enforcing criminal laws. Indeed, until 1959 when the Council of Europe members concluded the European Convention on Mutual Assistance in Criminal Matters there was no multilateral acceptance that there was a need for such co-operation. The European Convention was, as may be expected, designed to cater for the needs of the various legal systems in Europe and took limited account of the common law system. It has since been revised by the Council of Europe to take account of recent developments such as the interception of telecommunications.

By the early 1980's there was a marked transnational recognition of the need to establish proper methods of facilitating mutual legal assistance in criminal matters. Early efforts were bilateral but these were followed quickly by the development by Commonwealth Law Ministers of the Harare Scheme on Mutual Assistance in Criminal Matters and by the development of the United Nations model treaty on mutual assistance in criminal matters. Between 1985 and 1990 many countries embarked upon bilateral treaty negotiation programmes designed to ensure that they could co-operate effectively with those countries which either provided destinations for the proceeds of crimes or which were important to their efforts to combat drug trafficking and other serious crime.

These bilateral treaty negotiations and the development of the United Nations model treaty had two very important effects. The first was to familiarize lawyers with the essential features of the major legal systems and the second was to find ways to break down the real or perceived barriers to effective co-operation. So effective have been the efforts of some countries to increase co-operation across legal systems that, except for operational constraints and obstacles surrounding issues of dual criminality, one could say that many of the major problems of ten years ago have been solved.

A major obstacle remaining in the way of effective international co-operation to combat crime is that, despite the significant increase in bilateral and multilateral arrangements, many countries remain unable to render the assistance necessary to give effect to obligations under the 1988 Convention.

There appear to be various reasons for this. Perhaps the most pressing is the lack of resources—both financial and staff. Small and developing countries often see the conclusion of international arrangements as being lower in priority to the need to solve domestic problems. They are therefore unable to embark upon bilateral treaty negotiation programmes. Even when the costs of negotiating treaties are borne by the more developed countries, problems can be encountered in finding the resources to develop and implement laws to give effect to treaty obligations.

The issue of costs in mutual assistance cases is also causing concern to some countries—in particular small or developing countries which provide off-shore corporate or financial services and receive numerous requests from countries attempting to combat money laundering. It is quite possible that countries are not developing international co-operation regimes because they fear that the cost of dealing with the resulting requests will place an unsupportable burden on them. This is an issue which is being addressed by Commonwealth Law Ministers in an attempt to make more universal the participation of countries in international co-operation regimes.

Inter-Legal System Extradition Problems

It is the subject of extradition which perhaps most starkly highlights the conflict between legal systems which can lead to difficulties in international co-operation. It is no longer realistic, nor I believe is it necessary, for countries to insist that a country which seeks surrender of a criminal to be able to meet procedural requirements in a requesting country which are designed only for the purpose of the legal system of the requested country.

Perhaps the most significant advance made in recent years to achieve this aim is the relaxing, in many common law countries, of the strict rules governing the admission of evidence provided in support of a request for extradition. It is true that not all countries have reached this point yet and some insist that 'due process' legal requirements mean that they cannot surrender without satisfying themselves that there is a complete case against the fugitive. In my opinion this is a problem which, although solved in many countries, still presents an obstacle to effective international co-operation. It would be less than honest, however, to suggest that my views on the need for extradition reform are shared by all Commonwealth countries.

One of the reasons why countries insist on retaining strict rules in extradition cases may be that they believe that surrender to a country with a different criminal justice system could result in a denial of human rights or, expressed another way, that protection of human rights is inconsistent with effective international co-operation in criminal matters. This perception is unlikely to change when the punishment which can be imposed in the requesting country is a type of punishment not known in the requested country. But where the requesting country imposes similar punishments but simply describes its criminal justice procedures in different terms, there would seem to be no real basis for holding the view that surrender will result in a denial of human rights.

Another reason why surrender is refused by a number of countries is that there is a law or constitutional provision which precludes the surrender of nationals of the requested country. The original basis for these provisions was the parallel assumption of criminal jurisdiction over nationals regardless of where they committed offences and the actual exercise of that jurisdiction. In countries which do bring their nationals to trial for extra-territorial offences and which respond to requests for extradition of their nationals by, wherever possible, dealing with the alleged offender themselves, refusal of surrender on the grounds of nationality can be supported. There are, however, an increasing number of countries which are giving to their authorities a discretion to refuse surrender of nationals in cases where they have no legal basis for assuming jurisdiction over the alleged offender themselves or where they have no intention of so doing. The result is a growing concern that refusal of surrender on this ground should be gradually discouraged by the international community and that it should be either abolished or replaced with provisions which allow surrender for trial and return to the country of nationality to serve any sentence imposed.

A lack of understanding of the laws of other countries leads to confusion in extradition cases. It is for this reason that the both the Commonwealth and the United Nations believe strongly that countries need to establish national central authorities which deal with extradition cases. These offices, usually located in justice ministries, can develop an understanding of the laws of other countries and help to ensure that extradition requests do not go to the courts until they are in a form which is likely to meet the requirements of the local laws. They can also assist in putting before the courts information on the legal procedures in the requesting country so as to satisfy the courts that the request complies with the treaty or national law.

An example of the sort of difficulty which can be encountered was provided by a case in Australia which ran for some three years before being resolved in late 1995. It involved a request by Austria for the surrender of a person accused of misappropriation and malversion offences. In support of the request, and in accordance with the treaty between Australia and Austria, the Austrian government submitted a warrant for the arrest of the person sought. The fugitive argued that she was not an 'accused' person and, following various arguments on this issue the matter finally came before the High Court of Australia. In a judgment which recognized the special nature of extradition legislation, the court discussed the meaning of the word 'accused'. It stated that:

.. in the common law the term 'accused' is not a legal term of art. It may be used in purely domestic legislation to encompass terms such as charge, indict, impeach, arraign and incriminate as well as to refer to the laying of an information in a private prosecution. The need to construe extradition legislation in a fashion apt to accommodate criminal procedure of extradition countries which operate in a different fashion to that generally applicable in common law jurisdictions has long been recognized. ... A reasonable cosmopolitan interpretation must be given and the difference between the denomination or categorization of procedures should not be given too great a weight. The fundamental question is whether the person is one in respect of whom there has been taken by the competent authorities of the extradition country a decision to invoke the operation of the criminal law by taking whatever steps are necessary to initate what might fairly be described as a prosecution.[1]

This decision is the sort of decision which must be reached by courts if the extradition process is not to founder on obstacles created by slight differences in practice and procedure between the requesting and requested countries. But such a decision can only be reached where both the justice ministries and the courts make a concerted effort to understand the legal processes of other countries and to draw the necessary parallels between them so as to meet the traditional requirements of extradition treaties and arrangements.

Inter-Legal Systems Problems in Mutual Assistance in Criminal Matters

International models for combating and investigating cross-border crimes and corruption are posited on the proposition that a country which has information, evidence or witnesses needed by another country will be in a position to use the powers available to its own law enforcement agencies to gain that material and will be able to provide it to the prosecuting country. These models also work on the basis that once a conviction has been secured countries can work together to ensure that the proceeds of the crime can be confiscated under the laws of whichever country they are located in.

To work effectively these models must cater for differences in legal systems and ensure that the needs of a requesting country can be met to the maximum possible extent using the methods available in the requested country. The 1994 Commonwealth Secretariat Conference on Mutual Assistance in

[1] Director of Public Prosecutions and Anor v. Kainhoffer 132 ALR 483.

Criminal Matters considered the problems encountered in trying to administer mutual assistance laws, treaties and other arrangements. The delegates concluded that where the requesting and requested state belong to different legal systems, it is important that the requesting state includes in its request any details of procedure which must be followed in the requested state to ensure that the evidence provided can be used at the trial. Common law countries, in particular, must be aware of the differences in rules of evidence which apply in other legal systems and ensure that their procedural needs are properly explained to the requested state.

That Conference also noted that:

— the protections provided to witnesses in the requested state might limit the assistance which can be provided in response to a request;

— expressions familiar to one system of law could convey a totally different concept to recipients in another; with a number of countries now introducing a right to a speedy trial it is important to consider the effect of delays in making requests and of delay in response on the ability to bring a person to trial within the required time. Countries which must provide a speedy trial may need to consider how to balance this requirement with the needs of prosecutors who must obtain evidence overseas.

— the time may have come to question whether the same policy considerations for the grant or refusal of extradition should continue to apply to the granting or refusal of mutual assistance requests. The possibility of conflict between a country's obligations under, for example, the European Convention on Human Rights and a mutual assistance convention was recognized.

It goes without saying that a request for assistance in the investigation or prosecution of a foreign crime should be considered by authorities in the requested country to ensure that by granting it they will not jeopardize their own essential national interests. Opinions differ, however, on the scope of national interests. Most countries do not require that the offence being investigated be an offence known to the law of the requested country but some have insisted on this. Others have decided that the possibility of the imposition of the death penalty in the requesting country should preclude the provision of assistance unless the requesting country guarantees that such a penalty will not be carried out.

There is, however, general agreement that it is appropriate for requested countries to refuse assistance in cases where a political offence is the subject of the request or where there are substantial grounds for believing that the person may be prejudiced at trial on account of race, religion, nationality, political opinion or ethnic origin.

One of the issues now facing countries which have started to use mutual assistance in criminal matters is that the evidence they receive from other countries, particularly when it is in written form and the deponent is unwilling to travel to the requesting country to give oral testimony, may not be readily accepted by the courts of the requesting country. It is therefore important to ensure that domestic evidence laws allow the reception of foreign evidence and some countries have taken steps to amend their evidence laws to facilitate the admission of foreign documentary evidence, including written witness statements, when the witness cannot attend the trial. For example, documents obtained as a result of a mutual assistance request can be made prima facie admissible with the court being given a discretion to allow the admission of written material in certain circumstances and provided that admission of the evidence will not be contrary to the interests of justice.

Effective mutual assistance arrangements are based on the presumption that a requested country will make available to the requesting country all investigative and prosecutorial powers which can be exercised by local law enforcement agencies when they are dealing with a local offence. This means that countries not only need to allow their powers to be exercised on behalf of other countries, they must also ensure that the powers they have to investigate domestic offences are as wide-ranging and effective as their legal traditions allow. A country which does not, for example, have laws governing the lawful interception of telephonic and telegraphic communications cannot, obviously, provide this essential service to another investigating agency. Similarly a country which has no, or has limited, laws on the confiscation of proceeds of crime cannot assist another country to recover such proceeds.

Perhaps one of the major obstacles to the effective operation of mutual assistance arrangements between countries is the difference in the investigative powers available to the law enforcement authorities of countries.

The other obstacle is a lack of understanding of the laws of other countries. This can and does lead to misunderstandings and the only solution to this problem is for lawyers in justice departments to start to learn the fundamentals of the criminal justice systems of other countries—and particularly of countries from different legal systems. For this reason, just as in extradition, it is desirable for countries to establish central authorities in their justice ministries where a small group of lawyers can specialize in international co-operation issues. It is, for example, important to know that when one makes a request to Switzerland for information about a bank account the holder of the account will, in the normal course of events, be notified of the request and be entitled to appear in court when evidence about the account is being taken. If it is imperative that the inquiries be made confidentially, then the central authority of the requesting country must speak personally to the Swiss Central Authority and determine how, if at all in the circumstances of the case, the information required can be obtained while confidentiality is maintained. There is no point in jeopardizing an investigation by making a request and not knowing the rules under which it will be executed. Nor is there any point in making a request to a banking centre for banking information where the banks will not allow their staff to travel to give oral evidence unless the law of the requesting country has provisions which will permit the admission into evidence of banking records without the need for oral testimony.

Proceeds of Crime

In addition to mutual assistance laws which permit co-operation in the confiscation of proceeds of crime a more recent development is the growing number of 'asset sharing' agreements which allow countries to share proceeds with countries which assist in the recovery of proceeds located in a jurisdiction other than that in which the trial for the main offence is conducted.

Another way of tackling the issue of returning confiscated assets is to agree that confiscation orders made in one country as an incident of a conviction can be enforced in another country which will return all or part of the assets confiscated at the request of the other country.

But before there can be a sharing of assets or assistance in the enforcement of confiscation orders of other countries there must be domestic proceeds of crime laws and a willingness to assist other countries. When this happens and there is an increase in the number of agreements which permit co-operation in the confiscation and return or sharing of the proceeds of crime, we may be able to see those countries which have resource constraints but which have nevertheless been prepared to assist other countries finding themselves the beneficiaries of confiscated assets.

Co-operation in Customs Matters

Co-operation between customs authorities is really a form of administrative rather than legal co-operation and hence it is perhaps subject to fewer constraints than formal mutual assistance in criminal matters. The Customs Co-operation Council, now called the World Customs Organization, has been involved in the business of international co-operation for some years. In addition to the Nairobi Convention known properly as the International Convention on Mutual Administrative Assistance for the Prevention, Investigation and Repression of Customs Offences, the WCO has produced a model bilateral convention on the same subject which deals with issues such as surveillance, communication of information and actions by customs officials of one country in the territory of the other party to the agreement.

Customs co-operation is an essential part of the regime of international co-operation to combat drug trafficking and other serious offences. Because the information obtained as a result of customs co-operation may not be in a form which is admissible in court it is often necessary for the customs authorities to have mutual legal assistance requests made to ensure that they obtain admissible evidence to prove their cases. For this reason it is highly desirable that there is an effective working relationship between the mutual assistance central authority and the customs authorities.

Conclusion

Although much is said about the difficulties caused by different legal systems when countries are seeking to co-operate in the investigation or prosecution of crime or in extradition, the experience of many countries is that the differences between legal systems are more illusory than real and what is causing the problems is, as often as not, failure on the part of law enforcement and legal authorities to communicate effectively. What is needed, and what often solves problems, is an understanding of the meaning of terms used in other legal systems, together with a real effort to equate the processes of one legal system to those of another so that requests can be made intelligible to the requested country. If the central authority of one country can explain its processes in general terms to another country one often finds that there are as many similarities as differences and that the similarities occur in the important steps.

For example, despite the difference between the independent police in common law countries and the police operating under judicial or magisterial supervision in civil law countries, an examination of the stages of investigation, charge, committal for trial and trial (to use common law terms) are, in fact paralleled in most civil law countries but bear different names and have slightly different rules of procedure. A request which sets out the process which is being followed, describes its aims and objectives and gives advice on the stage reached and the material needed will be of much more use to a requested country than will a request couched in technical language and demanding that a particular procedure be followed without giving the necessary reasons. In fact, unless following a particular procedure is absolutely essential, the task of the requested country in responding to the request will be made easier if it is simply allowed to use its own procedure.

Equally, when responding to a request, the requested country can make the task of the requesting country much easier if, in its reply, it sets out the exact procedure followed so the court or other authorities in the requesting country can determine whether the rights of the accused have been adversely affected in a way which would make it unsafe to seek to rely on the material received.

A concerted effort on the part of countries to establish central authorities to handle their international co-operation in criminal matters and an effort to train officers in these authorities would undoubtedly go a long way towards breaking down the barriers which now exist.

BREAKING DOWN THE BARRIERS: INTERNATIONAL CO-OPERATION IN COMBATING TRANSNATIONAL CRIME

Kimberly Prost

In a 1989 case, United States of America v. Cotroni, the Supreme Court of Canada, made the following statement:

> The investigation, prosecution and suppression of crime for the protection of the citizen and the maintenance of peace and public order is an important goal of all organized societies. The pursuit of that goal cannot realistically be confined within national boundaries. That has long been the case, but it is increasingly evident today.[1]

With advances in technology and the ease of global travel, the world we live in has become in many ways as Canadian author Marshall McLuhan predicted 'a global village.' This has had a dramatic impact on many aspects of life and society, and law enforcement is no exception.

For the law enforcement community, in particular those who work to combat the importation, exportation and trafficking of narcotics and psychotropic substances, it is increasingly evident, that sovereignty, a fundamental principle which grounds the relations of states, is also a major tool in the armoury of the criminal element in our societies. Criminals depend heavily upon the barriers of sovereignty to shield themselves and the evidence of their crimes from detection.

International cooperation in criminal matters, vehicles such as mutual assistance and extradition are intended to provide ladders over the barriers of sovereignty and allow the international community to 'fight back.' Both extradition and mutual legal assistance are about countries building bridges to overcome the differences in their legal systems and assisting each other in law enforcement matters, by surrendering fugitives for prosecu-

[1]United States of America v. Cotroni (1989) 48 C.C.C. (3d) 193 at 215.

tion or service of a sentence or providing evidence of criminal activity for use in criminal investigations and prosecutions.

It is a constant struggle for States to provide this assistance in a useful and effective form, and at the same time respect the sovereignty of nations. The goal is to find ways to accommodate the differences in legal systems and traditions. This is no easy task which the world community faces and despite the recent advances in the development of mutual assistance and the enhancement of extradition, these programmes are still in their infancy or, at best, adolescence. There is much work to be done, particularly in liberalizing the approach taken by States in adopting and administering programmes for mutual assistance, restraint and confiscation of proceeds of crime and extradition, before any real progress can be made.

The criminal organizations which orchestrate the production, importation, distribution and sale of drugs and which then disperse and conceal the proceeds of their illicit activities the world over, have no regard for national borders. In fact, by structuring their organizations to span borders they are much better able to protect their interests and organizations. They are positioned to take advantage of the differences between legal systems, the clash of bureaucracies, the protection of sovereignty, and, at many times, the complete incapacity of nations to work together to overcome their differences.

International co-operation in criminal matters, which is a growing component of the relations between States, is the international community's response to this very alarming and real attribute of transnational crime. It encompasses many measures, such as extradition, mutual assistance, transfer of prisoners, transfer of proceedings, asset restraint and forfeiture. Historically, each measure has been viewed separately but there is now growing acceptance that such measures should be viewed, non-compartmentally, as part of an overall structure essential for the international community to respond to transnational drug trafficking and transnational crime generally.

For it is apparent that each of these measures is designed to achieve the same goal, that is, to allow for the efficient and effective investigation, prosecution and punishment of those who engage in transnational crime.

Pursuing the Evidence—Mutual Assistance

Background: Mutual assistance as a means of cooperation has advanced significantly over the last decade. It is a concept that is difficult to capture by precise definition. It must be examined in context.

Countries have long assisted each other in gathering information and evidence for criminal investigations and prosecutions. There are well established police channels through which much essential information has been and continues to be, shared. These channels range from direct relationships between police officers and police forces, to the posting of police liaison personnel in foreign States, to the auspices of Interpol. All of these measures remain critical to cooperation in evidence gathering and have not been replaced by the more formal process of mutual assistance.

But the reality is that there are types of assistance which cannot be provided between States, through informal channels. The most obvious is where the type of assistance sought will require resort to the legal process within the requested State; where some type of judicial order or compulsory measure must be applied to produce the desired information or evidence, in an acceptable form.

For example, where a country is seeking the production of bank records or the search of a residence, there is need for a process through which the appropriate authorization can be obtained.

For many years, States were required to rely entirely upon traditional letters rogatory, submitted through diplomatic channels, to gain access to such evidence. However, in our modern age, this method was insufficient to meet the growing demand for speedy and effective assistance in evidence gathering. Letters rogatory did not provide the scope of assistance required, nor were they efficient enough to allow for the production of the evidence, within a reasonable period of time.

Thus the development of mutual assistance as a mechanism of cooperation. It is intended to allow for a wide range of assistance between States in the production of evidence, in a direct and efficient manner. Generally rendered on the basis of bilateral treaty or agreement or multilateral convention,[2] mutual assistance provides a means for one State to obtain evidence from another State for use in a criminal investigation/prosecution. The range of assistance usually includes, *inter alia*, taking evidence or statements of persons, search and seizure, and the provision of documents or evidentiary items.

Mutual assistance is an idea whose time has come. Its development over the last decade constitutes a crucial step forward for the international community. And yet, it is a concept which has yet to be completely transformed from a great idea into an effective practice and the reasons for that merit consideration.

[2]In some countries, mutual assistance is provided for on the basis of domestic legislation which is either applied generally to all States or to designated States on the basis of reciprocity. Some States also provide for case by case assistance through administrative arrangement.

The Instruments of Co-operation

Over the last decade, great strides have been made in the development of a framework of instruments for the rendering of assistance.

The first significant instrument for mutual assistance was the *European Convention on Mutual Assistance in Criminal Matters*, developed by the Council of Europe, entered into on April 20, 1959, in force June 12, 1962.[3] It was an important achievement of its time in its recognition of the necessity for specific instruments for co-operation in evidence gathering. However, like all innovative instruments, it had limitations. Perhaps the most notable in this instance was that the Convention was designed to operate amongst States of like legal tradition, the civil law states of Europe, and it therefore did not address perhaps the most significant challenge to effective mutual assistance, bridging the differences between legal systems.

Similarly, within the Commonwealth, in 1986 Law Ministers in Harare, Zimbabwe,[4] adopted a scheme for mutual assistance. It is a non-treaty based scheme which depends upon States enacting domestic legislation to permit the rendering of assistance in criminal matters. It too, however, is based very much on the commonality of systems.

In between the creation of these two multilateral instruments of cooperation, individual States began to develop treaties on a bilateral basis, to allow for the provision of assistance and most notably, the provision of assistance between States of a different legal tradition. The oft cited example of the first 'break through' instrument is the treaty between the United States and Switzerland, which came into force in January, 1977[5]. Since that time there has developed a network of bilateral instruments between States of similar or diverse legal tradition. Those agreements are further supplemented by domestic legislation within some States, which allows for assistance to be rendered on the basis of reciprocity, designation or administrative arrangement.

There has also been an increasing development of regional agreements for mutual assistance such as the *Inter-American Convention on Mutual Legal Assistance in Criminal Matters*.[6]

Two other significant developments in the field of mutual assistance came with the adoption by the General Assembly of the United Nations of the

[3]European Treaty Series No. 30.

[4]Scheme Relating to Mutual Assistance in Criminal Matters within the Commonwealth, Commonwealth Secretariat, London, LMN (86) 13

[5]Lionel Frei and Stefan Freschal, Origins and Application of the United States—Switzerland Treaty on Mutual Assistance in Criminal Matters, Harvard International Law Journal 31 (1990) @ 77-79

[6]1996 *Canada Gazette*, Part 1, p. 2483, Vol. 130 No. 35.

Model Treaty on Mutual Assistance[7] and the coming into force of the 1988 *United Nations Convention Against Illicit Traffic in Narcotic Drugs and Psychotropic Substances (1988 Drug Convention)* which contains a 'stand alone' article on mutual legal assistance. The first provided an excellent guide for nations wishing to develop mutual assistance treaties and the second provided a multilateral instrument for assistance, an instrument which now has over 100 participant countries.

The inclusion of a stand alone provision on mutual assistance within the *1988 Drug Convention* also constituted recognition of the integral role mutual assistance plays in combating drug trafficking. That message has been continually reinforced with respect to transnational organized crime generally, within the international community, in various statements arising from international fora.[8]

The Practical Problems

No one would suggest that the network of instruments for mutual assistance is any way complete, such that efforts to develop further multilateral, regional or bilateral instruments for assistance should be curtailed.

However, no matter how complete the network of agreements may be and regardless of how well-crafted the instruments of cooperation are, little is gained if it is still not possible to present a request for assistance and receive evidence in an acceptable form, in an effective and timely fashion.

And unfortunately, very often that remains the reality. In a great number of cases, despite the existence of an applicable instrument, evidence is not forthcoming; it arrives in such a form that it is not useful to requesting authorities; or it is provided so late that it is of little practical value.

The problems stem from a lack of or inadequate programmes and procedures for implementation of mutual assistance and the provision of evidence on a practical, case by case level. There are a number of particular problems with approaches to implementation which could be identified and considered. Two of the most common and significant will be discussed below.

[7]General Assembly resolution 45/117, UN GAOR 45th Sess., Supp No. 49A at 215.

[8]See 'Naples Political Declaration and Global Action Plan' adopted at the World Ministerial Conference on Organized Transnational Crime, November 1994; Report of the Oxford Conference on Mutual Legal Assistance, September 1994, Christ Church, Oxford; Recommendations of the P8 Senior Experts Working Group on Combatting Transnational Organized Crime.

Central Authorities

To have a 'Central Authority' for mutual assistance is to have one central location through which all requests for mutual assistance will flow. The central authority will be responsible for coordinating and monitoring the progress of requests made and received.

The critical role of a central authority in mutual assistance cannot be overstated. Canada's experience, shared by many other states, is that efficient and knowledgeable central authorities are essential to effective and timely mutual assistance. Whether a state is seeking assistance or providing it there are immeasurable benefits to having an identified, direct and informed channel on both sides of the request.

For authorities seeking assistance, having an effective central authority to deal with in the foreign State can make the difference between success and failure. The immediate benefit is that delay in transmission of a request will be significantly reduced, as the central authority will provide an identifiable, direct entry point, within that foreign State, for the presentation of a request. As well, where the staff of the authority are specialized and, most critically, legally knowledgeable, they can provide, by fax or phone or some other mode of communication, critical information and advice about relevant legislation and the execution process within that State. In addition, if the central authority is properly resourced, in terms of numbers and qualification of persons, and has at least the capacity to influence the executing authorities the chances for timely processing of the request will be greatly enhanced.

Authorities within a country receiving a request for assistance, similarly require that the request emanate from a State with a strong and effective central authority. The central authority within the requesting State will be able to review outgoing requests to ensure they are presented in a workable and usable form for the requested State and that they contain sufficient information to allow for their execution in the foreign State. It can also provide a critical prioritization function such that the most urgent and significant requests will be submitted in a timely and efficient manner.

The integral role of a central authority has been recognized both in mutual assistance instruments, bilateral and multilateral, and in the commentary and recommendations of international conferences and expert meetings on the subject of mutual assistance.[9] Both the *United Nations Model Treaty on Mutual Assistance* and the *1988 Drug Convention* include a provision for a designated authority or authorities for the receipt and presentation of requests for assistance. At the *1994 Oxford Conference on Mutual*

[9]Supra footnote 8.

Assistance,[10] there was a working group dedicated solely to the role of a central authority, which made recommendations on that specific topic. The report of the *Expert Working Group on Mutual Legal Assistance and Related International Confiscation* hosted by UNDCP in February 1993 highlights the important role of a central authority, and makes specific recommendations for central authorities to help solve or alleviate problems in mutual assistance practice. Most recently, the *P8 Senior Expert Working Group*[11] on combating transnational organized crime recommended the establishment of a central authority which could provide speedy coordination of mutual assistance requests.

It is critical to note that the establishment of a central authority for mutual assistance does not require the creation of an elaborate structure that is resource intensive. The models for successful central authorities are as varied as the number of States which have created them. The possibilities range from a central authority created by statute, to a group of officials carrying out delegated functions within an establishment department, to a person who, by practice, is responsible for coordinating all such requests. There are, of course, advantages and disadvantages to each method. For example, legislated central authorities have the authority of statute, and can better control and influence the execution of requests. Legislation also provides an opportunity to clearly define the functions of the central authority.

On the other hand, legislation is costly and resource heavy and provides only limited flexibility to an authority which may be required to change and adjust as the practice of mutual assistance develops. For smaller countries, with limited resources, it may be more realistic to establish a central authority by practice or as a delegated authority of a minister.

Despite the very real practical benefits and the repeated recommendations for the establishment of central authorities, there are persistent problems. Many countries have yet to establish such authorities or have such authorities but they are simply not operational.

Possible Discussion Points

* Domestic barriers which prevent the establishment of or impede the work of a central authority;

* Central authorities within a state with multiple competent authorities that make or execute requests;

* Composition and characteristics of an effective central authority;

[10]Supra footnote 8.

[11]Supra footnote 8.

* Crucial functions of a central authority—coordination, communication, advice and information, etc.

Flexible Legislation and Procedures

It is perfectly normal to expect that authorities raised within a particular legal tradition have a natural bias for the approach and practices of that legal tradition. Also, in providing foreign states with access to compulsory process within a given State, there will be, whether by virtue of constitutional or legislative requirements, constraints on what measures are available and in what circumstances.

However, one of the most critical attributes of mutual assistance is that it is a mechanism designed to bridge the differences between legal systems. This goal can only be realized, however, if States approach mutual assistance with a view to overcoming the differences and not entrenching them.

The governing philosophy for mutual assistance must be to provide the widest scope of assistance possible and to provide that assistance in a usable form for the requesting State. Clearly, that assistance must be rendered in accordance with the law, but that law must be as flexible as possible, with the result that, unless the rendering of assistance would be contrary to a fundamental precept of the requested State, it should be provided and provided in the form sought. If those principles do not govern treaties, legislation and practice, quite frankly, at the operational level, mutual assistance will fail. This is unquestionably the central challenge and it is a very real challenge that practitioners face each day. These following examples illustrate the issue at the treaty and legislation level:

Canada has a common law criminal justice system where there are in essence two stages in the process: pre-charge; the investigation and post charge—the prosecution. The police conduct investigations and lay charges and the prosecutions are then conducted by Crown Attorneys, before a judicial authority.

There is no provision in Canadian domestic law for witnesses to be compelled to provide a statement to or answer the questions of authorities at the investigation stage. It is only during the prosecution phase, at preliminary hearing on trial, after charges have been laid, that a person can be compelled to appear and answer questions before a judicial authority. It is not contrary to or prohibited by Canadian law to provide for compelled statements from witnesses at an investigative stage, but rather by virtue of practice and tradition, there is simply no provision for it.

However, in the vast majority of countries-civil law countries and a growing number of common law countries-that is not the case. Compelled interviews of witnesses during the investigation are, in fact, common practice.

In enacting mutual assistance legislation, Canadian authorities had a choice; follow the Canadian tradition and provide only for post charge, compelled testimony before a judicial authority or provide for a more flexible mechanism, in the context of assistance to a foreign State. Fortunately, in this instance, Canada adopted the approach most consistent with the principles outlined above—the widest measure of assistance possible in a form sought by the requesting State. The legislation was drafted to allow for compelled statements from witnesses at any stage of a foreign criminal process and regardless of the type of authority (judicial, prosecutorial or police) seeking the statement. Thus, foreign authorities can take evidence in Canada in a form consistent with their laws and practice, regardless of the fact that the process is unknown in Canadian domestic practice.

A similar example arises from the difference in competent authorities between civil and common law systems. In many civil law countries, investigations are conducted by judicial authorities. Domestically, it is those judicial authorities who will require evidence for their investigations and thus, requests to foreign States for investigative assistance will originate and emanate from those judicial authorities.

In some civil law states, that practice is applied not only in domestic matters and outgoing requests for assistance but also to mutual assistance requests that are presented by foreign States. That is, by legislation or practice, some states require that requests for assistance from a foreign country emanate from a judicial authority. For common law countries that often presents an insurmountable barrier to assistance, as judicial authorities do not conduct investigations within those States and are not a proper authority to originate a request for assistance.

In those civil law states, however, that have accepted the underlying philosophy and principles of mutual assistance, solutions to this problem have been found. Some countries have provided, through treaty or legislation, that the requests presented by a proper central authority will be acceptable, regardless of the authority conducting the investigation or prosecution. Some have provided, by treaty or legislation, that the request will be acceptable if it emanates from a competent authority, as defined by the requesting State. And still other States have treaties which 'deem' a competent authority in a common law State, such as an Attorney General, to be a 'judicial authority.' This problem and the solutions found to it in some States provide an important illustration of how to reflect in practice the underlying principles of mutual assistance.

While these examples focus on treaties and legislation, it is equally important that the authorities reviewing, processing, and executing requests approach their day to day functions with a similar flexibility.

The challenge is to find similar solutions in treaties, legislation and practice for the problems that follow from the differences in our legal system.

Possible Discussion Points

* Other examples following from the differences in legal systems e.g. examination and cross-examination of a witness in a foreign State, requirements to demonstrate reasonable and probable grounds or probable cause;
* Provision for modified evidentiary rules for the introduction of evidence obtained outside the country;
* Flexible approaches to and provisions for implementing legislation and practices;
* Designing a system for assistance which meets legislative or constitutional standards for the issuance of search warrants or other court orders and at the same time is workable for authorities from another legal tradition;
* The advisability and practicality of designing implementing legislation for mutual assistance which includes all investigative measures available domestically e.g. wiretap, video surveillance etc.

Pursuing the Profits—Cooperation in the Restraint and Confiscation of Proceeds of Crime

Background: To effectively combat an economic based crime it is necessary to strike at that which motivates individuals to commit the crime—profit. To that end, cooperation in the restraint and confiscation of proceeds of crime is the fastest growing component of international assistance.

It was a significant step forward when the *1988 Drug Convention* obligated signatory States to create domestic mechanisms which would allow for the restraint and confiscation of the proceeds of drug-related crime. Perhaps even more importantly, the Convention provided that State parties must be in a position to respond to a request presented by other States, seeking the restraint and confiscation of the proceeds of the Convention offences.

That requirement is critical, because experience clearly demonstrates that sophisticated criminal organizations launder and deposit the proceeds of their activities through many countries and through a vast array of businesses, institutions and organizations. The reality is that without the assistance of other States, no country can successfully investigate, restrain and confiscate the profits of a sophisticated criminal organization. It is not enough that each country has its discrete domestic scheme for restraint and confiscation. There must be a developed network for fast and effective international cooperation, which allows for cross border restraint and confiscation. At the same time, that process must respect the rights of individuals—those whose property may be improperly restrained, and innocent third parties. This area of international cooperation presents perhaps the most significant challenge.

Contrasting Legislative Schemes: One of the central issues is the varying legislative approaches, adopted in response to the *1988 Drug Convention* and in particular in response to the obligations with respect to requests for restraint and confiscation presented by another State. Contrasting the Canadian and Australian models provides an appropriate illustration of the diversion in approach.

Canada has chosen to meet its international obligations to assist other States with the restraint and forfeiture of proceeds of crime by the application of a purely domestic scheme. Under Canada's legislative scheme, where there is a sufficient basis to believe that proceeds of crime are located in Canada, domestic authorities can seek a restraint order or special search warrant to hold that property pending charges and forfeiture proceedings.

To obtain confiscation of suspected proceeds of crime, Canada has adopted a purely criminal charge approach. That is, where a person is convicted of a specified type of offence (either a designated drug or enterprise crime offence) and the court is satisfied on the applicable standard that property or assets constitute proceeds of crime related to that offence or generally, forfeiture can be ordered. The only circumstances where forfeiture is possible without conviction is where the person was charged but absconded or died.

These domestic provisions are essentially the only means by which restraint and confiscation can be pursued. Aside from one quasi-measure for the enforcement of foreign orders described below, there is no separate scheme which allows for restraint and/or confiscation on the basis of foreign requests or through the registration of foreign orders.

To execute a request from a foreign state which seeks the restraint or confiscation of proceeds, Canada must initiate a domestic investigation with a view to charges and prosecution in Canada, and any resulting restraint and confiscation action.

Similarly, there is no provision for direct enforcement of a foreign restraint or confiscation order. The mutual assistance legislation comes close in providing that a foreign country can seek standing to enforce a pecuniary penalty, determined by a court in the foreign jurisdiction to represent the value or assets or other benefit, obtained through the commission of an offence. But that section is limited in scope and has yet to be used.

Canada's approach can be contrasted with that of Australia, where the mutual assistance and proceeds of crime legislation in combination provide for a detailed scheme in relation to requests from foreign States for the restraint and forfeiture of proceeds of crime. The legislative scheme permits the registration and enforcement of both foreign restraint, confiscation and pecuniary penalty orders. Also, there is provision for Australian authorities authorized under the mutual assistance legislation, to apply for a search warrant for tainted property or a restraining order in relation to a foreign serious offence.

Other countries have opted for schemes similar to the two examples or variations thereof, such as a mixture of reliance on domestic procedure and a specific scheme for the enforcement of foreign orders.

Problems in Implementation: The approach adopted in Canada has created a myriad of problems. Sole reliance on domestic process severely limits a State's capacity to provide speedy and effective assistance. In addition, it is cumbersome and time-consuming to try and apply a domestic process to a foreign request and often this discourages Canadian investigative authorities from vigorously pursuing or pursuing at all, investigations flowing from foreign requests. While this approach provides significant protections for individual rights, in that there is a uniform system and standard for restraint and forfeiture, it does so at the cost of an ineffective system for cooperation. In this regard, it is not clear that an appropriate balance between individual rights and societal interests has been achieved.

Again, in contrast, the Australian model provides, in theory at least, for a much more effective response to foreign requests. It will be useful to explore whether authorities there or within states that have adopted a similar system have encountered significant problems in the practical application of the legislative scheme.

Possible Discussion Points

* Balancing effective assistance and the protection of individual rights in a system that permits the registration and enforcement of foreign restraint and confiscation orders;

— what powers of review, if any, do the courts in the requested State have?

— what information, if any, must accompany the order?

— what undertakings must be provided by a foreign state in the case of a request of restraint?

* Liability in the case of wrongful seizure;

* General restraint, forfeiture and money laundering laws against drug related ones only.

Pursuing the Suspect—Extradition

Extradition is the oldest and most recognized form of international cooperation in criminal matters. As much has been written on this topic, this paper will touch only briefly on two issues of particular relevance to transnational organized crime.

In the prosecution of large scale, organized drug importation and distribution schemes or other similar transnational organized crime, there are two critical problems with extradition—the evidentiary requirements for obtaining extradition and the refusal of States to extradite their nationals.

Evidentiary Requirements

At issue is what evidence must be provided before an individual will be extradited to another State. This has been and remains a central issue in extradition, particularly as between civil and common law countries. For civil law States, the issuance of a warrant of arrest within a requesting State evidences that a judicial authority within that State has determined that there is sufficient evidence in the case. From that perspective it is logical to assume that the authorities in the requested state should accept and rely on that determination and not look behind it and reassess the underlying basis of the decision.

Traditionally, common law States have required that, in addition to the warrant, the foreign State must submit evidence to meet a prescribed domestic standard. This requirement flows not from a mistrust of the foreign State but the applicable domestic standards for any action that affects the liberty of an individual within the State. Many such States have also required that the evidence be adducted in a form consistent with the law of the requested State, before extradition will be granted. Historically, the result has been that many fugitives have escaped justice or found safe havens because it was impossible for civil law countries to generate the level of material required, in the form sought.

Fortunately much progress has been made in this area. Several common law countries have eliminated the requirement for evidence. Others have lowered the threshold that must be met and will accept evidence adduced in a summary form, without requiring that it meet the evidentiary standards of the requested State. At the same time, there remain a number of common law States that have yet to modify their process.

Possible Discussion Points

* The barriers which common law states face in modifying the evidentiary requirements;
* The response from the courts within common law states that have eliminated the requirement for evidence;
* The potential for states of a different legal tradition to meet the requirement to adduce some evidence, in a summary form.

Non-Extradition of Nationals

The problems which flow from the refusal of some states to extradite nationals are most acute in the prosecution of transnational organized drug trafficking or transnational organized crime generally.

When authorities of a given state conduct a successful investigation into the activities of a sophisticated transnational criminal organization, with resulting charges against multiple members of the organization, invariably some of those individuals will be located outside the country where the charges have been laid. Those individuals may be nationals of some other State and may never have entered the prosecuting State. For that is often the case with high ranking members of a criminal organization, who plan multiple, large scale importations or other criminal schemes, from a safe distance.

If one of those individuals is located in a State of nationality, that does not extradite its nationals, the result will be a splintered trial process. It will not be possible to bring before one court, all of the players in an organization, to provide a complete picture and allow a court to attribute liability and penalties in a proportional and equitable manner. In traditional thinking, the appropriate response for the State refusing extradition in such circumstances, is to prosecute the individual domestically for the offences for which extradition was sought. In the case of multi-party prosecutions, that is not a satisfactory solution.

In addition, for many reasons, that response is generally no longer an adequate one. In reality, it is difficult to conduct an effective prosecution in the State of nationality. In many instances, with scarce resources, such prosecutions do not receive high priority when competing with domestic territorial cases. The evidence of the offence must be gathered from the other State and this is both costly and time consuming. The result of these practical problems is that often, fugitives find safe havens in a country of nationality.

In recent years, a number of alternatives to unconditional refusal of the extradition of nationals have developed. For example, some countries which traditionally did not extradite nationals, have found it possible to agree to the extradition of nationals for trial in a foreign State, on the condition that any sentence imposed would be served in the requested State.

Possible Discussion Points

* Alternatives to the non-extradition of nationals;
* Domestic barriers to the extradition of nationals;
* Enhancing the process for prosecution in the requested State.

Conclusion

This paper provides only a brief consideration of some of the challenges for practitioners in the field of international cooperation. Those challenges, while significant, should not be viewed as insurmountable. International co-operation has come a very long way, in a very short time. There should be no doubt, that with the continued efforts of the world community, its effectiveness will continue to increase, as will the security of our 'Global Village:'

INTERNATIONAL MUTUAL LEGAL ASSISTANCE AND OTHER FORMS OF INTERNATIONAL LEGAL CO-OPERATION

Jan d'Oliveira

The 1988 United Nations Convention Against Illicit Traffic in Narcotic Drugs and Psychotropic Substances[1]

"is, and was intended to be, primarily a law enforcement convention ...'[2]

These are the words of Dr. W.C. Gilmore who further cites Stewart [3] as saying:

> 'The Convention is one of the most detailed and far-reaching instruments ever adopted in the field of international criminal law, and if widely adopted and effectively implemented, will be a major force in harmonizing national law and enforcement actions around the world.'

This gathering is no doubt acquainted with the Preamble to the 1988 Convention and the concerns therein expressed. And if there happen to be any who at the time of the conclusion of the Convention did not fully appreciate the real need for such a measure, surely events have overtaken us and we are sorely aware of the necessity of effective international co-operation on the legal front. The words of the poet[4] are apposite:

[1]Adopted in Vienna on 19 December 1988.

[2]W.C. Gilmore. *Combating International Drugs Trafficking: The 1988 United Nations Convention*. Explanatory Documentation: Commonwealth Secretariat, p. 42.

[3]Stewart, 'Internationalising the War on Drugs' (1990) 18 *Denver Journal of International Law and Policy*, at p. 388. (Cited by Gilmore, *op.cit.*, 42).

[4]John Donne. 'No man is an island, entire of itself; every man is a piece of the continent, a part of the main.'

'No man is an island ...'

Transposed, this means that, in order to counter the virulent scourge of drugs and drug trafficking, no country can afford to be an island.

This very Conference is an indication of the awareness of the manifold dangers of the global drug trade. The convenors are to be commended for their timely initiative to stress the pressing need for global strategy and active co-operation. As the Executive Chairmen have stated: the war on drugs has to be on the top of every nation's domestic agenda.

In a recent publication,[5] the journalist and writer Brian Freemantle somewhere states that the struggle is no longer between east and west, but between legality and illegality. He refers to the 1994 Naples speech of the UN Secretary General where the latter stated that the choice confronting *the entire world* was

> 'the rule of law over the rule of the jungle'[6]

and described illegal drugs as

> 'that bedrock upon which all organized crime is founded.'[7]

Recognition of the Necessity for International Cooperation

It is the experience of embattled jurisdictions or with countries struggling to cope with organized crime, particularly of the drugs trafficking variety, that they cannot go it alone. Certainly it is our experience in southern Africa.

With the UN Convention,[8] it ought to have been recognized by now:

> 'the links between illicit traffic and other related organized criminal activities which undermine the legitimate economics and threaten the stability, security and sovereignty of states,'

and

> 'that illicit traffic is *an international activity*, the suppression of which demands urgent attention and the highest priority,'

and

[5] *The Octopus—Europe in the Grip of Organized Crime*: Orion Books (ISBN 1857976096) 1995.

[6] *Ibid.*, 9.

[7] *Ibid.*, 36.

[8] Preamble.

'that the eradication of illicit traffic is the collective responsibility of all States and that, to that end, *co-ordinated action with the framework of international co-operation* is necessary.'

and also

'the importance of strengthening and enhancing effective legal means *for international co-operation* in criminal matters for suppressing the international criminal activities of illicit traffic.'

The question is: how do concerned jurisdictions go about securing that desired international co-operation in law enforcement and criminal justice? This presentation seeks to suggest some indications of what is practicable. It is based on the premise that there are many countries which have not acceded to, or which have not been able to accede to, the 1988 UN Convention.

Drug Trafficking: South Africa: Methaqualone—The Indian Connection

Permit me to use as illustration the drugs and drug trafficking situation in South Africa and its relation to the host country, India. The focus will be on the drug Methaqualone (Mandrax).

In its most recent overview of southern Africa, the South African Narcotics Bureau[9] attributes the escalation of drug trafficking in Africa, including South Africa, to such factors as:

— stricter laws aimed at curbing smuggling and greatly improved control at airports and harbours in Europe and the Americas;

— a renewed international investors interest in South Africa;

— South Africa's favourable geographical situation on the major trafficking routes between the Far and Middle East, the Americas and Europe;

— the country's accessibility via land, sea and air routes, especially since South Africa's re-entry into the international arena.

The report states further that the drug problem is exacerbated by the ability of South Africa and of other southern African countries to cultivate, manufacture and process drugs, unfortunately—in some instances—with the connivance and participation of government officials. Mandrax is now manufactured in South Africa, Zambia, Mozambique, Swaziland and

[9]South African Police Service: *The Extent of Drug Trafficking in South Africa*, 7 October 1996.

Tanzania; and cannabis is cultivated in the mountainous areas of Southern Africa, especially of Swaziland, Lesotho and South Africa.[10]

Cannabis (Dagga)

The cultivation, possession, use and dealing in cannabis are statutorily prohibited. Cannabis is the most widely used drug. The surge in the cultivation of the drug has been fuelled by its tremendous profitability. For many rural folk, the cultivation and use of cannabis are not regarded as illicit—to them it is a traditional herb. However, intelligence indicates that cannabis syndicates recruit the rural population to cultivate their crops.

Besides illegal domestic smuggling and transportation, cannabis is exported to the Netherlands and the United Kingdom.[11] The statistics in respect of law enforcement for the first six months of 1996 in respect of dealing are:

arrests	1,843
confiscated/abandoned	55,415 Kg
destroyed in cultivation areas	25,011 Kg.[12]

Hashish

The main indications are that the region is still a transit or conduit for hashish and that there is as yet no conversion to its becoming a consumer market.[13]

During 1995 there were 12 arrests for trafficking with just over 7 Kg being seized. In the first half of 1996 there were 4 arrests and a seizure of just over 1 Kg of hashish.[14]

Cocaine

Prior to 1992, cocaine was considered a status drug which was highly priced (USD 75-100 per g), although of low quality.

In 1992 Nigerian nationals started arriving in South Africa and a high quality of cocaine was introduced. A constant supply has caused the retail prices to fall by more than half and local traffickers have found it more rewarding to do business with the Nigerians at an even lower, wholesale rate.

[10]*Ibid.*, 2.
[11]*Ibid.*, 4-5.
[12]*Ibid.*, 3.
[13]*Ibid.*, 5.
[14]*Ibid.*, 3.

Consumption has spread to all levels of society, including the less affluent. The traditional snorting method was quickly replaced by 'free base,' and 'crack' has made its appearance.

West African nationals seem to have selected Johannesburg as their base. The Nigerians are primarily involved in the importation, wholesale distribution and street peddling of the drug. Additional, lesser role players are nationals from Malawi and Ghana.[15]

Arrests for dealing during 1995 were 269 (including 2 for dealing in crack cocaine). Confiscations amounted to 187 Kg. During the first half of 1996, the figures were 65 arrests and 77 Kg seized.[16]

Heroin

Although, at present, there appears to be no heroin-addiction problem domestically, the indications are that South Africa could become a transit country.

> 'A cause for grave concern is the phenomenon that traditional cocaine drug lords in Colombia and other coca-producing countries, are focusing their attention on heroin manufacturing and trafficking. The implication for South Africa is that established routes for cocaine trafficking can now be used by heroin syndicates. African groups, in particular from Nigeria, now participate actively in these operations, and act as conduits for sales in both Western Europe and the United States. The involvement of West Africans, especially Nigerians, are in this regard a further cause for concern when seen against the backdrop of United Nations (UN) estimates that approximately 51 per cent of the heroin market is controlled by syndicates. More alarming is the fact that they are not merely acting as couriers, but are behind and steering major drug syndicates. In addition, the same traders are opening up markets in South Africa and its neighbouring countries. South Africa has very good commercial air links with the rest of Africa, Asia, Europe and North America which work favourably for heroin traffickers. Couriers of diverse nationalities and backgrounds are recruited by Nigerian traffickers. These couriers use a variety of routes to smuggle heroin from the source-countries to Europe and the United States of America. A large number of couriers are dispatched who use 'body carry' techniques or swallowing and indigestion to conceal heroin. These couriers travel aboard commercial airlines from South East Asia, transiting through Africa and Europe,

[15] *Ibid.*, 9.
[16] *Ibid.*, 3.

bound for the United States. Concealment methods are to a large extent similar to that which are used to conceal cocaine, eg. false-sided luggage, containers, etc.'[17]

Statistics reveal that there were 21 arrests for trafficking, with almost 6 Kg heroin seized, during 1995. For the first half of 1996, there were seizures of 783 grams and 7 arrests.[18]

Designer Drugs

Ecstasy has rocketed to prominence in the space of just two years. Its use has grown at an alarming rate.[19]

SANAB reports 32 arrests for dealing during 1995 and 29 for the first half of 1996.

The comparable number of units confiscated in those periods are 2,117 units and 2,746 units, respectively.[20]

Methaqualone (Mandrax)

The aforementioned survey has thus far indicated South Africa's domestic position as cultivator and exporter of certain substances (such as cannabis), as importer of others (such as cocaine) and as conduit or potential conduit of yet others (hashish; heroin). In addition it has shown it to be both an importer and manufacturer of certain designer drugs.

The most significant problem where its relationship to India is concerned, is in the area of the importation and manufacture of Mandrax. The South African experience is that the original and continuous source of the drug in question is South East Asia, notably India, whose unlawful dealers have established a firm and profitable market. South Africa is the single largest consumer of Mandrax, and most of the global clandestine production is destined for our domestic market. According to UN reports, India seized 45 tons of Methaqualone during 1994, whilst seizures in other countries only amounted to 7 tons (This included South Africa's 667 Kg).[21]

The (ab)use of Mandrax continues to be a major problem in southern Africa. A possible explanation is that we were the first country in which a sub-culture evolved where Mandrax was ground to a powder, mixed with

[17] *Ibid.*, 12.
[18] *Ibid.*, 3.
[19] *Ibid.*, 13.
[20] *Ibid.*, 3.
[21] *Ibid.*, 7-8.

cannabis and smoked as a concoction called a 'white pipe.' Mandrax manufactured in illicit laboratories in India is smuggled by sea and air to either Kenya, Mozambique, Tanzania, Zimbabwe or Zambia and thence ultimately to South Africa. Stolen motor vehicles are increasingly being bartered for illegal drugs (especially Mandrax) in Kenya and the neighbouring SADC countries.[22]

The good news is that the exchange of intelligence and informal international co-operation between the police authorities of South Africa and India has demonstrated the value of finding ways to implement the spirit of the 1988 UN Convention. Indian authorities, acting on information provided by the South African Police Services, closed down an illicit manufacturing facility in Hyderabad on 3 January 1995 and confiscated 1,820 Kg Mandrax (i.e. more than 3 million tablets) destined for the South African market.

The significant successes achieved by the Indian authorities in detecting and closing down clandestine laboratories, may—it seems—be shifting the producers to Southern Africa. The involvement of nationals of both countries still calls for continued collaboration. The appearance on the scene of other nationals requires that collaboration to include other jurisdictions.

Illustrations of the moving of laboratories (which, however, still require the importation of the precursors or chemical components) are as follows:

— Following on an investigation of almost 2 years, SANAB, acting in conjunction with the Royal Swazi Police, in May 1995 seized laboratory equipment in Mbabane, Swaziland. Fifty punches used in the production of Mandrax tablets were seized and the leader of an international drug syndicate arrested.

— In October 1995 the Mozambican Police dismantled a clandestine laboratory that was controlled by an Asian syndicate.

— A month later a clandestine Mandrax laboratory was uncovered between Pretoria and Johannesburg. The precursors were found on the premises. The laboratory was capable of producing 500,000 tablets (with street value R11 million, or USD 3.5 million).

— In September 1996, after surveillance following on intelligence received from the United Kingdom,[23] a major operation was dismantled in the North West Province. Whilst the origin of the precursors was the UK and Germany, two of the arrestees were Indian nationals one of whom was an escaped convicted trafficker from the UK. The apparent local head of the operation is a businessman with strong Indian connections.

[22] *Ibid.*, 7.

[23] UK customs authorities had specially marked consignments of chemicals to be exported; the exact same containers were seized on the premises.

Statistics for 1994, 1995 and the first six months of 1996 serve to indicate the extent of SANAB's law enforcement activities:

	1994	*1995*	*1996 (1st Half)*
Arrests (possession)	324	172	105
Tablets Confiscated	27,124	683	17,314 plus 101g powder
Arrests (Dealing)	2,459	1,288	527
Tablets Confiscated	2,841,100 plus 2,085,000 in Swaziland	886,162 plus 30Kg powder	289,521 plus 3.8Kg powder

International Co-operation in the Absence of Accession to the 1988 UN Convention

Prior to, and in the absence of accession to the UN instruments,[24] the various jurisdictions had, where criminal law is concerned, only traditional bilateral extradition treaties (where in existence) and the sometimes frustrating Rogatoire Procedure to rely on to secure international collaboration. Informally, grassroots reliance had to be placed on whatever police liaison, of which Interpol is an illustration, existed.

Except where regional co-operation was formalized, any co-operation was largely dependent on mutual goodwill and comity. The inadequacy thereof, in the face of spiralling global crime, has become only too apparent in recent times. Even the existence of the older type treaties have proved to be inadequate: more likely than not, drug offences were not extraditable. Hence Articles 6(2) and 6(4) of the Vienna Convention.

Extradition

There exists no bilateral treaty between India and South Africa.

Granted, this does not preclude informal assistance between police authorities as illustrated above,[25] but such assistance is naturally no substitute for extradition.

It may be of some interest to mention that the South African Extradition Act[26] has always provided for extradition *in the absence of any extradition agreement* under the written authority of the Head of State.[27] This

[24]The 1988 Vienna Convention and the 1961 Convention, as amended—1971.

[25]See under Methaqualone, above p. 182.

[26]Act No. 67 of 1962, s 3(2).

places us in a very favourable position to co-operate with other jurisdictions.

Pursuant to a comprehensive study by the Law Commission of the issue of international co-operation in criminal prosecutions, South Africa is poising itself to become a full partner in the fight against transnational crime. The Extradition Amendment Act is the first of three statutes to have been put into operation.[28]

Ultimately, where global drug trafficking is concerned, the ideal is accession to the 1988 Convention. In the meantime, Article 6 thereof serves as the benchmark for the regulation of extradition whilst the several jurisdictions commit themselves to upgrading their domestic laws.[29]

Mutual Legal Assistance

Here Article 7 of the Vienna Convention sets the benchmark. It can no longer be said that the subject matter of Mutual Legal Assistance (MLA) is one with which the common law world is unfamiliar.[30]

Following on the positive experience of the United States, a number of bilateral MLA Treaties (MLAT's) were concluded. The Commonwealth followed suit with the conclusion in Harare in August 1986 of the Commonwealth Scheme on Mutual Assistance in Criminal Matters. Since then a number of Commonwealth jurisdictions have enacted the necessary domestic legislation and have been active in the negotiation of bilateral agreements.[31]

[27]Act No. 67 of 1962 has recently been amended by Act No. 77 of 1996. Section 3(2), which has been streamlined, reads as follows:

'Any person accused or convicted of an extraditable offence committed within the jurisdiction of a foreign State which is not a party to an extradition agreement shall be liable to be surrendered to such foreign State, if the President has in writing consented to his or her being surrendered.'

[28]Act No. 77 of 1996. The other two Acts, passed but not yet in operation are: the International Co-operation in Criminal Matters Act, No. 75 of 1996 and the Proceeds of Crime Act, No. 76 of 1996.

Vide: The First 1000 Days, presentation by the Minister of Justice, 13 February 1997 (Cape Town), p. 23.

[29]Cf Gilmore, *op cit.*, 18-23.

[30]*Ibid.*, 23.

[31]*Ibid.*, 23. Gilmore mentions the example of Australia and points to the UK as having subsequently taken the required steps (*See* Criminal Justice/International Cooperation Act 1990, Chapter 5).

Gilmore[32] states that the text of Article 7 of the 1988 UN Convention is fully compatible with the provisions of the 1986 Commonwealth Scheme.[33]

Where does South Africa stand at present in regard to MLA, assuming it receives a request for assistance from a jurisdiction such as India? A distinction needs to be drawn between present operative legislation and laws passed but not in operation. Additionally, consensual as against coercive steps must also be borne in mind.

Consensual (Informal) and Coercive (Formal)

One tends to underestimate what can be achieved through informal co-operation. To assist in tracking down a witness or locating exhibits is something that does not require legislation or a treaty. It is on a par with the exchange of intelligence by police authorities.

Experience also shows that there are witnesses who are quite prepared to make a statement for, or even testify in the foreign jurisdiction, or perhaps even surrender an exhibit. *This consensual approach should always be exhausted.*[34]

It is, however, in the matter of the reluctant witness or of confiscation where coercive or formal means need to be employed that legislation and/or treaty became important.

South African Assistance: At Present

Apart from a readiness to assist informally, there are two pieces of legislation readily available for assistance of the coercive variety.

(1) The first is an oft-overlooked provision of the Criminal Procedure Act[35] which provides that a magistrate may order that an 'article' seized be handed over to a member of a foreign police authority who may remove it from the country. The circumstances must be that the article seized is one used in the commission of an offence

[32]*Ibid.*, 23 note (101).

[33]The Commonwealth Secretariat has been active in promoting MLA with the support of UNICRI and UNDCP: witness the Oxford Conference on MLA (Sept. 1994) and a number of regional initiatives such as Conferences on Cross-Border Co-operation held in the Southern African Region.

[34]Prosecuting authorities have received much assistance in using this approach. Recently both UK and German authorities have been very amenable in the investigations of the North West Province Mandrax case. It is, however, always understood that the requested state will dictate whether the informal or formal avenue is to be followed.

[35]Act No. 51 of 1977, s 36.

outside the Republic or suspected on reasonable grounds to have been so used; and there are likewise reasonable grounds to believe that it will serve as proof of the commission of an offence, or that it was used for the purpose of *or in connection with*, such commission.[36] 'Article' is very broadly defined[37] and may be construed to include not only money or negotiable instruments, but even the bank statements of the account in which the exhibit was deposited.

(2) The second is the Foreign Courts Evidence Act,[38] whereby depositions may be taken from witnesses for use in the requesting state. An application is made to the High Court, which—in the case of criminal proceedings—will direct that a magistrate examine the witness(es). The Magistrate

'shall cause any person whose evidence is required, to be summoned to appear and give evidence or produce any book, document or object before him ... and take his evidence upon interrogatories or otherwise as ordered or requested ...'

[36] Section 36(1) provides in full:

(1) Where an article is seized in connection with which

(a) an offence was committed or is on reasonable grounds suspected to have been committed in a country outside the Republic;

(b) there are reasonable grounds for believing that it will afford evidence as to the commission in a country outside the Republic of any offence or that it was used for the purpose of or in connection with such commission of any offence, the magistrate within whose area of jurisdiction the article was seized may, on application and if satisfied that such offence is punishable in such country by death or by imprisonment for a period of twelve months or more by a fine of five hundred and or more, order such article to be delivered to a member of a police force established in such country who may thereupon remove it from the Republic."

[37] Section 20 of Act No. 51 of 1977 provides:

'The State may, in accordance with the provisions of this Chapter, seize anything (in this Chapter referred to as an article)

(a) which is concerned in or is on reasonable grounds believed to be concerned in the commission or suspected commission of an offence, whether within the Republic or elsewhere;

(b) which may afford evidence of the commission or suspected commission of an offence, whether within the Republic or elsewhere; or

(c) which is intended to be used or is on reasonable grounds believed to be intended to be used in the commission of an offence.'

[38] Act No. 80 of 1962, ss 2 and 4.

The Drugs and Drugs Trafficking Act[39]

The 1992 drugs legislation endeavoured, in so far as is possible, to be compatible with the 1988 UN Convention although there was no likelihood of accession at the time. In accordance with, particularly, Article 3 of the Convention the manufacture and supply of scheduled substances,[40] the use and possession of drugs,[41] dealing in drugs,[42] the knowing acquisition of the proceeds of defined crime[43] and the conversion of known or reasonably suspected proceeds of crime[44] were proscribed[45] and severe penalties provided for.[46] Police officials were given wide powers of entry, search, interception, questioning, access to records, and seizure.[47]

Concerning the present subject-matter, the only explicit reference to 'mutual assistance' is found in Chapter VI of Act No. 92 of 1992 (ss 54-60). Somewhat surprisingly, the chapter does not deal with the MLA envisaged by Article 7 of the Convention, but seeks to provide for the registration and execution of foreign confiscation orders, in anticipated implementation of Article 5 of the UN Convention. Indeed, Chapter V of our Drugs Act[48] contains extensive provisions relating to the Proceeds of Drug Trafficking, particularly to confiscation orders,[49] restraint orders[50] and the realization of property.[51]

The mutual assistance in Chapter VI is restricted to a certain topic, albeit a very important one. However, as its application depends on the designation of 'any country outside the Republic as a designated country'[52]

[39]Act No. 140 of 1992.

[40]*Ibid.*, s 3.

[41]*Ibid.*, s 4.

[42]*Ibid.*, s 5.

[43]*Ibid.*, s 6.

[44]*Ibid.*, s 7.

[45]*Ibid.*, ss 13 and 14.

[46]*Ibid.*, s 17.

[47]*Ibid*, s 11. Section 11(1)(g) provides that a police official may 'seize anything which in his opinion is connected with, or may provide proof of, a contravention of a provision of this Act.'

[48]*Ibid.*, s 28 *et seq.*

[49]*Ibid.*, ss 35-40

[50]*Ibid.*, ss 41-45.

[51]*Ibid.*, ss 46-47.

[52]*Ibid.*, s 55(1)(a).

and since no designations have as yet been made, the only credit we can claim is that the machinery is in place. The Minister of Justice has however declared his serious intention in this regard.[53]

International Co-operation in Criminal Matters Act[54]

Domestic legislation has recently been enacted, but is not in operation yet. The above Act will not only find specific application to drugs and drug trafficking (and therefore be a response to Article 7 of the Convention), but will apply to all crimes. This is one of the pieces of legislation following on the comprehensive report of the Law Commission, referred to earlier.[55]

Practical Means of Assistance

Delegates to this august Conference will, no doubt, take home with them a renewed awareness of the 1988 UN Convention and a realization of its beneficial use as a framework for the purposes of harmonizing and updating domestic legislation. They will probably seek to enter into or augment bilateral and multilateral agreements. Some countries may position themselves to accede to the Convention.

[53]*The First 1,000 Days, supra*, p.45:

'Before designations are made for the purposes of the Drug Trafficking (Mutual Assistance) Regulations, 1995, it is necessary to conclude mutual assistance agreements with the countries concerned to, *inter alia*, provide for the respective authorities in each country which will deal with requests for assistance, the format and content of such requests, documentary proof that shall accompany such requests, the language to be used and the requirements regarding the authentication of documents. A comprehensive mutual assistance agreement has been concluded with the United Kingdom of Great Britain and Northern Ireland, but has not yet come into force.

As soon as the Republic is in a position to grant assistance in the investigation process, the necessary steps will be taken for the entry into force of the agreement. Mutual assistance agreements are also being negotiated with Argentina, Brazil, Chile and Paraguay. The Republic has also agreed to designate Zimbabwe in terms of the Drug and Drug Trafficking Act, 1992, and a mutual assistance agreement must still be negotiated and agreed on in this regard. In respect of Namibia the Republic has agreed on the launching of a joint investigation to promote legislation which on the basis of reciprocity will *inter alia* provide for mutual assistance regarding the confiscation of the proceeds of crime.'

[54]Act No. 74 of 1996.

[55]Above, note 28.

Yet there is a major benefit to be derived from international gatherings where international co-operation in criminal justice matters are concerned. The benefit is that one learns *to collaborate informally* whilst the formal mechanisms are being put in place. Informal collaboration is a justifiable and necessary form of international co-operation. Much can be achieved whilst recognizing the exclusive preserve of the other jurisdiction.[56]

A. Central Office

One ingredient of a MLA arrangement is the designation of a central office or authority to which all requests are directed. A jurisdiction could, in the absence of a formal MLAT, agree internally on a central point for the processing of, or onward referral of requests and enquiries.

B. Prosecuting Authorities—Direct Communication

Irrespective of the designation of a central office, chief prosecutors should take the liberty of contacting their counterparts in other jurisdictions.

It is the nature of the function common to them that prosecutors will more readily know what it is they seek and, corollarily, what could be done to assist the counterpart who seeks assistance.

One benefit of the recently formed International Association of Prosecutors (IPA)[57] is that avenues of personal communication have been opened. It is amazing what can be achieved through the modern means of direct communication. On more than one occasion such contacts have borne fruit in investigations.[58]

C. Contact and Cooperation on a Regional or Common Interest Basis

The initiatives and exhortations of such bodies as the Commonwealth Secretariat and the UNDCP at regional meetings in southern Africa have led to regularized contact between the region's police chiefs. The formation of a chief prosecutors' forum has been agreed upon. Such associations are ideal for the exchange of intelligence, the sharing of experience, the pro-

[56]Cf Article 2(3) of the Convention: '*A Party shall not undertake in the territory of another Party the exercise of jurisdiction and the performance of functions which are exclusively reserved for the authorities of that other Party by its domestic law.*' Cf Gilmore, *op cit.*, 3.

[57]Not only the IPA, but gatherings such as the Oxford Conference on MLA and other regional meetings have had this beneficial effect.

[58]In many cases the direct communication may be in parallel with, or precede, the making of a formal request.

motion of the harmonization of laws and, naturally, the cementing of direct liaison. Very little, if anything, in the line of enabling legislation is required for such avenues of co-operation.

D. Police Authorities

Vital to any form of co-operation, whether formal or informal, is collaboration at the grass-roots between the police authorities of different jurisdictions. Whether the vehicle be Interpol or any similar association, the fact is that such collaboration does not require enabling legislation. The successes in investigating and prosecuting drug traffickers are due to the bond between police officers of different countries.

Gilmore[59] reminds one that

> 'Article 9 (of the 1988 Convention) makes it clear that formal mutual legal assistance procedures should not be seen to be in any sense a substitute for existing police-to-police co-operation.'

By the same token, reliance must be placed on such co-operation in the absence of formal procedures. Illustrations of what is possible are:

— *Controlled Delivery*

This technique, endorsed and promoted by the Vienna Convention,[60] is applied by police authorities, usually pursuant to some form of operational agreement (in terms of which undercover operations are also undertaken).

— *Operational Co-operation*

(1) About 18 months ago, clandestine laboratories in the Philippines were shut down and 11 tons of Mandrax seized. Both Indian and South African assistance was rendered to the Philippine police authorities (The South African link was an Indian national resident in our country). Photographs of suspects who fled have been given to our police for purposes of the ongoing effort to apprehend them.

(2) Intelligence received from HM Customs Officer stationed in India, on Indian-based activities in Kenya and Zambia, ensured the recent apprehension of traffickers and the seizure of Mandrax and equipment.

[59] *Op cit.*, 25.
[60] Article 11, see Gilmore, op cit., 35-36.

— *Drug Liaison Officers*

The posting of liaison officers in each other's country is a very concrete form of international co-operation. South African drug liaison officers will soon be posted to India and Pakistan. In South Africa the DEA (US) has opened an office in the US Embassy in Pretoria.

— *Customs Authorities*

The 1994 Oxford Conference on MLA recognized the importance of co-operation between the customs authorities of the respective jurisdictions and urged that some degree of co-ordination was needed, both internally and between requesting and requested states. Whilst South Africa has yet to attend to the matter of internal co-ordination, it should be mentioned that our police authorities have taken the lead in liaising with customs authorities abroad.[61]

E. Conferences and Training

The first major Methaqualone Conference in Africa was held at Sun City, in the North West Province, just over two years ago. A strong Indian delegation was among the large number of international participants. This confirmed the mutual earnest with which South Africa and India regard the Mandrax problem and opened valuable avenues of communication.

Training seminars are yet another vehicle of co-operation. South African prosecutors and investigators have, on a number of occasions, benefitted from seminars held in our country by the DEA (US) and by H M Customs. The seminars have served to bolster motivation and develop expertise, and to establish yet further transnational contacts.

Progress with Accession to the UN Convention

I can do no better than quote from the recent presentation by Dr. A.M. Omar, Minister of Justice, to illustrate South Africa's progress in positioning our country to accede to the 1988 Convention:

> 'The Vienna Convention was adopted during December 1988 as a result of growing international concern about the magnitude and rising trend in the illicit production of and traffic in narcotic drugs. The Con-

[61]Cf. Collaboration in the African and North West Province Mandrax cases mentioned previously.

[62]*The First 1000 Days, supra,* 44.

vention *inter alia* aims to deprive persons engaged in illicit traffic of the proceeds of their criminal activities, improve international co-operation, and to strengthen and enhance effective legal means for international co-operation. The commencement of the Drugs and Drug Trafficking Act, 1992 (Act 140 of 1992), which *inter alia* provides for the confiscation of the proceeds of drug trafficking and international co-operation is but one of the steps necessary to comply with the provisions of the Vienna Convention. Necessary legislation (that is the legislation referred to above in relation to proceeds of crime, international cooperation, and extradition) has been approved by Parliament. It is intended to put this legislation into operation during the first quarter of 1997, whereafter steps will forthwith be taken to accede to the Vienna Convention.'

Conclusion

The 1988 UN Convention and its predecessors comprehensively set benchmarks for domestic and international endeavours to counter the attack on humanity occasioned by drug abuse and drug trafficking. It is a framework for a proper formal response. Yet the matter cannot be allowed to rest at that. Innovative thinking is called for in order to buttress the aims of the Convention. There are a number of avenues of informal international co-operation which can successfully be explored and used in order to secure effective results. It requires only genuine goodwill on the part of each jurisdiction.

If this paper has succeeded in creating an awareness of possibilities of informal co-operation, it will have contributed in a small way towards the objectives of the organizers of this timely Conference.

COUNTER-NARCOTICS LAW ENFORCEMENT CO-OPERATION: A NECESSITY

Michael E. Fredericks

After having spent more than twenty-five years in federal narcotics law enforcement, whenever the question of inter-agency or international co-operation in counter-narcotics law enforcement arises, it brings to my mind one of the great military philosophies: Divide and Conquer. Or possibly the other adage: United We Stand, Divided We Fall.

Co-operation in counter-narcotics law enforcement efforts, whether it be between multiple agencies within a single city or state government, or between federal or central government organizations working on an international plane, is indeed, a necessity. A necessity especially in today's world when the resources of many government agencies committed to prevent the spread of narcotics use and abuse are significantly less than the resources of those trafficking organizations which infect our cities, countries, states, provinces, departments, territories, and countries with illicit controlled substances.

Whether talking about the individuals and organizations who traffic in opiates (heroin and morphine); cocaine; psychotropic substances such as LSD (acid), MDMA (ecstasy), methamphetamine (speed, crank, crystal), methaqualone (Mandrax), or the cannabis derivatives of marijuana (ganja) and hashish (charas), they share a common denominator. They are beating us to death every day. There are many reasons for this, but make no mistake-without co-operation between agencies and governments in our efforts to combat the spread of illicit drug use there is no hope of holding our own in the battle, much less winning it.

There are many ways to achieve better co-operation between agencies and national governments. One of the most important, in my opinion, is through training. When law enforcement officers are brought together from many different agencies (police, customs, etc.) or from many different countries, an amazing thing happens. The manifestoes and prejudices dictated by politicians and bureaucrats seem to dissolve as those enforcement officers learn that their counterparts on the other side of the border, or their rivals on the other side of town, or in that other ministry or department, confront the same or similar problems as they do.

One of the most important aspects of training seminars and conferences is, contrary to the belief of many, not the 'perks' of international travel or the chance to shop or visit Disney World, but rather the ability to forge long-term relationships through the 'networking' which takes place in such meetings. Once an officer has made personal contact with a counterpart agency, whether in another State or in another country, the way has been paved to continue that personal relationship in the pursuit of criminal investigations which present a common professional interest. Often a conference delegate may meet another officer who has solved the same or similar problems with which he has been grappling for some time. Exchange of ideas, methods of operation, and most importantly, intelligence on the criminals and their organizations, are a goal of such training seminars.

In the past fourteen years that I have worked in international counter-narcotics law enforcement and lived outside the United States, I have personally experienced both the successes derived from international co-operation between agencies and governments, and the failures due to a lack of it. By way of example, consider these two scenarios:

Country A was one of several within my office's area of responsibility which received specialized training for counter-narcotics enforcement officers. As a result of Country A's specific interest and need, subsequent training was provided in airport interdiction procedures, along with an intelligence profile of selected groups of suspected drug couriers operating in the area. Some time later, the customs officers at Country A's primary international airport arrested a subject who met the intelligence profile for a suspected courier when he was found attempting to smuggle eight (8) kilograms of white heroin through the airport. As a result of that arrest and the subsequent follow-up investigation, which was conducted jointly between U.S. officials and host country counterparts, the courier was identified as an active member of an organization sending heroin to Chicago, Illinois. He was also linked to other multi-kilogram seizures of heroin in San Francisco, California and Portland, Oregon, and subsequently indicted in the U.S..

Country A did not at that time, and does not currently, have an extradition treaty with the United States which would have provided for the fugitive's formal return to the U.S. to face criminal charges. In spite of the lack of a formal treaty, however, the government of Country A expelled the heroin courier to another cooperative country, which in turn sent him to the U.S. to face narcotic trafficking charges. This decision to support international and multi-lateral counter-narcotics co-operation was reached in the highest office of the government of Country A. That decision was further supported by multiple government ministries, including the foreign ministry and the domestic ministries under which the customs and police organizations served.

In Country B, another heroin trafficker was detained when he attempted to depart through that country's primary international airport and was found to be in possession of multiple kilograms of heroin. He was subsequently arrested and charged with the offense. Six years later, that same trafficker came to the attention of domestic counter-narcotics law enforcement officers in New York City when it was determined that he was the ongoing supplier of multiple multi-kilogram consignments of heroin to local distributors on the east coast of the U.S. No fewer than ten individuals arrested in the U.S. named the foreign trafficker as the source of supply for their heroin. That intelligence was corroborated when a Drug Enforcement Administration (DEA) informant initiated contact with the drug trafficker by telephone and was told that the drug trafficker would, indeed, provide substantial quantities of heroin for distribution in the U.S.

A joint investigation was initiated between the local DEA office and its host country counterparts at the designated counter-narcotics enforcement agency. The investigation disclosed that the trafficker had never gone to trial on the original charge made six years ago, was still free on bail, and was continuing his heroin trafficking activities. The investigation subsequently brought the U.S. based informant to the host country to meet and negotiate with the heroin trafficker for a quantity of heroin. A 500 gram (1/2 kilogram) sample was delivered to the informant under visual and electronic surveillance of enforcement officers. The trafficker was again arrested and charged with the offence. That arrest occurred in early 1995. The trafficker was again released on bail, has not been brought to trial, and is still not incarcerated. This, in spite of two arrests with substantial quantities of heroin in his possession and an outstanding criminal indictment in the United States.

In the first case with Country A, the participating enforcement officers were able to feel a sense of accomplishment. In the second case with Country B, frustration was the key word. What was the primary difference between these two examples? A combination of awareness, commitment, and co-operation between agencies, ministries and countries. Country A exhibited all three traits, from the customs officer who detected the heroin, all the way to the highest office of government. In Country B, all three traits were present at the enforcement level. Awareness, commitment, and co-operation were all demonstrated throughout the joint investigation which resulted in the arrest of the trafficker and seizure of the heroin sample. Once the case was submitted for prosecution, however, it became very unclear where in the judicial system either awareness, commitment, or co-operation, or a combination of any two or all three failed to exist.

The second example brings us to what is probably the largest single threat to total co-operation between agencies and/or countries in pursuing their individual counter-narcotics enforcement goals. The spectre of compromise. Take away all the banter and self-righteous indignation which accompanies the arguments and 'turf-battles' between agencies with their claims of expertise, better intelligence sources and analysts, more effective undercover officers, more sophisticated equipment, etc., and all else will come down to the simple question, 'Can we trust them?'.

That is not necessarily to imply corruption, although the possibility of corruption must always be a consideration when deciding whether or not to share sensitive sources or intelligence with another agency. Consider the foregoing examples once again. If the question, 'Can we trust them?' is asked in each case, what are the respective answers? I submit that in the case of Country A, it is obvious from the results achieved that the answer must be an unhesitating 'Yes'. In the case of Country B, however, the answer is not so clear. It becomes necessary to answer a multiple part question. The question is broken down to 'who to trust?'. And once the answer to that question is found, will we be willing to again pursue a similar joint investigation with this agency, or will we decide that our commitment of resources (both financial and manpower) is not worth the chance of facing failure again in our mission to arrest, *convict* and *incarcerate* the offender?

In the latter instance described, it was obvious to me that the counterpart law enforcement agency was aware, committed and cooperative. Somewhere in the prosecution or the judiciary, however, the ball appears to have been dropped, to use an American phrase. There is something basically wrong in a system which lets a drug trafficker walk the streets after two arrests for quantities of a drug which would, in theory, bring the death penalty upon conviction, while also being under indictment in another country for similar offences. The obvious argument is that the man has not been convicted of a crime and should not, therefore, be deprived of his freedom. That is the point. Why hasn't he been convicted?

In this case, specific allegations arose concerning the deciding judicial officers. Speculation within the enforcement community was fueled by allegations made by an informant. Ultimately, there was no evidence of corruption or conflict of interest, but the informant providing the information had proved reliable in multiple drug-related investigations for which he had been utilized by counter-narcotics law enforcement agencies over the past several years. Whenever such accusations or allegations are made within the community of law, whether in the realm of enforcement or judicial responsibility, it is cause for concern. Such schisms cause distrust, suspicion, and a loss of faith between those entities which should be working closely together toward a common goal.

So we come full circle to the necessity of co-operation, as enhanced by training seminars and conferences. Co-operation between agencies and ministries through the exchange of ideas and experiences. Through understanding. An ongoing learning process wherein the judge, the policeman, and the prosecutor all become students. Co-operation between nations and their governments is paramount in the international battle against drug trafficking. Before we can have co-operation, however, there must be education, interest, and a commitment. The police officer and the customs officer must not only believe in, and be committed to the job he or she is doing, but also be especially trained in drug investigation techniques. The robed jurist must make his or her final judgement upon rule of law, but must further understand the entire process and circumstances by which the defendant appears before the bench. And the criminal prosecutor must have not only complete knowledge of the statute of law he is prosecuting, but must also have a complete understanding of all aspects of the investigation in order to prosecute the violation to its fullest extent, while simultaneously educating the courts on elements of the case which will not otherwise come to the attention of the bench.

As long as we fail to fully cooperate with each other; as long as agencies refuse to share information among themselves; as long as participants within the criminal justice system fight and bicker with each other over inconsequential issues; and as long as some countries refuse to deal reasonably with others in matters of international drug trafficking, the battle will indeed be long and difficult. For with all the achievements and accomplishments that we as an international counter-narcotics law enforcement community have made in the past several years, and for all the improvements we have made in cooperating with each other, we still have a long way to go. And unless we are able to 'stand united' as a unified force to confront the international drug trafficking cartels, we will certainly 'fall divided' in our efforts.

ESTABLISHING PRIORITIES AND POLICIES TO ENABLE THE CRIMINAL JUSTICE SYSTEM TO RESPOND MOST EFFECTIVELY TO THE REQUIREMENT OF DRUG CONTROL

Herman Woltring

The additional demands and requirements placed on the agencies and arms of the criminal justice system by the continuing growth in the trafficking and abuse of prescribed drugs has been documented. It has principally been referred to in criminological materials. From these materials it would seem that drug control policy makers have simply assumed the capacity of the criminal justice system. It is already in place to provide services of processing and punishing those who transgress the law; and it can therefore be properly called upon to perform those functions for persons who break the law in respect of controlled substances.

However, the criminal justice system has a dual problem. First, in most countries, the term 'system' is a misnomer, as the various agencies including the police prosecutors, courts and corrections personnel, work independently from each other without any co-operative or co-ordination mechanisms in place. When one adds the international dimension, including differences in legal systems, these problems are aggravated. Secondly, the assumption appears to have been that the criminal justice 'system' can deal with any imposts placed on it. This has, in many countries, proved to be a fallacy, and is now being utilized by the legalization lobby which points to either an alleged incapacity of the system to cope, or to 'economic costs' arguments, for the abandonment of a supply reduction approach. Whilst this economic cost approach argues that law enforcement is too costly, the lobby has not provided the alternative costs involved in legalization. What is the point of transferring the costs from one public sector to another, for example higher pension and health care costs, not to mention the added social costs?

For various reasons the problems are even more acute for developing countries and those countries in transition to pluralist democratic market economies. Many of these countries were to a degree sheltered from the drug abuse phenomenon; it was perceived to be a 'developed world' problem, at least insofar as drug use was concerned. Developments over the past years indicated this to be no longer correct—traffickers are intent on increasing the size of their markets, including in countries where they previously did not, or could not, operate. Evidence from Central and Eastern Europe is particularly stark in this regard.

Secondly, the evidence is clear that the cost of operating criminal justice systems in developing countries is comparatively more expensive than in developed countries. Thus, for example, the then United Nations Committee on Crime Prevention and Control found in 1990 that 'developed countries expended an average of 2 to 3 per cent of their budgets on crime control. In developing countries an average of 9 to 14 per cent of the budgets is consumed by the attempt to provide crime prevention and criminal justice services'.[1] In other words, the growing drugs phenomenon will place extra burdens on systems already swallowing up a substantial part of the national budget.

The question which I believe is central to all the Conference themes is how can we upgrade our systems of administration of justice at both the national and international levels without necessarily allocating significantly higher resources, which would involve an opportunity cost away from other developmental activities. Put another way, how can we, at minimal cost, equate the capacity of the system with the needs arising from the impact of, *inter alia*, the drug phenomenon?

As mentioned earlier, with minor exceptions prior to this Conference, the problem has mainly been addressed in criminological terms and not at the policy and managerial levels—at least not in a co-ordinated manner involving all components of the criminal justice system. The criminological literature itself has largely taken the form of narrative descriptions of some aspects of the problem rather than any in-depth analysis with a view to the development of counter strategies. It does, however, make clear that in many countries the drug phenomenon has been the most significant source of extra pressure and other negative influences on the criminal justice system in recent decades.

In 1995, the United Nations International Drug Control Programme, later with the involvement of UNICRI, conducted a series of small pilot studies in the United States and Western Europe aimed at identifying the main stresses imposed on the agencies of the criminal justice system. The stud-

[1]UN document E/1990/31/Add. 1

ies were limited to the police and prison components of the system. The objective was to obtain more precise and focused information on the additional pressures and factors arising from drug related crime, where in each agency these occur, what form they take and the impact they create on the relevant agencies. The prisons studied included those in Texas and Maryland in the United States and others in the Nordic Countries, whilst the police agencies were those in Chicago and Maryland in the United States and the Thames Valley Police Service in the United Kingdom.

The pilot studies involved a 'bottom-up' approach in that the participants were active members of the prison and police services who identified particular problems together with possible solutions, including the advantages and disadvantages associated with each option for change, including resource implications. An important feature of these pilot studies was that no 'solutions' or 'answers' were suggested to the participants, so that the findings were based entirely on their practical knowledge and expertise. The role of the UNDCP and UNICRI staff was only to bring out the problems and possible solutions in a structured way, and not to impose preconceived ideas or information.

A final comparative workshop was held by the Prompidou Group of the Council of Europe at Strasbourg and was, we believe, the first meeting of international groups of senior police and prison officials. Interestingly enough, the results were remarkably similar to those of the earlier meetings conducted with culturally homogeneous groups, suggesting that the problems may have similarities even in different settings.

The pilot phase was completed with an Expert Meeting hosted in Budapest by the Government of Hungary, attended by representatives of most Pompidou Countries, the Visegrad Countries, some Eastern European countries as well as representatives from India, Costa Rica, Egypt and Malawi.

The 'macro' conclusions were as follows:

(1) the additional demands placed on the criminal justice system stemming from the requirements of drug control activities are real and of sufficient seriousness to threaten the quality of the administration of justice;
(2) both the nature of the problem and their point of impact within at least the prison and police agencies are capable of precise determination
(3) alternative responses, together with positive and negative consequences, can also be defined;
(4) the outputs of such studies can form a good foundation for informed policy development to minimize the problems arising by the ever increasing number of drug related cases; and

(5) unless such steps are taken, the ability of the criminal justice system to function effectively as an instrument of drug control could be at risk.

At the agency level, the pilot phase identified four major impacts of drug control:

These were:

(1) an increase in agency workload disproportionate to the increase in number of cases dealt with. In the case of the police, for example, drug cases were frequently seen as more confrontational with a far lower number of suspects prepared to plead guilty but insisting on the prosecution establishing guilt beyond reasonable doubt in a court of law. For the prison service, additional behavioural and disciplinary issues were identified as well as the need for searching visitors in order to prevent the spread of a drug culture within the corrections service.
(2) a deterioration in the quality of the conduct of the normal activities of police and prison services;
(3) a significant increase in the demands made on the resources of the agency, especially staff resources at both the institutional and personal level; and
(4) not surprisingly, the impact of drug control functions on an agency is directly linked to the scope and intensity of the drug phenomenon in the given jurisdiction.

As a result of the pilot phase and the Strasbourg and Budapest meetings, UNICRI has been requested by the Government of Hungary to replicate the study in Hungary, involving all four principal criminal justice agencies, namely the police, prosecutors, courts and correction. We hope to commence that activity this year.

Given the apparent cross-cultural similarities discovered in the Strasbourg and Budapest meetings, UNICRI believes that these studies should be made on a wider basis, encompassing at least one Asian and a Latin American country, possibly followed by a larger inter-regional meeting. Given the initiative shown by the Government of India in organizing this Conference, I would like to suggest that India be the representative Asian nation in which these studies be carried out. Subject, of course, to the consent of the Government of India, I can state that UNICRI would be prepared to undertake the task with the only cost to the Government of India being the time, approximately one week, of the practitioners from the various agencies which it nominates to participate.

UNICRI would hope to carry out these studies in collaboration with both the United Nations International Drug Control Programme and the Crime Prevention and Criminal Justice Programme as well as with other relevant inter-governmental organizations including the Pompidou Group of the Council of Europe, the Phare Program of the Commission of the European Union and the Commonwealth Secretariat.

UNICRI believes that countries and regions in which the project is implemented can benefit from an improved and innovative capacity in policy planning, including specific and detailed needs assessment activities leading to better insights into resource allocation, training, curricular agency planning and enhanced law reform opportunities.

All countries can benefit from an enhanced ability to exchange information and experience at the international level in a clear, precise and structured format to assess what has been attempted, with what outcome, and how those measures, tailored to local conditions, may be replicated with a good chance of success.

More importantly, countries where the level of drug abuse is increasing could be given the opportunity to pre-empt some of the negative effects on their criminal justice systems by developing pro-active strategies and law reform based on the experiences of other countries recorded in precise terms.

The last point is particularly significant because, as I have previously mentioned, of the strong evidence that as countries develop, drug abuse and the concomitant trafficking develop also. The United Nations crime prevention and criminal justice programme has shown that the cost of the administration of justice in developing countries is higher in terms of the percentage of gross national product than in the industrialized world. The additional impact of increasing drug control activities would be capable of diverting even more resources from other development activities. Therefore, opportunity cost will be highest in developing countries. One aim of this project is to minimize these costs.

At a more detailed level, at the end of the implementation of the project in their country, the managers of the agencies of the national criminal justice system, at both the policy and operational levels, will be better equipped for the following tasks:

(i) The optimal allocation of existing resources within their agency to minimize the heavy strains to which the growing demands of drug control will inevitably subject them; (ii) to set up training programmes for different levels of staff within their agency to enable them to respond better to the new demands. The syllabi and nature of such programmes will be based on the material generated empirically by the project, and focused on the precise points of greatest needs; (iii) to request assistance from inter governmental bodies or other countries in programmes of technical co-operation for training and other activities, in specified and precise areas; and (iv) to co-ordinate the staff training activities of the agency with those of other relevant agencies, and to communicate more precisely with their opposite numbers in the agencies of other jurisdictions on these matters, and perhaps to take a leading role in the development of common strategies on these matters in their region or sub-region.

A major product of the project will be a set of manuals, one for each agency, listing the options available and their respective predicted advantages and disadvantages, to be prepared and expanded after each iteration of the project. After the experience of implementation in several countries, the project team will also publish model methodologies, in manual and perhaps computerized form, to be used by nationals agencies wishing to carry out such needs of some area or topic of particular urgency in that agency. Governments will also benefit directly and indirectly through the increased technical co-operation capacity of inter governmental bodies and in respect of identifying proposals for law reform.

PART III

OVERVIEW: NATIONAL

CRIMINAL JUSTICING IN INDIA TO CONTROL THE DRUG MENACE

Ashok A. Desai

Intoxicants have a longer history on this planet than that of the human race. In the pre-historical era, intoxicants were used to invoke the divine power. Certain intoxicants had also medicinal value. In those days, herbs and plants were carriers of intoxicants. As civilization advanced intoxicants have artificially been converted into narcotic drugs.

Legislation, such as the Opium Acts of 1857 and 1878; the Dangerous Drugs Act, 1940; the Drugs & Cosmetics Act of 1940; and the Drugs (Control) Act of 1950 attempted to regulate the dealings in relation to certain types of intoxicants. However, there has never been complete prohibition.

To satisfy the psychological and physiological requirements, intoxicants have a formidable place in human life. Industrial civilization has, however, aggravated the situation. In the world of technology, man has lost proximity to the spiritual world. This has increased dependency on intoxicants to gain relief from psychological strain or mental tension. This has further led to drug addiction, which, in turn, has brought about mental instability and disorder. Legislative measures so far taken are only a minor step in the crusade against the drug menace.

The Constitution of India took cognizance of the devastating effects of the drug menace. It called upon the State (Article 14) to prohibit consumption of intoxicants which are injurious to health. Pursuant thereto certain prohibition laws attempted to deal with the transactions. But they were more keen in introducing a licensing and permit system in order to have state control over the transactions. The government also could not disregard the revenue being earned through excise duty. The drug menace went ahead without formidable legislative obstructions.

In 1985, the Central Legislature, with high ambitions, enacted the Narcotic Drugs and Psychotropic Substances Act, 1985. It repealed the earlier Opium Act and the Dangerous Drugs Act of 1940. The legislature endeavoured to make the provisions very stringent. The punishment prescribed has been made more severe so as to carry a deterrent effect. The legislature, however realized the possibility of grave abuse of the provisions by the enforcing agency. It has, therefore, provided various mandatory devices to minimize such possibilities.

Besides the peddler, the Act has also classified the consumer of the drugs as an offender. There has been criticism that the legislative approach in this regard is wholly unjust. It has been urged that the consumer of a drug needs to be viewed as a patient, rather than as a criminal. The consumer ought to be treated psychologically and medically. India's criminal jurisprudence could not develop such an insight for the legislation. As to whether the law could undertake such a mission, the question needs to be examined dispassionately. Criminal jurisprudence has, no doubt, marginally attempted to introduce the reformative theory, but it puts more emphasis on prohibition and penology.

Punishment of individual drug consumers deters others. That effectively serves the interests of society. Pursuing one to relieve him or herself from drug addiction by the reformative method would not be free from risks. It would offer chances to others to consume drugs out of curiosity. Law alone cannot change the behaviour pattern of the community or wipe out the urge for drug consumption. The enactment could not control the devastating effect of the drug menace. The growing abuse of drugs has fertilized criminality in the society.

In 1988 the Central Legislature introduced the Prevention of Illicit Traffic in Narcotic Drugs and Psychotropic Substances Act to provide for detention of a person engaged in illicit narcotic drug trafficking. Obviously, the enforcing agency could not deal with such persons effectively with the aid of the Act of 1985.

The law enforcing agency has certain problems which are inherent in its working. It cannot initate action on its own. Moreover, society does not look at the enforcing agency with faith and confidence. The general atmosphere is more of distrust. Another factor is that we do not have adequate resources for law enforcement in developing countries. As against that, the offender is highly resourceful. For developing countries, law enforcement has become more a ritual than a matter of deterrent.

Society has to evolve a mechanism with multiple perspectives, of which criminal justice would be one part, to eliminate completely the benefits of drug trafficking and also the demand for drugs.

INDIA'S DRUG LAWS—A SURVEY

A. Abdul Hadi

Today, the world is facing the twin problems of drug abuse and drug traffic on an unprecedented scale. The illicit production, distribution and consumption of drugs have intimidated and corrupted public servants and even destabilised governments. The sheer volume of "drug money" has also affected the money supply and exchange markets. Illicit money-laundering on an international scale is another criminal activity associated with drug trafficking. Terrorists thrive through drug trafficking, so too, under-world crime and violence. It is also well known that those who use these drugs become their slaves and slowly, but almost irretrievably, push themselves into graves of their own making. We also find that India has emerged as a transit country for illicit traffic in drugs. The 'spill over' from such traffic has caused problems of abuse and addiction.

Two Central enactments have been recently passed to combat the menace in our country: (1) The Narcotic Drugs and Psychotropic Substances Act, 1985 and (2) Prevention of Illicit Traffic in Narcotic Drugs and Psychotropic Substances Act, 1988. The former Act of 1985 consolidated and amended the existing laws relating to narcotic drugs, strengthened the existing controls over drug abuse, provided for rebuttable of the presumption of *mens rea*, considerably enhanced the punishments particularly for trafficking offences, made provision for exercising effective control over psychotropic substances and provided for the implementation of the international conventions. Pursuant to Notification under Section 5 of the above said Act, the Central Government constituted in February, 1988, the *Narcotic Drugs and Psychotropic Substances Consultative Committee*, to advice the Central Government in keeping the law relating to drugs under review and effect necessary changes thereto, and also to formulate a national policy on cultivation and production of narcotic drugs and psychotropic substances.

Yet, the transit traffic in illicit drugs could not be eliminated to any great extent. It was, therefore, felt that a *preventive detention* law should also be enacted with a view to effectively immobilising the traffickers. The

Conservation of Foreign Exchange and Prevention of Smuggling Activities Act, 1974 provided for detention in relation to *smuggling* of drugs and psychotropic substances, but, it could not be invoked to deal with persons engaged in illicit traffic of drugs and psychotropic substances *within the country*. Hence the Prevention of Illicit Traffic in Narcotic Drugs and Psychotropic Substances Act, 1988 was enacted.

By the said Act of 1988, the Central and State Governments have been empowered to make orders of detention with a view to preventing persons including foreigners, from committing illicit traffic in narcotic drugs and psychotropic substances. The expression "illicit traffic" has been defined to include cultivation of any coca plant, or gathering any portion of coca plant, cultivating opium poppy, or any cannabis plant, or engaging in production, manufacture, possession, etc. of narcotic drugs and psychotropic substances. Detention could be made without obtaining the opinion of the Advisory Board, for a period not exceeding one year from the date of detention, if the detaining authority is satisfied that such persons are engaged in illicit traffic "in any area highly vulnerable to such illicit traffic."

In 1989, the following *amendments* were made to the abovesaid Act of 1985:

(1) making most of the offences under the said Act non-bailable (Sec. 37);

(2) providing death penalty for certain offences after previous conviction; (Sec. 31A)

(3) introducing a new Chapter, viz. Chapter VA in the said Act, providing for forfeiture of property, derived from or used in, illicit traffic.

(4) constituting a National Fund for Drug Abuse to meet the expenditure in connection with the measures for combating the illicit traffic and preventing drug abuse.

(5) bringing certain "controlled substances" (viz., certain specified chemicals), which are used for the manufacture of narcotic drugs and psychotropic substances, under the ambit of the above said Act of 1985, and giving power to the Central Government to regulate or prohibit their production, manufacture or supply.

Pursuant to the above power given to the Central Government, the Government issued the Narcotic Drugs and Psychotropic Substances (Regulation of Control Substance) Order, 1993. The contravention of this order was made punishable under Section 25A of the abovesaid Act with rigorous imprisonment for a term, which may extend to ten years and a fine which may extend to two lakhs rupees.

We may also note that the above referred to Chapter VA of the Act dealing with forfeiture of property, derived from or used in, illicit traffic, was introduced, as a consequence of the Convention Against Illicit Traffic in Narcotic Drugs and Psytropic Substances, adopted by the United Nations Conference held at Vienna in December, 1988. The preamble to the said Convention reiterates that illicit traffic generates large financial profits and wealth, enabling transnational criminal organizations to penetrate, contaminate and corrupt the structures of government, legitimate commercial, financial business and society at all levels. The said Convention also provided for extradition and mutual legal assistance between the countries and for transfer of proceedings from one country to another and for other forms of international cooperation.

It may also be pointed out in particular that Section 68C in Chapter VA of the 1985 Act prohibits holding "illegally acquired property." If any person holds such property, which was acquired within a period of six years preceding the date on which he was charged for an illicit traffic offence, that property stands liable to be forfeited to the Central Government. Certain other provisions in the said Chapter provide for interim measures so as to ensure prevention of transfer, concealment, etc., of such property during the pendency of the prosecution.

Despite all the statutory provisions, the view that still prevails is that the desired effects have not materialized so far. It is well known that the efficacy of a law depends on its proper implementation. A law that is not vigorously enforced is not a deterrent. It is *not the existence of a law* that is a deterrent but its *enforcement*. Unlicensed cultivation in the Himalayas and the Western Ghats among other areas is good agricultural business. The staff for narcotics control is inadequate as are the funds. The drug networks keep on expanding. The courts are over burdened with dockets and since special Drug Courts, and funds from the Centre, are not forthcoming, the arrestees (who are only few now) languish in jail for years because of long delays in trial.

Half-hearted investigation without going into the origin of the contraband exposes both the law and the law enforcement agencies to the comment that either it is perfunctory or that the "law governs the poor, and the rich and influential govern the law" as the influence of the mastermind and mighty hands in the distribution of these deadly drugs or substances remains undetected and at safe distance.

Further the sentences prescribed for various offences under the Act of 1985 are quite illogical. One may be found in possession of five grams or five kilograms of heroin, but the sentence prescribed remains the same. The sentence should be commensurate with the nature and quantity of the contraband as is the case in the United Kingdom and the United States of America.

Sections 68A and 68E of the 1985 Act (in the above referred to Chapter VA) have created an anomalous situation regarding persons whose property (derived from or used in illicit traffic) can be forfeited. Section 68E (1) of the Act provides that every officer, empowered under section 53 and every officer-in-charge of a police station, shall, on receipt of information that any person, to whom Chapter VA applies, has been charged with any offence punishable under the said Act, whether committed in India or outside, proceed to take all steps necessary for tracing and identifying any property illegally acquired by such person. Section 68A(2) enumerates the persons to whom the said Chapter shall apply. The persons referred to in Section 68A(2), *inter alia*, include (i) a person, who has been convicted of an offence punishable under this Act with imprisonment for a term of five years or more, (ii) a person, who has been convicted of a similar offence by a competent court of criminal jurisdiction outside India, and (iii) a person against whom a detention order has been passed under the Prevention of Illicit Traffic in Narcotic Drugs and Psychotropic Substances Act, 1988 or under the Jammu and Kashmir Prevention of Illicit Traffic in Narcotic Drugs and Psychotropic Substances Act, 1988 and the said order has not been revoked, set aside or quashed by any competent authority of the court. Thus, action under S. 68E regarding tracing and identification of the illegally acquired property or under Section 68F relating to seizure and freezing of such property, can be initiated *only when* a person already convicted of the requisite offence under NDPS Act, 1985 is again charged with any offence under the said Act, or, when a person against whom a detention order has been passed is charged with the commission of an offence under this Act after the issuance of the order for his preventive detention. This is what the plain language of Sections 68-A(2), 68E and 68F envisages. It cannot be stretched further so as to include a person against whom a charge for an offence under the Act has been framed but who is not covered by any one of the categories mentioned in Section 68-A(2) of the said Act.

Further, it is important to note that the provisions of Sections 42, 43, 44 and 49 of the Act are not applicable for search, seizure, etc., in respect of the above referred to *Controlled Substances*. These sections will have to be suitably amended. Unit such time, the seizure of controlled substances and the relevant documents, as evidence of the commission of the offence in respect of *controlled substances*, can be effected under the Criminal Procedure Code.

In two recent decisions of the Supreme Court, viz., *State of Punjab* v. *Balbir Singh* reported in *J.T. 1992 (2) SC 108* and *Saiyad Moh. Saiyad Umar Saiyad* v. *State of Gujarat* reported in *1995 (3) SCC 610* the Supreme Court held in relation to Section 50 of the 1985 Act that the requirement on the part of the officer conducting the search to inform the accused of his right to be searched in the presence of a Gazetted Officer or a Magistrate is mandatory and the prosecution *must prove* that the accused was made aware of this right, but he did not choose to be so searched, and that *if no evidence to this effect is given, the Court must assume* that the accused was not informed of his right and *must find* that the possession of the illicit articles was not established. The Supreme Court observed that instructions in this behalf need to be issued, *so that investigating officers take care* to comply with the abovesaid requirement under Section 50, and drug peddlers do not go scot-free due to non-compliance thereof.

It is needless to add that all concerned must make sincere efforts to implement the Directive enshrined in Article 47 of the Constitution of India to bring about prohibition of the consumption of intoxicating drinks and drugs.

DRUG SCENARIO: OVERVIEW

Rakesh Munjal

India has been facing the problem of *transit traffic* in drugs. India is increasingly used as a transit country for *opiates* (opium) and cannabis destined for other regions of the world and New Delhi and Bombay are reportedly the most important exist points for these drugs. Seizures of opium, heroin and hashish (charas) are indicators in this regard. India is used as a transit country for illicit traffic in heroin orginating in parts of Near and Middle East and South West Asia.

The government has been seriously concerned with the illicit drug trafficking situation and has taken various measures to prevent illicit drug trafficking. A comprehensive legislation called the Narcotic Drugs and Psychotropic Substances Act, 1985 is in force.

Stringent penalties have been provided for drug trafficking offences under the Act. It provides for a minimum punishment of 10 years RI and fine of Rs. 1 lakh which may be extended to Rs. 2 lakh and an imprisonment of 20 years RI in respect of *repeat offences*. It provides for a maximum punishment of 15 years RI extendable up to 30 years and also a minimum fine of Rs. 1.5 lakh which may go up to Rs. 3 lakh. The courts have been empowered to impose fines exceeding these limits for reasons to be recorded in their judgements.

Separate Narcotic Cells have been created in all the collectorates of Customs & Central Excise through out the country for exclusively dealing with drug-related offences. Customs and Border Security Force also keep a strict vigil on our borders/sea ports and airports to check smuggling of narcotic drugs.

In 1976 India enacted specific legislation providing for the forfeiture of the property and assets of smugglers, including traffickers and foreign exchange manipulations. This legislation known as Smugglers & Foreign Exchange Manipulations (Forfeiture of Property) Act, 1976 enables the enforcement authorities to confiscate all property, both movable and immoveable, illegally acquired or accumulated or for which investment is made from unlawful earnings resulting from the smuggling of foreign exchange. It covers all such property held not only in the names of smugglers and traffickers themselves but their relatives and associates as well. The Act provides for principles of natural justice to be followed for all forfeiture proceedings and appeals to a higher tribunal.

Illicit drug trafficking is sophisticated and complex in nature involving a wide variety of drugs from many sources throughout the world. The illicit traffic not only violates national drug laws and international conventions but also involves many other criminal activities including conspiracy, bribery, corruption of public officials, tax evasion, banking law violations, illegal money transfers, import/export violation, violence or terrorism. Narcotics are often used in lieu of money in exchange for weapons. Many large drug trafficking networks have become powerful links in certain regions of the world.

POSSESSION AND TRAFFICKING OF DRUGS AND THE INDIAN JUDICIARY

Raghunath Patnaik and B. B. Panda

India holds a special significance in the illegal drug trade, primarily due to its geographical location. Illicit drug trafficking is complex in nature and it violates national as well as international laws and conventions. The manufacture, possession and trade in drugs, except for its medicinal use, is a criminal offence that attracts penal sanctions.

The implementation of the legal statutes has revealed some problems. Due to the mandatory prescribed punishment of a minimum of ten years imprisonment, the Judiciary has shown a disinclination to apply such harsh laws and a large number of offenders are acquitted on technical grounds. Some of the procedures to which recourse is had by the authorities lead to a violation of the constitutional rights of individuals, on whose behalf the Judiciary then intervenes. Such situations ultimately frustrate the legislative goal of preventing the illegal trade in narcotic drugs and psychotropic substances. An example is that of Section 50 of the Act which compels the concerned officer, about to search an accused person, to take such person without further delay, to the nearest Gazetted Officer or a Magistrate 'if the person so requires'. Failure to do so could be prejudicial to the accused and would warrant his acquittal in respect of the offence charged. The accused has to be made aware of his right, prior to the search. There was no uniformity in the application of this section until a landmark case, the *State of Punjab* v. *Balbir Singh*, wherein the Supreme Court ruled that the accused should be made aware of his right in unambiguous terms and that a search before a Gazetted Officer or a Magistrate would confer much more authenticity to the testimony and would also provide a safeguard to the accused.

It is imperative that correct procedures are followed and ambiguities and anomalies in the administration of the law are removed.

DRUGS, THE SAVIOUR VERSUS DRUGS, THE KILLER: ARENA - LIFE AND LAW

Susanta Chatterji

International measures to control drug use and abuse have grown more complex and more comprehensive over time. Starting with the first International Opium Convention of 1912, international conventions today address contemporary problems of drug abuse, trafficking, sale and the need for rehabilitation and social re-integration of drug addicts. The Comprehensive Multidisciplinary Outline of Future Activities in Drug Abuse Control (CMO) of 1987 provides clear guidelines and procedures for practical action and the 1988 UN Convention addresses the important issue of international cooperation and coordination in dealing with drug abuse and trafficking. Such international conventions mobilize the community of nations that abide by certain laws regarding drug abuse and thus enable them to combat an international problem of dangerous proportions.

India has been concerned with the indigenous manufacture and import of drugs from the turn of the century. Section 103 of the Government of India Act of 1935 sought to regulate indigenous medicine manufacture and drug import by prescribing standards for drugs distributed in India, and by monitoring the distribution system and price structure. The Drug Policy of 1986 adopted measures for the rationalization, quality control and standardization of drugs and the pharmaceuticals industry. There is a need to establish a National Drug Authority to set standards for manufacture, import, supply and use of drugs; to approve and register pharmaceutical imports and products only if they are safe and medically necessary; to establish stringent quality controls on all aspects of the pharmaceutical industry including prescription practices of medical practitioners; and to ensure the dissemination of necessary information to consumers and prescribers regarding specific drugs and their appropriate use.

The Narcotic Drugs and Psychotropic Substances Act of 1985 addressed the problem of drug trafficking and narcotics abuse. Placed between the

Golden Triangle and the Golden Crescent, India faces the peculiar problems of being a major transit state. The long borders are used as drug trafficking routes. The 1985 Act was amended in 1988 to overcome certain deficiencies. The 1988 Act was also passed to implement the provisions of the United Nations Convention on Narcotic Drugs and Psychotropic Substances.

The participation and cooperation of different branches of the government machinery—legislative, public health, social welfare, education, law enforcement and economic affairs bodies—is required to effectively deal with the problems of drug abuse and drug trafficking. The national authority responsible for implementing the recommendations of the CMO may be guided by certain general principles such as the need for research in drug abuse, its aetiology and consequences; the need for coordination; the need for clear achieveable targets and defined target groups; and the need for an approach which balances efforts against trafficking, supply and demand.

*CONVICTIONS FOR DRUG-RELATED OFFENCES: A SOCIO-LEGAL STUDY**

Daljeet Singh and *Subhash Sharma*

Illicit drug production, trafficking and abuse have assumed dangerous dimensions practically in all the countries on the globe. Day after day, the graphs of drug abuse and illicit drug trafficking are rising at alarming rates. This problem has attracted a relatively more serious note due to its broader ramifications on the socio-economic-political health of the nation.[1] The problem further gains significance for the reason of its important role in the development of criminal, delinquent and other anti-social behaviour among drug addicts. In India[2] and many other countries of the world, drug offences have been found to have a direct link to terrorism and other political upheavals.[3]

With the dawn of the 20th century drug abuse surfaced at the international level. To curb this problem, it was realized by most societies that co-operation at regional and international levels were required to fight the drug menace in an integrated fashion. With this objective in view, it was considered that international control treaties should provide the basis and the mechanism for such co-operation. A beginning was made at the meeting of the International Opium Commission in 1909 at Shanghai. The signing of the Opium Convention in 1912, the Single Convention on Narcotic Drugs in 1961 and the 1971 Convention on Psychotropic Substances are a few milestones in international co-operation to curb narcotic drug trafficking.[4]

*A synopsis of the paper with the original title "India's NDPS Act vis-a-vis Convictions: A Socio-Legal Study"

[1]See: Govt. of India publication, Drug Menace, Lok Sabha Secretariat, 1988, pp. 1.4 See also: *State of H.P. v. Prithi Chand, 1996 (2) SCC 37* at p. 42.

[2]See: Rajya Sabha Debates, July 24, 1986, cc. 1981-1982.

[3]Commission on Narcotic Drugs, UN: Economic and Social Council Report of 31st Session, 1985, Supplement No. 3, pp. 63-64.

[4]WHO Chronicle, Vol. 138, No. 11, 1984, pp. 17-20.

India, on its part, has from time to time taken legislative initiatives to curb the drug menace in all its dimensions. In the pre-independence period, it was the Opium Act, 1867 that consolidated and amended the law for regulating and preventing the illicit cultivation of poppy and manufacture of opium. This was followed by the Opium Act, 1878 to deal with the power of the State Government to regulate possession, transport, inter-state import and export, and the sale of opium. The Dangerous Drug Act, 1930 was enacted to centralize and vest in the Central Government the control over certain operations relating to dangerous drugs and to increase and render uniform the penalties for offences relating to such operations. It dealt with the entire range of narcotic drugs. In the post-independence legislative history of India, the Narcotic Drugs and Psychotropic Substances Act, 1985 (in short NDPS Act) is a milestone towards curbing the drug menace. This comprehensive piece of legislation, aimed at overcoming the weaknesses of the earlier three laws and to make the Indian law meet the demands of various international treaties and protocols to which the Government of India is a signatory and to cover the new drugs of addiction offences. The law is quite different in its nature and consolidates as well as amends the laws relating to narcotic drugs. This Act strengthens existing controls over the drugs of abuse, it considerably enhances the penalties particularly in the areas of trafficking offences and makes provision for exercising effective control over the psychotropic substances in an attempt to meet the requirements of international conventions.

Convictions under NDPS Act

Though the NDPS Act is quite comprehensive and shows its teeth in its stringent penalties it must be noted that the objective of this law has not been fully served. The violations of the law can be seen as quite rampant. The convictions are far less than the acquittals under this law and in the area of convictions too, there are problems. The deterrent punishments are proving to be counter-productive. All this prompts us to have a fresh look at the provisions of this law as implemented. We studied the decisions of the trial courts in Jalandhar decided during the period 1986 to 1996, as well as the decisions of the High Judiciary reported in various law journals in the years 1995 and 1996. We also interviewed the investigating officers and the members of the judiciary and bar.

Convictions under NDPS Act

Table A[5]
Proportion of Convictions under NDPS Act at Jalandhar during 1986 - 1996

Total Cases Decided	*Acquittals*	*Convictions*
1156	1112 (96.20%)	44 (3.80%)

(a) Trial Court Conviction Rate

As is evident from Table A, during the period 1986 to 1996, 1156 NDPS cases were decided by the trial courts at Jalandhar. Only in 44 cases (constituting 3.80 per cent of the cases tried by the trial courts), the accused persons were convicted and all the remaining 1112 accused persons (i.e. 96.20 per cent of the total) were acquitted on technical and procedural grounds. Therefore, acquittal remains the practical rule.

Table B[6]
Details of Cases registered and Decided under NDPS Act at Jalandhar during 1986-1996

Year	*Cases (Registered)*	*Cases (Decided)*	*Acquitted*	*Percentage*	*Convicted*	*Percentage*
1986	357	-	-	-	-	-
1987	220	-	-	-	-	-
1988	171	56	40	71.40	16	28.6
1989	141	158	157	99.36	1	00.64
1990	125	224	223	99.55	1	00.45
1991	154	185	185	100.00	-	-
1992	169	91	88	96.60	3	03.40
1993	170	106	104	98.10	2	01.90
1994	127	168	161	95.84	7	04.16
1995	55	112	102	91.00	10	09.00
1996	80	56	52	92.80	4	07.20

[5]Source: Record SSP Office, Jalandhar. We are thankful to Mr. Dinkar Gupta, IPS, S.S.P. Jalandhar for his valuable assistance and for providing necessary information.

[6]*Ibid.*

From Table B it further comes to light that during the years 1986 to 1996, a substantial number of cases were registered every year in Jalandhar. But from the year 1988 onwards when the trial courts started giving its decisions, it is on record that acquittals became the rule and convictions the exception. From this Table, we can further notice that in the year 1989 out of 158 decided cases, in only 1 case the accused was convicted (i.e. an acquittal rate of 99.36 per cent). The same negligible conviction rate occurred in the following years: 1990, 1992, 1993, 1994, 1995 and 1996 (being less than 10% in all the years). In 1991, out of 185 decided cases not even a single accused was convicted (the acquittal rate being 100 per cent).

On further study the following reasons for this were observed:

(a) the police personnel remained non-conversant with the provisions of the new law; and

(b) the hesitation of the trial courts to convict the accused due to the reason of heavily enhanced punishment i.e. from a maximum of three years imprisonment and a fine under the Opium Act, 1878[7] to a maximum of 20 years rigorous imprisonment and a fine upto Rs. 2 lacs; a mandatory minimum punishment of rigorous imprisonment of 10 years as against no minimum imprisonment under the old Opium Act; and, a mandatory minimum fine to the tune of Rs. 1 lac fixed over 10 years ago as against no such provisions under the old Opium Act;

(b) Convictions by Higher Judiciary

Table C[8]

Cases Decided by the High Courts and the Supreme Court in appeals under NDPS Act (as reported in Indian law journals during the years 1995-96)

Total Reported Cases	*Appeal by State in Acquittals by Trial Courts*	*Appeal by Persons Convicted by Trial Courts*
74	11 (14.87%)	63(85.13%)

Table C indicates that during 1995 and 1996, out of 74 cases reported in law journals, the State appealed only in 11 cases (14.87%), while in 63 cases (85.13%) appeals against convictions were lodged by convicted persons.

[7]Section 9 of the Act.

[8]Source: Recent CR: S.C.C. Cr. LJ: AIR

Table D shows the outcome of the appeals-in all 11 cases where the State lodged an appeal against an acquittal, the acquittals were upheld, while in 57 out of the 63 cases where appeals had been lodged against convictions, the appellate courts reversed the convictions.

Table D[9]

Nature of Case in Appeal	*Total Cases*	*Acquittals by the Appellate Courts*	*Convictions by the Appellate Courts*
Acquitted by the Trial Courts	·11	11-100%	NIL
Convicted by the Trial Courts	63	57-90.47%	6.09-53%

On a number of occasions, the higher courts have pointed out the need for acquittals due to non-compliance with technical requirements of the law. For instance, in the recent case of *State of Punjab* vs. *Jasbir Singh*[10], the Supreme Court stated that:

> Under the circumstances, we are constrained to confirm the order of acquittal though the High Court unfortunately did not deal with the case properly.

Does not this indicate that the words and provisions of the NDPS Act should be made more unambiguous and explicit when even the Hon'ble Judges of the High Court can also not appreciate them fully?

Court rulings indicate the need for more explicit legal provisions, as well as for due compliance with the technical requirements of the law. There is a need to redraft certain provisions; to reconsider the penalties provided under the legislation; to better inform the public, law enforcement officers and the lower judiciary about the legal requirements; and to establish Special Drug Courts.

[9] *Ibid*

[10] 1996 (1) S.C.C. 288

DRUG ADDICTION AND ADOLESCENTS

Meena H. Rao

The growing drug abuse problem, which has already affected the adolescent population of the country, calls for the effective implementation of the country's drug abuse laws. However, there are a number of problems with implementation that must receive attention. A particularly serious problem is that accused are often granted bail even for drug-related offences that should be regarded as non-bailable. Influential persons released on bail for major offences can interfere with investigations.

With the increasing involvement of adolescents with the criminal justice system on account of drug-related offences, particularly for possession for personal use, it is necessary to review sentencing policies and procedures for their integration into society. It is not in the interest of society that they be kept in regular jails along with other major criminals.

LEGISLATIVE AND ADMINISTRATIVE MEASURES FOR PREVENTION OF DRUG ABUSE IN PAKISTAN

Sajjad Ali Shah

Drug abuse is a social issue and a human problem. It does not just affect the individual drug addict. Its consequences and ramifications extend far beyond the person and family of the individual addict, and afflicts the society at large. It destroys the addict's productive potentialities and ultimately takes his or her life. It breaks the family, destroys family values and ruins the society. No individual person or country is immune or safe from its harmful effects and devastating consequences. Seen in this context, human beings are to realize that the eradication of drug abuse is in the interest of the entire humanity, irrespective of any distinction on the basis of colour, creed, culture or nationality; and that joint struggle and collaborative efforts are required to win the fight against it. The account that follows is a situation analysis of the intensity and prevalence of drug-abuse in Pakistan and our national efforts to control and combat the same.

The terrain and climate of the Indo-Pakistan subcontinent suit the growth of the hemp plant and cultivation of poppy crop. Before 1979, poppy was cultivated in parts of North West Frontier province of Pakistan under a system of licences issued to farmers. Almost the entire produce was purchased by the government for medicinal and scientific purposes. With the enforcement of the Prohibition (Enforcement of Hadd) Order 1979, however, the licencing system was discontinued, and consequently, poppy cultivation became illegal.

With the emergence of heroin in the late 1970s, which incidentally coincided with the Soviet involvement in Afghanistan and the resultant Afghan resistance against foreign interference, poppy became a very valuable and most precious crop. Demand for the crop increased and consequently supply also increased. The cultivation was restricted mostly to the far-flung and inaccessible tribal territories of Pakistan; and since such cultivation was illegal, it was done in a clandestine manner. The areas where this crop were grown were traditionally known for the produce of poppy, as the climate and land in such areas were favourable to the growth of poppy. The government efforts to prevent its cultivation were not fully successful, partly due to disturbed conditions on the border and partly due to lack of proper administrative structure in such areas. The smuggling from across the border was an added factor to its easy availability in Pakistan. The farmers also put up strong resistance against any move to stop its cultivation, as the livelihood of their families depended on this product. The government, therefore, had to devise appropriate measures for eradicating its cultivation. Such measures included land development projects, provision of canal water to such areas, crop substitution schemes and offering incentives to farmers to grow alternative crops. In some such places, industrial estates were established so as to provide alternative means of income to the people. Side by side with such curative measures, the government also took administrative measures so as to strictly impose the ban on poppy cultivation. At times, operations were carried out, with the help of para-military forces to destroy the cultivated crop. Tribal elders were taken into confidence to support such actions. The use of carrot-and-stick policy yielded positive results and poppy production was gradually reduced. The land under cultivation was reduced from 80,500 acres in the year 1978-79 to only 2,565 acres in 1995-96. Similarly, for the same period, the production of the crop fell down from 800 tonnes to only 23 tonnes. Having said so, however, let it also be clarified that unstable conditions on our western frontier and unguarded long border, made it highly difficult for the government to check its smuggling from across the border.

Pakistan has been severely hit by the destructive effects of drug addiction. Drug addiction is intense and pervasive, both in the urban and rural areas and has affected all strata and groups of population. As per a survey conducted by the integrated Drug Demand Reduction Project of the United Nations Drug Control Programme, there are a total of 3 million drug addicts in Pakistan, among which a high percentage i.e. 51 per cent are hooked to heroin—very hazardous and the most lethal of all drugs. The economic and social consequences of this problem are very disturbing. It is painful to see and bear the ordeal of drug addicts, the bulk of who are in their prime youth. The society is, thus, deprived of their productive capacities and is paying for their dereliction in the shape of family break-downs and rise in crime graph. The government, naturally, is cognizant of the drug-addiction problem and is taking all necessary measures to combat it.

We are also aware of the global dimension of drug abuse. We understand that drug issues are indeed global issues and require a coordinated global approach to address them. Thus, the Government of Pakistan has ratified several international as well as regional instruments on the elimination of narcotic drugs and psychotropic substances. It has signed the Single

Convention on Narcotic Drugs 1961, United Nations Convention on Psychotropic Substances 1971 and United Nations Convention against Illicit Traffic in Narcotic Drug and Psychotropic Substances 1988. It has also signed the SAARC Convention on Narcotic Drugs and Psychotropic Substances 1993. At the initiative of the Government of Pakistan, the Economic Cooperation Organization established the ECO Technical Committee on Narcotic Abuse Control, whose regional plan of action is currently being implemented in the member states. Besides, Pakistan has entered into bilateral arrangements with its neighbours namely India and Iran for a regular dialogue on addressing the problem of controlling the trafficking in narcotics across the border. The United Nations International Drug Control Programme is the coordinating agency for ensuring periodic meetings among the officials so as to pass information and extend assistance in the area of controlling drug trafficking.

The United Nations instruments and regional conventions oblige the member states to cooperate with each other and coordinate their efforts so as to eliminate the cultivation, production, transportation, distribution and abuse of narcotic drugs, psychotropic substances and chemicals used in the production of such drugs or substances. The members are further obliged to assist one another in the investigation, prosecution and judicial proceedings in respect of drug-related cases so as to ensure that such offenders do not escape punishment. The conventions further require the members to make arrangements for the treatment, education, rehabilitation and social integration of drug addicts.

In compliance with international obligations, the Government of Pakistan has updated its laws on drug trafficking and abuse and taken necessary administrative measures for implementing the same. Its resolve to eradicate drug abuse is strengthened by the fact that our religion i.e. Islam prohibits the use of narcotic drugs or other intoxicants. The Quranic injunctions on the subject are very specific and categorical, leaving no room for doubt or ambiguity. The Constitution of Pakistan also provides that the State shall prevent the taking of injurious drugs and consumption of alcoholic liquor otherwise than for medicinal purposes or use by the non-Muslims in religious ceremonies. Consequently, the Prohibition (Enforcement of Hadd) Order 1979 was adopted which prohibits the processing of any intoxicant or intoxicating liquor, its possession, use or transportation. Stringent penalties are prescribed for offenders. Depending on the kind of contraband and quantity involved, penalties range from two years imprisonment to imprisonment for life. Exemptions, however, are provided to non-Muslim citizens who may consume a reasonable quantity of such intoxicants as part of religious ceremony. A similar exemption is also available to non-Muslim foreigners, subject to the condition that they do not consume it in public places.

The earliest law on the subject of drug abuse was the Dangerous Drugs Act 1930. This law, however, was found to be inadequate to meet the present-day challenges of widespread abuse of narcotic drugs and its easy availability. As a result, in 1995, a new, more modern and fairly comprehensive law entitled Control of Narcotic Substances Ordinance was promulgated. This law prohibits the cultivation of narcotic plants and manufacture, possession, transportation or use of narcotic drugs and psychotropic substances and prescribes severe penalties for breach including death penalty and confiscation of assets for drug trafficking. The law obliges the government to open and operate centres for the treatment, aftercare, rehabilitation and social integration of drug-addicts. The government is bound to provide necessary medicines for the detoxification of such addicts. The law is strictly enforced by a special force called Anti-Narcotic Force. The Anti Narcotic Force is indeed in addition to the normal law enforcement agencies such as Police, Federal Investigation Agency, Custom Officials and Coast Guard, etc. who are equally responsible for the enforcement of drug laws.

As regards netting fugitive offenders involved in drug-related crimes, the Extradition Act 1972 holds the ground. An offence against the law relating to dangerous drugs or narcotics is mentioned as an extraditable crime in this Act. It provides for the procedure to extradite into or outside Pakistan, any fugitive offender against whom prima facie evidence is produced. The request for the purpose is made through the diplomatic channels and processed through the Ministry of Foreign Affairs and Ministry of Interior. Enquiry against the accused is conducted by a Magistrate of the Ist Class who reports his finding to the Federal government. The government may, if it accepts such finding, issue a warrant for the custody and removal of such fugitive offender. Several cases came for consideration before the superior courts of Pakistan which involved the validity of the extradition law as well as proceedings conducted thereunder. The law survived a challenge on the ground that it violates the right to freedom of movement guaranteed by Article 15 of the Constitution. The Supreme Court observed that the said right was never intended to provide protection to an accused person involved in serious crimes such as the abuse of or trafficking in narcotics. The Court further expressed the view that Pakistan being an honourable member of the international community, is bound to fulfil its international commitments, thus its territory cannot become a safe-haven for offenders and criminals. Thus, subject to the conditions that prima facie evidence is produced and the procedural requirements for extradition are fully observed, the courts in Pakistan have generally allowed extradition, thereby facilitating the full and effective enforcement of drug laws. Again, except when sufficient evidence was not produced or the charge appeared to be trivial or false or *mala fide*, the courts have not hesitated to award stringent punishments, including imprisonment and seizure or confiscation of assets of the drug-barons.

The government also launched cleaning up operations in the tribal territory with a view to destroying drug manufacturing laboratories. As of 1992, a total of 146 such laboratories have been destroyed. The Anti-Narcotic Force, in collaboration with the Frontier Corps, raided the hideouts of drug traffickers and recovered a huge quantity of heroin, cannabis and other contraband goods.

Besides the law enforcement measures, the government also gave attention to the treatment, aftercare and rehabilitation of drug addicts. Special wards have been established in the public hospitals. Some private clinics were also created for the purpose. The government plans to establish one fully equipped detoxification centre at each district headquarter. The Provincial Governments are in the process of preparing PC-1 document for the purpose.

The government included in its 8th Five Year Plan, which commenced in 1993, the objective of eradicating the cultivation of narcotic crops, production of narcotic drugs and treatment as well as rehabilitation of drug addicts. Rs. 3.3 billion have been allocated for the purpose of achieving such goals.

The government has also launched fairly successful mass education and awareness campaigns through the print and electronic media, informing the public of the harmful effects on the lives and families of drug addicts and its social consequences for the society. As of 1990, a programme planned under the Drug Abuse Prevention Resource Centre is being implemented so as to bring about general awareness and provide training for controlling drug abuse. The government's efforts are also being supplemented by the NGOs, CBOs and other professional groups, operating in the area of drug prevention and treatment of addicts.

AMERICAN DRUG COURTS: A COMMON SENSE APPROACH TO THE DRUG-USING OFFENDER

Jeffrey Tauber

Interest in Drug Courts is sweeping the United States as over 200 innovative Drug Court programmes have been implemented since 1990. Many of these programmes have reportedly achieved remarkable success in reducing the levels of drug abuse, incarceration and criminal recidivism among drug-using offenders. That interest is heightened by the realization that these same offenders clog our court calendars, strain our treasuries, and flood our jails and prisons. (According to an American Bar Association report, imprisonment of drug offenders alone increased by 32 per cent between 1986 and 1991).

Even so, some have criticized Drug Courts as a radical and unwarranted departure for the courts. However, there is nothing radical or even particularly new about how a Drug Court works. A single Drug Court Judge and dedicated programme staff, applying a direct, immediate, and personal approach to the drug offender, handles all Drug Rehabilitation cases from start to finish (*Section I, A Judicial Intervention Strategy*). Court procedures are adapted to reflect the realities of the offender's substance abuse (*Section II, Reality-Based Design Principles).* A cost-effective approach to the use of sanctions and incentives is applied (*Section III, Smart Punishment*). And coordinated programmes are created, where all participants (not just the offender) are held accountable for their performance (*Section IV, Structural Accountability*). Government agencies and community organizations work closely together as a part of a Unified Drug Court System (*Section V, Unified Drug Court System).*

Drug Courts, in fact, mark a turning back of the judicial clock to a time when judges ran their own calendars and were responsible for their court's operations, defendants had to answer directly and immediately to the judge for their conduct, and cases moved slowly and purposefully through the judicial system (instead of relying on sentencing guidelines, mandatory minimums, and negotiated pleas to speed up the court process).

This paper will attempt to describe how Drug Courts work, how they are different from most American courts, and what the underlying principles are that make them successful.

The Judge's Role in a Drug Court: Implementing the New Judicial Intervention Strategy

There is a persistent belief in the judicial community that a drug using offender's failures while under court supervision are willful and deliberate and consequently ought to be dealt with severely. Unfortunately, this belief minimizes the compulsive nature of drug abuse and exaggerates the offender's ability to refrain from continued drug usage (as well as the court's ability to coerce abstinence).

The Drug Court Judge recognizes the limitations of judicial coercion as a drug rehabilitation tool and rejects the notion that programme failure is necessarily the result of the willful defiance of judicial authority (and therefore, punishable as a kind of contempt of court). In its place, Drug Court Judges have adopted a new pragmatic *Judicial Intervention Strategy*. That strategy relies on the development of an ongoing, working relationship between the judge and the offender and the use of both positive and negative incentives to encourage compliance.

The Drug Court as Theatre

In a Drug Court, communications between judge and offenders are crucial. By increasing the frequency of court hearings, as well as the intensity and length of judge/offender contacts, the Drug Court Judge becomes a powerful motivator for the offender's rehabilitation.

A successful Drug Court depends on the willingness of the judge and staff to work together as a team. The defense attorney (literally and figuratively) takes a step back, rarely getting between the judge and the offender. The prosecuting attorney adopts a conciliatory position. All staff see their jobs as the facilitation of the offender's rehabilitation.

A Drug Court Judge performs on the courtroom stage before an audience full of offenders. As appropriate, the judge assumes the role of confessor, task master, cheerleader, and mentor; in turn exhorting, threatening, encouraging and congratulating the participants for his or her progress, or lack thereof.

The court hearing itself is used to educate the audience (as well as the offender) as to the potential consequences of the programme. In-custody offenders who have failed the programme are seen early in the hearing before a full audience of participants, while successful graduates are often handed diplomas by the judge accompanied by the applause and congratulations of staff.

The Importance of Judicial Leadership

A Drug Court provides direction and focus through the leadership of a single judge. Such focused leadership ensures consistency in judicial decision-making and programme implementation, coordination and accountability of participating agencies and staff, and cost-effectiveness through direct calendering and efficient case management.

Many judges tend to regard any judicial activity outside the courtroom with suspicion. The truth is, however, that judges can only be as effective in their courtroom as the systems they build outside that courtroom will allow.

By way of example, in Oakland, California, more than 1/3 of defendants failed to appear for their diversion eligibility hearing when that hearing was held 6 to 8 weeks after their arraignment and release from custody. It didn't matter how fair, competent or effective the judge was in court (nor, for that matter, how effective the programme was), when the defendant failed to appear in court to be placed in the rehabilitation programme. With the advent of the FIRST Diversion Programme, the delay between arraignment and diversion eligibility hearing was reduced from six weeks to a single day, facilitating the immediate intervention in the offender's drug usage. Consequently that failure to appear rate dropped from approximately 36 per cent to 3 per cent.

Sharing Power

Judicial leadership involves more than a willingness to lead. Drug Court programmes look beyond traditional relationships to the forming of innovative partnerships and feature collaboration in decision-making, sharing of resources, and coordination of efforts.

It is crucial that all programme staff participate fully in the design and implementation of the programme. (Nothing will defeat a Drug Court programme faster than a reluctant bureaucracy.) Supervision and/or other programme staff share in the ownership of the programme and understand that programme success is in both their institutional and personal interest. Such staff commitment to programme success is one of the most valuable assets a Drug Court programme can have.

The Reality-Based Design Principles of a Drug Court

Court ordered drug rehabilitation programmes suffer from the generally held belief that 'nothing works' in the treatment of drug using offenders. Unfortunately, that perception (although untrue) becomes a self-fulfilling prophecy when financially strapped communities inadequately fund court-ordered treatment programmes and skeptical judges half-heartedly implement those programmes (often terminating participants with the first sign of drug relapse).

It takes more than increased funding and full judicial support (although extremely important) to create an effective Drug Court programme. Successful Drug Court programmes are based on an understanding of the physiological, psychological and behavioral realities of drug abuse and are implemented with those realities in mind.

Such programmes recognize that drug abuse is a serious debilitating disorder; that relapse and intermittent progress are a part of most successful drug rehabilitations; that as drug addiction is not created overnight, it cannot be cured overnight; that a drug user is most vulnerable to successful intervention when he or she is in crisis (i.e., immediately after initial arrest and incarceration); that drug users are in denial and will do everything possible to avoid responsibility, make excuses for programme failure, and evade the court and its programmes (Consider for example, how profoundly difficult it is for many judges, lawyers, and other criminal justice professionals to give up cigarettes or alcohol.)

Model Drug Courts that Share Reality-Based Design Principles

Several jurisdictions across the country have developed successful Drug Courts and court ordered drug rehabilitation programmes that recognize and work with (rather than against) the realities of drug usage. *Although these programmes often have substantially different programme characteristics reflecting their individual circumstances* (i.e. Miami, Fort Lauderdale, and Portland have replaced a Probation Department presence with direct court/treatment linkages, while Oakland, Phoenix, and Kansas City use a court/probation partnership model), *what is crucial is that they share the same underlying 'reality-based' principles.*

Features of Reality-Based Drug Courts

Immediate and upfront Intervention Reality: A drug addict is most vulnerable to successful intervention when he or she is in crisis (i.e., immediately after initial arrest and incarceration).

Principle: *Intervention should be immediate and front-loaded*

Even the best designed court-ordered drug rehabilitation programme will be less than effective when intervention is delayed. Recognizing this, Drug Courts order participants to begin treatment immediately after their court hearing. (In Miami, participants are transported by van, in Oakland they are ordered to appear within 15 minutes of the court hearing.)

For the same reason, supervision and treatment should be front-loaded; to engage the participant early and often, giving the programme and treatment the opportunity to take root. In Miami, offender contact with the programme is required five times a week for the first three weeks, while in Oakland, an average of three contacts per week is required over the first ten weeks.

Coordinated, Comprehensive Supervision

Reality: *If there are gaps in programme supervision, the offender will find and exploit them.*

Principle: *Supervision must be comprehensive and well-coordinated to ensure accountability.*

Few offenders enter the court's programmes with rehabilitation on their minds. They are in denial, and are there mostly to beat the system and avoid incarceration. The challenge is to keep them in the programme until sobriety, and attitudinal changes can occur. This may be difficult to accomplish, since the drug-using offender is often an expert at avoiding responsibility, making excuses for his or her failures, and evading the court and its programmes.

The drug offender must be held accountable for his or her conduct, if rehabilitation is to be successful. A Drug Court programme builds a chain-link fence around the drug using offender whose links consist of frequent supervision contacts and drug testing, direct access to full information on the drug offender's progress, immediate responses to programme failures, and frequent progress report hearings before a single Drug Court judge and permanent staff (Oakland allows a maximum of ninety days; Miami no more than sixty days between hearings.)

Long-Term Treatment and Aftercare

Reality: *A drug addict is not created overnight, and therefore cannot be cured overnight.*

Principle: *The drug-using offender needs intensive long-term treatment and aftercare.*

Drug addiction is a serious, debilitating disorder that demands intensive long-term treatment (Miami and Oakland participants average approximately one year to graduation). Treatment preferably begins in a medically supervised jail drug detoxification unit. For most participants, however, a community-based non-residential treatment programme is the initial treatment experience. More costly residential treatment programme is the initial treatment experience. More costly residential treatment spaces are generally reserved for those who have not responded well to non-residential treatment.

Without adequate aftercare, an offender's sobriety may be short-lived when he or she faces the same problems that contributed to their drug usage in the first place. A Drug Court Rehabilitation Programme should include ongoing drug treatment and counselling, as well as educational opportunities, job training and placement, and health and housing assistance.

Progressive Sanctions and Incentives Programme

Reality: *Relapse and Intermittent Progress are part of most successful drug rehabilitation.*

Principle: *The Court must apply a patient, flexible approach in monitoring compliance*

In most cases, progress toward rehabilitation will be slow starting and fitful, with sobriety only taking hold over a period of months. Progressive sanctions and incentives are incrementally applied in response to success and failure to move participants toward sobriety.

Smart Punishment: A Drug Court's Sentencing Philosophy

The judge who uses extended incarceration as the only response to drug usage is like a carpenter who shows up at a jobsite with only a hammer; he doesn't have the tools to get the job done. The Drug Court Judge carries intensive supervision, counselling, educational services, residential treatment, acupuncture, medical intervention, drug testing, and programme incentives, as well as incarceration in his or her tool box.

The problem is not in the use of incarceration, but in our overdependence upon it. Incarceration works for drug-using offenders. It works by providing the offender with the opportunity to detox from drugs. It works as a deterrent, by presenting the offender with the stressful, anxiety producing experience of incarceration. It works by coercing drug using offenders to enter and complete rehabilitation programmes.

The use of extended periods of incarceration, however, does not appear to increase the value of incarceration and may in fact be counter-productive to sentencing goals. Extended incarceration may disrupt whatever stability exists in a drug-user's life (needed for successful drug rehabilitation), initiate him or her into a criminal lifestyle, and reduce the deterrent effect of incarceration, thus limiting the effectiveness of court-ordered rehabilitation.

Smart punishment is the imposition of the minimum amount of punishment necessary to achieve the twin sentencing goals of reduced criminality and drug usage. It relies on the use of Progressive Sanctions, the measured application of a spectrum of sanctions, whose intensity increases incrementally with the number and seriousness of programme failures. Like a surgeon using a scalpel, progressive sanctions are used surgically to achieve sentencing goals.

Progressive Sanctions

In a Drug Court, there are immediate and direct consequences for all conduct. Sanctions follow violations and are applied as close to the time of failure as possible. This calls for frequent court hearings to monitor the offender and mete out sanctions.

In many Drug Courts, less serious violations, such as inadequate participation in a court-ordered programme, call for sanctions that start with the intensification of supervision, treatment, and/or a single day's incarceration. Those sanctions increase incrementally (i.e. 1 day, 2 days, 4 days, etc.) with continued violations. At the other end of the spectrum, complete programme failure (represented by an offender permanently absenting him or herself from court or treatment programme) may call for a substantial period of incarceration (at least one week) to detox the offender, as well as deter the offender from future programme failure and/or drug usage.

Diversion and Other Incentive Programmes

Drug rehabilitation is at best a difficult, demanding, and lengthy process. In order to motivate defendants to complete that process, Drug Courts offer them substantial positive, as well as negative, incentives to do so. Encouragement and appreciation, as well as real incentives (as described below), are given to participants for positive behaviours.

A diversion programme (statutory or otherwise) provides a powerful motivational tool for drug rehabilitation, offering the defendant the opportunity to work toward a complete dismissal of a felony drug charge. Hybrid Diversion programmes that do not offer a complete dismissal are common (i.e. offering to reduce felony convictions to misdemeanours), but provide less incentive for participants to succeed. Even where a Diversion Programme is not available at all, significant incentives are often offered to offenders through the innovative application of probation terms (i.e. offering participants reductions in the length, intensity or cost of probation supervision).

Structural Accountability: Structures that Promote Coordination

Government agencies tend to see their interests narrowly, be distrustful of other agencies, resentful of outside pressure, and jealous of their prerogatives and resources. For a Drug Court and its accompanying court-ordered drug rehabilitation programme to be effective, participating agencies must be able to look beyond those narrow interests (i.e. distributing information freely, collaborating in decision-making, sharing resources, and coordinating their efforts.)

While strong leadership and individual commitment may initially create a climate conducive to coordination, over time programmes unravel and agencies tend to revert to accustomed ways (when personnel change). It is crucial, therefore to develop permanent structures that will ensure continued programme coordination, stability, and effectiveness over time.

Structural Accountability: Where Structure is Accountable for Programme Coordination

Structural accountability exists where participating agencies share programme responsibilities and are accountable to each other for programme effectiveness. Each part of the system (supervisory staff, public defender, prosecuting attorney, treatment provider, court staff and judge) is directly linked to, dependent upon, and responsible to the others.

The Structurally Accountable Characteristics of a Drug Court

1. *A Unified Court*: A single Drug Court Judge and dedicated court staff (handling all Drug Rehabilitation cases from start to finish) is the focus for programme design, implementation, and monitoring.
2. *Co-Funding of a Coordinated System*: Joint responsibility as to funding decisions for the programme promotes as integration of function and sense of responsibility for the total programme.
3. *Inter-Agency Planning*: Full interagency and personnel participation in the design and implementation of the programme promotes agency and personal commitment to, and ownership of, the programme.
4. *Programme Procedures and Guidelines*: The setting of clear procedures and guidelines describing programme requirements and consequences informs all participants (including offenders) as to what is expected of them.

5. *Setting a Mission and Goals*: Court and staff develop and agree on programme goals that they can work towards and measure their progress against.

6. *Periodic Review*: Inter-agency review of the programme permits continuous evaluation of programme and agency effectiveness, trouble shooting for problems and the maintenance of inter-agency relationships.

7. *Hands-on Vertical Participation*: The offender is seen by the same agency personnel throughout the process promoting personal responsibility and commitment to the offender's progress.

8. *Developing Partnerships*: Participating agencies look beyond traditional relationships, redefining their roles, and sharing in decision-making formerly reserved to a single agency.

9. *Data Collection*: The collection of pertinent data is essential in determining whether the goals of the programme are being met, and in planning for new ones.

10. *Full Access to Programme Information*: Complete access to information on the work of participating agencies allows them to better understand each other's role and work together more effectively.

11. *Direct Linkages:* Developing mechanisms for the face-to-face meeting of all participants (including offenders) promotes the monitoring of the offender's progress and the work product of staff.

12. *Personnel Incentives*: Providing incentives for the effective performance of work done and rewards for the special contributions of individuals, promotes staff innovation and productivity.

Contingency Contracting in Oakland's FIRST (Fast, Intensive, Report, Supervision and Treatment) Diversion Drug Court: An Example of Structural Accountability

A contingency contract is developed cooperatively by the Drug Court Judge, the supervision and treatment staff, and other participants agencies. It sets out the standards of and consequences for offender conduct during the programme. Both positive and negative behaviours are rewarded or penalized according to the number of rehabilitative tasks completed.

In Oakland's FIRST Diversion programme, the number of points achieved under the contract reflect the number of rehabilitative tasks completed. Over the life of the programme, that point total translates into rewards (where diversion may be reduced from 24 months to as little as 6 months, and the diversion fee reduced from \$ 220 to as little as \$ 20) or sanctions (where the court increases the intensity of supervision, treatment and/or remands the offender).

All participants are responsible for the creation of the contingency contract, and accountable to each other for its effective operation. In designing a contingency contract, participants share the responsibility of establishing treatment and supervision requirements (traditionally the province of the supervision and treatment staff). Similarly, by creating a contingency contract that sets out the consequences of the offender's conduct, participants share in the making of sentencing decisions (formerly the court's sole responsibility).

The contingency contract is the structural cornerstone of the programme, requiring collaboration in decision-making and coordinated agency action and providing ground rules that reduce confusion over programme implementation and promote long term programme stability and effectiveness. The contract makes the offender accountable for his or her behaviour and gives the offender control over his or her own rehabilitation (ultimately making the offender a participant, rather than a self-described victim of the rehabilitation programme). Importantly, the court, supervision and other participating agencies have also committed themselves to the terms of the contingency contract, making themselves accountable to the offender and to each other for the contract's promised consequences. (See Contingency Contract)

The Success of Oakland's Drug Court

The Oakland FIRST Diversion programme has achieved a 50 per cent graduation rate, approximately twice the number of successful diversions of the previously existing programme, as well as half the felony recidivism. Perhaps, most importantly, for the first time Alameda County has been able to rent empty jail cells to neighbouring counties, as FIRST Diversion participants spent approximately 35,000 fewer days in custody over the two-year Diversion period (a 45 per cent reduction), earning over 2 million dollars for the country. (See the Importance of Immediate and Intensive Intervention in a Court-Ordered Rehabilitation Programme: An Evaluation of the FIRST Diversion Programme (Fast, Intensive, Report, Supervision and Treatment) After Two Years, Judge Jeffrey Tauber, Oakland Criminal Court, California, 1993.)

A Unified Drug Court System

All government programmes require the effective operation of participating agencies. But because the task involved in the rehabilitation of drug-using offenders is an extraordinarily difficult one, a higher degree of competence, coordination, and accountability is required of both programme personnel and the structures they create. A Unified Drug Court System provides the opportunity to coordinate a wide range of anti-drug strategies, from rehabilitative to treatment services, probation and parole, education and job training, and police service.

The most basic Drug Court design requires the daily communication, cooperation, and linkage of judge and court staff, supervising agency, treatment providers, and prosecution and defense bar. Attributing the success of a Drug Court to the judge alone is like saying the safety record of a jet airliner is the sole responsibility of the pilot (leaving out the crew, mechanics, air flight controllers, etc.). A Unified Drug Court System is a circular system, with each participant linked to, dependent upon, and responsible to the other.

Drug Courts as the Focus of an Anti-Drug System

The courts stand in a unique position among service agencies, they are at the fulcrum, where service agencies meet. Participating agencies are used to working closely with or under the supervision of the courts. Judges, too, have a special position in their communities that make Drug Courts the logical place to focus anti-drug efforts. In fact, the court is the only place that some agencies (such as police and treatment) ever have significant contact. Even agencies that are hostile and uncooperative with each other work effectively and cooperatively within the court's orbit.

Conclusion

The development of Drug Courts is a major innovation for the American Criminal Justice System, as Drug Courts work with drug using offenders in their communities, with minimal incarceration, criminal recidivism and cost. In the United States, Attorney General Janet Reno's championing of Drug Courts has drawn attention to the idea that we can do better than simply warehousing drug using offenders in the U.S. jails and prisons. Similarly, Governments around the world can play an important role in the development of Drug Court models by providing technical assistance and funding incentives necessary to promote the adoption of proven design strategies.

As the international community begins its consideration of the American Drug Court model, it should be acknowledged that the model may need to be modified substantially to meet differences in cultural, local conditions and resource availability. However, it is my belief that more traditional societies and cultures, with their strong cultural and family ties, are in an excellent position to develop uniquely effective Drug Court models.

A SYSTEM PARTICIPANTS GLOSSARY OF DRUG COURTS

A *Unified Drug Court System* is a circular system, with each part of the system linked to, dependent upon, and responsible to the others.

Unified Drug Court Provides direction and focus through the leadership of a single judge, ensuring consistency in judicial decision-making and programme implementation, and the coordination and accountability of all participants through the handling of all drug rehabilitation cases by a single court.

Specialized courts (Domestic Violence, Drunk Driving, Family and Juvenile Courts). Work closely with the Drug Court, providing each other with information essential for the comprehensive, direct, and immediate supervision of offenders.

Supervision agency Probation, parole, and/or other supervisory agencies maintain continuous contact with offenders and provide frequent reports on the offender's progress.

Treatment providers. Providing treatment to offenders, communicating complete and timely drug testing and other information on the offender's participation.

Public agencies. Providing health services, social services, and housing services so that offenders can begin the process of re-entry into society.

Educational Institutions. Community colleges and other educational institutions provide educational services to participants.

Community participation. (Bar Associations, Anti-Drug Coalitions, etc.) A monitor of programme effectiveness and advocate for the programme; involved in systemic decision-making.

Job training/placement. Providing the skills, as well as the jobs, to enable participants to take control of their lives.

Local government. (Mayor, county, government, etc.) Providing oversight and local government involvement in the system.

Law enforcement. Providing information to the system on community drug usage and programme success. Offenders must initially report to a beat officer and maintain; failure to participate or other problems are communicated directly to the beat officer for follow-up.

Custodial agency. Providing separate facilities, as well as drug and alcohol education and treatment services for participants remanded into custody. Offenders released from custody are directly linked up with supervision, treatment, and law enforcement agencies.

Court staff. The District Attorney and Public Defender (and/or Defense Attorney) work as a team, to facilitate the programme. They jointly determine initial eligibility.

CONFISCATION AND MONEY LAUNDERING IN THE UK

Kennedy Talbot

Confiscation

The Crown Court has the power to make a confiscation order. This power arises in all types of crime dealt with in the Crown Court on indictment. A unique feature of confiscation is the availability of High Court civil powers, adapted from civil procedure, on the application of the prosecution, to make a restraint order to freeze the defendant's assets, regulate his financial affairs, force the disclosure of information to the prosecution and, ultimately to realize property to enforce payment of the confiscation order.

Drug Trafficking: Originated with the Drug Trafficking Offences Act 1986. The law has recently been strengthened against defendants charged on or after 3 February 1995, with the introduction of the Drug Trafficking Act 1994 (DTA). The old law—the Drug Trafficking Offences Act 1986 (DTOA)—still applies to defendants charged before 3 February 1995.

Other Crime—The Criminal Justice Act 1988 (CJA): Less common-but now increasingly used-is confiscation in crime other than drug trafficking. These provisions were originally much more favourable to the defendant than those under the DTA. However, significant change has been enacted in the shape of the Proceeds of Crime Act 1995. This became law in the Autumn of 1995, bringing CJA confiscation closer to drug trafficking confiscation. The Crown Court now has the power in all cases to make a confiscation order in respect of benefit from crime of which the defendant is not convicted, does not admit and in the absence of any evidence of its commission. Both the DTA and the CJA permit the High Court to make orders to render Crown Court confiscation orders effective. These powers are considered together in this paper. Then the Crown Court confiscation powers will be discussed.

The High Court Powers

Although these powers are to support criminal proceedings the High Court proceedings are civil. If the prosecution decides to invoke confiscation, it will invariably make use of the High Court powers. The High Court powers are:

Restraint

This is to prevent disposal of assets. It is similar to, but more Draconian than a *Mareva* injunction. Such an order may be made even before charge, provided the defendant is to be charged. A few points are worth mentioning.

* Any person may be restrained from dealing with 'realizable property'. Realizable property is any property in which the defendant has any interest, legal or equitable and any property in which the donee of a gift from the defendant has an interest. The High Court power to restrain is not, therefore, restricted to restraint of the proceeds of the offence.

* The value of the property restrained should not exceed the amount required to satisfy any confiscation order which may be made. But in all drug trafficking cases and some CJA cases it will be proper for all the defendant's assets to be restrained as the burden will lie on the defendant to show that they are not derived from crime.

* Restraint orders should provide for living expenses. Broadly the defendant is entitled to ordinary and reasonable living expense.

* The defendant is entitled to the release of funds for the payment of legal costs. The prosecution may however insist on the costs being taxed, i.e. the amount assessed by the court if necessary.

* The restraint order is normally granted *ex parte*. There is therefore a duty of the prosecutor for full and frank disclosure to draw to the court's attention to all relevant matters. This duty extends to the prosecutor drawing to the court's attention material developments subsequent to the granting of the order.

* Third parties affected by the order are entitled to have the value of their interest in any property restrained released to them.

* The restraint order may apply to property situated outside England and Wales. If it does, there will usually be a paragraph in the order preventing it affecting third parties wholly outside the jurisdiction who are not named in the order and who cannot prevent a breach of the order within the jurisdiction. Of course this will not assist the defendant as the order operates *in personam* against him. Further, international conventions are in force between the UK and other countries. It may well be, there-

fore, that the prosecution will seek the enforcement of the restraint order in the other country by means of a formal letter of request.

Disclosure

If a restraint order is made, the court may make an order requiring the defendant or any person to disclose, by affidavit, to the prosecution the nature and whereabouts of his assets, wherever they may be in the world. This power is likely to be used in most cases and in particular to require the defendant to explain various transactions and identify assets where the prosecution only have limited information.

* Such an order may be made against any person who has knowledge of the defendant's assets.

* Any affidavit supplied cannot be used as evidence in a criminal trial against the person required to make disclosure. The extent to which any evidence obtained as a result of the disclosure can be used in the trial is not entirely clear but probably cannot be used before the jury to determine guilt or innocence.

* The affidavit may be used by the prosecution to police the restraint order and in the course of the confiscation hearing at the Crown Court.

Receivership

The Court can appoint a receiver, either pre-conviction to manage a defendant's estate, or post conviction to ensure that the order is satisfied.

Management Receiver:

The receiver is an officer of the court and must exercise his powers with a view to making the defendant's assets available to satisfy the confiscation order. In cases where a business needs to be run or urgent or complex action has to be taken to preserve assets of the defendant the court may be invited to appoint a receiver. A receiver may only be appointed over realizable property—property in which the defendant has an interest or the value of gifted property. In cases involving incorporated businesses, prima facie the receiver may only be appointed over the shares of the company as a person's interest in a company are the shares in it.

Once appointed, the usual order enables the receiver to take most management decisions in relation to the defendant's property. However, in the absence of specific empowerment in the receivership order or if the receiver wishes to ensure his decision is sanctioned by the court, he may apply to the court for directions.

Enforcement Receiver—See the section on enforcement.

Drug Trafficking—The Crown Court Confiscation Hearing

Confiscation should always be approached with care and it should not be assumed that experience in other areas of litigation will be of application. Many traditional rules relating to criminal law are discarded. The legislation is intentionally Draconian reversing the burden of proof, removing the privilege against self-incrimination and removing finality of litigation.

In summary, a conviction for a drug trafficking offence, together with a prosecutor requirement operates as a trigger, obliging the court to order the defendant to pay a confiscation order equal to the total value of the proceeds of the defendant's drug trafficking at any time (even before the Act came into force) and whether or not the defendant has been convicted in respect of that drug trafficking. The court has no discretion to reduce the amount of the order and must make it in the amount it assesses to be his benefit, unless the defendant proves to the court that he cannot pay the amount assessed.

In carrying out this function the court is obliged to follow a statutory regime. Broadly, the court must determine in this order:

(a) Whether or not the defendant has benefited from drug trafficking.

(b) If the court finds that the person has so benefited, it must then assess the amount of the benefit.

(c) The court then, at the defendant's initiative, assesses the amount that might be realized—what assets the defendant has, from wherever they are derived.

(d) The court must make a confiscation order in the amount of the defendant's benefit, unless satisfied that the amount that might be realized is less. If satisfied the amount is less the order must be made in the lesser amount.

Although the court is only obliged to carry out a confiscation inquiry if the prosecution requires it, once the requirement is made the regime is strict; the prosecution cannot agree an amount of a confiscation order. Any such agreement must be rejected by the court.

Calculation of Benefit (a) and (b)

The burden is on the prosecution to prove the fact and amount of benefit to the civil standard. The court has to calculate the aggregate of all payments made to the defendant in connection with drug trafficking whether or not the defendant has been convicted of an offence in connection with that trafficking. The duty on the court extends to trafficking carried out at any time—since the defendant was born. This is obviously an onerous responsibility and as a matter of practice the court will rely heavily on the assumptions in s. 4 of the DTA. In summary, these assumptions oblige the court to assume that:

— all the defendant's assets held by him since his conviction, and

— all the defendant's income and expenditure since 6 years prior to when he was charged,

are derived from drug trafficking. It is then for the defendant to prove that the assumption is incorrectly made i.e. legitimacy of the source of his assets, income and expenditure.

The Amount That Might be Realized (c)

The defendant cannot be ordered to pay by way of a confiscation order more than he can afford. Therefore, once the court has decided upon the amount of benefit from drug trafficking, it must then go on to consider the value to the defendant of all property in which he has an interest. The court is concerned with civil property interests. Additionally, to ensure defendants cannot escape the operation of the statute by transferring their interest in their assets to others such as friends and relatives, the court must take into account and calculate, as part of the amount that might be realized, all gifts made by him to any other person. The burden of proof to satisfy the court that the amount that might be realized is less than the benefit is on the defendant.

Procedure

In deciding what the confiscation order should be, the court will have regard to:

* Any evidence given in the trial.

* The contents of the prosecutor's statement and any defence statements under s. 11 of the Act.

* Any evidence given in the confiscation hearing.

* Any information the court requires the defendant to provide.

The prosecution are now obliged to provide a statement in every case where they made a confiscation hearing requirement. Although the Act refers to this document as a statement, it is really in the nature of a pleading: its purpose is to narrow the issues between the parties. Any factual matter relating to the defendant's proceeds from drug trafficking may therefore be set out in the s. 11 statement. The statement itself is not evidence and question of admissibility of facts alleged in the statement do not arise.

The point of the prosecutor's statement is that once served

* the court may require the defendant to indicate the extent to which he accepts any allegation in the statement and if he does not accept the

allegation upon what he intends to rely. If the defendant fails to comply with this requirement the court may treat him as accepting the allegation, and,

* acceptance by the defendant of allegations in the statement may be treated by the court as conclusive.

If the defendant denies an allegation, the issue is joined and any facts to be proved have to be so proved according to the normal rules of criminal evidence.

It is notable that third parties do not have a right of audience in the Crown Court to be heard on the extent of their interest in assets in which the defendant also has an interest. This is not unjust as a confiscation order is just an order against the defendant to pay a sum of money. It is only if the defendant does not pay the confiscation order voluntarily that the court (the High Court) may make an order forcing the sale of particular property. At that stage the third party has a right of audience.

Further it may be unwise for third parties to seek to make representations at the Crown Court. If they do and do not succeed on the merits, they may be bound by the decision against them so that any attempt to reargue the point in the High Court would be an abuse of process.

All Crime Other Than Drug Trafficking-The Crown Court Confiscation Hearing

Like drug trafficking, a confiscation order is an order to pay a sum of money, Again like drug trafficking, a defendant cannot be ordered to pay more than the value of the property he has unlawfully obtained ('benefit') or more than the value of his assets ('amount that might be realized').

The making of a confiscation order is a two stage process. First, the court calculates the benefit. Then the court calculates the amount that might be realized. The court must then order the defendant to pay a sum equal to the lower of the two.

Benefit

Simple Benefit—Defendant convicted of only one offence

This is the total value of the property obtained as a result of or in connection with the offences s. 71(4) and (5).

* The court is confined to benefit from the offences plus any offences formally admitted by the defendant.

* The court is concerned with the gross value of the property obtained, not profit.

* If the defendant obtained property for another he has still obtained it. This obviously covers cases where the defendant obtains property for a limited company.

* The amount is increased to take account of inflation or increase in the value of the property between when it was obtained and the date of the confiscation hearing.

Extended Benefit—Defendant convicted of more than one offence one of which may be a previous conviction.

* If the defendant is convicted of two offences on the indictment, or has a previous conviction within the last 6 years, the court can assume (without any evidence from the prosecution) that all assets held by, and income and expenditure of, the defendant was derived from the proceeds of 'criminal conduct' and make a confiscation order accordingly. There will be no need to convict the defendant of any offence in relation to that criminal conduct. The burden is on the defendant to prove the legitimate origin of his assets of his transactions.

The Amount that Might be Realized

This is calculated in almost exactly the same way as drug trafficking and is the aggregate of the value of the defendant's interest in all his assets and the value of any transfer to any other person for insignificant consideration since the commission of the first of the offences.

This is a stage where civil property law applies. The court must determine what the defendant owns and what the value is of his interest in all his property. The burden of proof is on the defendant to prove that the amount that might be realized is less than the benefit.

It obviously follows that when assessing the amount the defendant can pay it is irrelevant that the court is considering legitimately acquired assets.

Variation of Confiscation Orders

Both types of order can be adjusted

* by the Crown Court within 28 days of the order being made,
* by an appeal to the Court of Appeal against sentence, and
* by 'double application' to the High Court, then Crown Court, where the assets turn out to be insufficient to pay the confiscation order.
* upwards by application to the Crown Court where the prosecution acquires evidence of further benefit from drug trafficking carried out before the confiscation order was made. Such an application can be made up to six years after conviction.

Drug trafficking orders can also be adjusted by

* 'double application' of the prosecution to the High Court, then Crown, Court where the benefit was originally assessed by the Crown Court in excess of the assets and the defendant later at any time acquires further assets.

The most frequent application experienced is for a reduction of a confiscation order. The basis for the application is that the defendant has insufficient assets to satisfy the confiscation order. The application has two stages. First, the defendant must apply to the High Court for a certificate of inadequacy. At this stage the High Court is simply concerned with whether or not the value of the property is sufficient to satisfy the order. The burden of proof is on the defendant, who will usually have to point to a change since the question was determined in the Crown Court. The defendant cannot re-litigate a point already determined against him.

Once the certificate is issued the defendant must then apply to the Crown Court for the order to be actually reduced. The Crown Court have a broad discretion and may substitute such lesser sum as they think just.

Enforcement of Confiscation Orders

A confiscation order is enforced by the magistrates' court as if it were a fine. This means orders to seize and sell goods, orders to attach earnings or bank accounts and ultimately imprison in default of paying. However and exclusively to confiscation orders the prosecution have a role. They may apply to the High Court to appoint a receiver to realize the assets. A receiver is an officer of the court, who will usually on appointment be grated fairly broad powers to take decisions in relation to the realization of property.

The prosecution may invite the court to appoint a receiver simpliciter, leaving it to the receiver to litigate any disputes between the defendant and others relating to the extent of the defendant's interests in the assets. Alternatively, the prosecution may seek a declaration of the property interests, thereby streamlining the receivership.

* There is no protection in the legislation for family homes and so the court will usually appoint a receiver to sell a family home if it is necessary to satisfy a confiscation order.

* The appointment of a receiver is (probably) an equitable remedy and so the court should only make an appointment if it is just and convenient.

Money Laundering Offences

Parliament has legislated for identical money laundering offences in both drug trafficking and proceeds of crime cases. The offences, fall into distinct categories with identical wording except that the section numbers and the object of the offence are different. Plainly, in money laundering cases under the DTA the allegation will be one of 'laundering' the proceeds of drug trafficking whereas under the CJA the allegation will be one of 'laundering' the proceeds of criminal conduct not being drug trafficking or terrorism. This immediately causes a problem for the prosecutor seeking to prove a case of money laundering as it will have to be proved to a jury that the launderer is dealing in the proceeds of drug or other criminal conduct activity (depending on the way the indictment is expressed). If the prosecutor cannot tie the proceeds in with the allegation on the indictment then it follows that a defendant will be acquitted even if the fact of laundering is proved.

The offences fall into the categories set out below but will be dealt with separately in a section dealing with drug trafficking and another for the proceeds of criminal conduct.

S49DTA/s93C CJA	Concealing or transferring the proceeds of drug trafficking/criminal conduct (whether one's own or another's) for the purpose of avoiding prosecution or to avoid the making or enforcement of a confiscation order.
S50DTA/s93A CJA	Entering into an arrangement with another to retain, control, conceal, remove, transfer, or invest the proceeds of drug trafficking/criminal conduct knowing or suspecting that the other carries on or has carried on or has benefited from drug trafficking/criminal conduct.
S51DTA/s93B CJA	Knowing acquisition, possession or use of proceeds of drug trafficking/criminal conduct for inadequate consideration
S53DTA/s93D CJA	Tipping off in respect of an investigation into drug money laundering/criminal conduct money laundering.

There are two further offences relating to the knowledge or suspicion of drug money laundering and the interference with an investigation into drug trafficking; both these offences are specific only to drug trafficking.

S.52DTA-	Failure to disclose to the police knowledge or suspicion of drug money laundering where the knowledge or suspicion came to the "launderer's" attention in the course of his employment.
S.58DTA-	Prejudicing an investigation into drug trafficking.

Observations on UK Drug Trafficking Confiscation

Key elements of the UK Confiscation System

* Judicial system—no administrative confiscation.

* Criminal conviction based.

Save in exceptional circumstances—a defendant who absconds or cash seized at borders—a conviction for an offence proved beyond reasonable doubt is necessary before a confiscation order can be made.

* Assumptions.

Reversal of the burden of proof requiring a convicted trafficker to prove the legitimate origin of his assets and money passing through his hands over a prior 6 year period.

* Value system.

The Court assesses the value of the defendant's proceeds of drug trafficking. Thereafter the court can enforce the order against any assets of the defendant including those legitimately derived.

* Third party protection.

The effect of a value system is that innocent third parties have their property interests fully protected.

* Preservation and enforcement powers.

High Court powers to restrain assets and appoint receivers to manage and realize assets.

* Payment to central government.

Confiscated monies paid to central government, not to police or prosecuting authorities.

Strengths of the UK Confiscation System

* Flexible—domestic and international.

The value system allows convicted traffickers to have orders made against them where they have disposed of their ill-gotten gains because the order can be enforced against legitimate property.

* Reversal of burden of proof.

It is absolutely vital to ensure that confiscation laws are effective. It is impossible for the prosecution to prove source of assets derived by sophisticated organizations who take deliberate and elaborate steps to hide or launder assets.

* Use of existing civil preservation and recovery methods.

This saves money and limits the requirement to train judiciary and law enforcement officers. An established law in place can be adapted to new circumstances.

Weaknesses of the UK Confiscation System

* Complexity.

If defendant does not pay order voluntarily further applications are necessary for other courts to enforce. This is probably an unavoidable by-product of a value system that seeks to be fair.

* Separation of drug trafficking from other crime.

Confiscation laws should be the same for all types of crime. Is serious fraud, corruption, contract kiliing etc. necessarily less serious than drug trafficking? Separation of the two leads to complexity and loopholes for traffickers and money launderers.

* Funding and resources.

Investigation and funding of the confiscation system is expensive but cost effective because of monies recovered. Payment to central government removes the incentive to property resource.

* Training and education.

The UK experience is that investment made in training for prosecutors and judiciary is insufficient.

Lessons to be Learned

* Fair.

An unfair system loses public and political support. It is important to strike the right balance between depriving the trafficker of ill-gotten gains and protecting the innocent.

* Confiscation fund.

Incentive to investigators and prosecuting authorities to invest in confiscation is essential. It is wrong to have direct payment by defendant or court to police/prosecutors on a case by case basis. The solution is a managed fund resourced from recovered proceeds to which police and prosecutor may apply for funding.

* Value system.

This makes it easier to co-operate internationally and ensures traffickers who dispose of ill-gotten gains can be dealt with.

* Educate judiciary and senior investigators/prosecutors.
* Simple—adapt existing laws.
* All crime together.

CANADA'S PROCEEDS OF CRIME LEGISLATION-AN OVERVIEW

D. D. Graham Reynolds

Canada's proceeds of crime legislation is principally found in Part XII. 2 of the Canadian *Criminal Code* (the Code)[1] which was amended effective January 1, 1989 by Bill C-61 to incorporate a number of specific amendments designed to enhance the enforcement of Canadian drug legislation as well as strengthening the then-existing provisions on search and seizure and offences prohibiting the possession of property obtained by crime. The aim of the legislation is to deprive criminals of the enormous profits derived from illegal activities associated with drug trafficking and other organized crime activities. As put in a recent judgment of the Court of Appeal for Ontario:

> The purpose of Part XII. 2 is clear. It is intended to give effect to the age old adage that crime does not pay. It is now recognized that some crime is big business, and that massive profits, both direct and indirect, can be made from criminal activity. Part XII. 2 is a response to that realization and provides a comprehensive scheme whereby those direct and indirect profits may be located, seized, and eventually forfeited to the Crown.[2]

A combined study by both Federal and some Provincial Attorneys-General and other officials concluded as early as 1982 that new approaches to the challenges posed by organized profit-making criminal activity were required. The culmination of the recommendations of the study were to enact amendments to the *Code* granting new powers to law enforcement agencies similar to those granted to U.S. authorities under their *Racketeer Influ-*

[1]R.S.C. 1985, c. C-46, as amended.

[2]*R.* v. *Wilson Nakatsuru & Doucette* unreported decision of Court of Appeal for Ontario, released October 27, 1993, at p. 5.

enced and Corrupt Organizations Statute (RICO), the *Continuing Criminal Enterprise Statue* (CCE[3]) and, in the United Kingdom, the *Criminal Justice Act, 1988.*

The context for the introduction of such legislation was clearly established. As observed by a former Attorney General for Canada on the introduction of legislation creating Canada's proceeds of crime laws:

> Increasingly we are seeing the effects of criminal organizations operating both from within and without the country that are totally dedicated to the commission of crime for profit. These organizations take advantage of modern communications, transportation and corporate structuring to frustrate the reach of national legal systems to amass illicit and illegal wealth.
>
> One of the reasons why this type of criminal activity is spreading is that the various administrations have been slow in adapting their legislation to changing circumstances. But now the western world acknowledges ever more readily that it is becoming imperative to adapt and revise national legislation and to negotiate international agreements to fill the gaps which now favour criminals.
>
> On an international level, this legislation is in compliance with the draft United Nations Convention against Illicit Traffic in Narcotic Drugs and Psychotropic Substances. Similar legislation has either been passed or has been presented to the legislatures of Britain, Australia and the United States. This uniquely Canadian proposal will strike a balanced middle ground in dealing with the reality of enterprise crime. Except for very limited situations, Canadian courts are powerless to strip an offender of the proceeds of criminal activity.[4]

An example of the historic frustration of law enforcement officials in this area was noted in a paper produced by one of my Federal colleagues on the proclamation of the Canadian legislation:

> What was lacking prior to C-61 was the power to seize the proceeds of illegal acts which were neither evidence, instruments, nor the direct subject of the offence. This meant that mixed, indirect, or converted proceeds of illegal acts were generally beyond the reach of law enforcement agencies. Moreover, even direct proceeds which were evidence but were in the

[3]19 U.S.C. Title II.

[4]Remarks of Minister of Justice and Attorney General for Canada, second reading, Bill C-61, 'Act to amend the Criminal Code, the Food and Drugs Act and the Narcotic Control Act,' 2nd session, 33rd Parliament, Vol. vii, p. 8888.

form of a chose in action or an intangible were beyond the reach of the general *Criminal Code* and narcotic search provisions. The shortcoming of the pre C-61 legislation is exemplified by the case of *Re Banque Royale du Canada and the Queen*[5]. There, R.C.M.P. officers obtained a warrant to search for and seize some $600,000.00 deposited in the account of Luis Pinto in the Royal Bank, alleging that the money was the direct proceeds of drug trafficking. The warrant was quashed on the basis that the credit balance in a bank account was an intangible, mere proof that the bank has some unsegregated funds on deposit, and therefore not subject to seizure pursuant to the pre C-61 legislation.[6]

The introduction of this legislation also conformed with Canada's commitments pursuant to the *United Nations Convention Against Illicit Traffic in Narcotic Drugs and Psychotropic Substances* (the Vienna Convention, December 19, 1988) which mandates the forfeiture of proceeds of crime. Thus, prior to the amendment of the Canadian *Criminal Code*, there existed no power by the Crown to seize intangible or converted proceeds of crime. As for forfeiture, this device was restricted to such items as conveyances used to transport narcotics, instruments, or other evidence through which criminal offences were committed. There was no ability to seize or 'freeze' suspected proceeds of criminal activity prior to conviction. The then existing power of law enforcement agencies did not reflect the scope of organized criminal activity, and represented a serious imbalance against the State's legitimate interest in confiscating the fruits of crime.

A Word About Jurisdiction, the Organization of Canadian Courts, and Prosecutorial Responsibilities in Canada

It may be appropriate at this point to offer some brief comments on certain aspects of the Canadian Criminal Justice System. As in other Commonwealth nations, prosecutions in Canada are undertaken by the Attorney General, who is independent from his or her cabinet colleagues as a matter of constitutional principle. As such, Canada is bound by tradition and jurisprudence to the 'Shawcross Principle'[7] on the role of the Attor-

[5](1985) 18 C.C.C. (3d) 98 (Que. C.A.).

[6]'Bill C-61, Canada's Seize and Freeze Legislation,' undated paper prepared by Richard Mosley of the criminal law policy section, Department of Justice, Ottawa, March, 1989.

[7]U.K., H.C. debates, vol. 483, cols, 683-84 (29 January, 1951), *per* Lord Shawcross.

ney General. One Province in Canada, Nova Scotia, has created a D.P.P. position akin to that in the United Kingdom. Both federally and in other provinces, however, the Attorney General operates with all the traditional powers and responsibilities.

Under our *Constitution Act, 1867*, there exists a division of powers between the provinces and the federal governments in matters of criminal prosecution. Section 91 (27) of this *Act* provided the federal parliament with the power to enact criminal law, including procedure, while under section 92 (14), the provincial legislatures were given power over the administration of justice within the provinces. Also, our *Criminal Code* has a statutory definition of the term 'Attorney General'[8] which differentiates between the federal and provincial roles. This brief paper does not pretend to be an analysis of Canadian constitutional law but it is now clear as a matter of law that the Provincial Attorneys-General have the constitutional authority to prosecute all *Criminal Code* offences (which include the 'typical' criminal offences of murder, robbery, theft, fraud, and the like) as well as federal non-*Criminal Code* offences, except where such offences are conducted by or on behalf of the Government of Canada.

At the operational level in Canada, it is customary for all *Criminal Code* offences to be prosecuted by provincial Attorneys-General (and, in our Province of Ontario, by Provincial 'Crown Attorneys') while all non-*Criminal Code* offences are prosecuted by Federal Prosecutors. The proceeds of crime amendments to the *Code* insofar as they are made applicable to drug or other federal prosecutions are conducted by federal prosecutors. In the language of Part XII. 2 of the *Code*, provincial Attorneys-General are concerned with 'enterprise crime' offences while the federal Attorney General is concerned with 'designated drug' offences. (see, *infra.*)

The courts in each Province are organized into superior and inferior courts. Superior courts have exclusive jurisdiction over a limited number of certain offences such as murder[9] while inferior courts may preside over a broad range of criminal and other offences. Appeals[10] in indictable proceedings may be brought from convictions (on questions of fact or of law) or from sentences imposed or by the Crown (from acquittals or stays of proceedings upon questions of law alone) or, with leave, from sentences imposed. Courts of Appeal have been established for each province, with a further appeal provided either as of right (in certain defined circumstances) or by leave to the Supreme Court of Canada, which is the final court of resort in our country.

[8]*Code* s. 2 'Attorney General.'
[9]*Code*, s. 469.
[10]*Code*, Part XXI.

With certain limited exceptions, an accused person has the right (in indictable offences) to trial by judge alone (either of a superior or inferior court) or to a trial by jury. In the event of election by a superior court, the inferior court will conduct a preliminary inquiry into the charge,[11] at the conclusion of which the accused may be committed for trial by the inferior court, or discharged. At the trial, an accused has the right to 'full answer and defence' which comprises a bundle of substantive and procedural rights both under the *Code* and under the *Canadian Charter of Rights and Freedoms*[12] (the '*Charter*'). A complete discussion of the Canadian *Charter* is beyond the scope of this brief paper; however, this constitutional document, proclaimed in 1982, provides the source of specific rights to persons accused of offences. If evidence is obtained in the course of a breach of an accused's *Charter* rights, it may be excluded from the proceedings provided that the accused demonstrates that admission of the evidence would bring the administration of justice into disrepute[13] (this provision of our *Charter* thus preserves the common law rule on the admissibility of illegally obtained evidence). Some of the *Code* provisions dealing with proceeds of crime have been evaluated against the requirements of the *Charter*[14], which has been determined by our Supreme Court to be applicable to both procedural and substantive aspects of legislation.[15]

Definitions and Main Features of the Legislation

Two major themes of the proceeds of crime amendments to the *Code* may be observed: the pre-trial power to seize, 'freeze,' and ultimately forfeit proceeds of crime and the creation of new offences of 'money laundering.' These amendments are set out in Part XII. 2 of the *Code*, as well as the consequential changes to our *Food and Drugs Act* as well as the *Narcotic Control Act*.

These provisions are made applicable to two broad categories of offences: 'enterprise crime' offences and 'designated drug' offences.[16] Enterprise crime offences comprise a large number of profit-making *Code* offences such as theft, robbery, fraud, forgery, uttering, possession of property ob-

[11]*Code*, Part XVIII.

[12]*Constitution Act 1982*, R.S.C. 1985, Appendix II, No. 44, Schedule "B."

[13]See *Charter*, section 24(2).

[14]See (re: s. 462.33-no violation of s. 8 *Charter*) *Serrano et al v. R.* (1992) 73 C.C.C. (3d) 437 (Ont. Gen. Div.) and (re: s. 462.37 no violation of s. 8 *Charter*) *R. v. Shah* (B.C. Prov. Ct.) (unreported) November 30, 1992.

[15]See *Reference re: s. 94(2) Motor Vehicle Act* [1985] 2 S.C.R. 486 (S.C.C.).

[16]*Code*, s. 462.3.

tained by crime, extortion, keeping a common bawdy-house, and betting and gaming offences. Under our constitutional division of legislative responsibilities, these offences are prosecuted by the Attorneys-General of the Provinces. Designated drug offences such as trafficking in narcotics, controlled or prohibited drugs, possession for the purposes of such trafficking, importing, or cultivating (or conspiracies to effect these offences) are prosecuted by the Attorney General of Canada. The Department of Justice's offices in Toronto, Canada are engaged daily in prosecutions of this nature.

Definitions

The term 'proceeds of crime' is defined very broadly[17] as follows:

> ... any property, benefit or advantage, within or outside Canada, obtained or derived directly or indirectly as a result of (a) the commission in Canada of an enterprise crime offence or a designated drug offence, or (b) an act or omission anywhere that, if it had occurred in Canada, would have constituted an offence referred to in paragraph (a) or a designated drug offence.

The *Code* now also provides for the new offence of 'laundering' which is very broad in scope:

S. 462.31 (1) Every one commits an offence who *uses, transfers the possession of, sends or delivers to any person or place, transports, transmits, alters, disposes of or otherwise deals with in any manner and by any means* any property or any proceeds of any property with intent to conceal or convert that property or those proceeds and knowing that all or a part of that property or of those proceeds was obtained or derived directly or indirectly as a result of:

(a) the commission in Canada of an enterprise crime offence or a designated drug offence; or

(b) an act or omission anywhere that, if it had occurred in Canada, would have constituted an enterprise crime offence or a designated drug offence. [emphasis added]

The same offence is also contained in the *Narcotic Control Act*[18] and the *Food and Drugs Act*[19].

Two features emerge from these definitions: the potential enforcement

[17]*Code*, s. 462.3.
[18]Section 19.2
[19]Section 44.3.

scope of our legislation is extremely broad and may be easily adapted to trans-national crimes. That is to say, proceeds of crime or the laundering of property constituting proceeds of crime is defined in such a manner as to clearly implicate a 'warehouser' or 'launderer' whose funds or property have been derived from drug trafficking activities in other countries. The legislation is constructed in a manner to eliminate any requirement of 'double criminality' on the underlying offence; proceeds lodged in Canada are seizable if the underlying conduct giving rise to them would constitute an offence in Canada, irrespective of whether the conduct is contrary to law in the originating jurisdiction. This is extremely significant in the world context of agreements or treaty arrangements to combat the international flow of narcotics and the illegal funds derived therefrom.[20]

It is also significant to note that Canadian jurisprudence to date has established that in determining whether proceeds of crime will ultimately forfeit to the State, it is unnecessary for the prosecution to prove a specific link between an act of drug trafficking (or other designated offence/ enterprise crime) and the *particular* asset or property sought to be made forfeit.[21] Thus, the 'luxury assets' of a drug trafficker may be forfeited to the State irrespective of whether they may be linked, dollar-by-dollar, to particular acts of drug trafficking, either domestically or internationally.

It is important at this point to indicate what Canada's seizure and forfeiture scheme enacted in the *Code* is not: it is *not* a civil forfeiture system akin to that available to U.S. prosecutors in defined circumstances.[22] The Canadian scheme is a *conviction-based* system, in that the ultimate forfeiture of property adjudged to be proceeds of crime will be made only after a conviction has been registered against the 'target' accused or, where that person has died or absconded, on proof that the impugned property is *beyond a reasonable doubt* proceeds of crime. This has important implications for law enforcement and particularly upon the preparation of 'proceeds of crime' prosecutions where forfeiture of tainted property is anticipated.

[20] See, generally, on the issue of Canada's obligations arising from a signatory to the *Single Convention on Narcotic Drugs Treaty*, 1961, *R.* v. *McPartland* (1981) 63 C.C.C. (2d) 88 at pp. 90-91 (Ont. C.A.) and *R.* v. *Pasha & Pasha* (1981), 61 C.C.C. (2d) 340.

[21] See *R. v. Tortone*, (1993), 84 C.C.C. (3d) 15, *per* Major, J. at p. 15.

[22] See, for example, 18 U.S.C. s. 981, s. 1956, 1957; s. 1963 (Racketeer Influenced and Corrupt Organizations) [RICO];

Pre-Trial Seizure or Restraint

The amendments to the *Code* also provide for expanded powers of search, seizure, and forfeiture. Pre-trial seizure or 'freezing' of property which, upon a 'probable cause' basis an order of forfeiture may be made is effected through two mechanisms: the *special search warrant*[23] and the *restraint order*[24]. While both measures obtain the same practical result, they are directed to different species of property: special search warrants deal with *tangible* property such as vehicles, currency, jewellery, furniture and the like; the restraint order, while in its legislative description would encompass items of tangible property, is in practice directed to *real property and intangibles* such as bank accounts, stocks and bonds, certificates of deposit, cheques, or choses in action such as mortgages, pledges, or other rights.

In Canada, the special search warrant differs from our 'regular' search warrant in several important respects. The warrant is to be obtained on the application of the Attorney General and not by a police officer or investigator alone, and is to be obtained from a superior court judge, not a provincial judge or magistrate.[25] The information founding the warrant must set out reasonable grounds upon which the informant bases his or her belief that

> ... there is in any building, receptacle, or place any property in respect of which an order of forfeiture may be made.[26]

The information is to be accompanied by an undertaking by the Attorney General as to damages arising from the issuance and execution of the warrant:[27] this undertaking is mandatory. There is a provision authorizing the issuing judge to give notice to any person who, in the opinion of the court, appears to have a valid interest in the property; this may be overcome on a showing that such notice would result in the '... disappearance, dissipation, or reduction in value of the property or otherwise affect the property so that all or a part thereof could not be subject to an order of forfeiture ...'[28].

[23]*Code*, s. 462.32.
[24]*Code*, s. 462.33.
[25]*Code*, s. 462.32(1).
[26]*Code*, s. 462.32(1).
[27]*Code*, s. 462.32(6).
[28]*Code*, s. 462.32(5).

These restraint order provisions of the *Code* are similar,[29] with several important differences which reflect the different nature of the property sought to be restrained thereunder. First, the order obtained is not merely one mandating the restraint of the property, but authorizes the judge to appoint a person to take control of and to manage or otherwise deal with all or part of that property, and requiring any person in possession of the property to give it up to such a person.[30] The formalities of the application, notice provisions, and undertaking are all in the same form as that provided for the special search warrant. A copy of the order must be served upon the person to whom it is addressed (typically the person in possession of the property)[31] and must be registered against the property according to the property registration scheme in effect in the particular province.[32]

It is an offence to contravene or fail to comply with the order,[33] which remains in force until it is revoked or varied under the review provisions (see, *infra.*), it ceases to be in effect pursuant to the limitation period (six months), or an order of forfeiture is made against the property under the *Code* or other federal statute.[34] The limitation period may be extended upon *ex parte* application by the Attorney General.[35]

The legislation contains review provisions[36] which enable any person with an interest in the seized or restrained property to apply, upon three days' notice to the Attorney General, for the release in part or in whole of the property (importantly, these provisions are *not* applicable to funds or property seized through other statutory instruments such as *Code* search warrants or *Narcotic Control Act* powers).[37] A court hearing such an application has broad powers to vary or revoke the original order and to order the return to property. The application may be brought for the purposes of meeting reasonable living expenses[38] of a person who was in pos-

[29]*Code*, s. 462.33.

[30]*Code*, s. 462.33(3).

[31]*Code*, s. 462.33(8).

[32]*Code*, s. 462.33(9).

[33]*Code*, s. 462.33(11).

[34]*Code*, s. 462.33(10).

[35]*Code*, s. 462.35; see *A-G Canada v. 162491 Canada Inc. & 162461 Canada Inc.*

[36]*Code*, s. 462.34.

[37]See *R.* v. *Wilson, Nakatsuru & Doucette*, *supra.* at pp. 23-28; *R.* v. *Love*, unreported decision of Queen's Bench Court, Alberta, November 2, 1990; *Gaudreau* v. *Her Majesty The Queen*, unreported decision of Queen's Bench Court, Regina, Saskatchewan, June 16, 1993.

[38]*Code*, s. 462.34(4)(c)(i).

session of the property at the time of seizure or restraint or any person who has a 'valid interest' in the property, or for the reasonable business and legal expenses[39] of such a person. In the latter case, the statute mandates a further *in camera* hearing for purposes of determining the reasonableness of legal expenses, at which the Attorney General is not permitted to appear.[40] This latter provision has been the subject of concern among prosecutors involved in proceeds of crime cases as it arguably permits a 'judicial laundering' of funds upon which a court has already determined, on a probable cause basis to be, proceeds of crime.

Forfeiture

As noted above, forfeiture in Canada is essentially a *conviction-based* system. In the *Code* there are two general categories of forfeiture. The first relates to circumstances in which there is a prosecution of an individual and forfeiture may occur in the following ways:[41]

(a) if the offence was committed in relation to the subject property, the court is required to order forfeiture; or

(b) if there is no connection between the subject offence and the property, but the court is otherwise satisfied *beyond a reasonable doubt* that the property constitutes proceeds of crime, forfeiture may be ordered.

The second type of forfeiture has been termed the *in trem*[42] method and involves circumstances where an accused has died or absconded prior to the application for forfeiture. For absconding accused where information has been laid and reasonable and unproductive attempts to arrest have been made during a six-month period following the issuance of a warrant, a court may order the forfeiture on the applicable standard.[43] This application must be made before a superior court judge.

[39]*Code*, s. 462.34(4)(c)(ii); see *Rossi* v. *R.* (B.C.S.C.) (unreported) May 14, 1992, February 5 & 19, 1993; *R.* v. *Morra* (1992) 77 C.C.C. (2d) 380 (Ont. Gen. Div.).

[40]*Code*, s. 462.34(5); amendments currently pending before Parliament would require a presiding Judge to take into account the legal aid tariff of a province in assessing the reasonableness of the particular fees and to permit the Attorney General to apply for the making of an order to tax the fees forming part of the expenses applied for

[41]*Code*, s. 462.37(1); 462.37(2).

[42]For an interesting case where this method was used, see *R.* v. *Clymore & Clymore* (1992) 74 C.C.C. (3d) 217 B.C.S.C.

[43]*Code*, s. 462.38(2); also see *R.* v. *Petersen et al* (1992) 15 W.C.B. (2d) 438.

Where property cannot be made subject to forfeiture as a result of its being secreted, destroyed, converted, or placed in the hands of third parties, the statute provides for the imposition of *fines in lieu* of forfeiture.[44] The criteria for imposition of such fines are that the property:

(a) cannot, or on the exercise of due diligence, be located
(b) has been transferred to a third party,
(c) is located out of Canada;
(d) has been substantially diminished in value or rendered worthless, or
(e) has been commingled with other property that cannot be divided without difficulty.[45]

The punishment provided under these provisions is onerous because the amount of the fine is limitless and is to be accompanied by a sliding scale of *mandatory* consecutive periods of incarceration which mirror the escalating value of the property and range from less than six months to five years in default of payment.

Another provision in the legislation which is of assistance in law enforcement is the 'inference provision'[46] which enables a court to infer that the property obtained by an accused was derived from commission of designated drug offences or enterprise crime offences in circumstances where the 'net worth' of the accused after commission of the offence exceeds that prior to commission of the offence and the court is satisfied that the income of that person from 'legitimate' sources cannot account for the increase in value. This is the 'net worth' method of establishing increases in wealth, often used in the revenue setting.

The court ordering forfeiture also has the power to set aside any transaction made after the seizure or restraint if not made for valuable consideration in good faith and without notice.[47] This provision is akin to the fraudulent preference provisions of many bankruptcy statutes and it is likely that the law in this area will be developed in a similar fashion.

Relief of Forfeiture

The *Code* also provides protection for third-party claims in the course of and even after forfeiture has been made. At the forfeiture hearing, for example, the Crown is required to provide notice to any person who appears to have a valid interest in the property. At the hearing, a person who

[44] *Code*, s. 462.37(4).
[45] *Code*, s. 462.37(3).
[46] *Code*, s. 462.39.
[47] *Code*, s. 462.4.

proves lawful entitlement to the property or any part thereof, other than a person charged with an enterprise crime or designated drug offence or a person who acquired title to or a right of possession of that property from a person charged with such an offence '... under circumstances that give rise to a reasonable inference that the title or right was transferred for the purpose of avoiding the forfeiture of the property,' may obtain relief from forfeiture.

Post-forfeiture claims of third parties may also be advanced within a period of 30 days following the making of an order of forfeiture; however, the terms for relief are somewhat more stringent, in that the person is not only required to establish the absence of 'taint' in the manner required by the pre-forfeiture relief provision, but also that he or she '... appears innocent of any complicity in any enterprise crime offence or designated drug offence that resulted in the forfeiture, or any collusion in relation to any such offence.'[48]

Any person aggrieved by an order to forfeiture may appeal to the Court of Appeal of the province.

Other Investigative Aids

There are additional provisions of Part XII. 2 of the *Code* which are of assistance to law enforcement agencies in proceeds of crime investigations. These include:

(a) the ability (in the case of investigations of designated drug offences) to apply to a superior court for release of relevant *Income Tax Act* information, which ordinarily would remain confidential;

(b) the ability to obtain an order for the interception of private communications ('wiretapping') for evidence of offences of money laundering and possession of proceeds of crime;

(c) a statutory protection for informants (typically, employees of banks or of financial institutions) who provide information to police or to the Attorney General on proceeds of crime matters; this provision is designed to counter allegations of breaches of client confidentiality made by customers who may be under investigation.

[48]In the context of Canadian Customs jurisprudence, a requirement to demonstrate innocence to obtain the return of seized goods was determined to be valid as a reasonable attempt to limit drug importation: *Knies* v *Deputy Minister of National Revenue, Customs and Excise* (1986), W.C.B. (2d) 353 (B.C. Co. Ct.).

The Mutual Legal Assistance in Criminal Matters Act

This legislation was proclaimed in 1988 and empowers Canada to enter into treaties to facilitate investigations in criminal matters. This statute enables the formation of treaties such as the one promulgated between Canada and the United States in January of 1990. This legislation considerably streamlines the process for obtaining judicial and other assistance in investigative matters and may include examining exhibits, exchanging information, locating or identifying persons, the execution of warrants to search, taking the evidence of persons, requiring production of documents, and transferring persons in custody for purpose of testimony. Requests under the treaties pursuant to this legislation are routed through the competent central authorities of each signatory. Presently, Canada is a signatory to treaties with the U.S., the U.K., Australia, Mexico, France, Hong Kong, the Bahamian Government, and the Netherlands.

Some Cases Conducted by the Toronto Regional Office

The Toronto Regional Office of the Department of Justice has conducted several proceeds of crime cases which have resulted in substantial forfeitures. In one of the first restraint-order cases in Canada, our offices obtained in April of 1989 an order 'freezing' some $13.5 million in U.S. funds on deposit in the Swiss Bank Canada which were linked to the U.S. operation 'Polar Cap' involving world-wide money laundering of funds derived from cocaine trafficking by the Medellin drug cartel. The order was obtained largely upon the strength of affidavit material supplied by the U.S. Drug Enforcement Administration and arose out of a primary investigation by the U.S. Attorney's Office in Atlanta, Georgia involving a Panamanian Bank, the *Banco Occidente*. At the time of the making of the Order in that case, our information was that the funds were to be the subject of a further transfer to an overseas account; our quick action in this case (the order was obtained the day after the request for assistance by the U.S. was received) enabled these funds ultimately to be transferred to a supervised account in Atlanta, Georgia where they were forfeited to the U.S. Government as part of a plea agreement which saw the offending bank plead guilty to the (then) largest money-laundering fine in U.S. history. As a result of the assistance rendered to U.S. prosecutors in this case, the Government of Canada received $1 million from the U.S. Government.

In the case of *Kutub Mesiwala*, an amount of $294,000.000 (U.S.) was ordered forfeited upon a plea agreement with U.S. authorities after a joint U.S.-Canada investigation of the accused, a medical doctor who was trafficking in "street" narcotics out of a medical clinic in a suburb of Detroit,

Michigan. The accused used family members to transport funds derived from this activity to Windsor, Ontario, where they were deposited in U.S.-dollar accounts. A 'tip' from a bank employee to the R.C.M.P. initiated the Canadian investigation. Ultimately, the accused entered a plea of guilty to a number of offences in the U.S. and was sentenced to a term of imprisonment, with virtually all his U.S. assets forfeited.

In October of 1989, a residence in North York, Toronto worth approximately $500,000.00 as well as a Mercedes vehicle were restrained and seized under the *Code* as part of a drug and proceeds of crime investigation involving a gang of Russian immigrants to Canada who were in the business of importing cocaine to Vancouver and using the proceeds of drug sales to buy real estate in the Toronto area (the *Filonoy* case). The residence in question was placed in the name of the father of the accused. Substantial evidence was accumulated showing an active cocaine-trafficking ring, as well as thorough documentary and financial evidence establishing a large increase in the 'net worth' of family members during the period of drug dealing. The case took a long time to resolve and during this period, two of the accused (the two sons) were murdered in underworld conflicts in the Vancouver area. Ultimately the father entered a plea of guilty and consented to the forfeiture of the residence, which was later sold.

The Toronto Regional Office has also recently successfully concluded prosecutions against money launderers. In one of the these cases, the accused (*Stefanelli*) had laundered monies derived from trafficking in cocaine through purchasing bank drafts in an estimated amount of from $300,000.00 to $400,000.00 over a period of about six months. The monies were derived from a sophisticated smuggling scheme in which hollowed-out compartments of Toyota cars were used by a syndicate to transport cocaine from Florida to Toronto for U.S. currency in return. This organization operated on a large scale, bringing in approximately 300 kilos of cocaine into Canada each month. The profit per kilo was in the range of $8,000.00 to $10,00.00. The accused in this case, who was actually linked to 32 bank drafts totalling some $176,00.00, received a sentence of 15 months' custody.

Conclusion

The amendments to the Canadian *Criminal Code* dealing with proceeds of crime represent a substantial initiative by the Government of Canada to combat the international and domestic profit made through crime. They offer law enforcement agencies substantial contemporary weapons with which to counter this international menance.

DRUG ABUSE LAWS OF BOTSWANA

P.T.C. Skelemani

The nations of the world have long realized that the fight against illicit drug trafficking and abuse has to be multidisciplinary. This also means that our several justice systems must always be reviewed to keep pace with the drug problems which are growing and becoming more complex by the day.

Each country, each region and continent must reexamine its system of justice. It is now clear that severe penalties alone cannot arrest the situation. It appears to me that a combination of the following measures in any justice system would go a long way towards meeting the drug challenge beyond the year 2000:

1. Appropriately severe sentences both in terms of imprisonment and fines.
2. Forfeitures of all proceeds of crime.
3. Rehabilitation of criminals and of the victims of illicit drug trafficking, that is, those who use or rather abuse the drugs.
4. Achievement of certain minimal developments to ensure provision of acceptable minimum standards of living. Employment creation.
5. Substitution of habit-forming plants with acceptable cash crops, for example, destroy poppy growing fields and replace these with other marketable cash crops.
6. Sustainable economic development with proper or equitable income distribution.

Regarding the penal provisions, we in Botswana have some experience. Our situation may not be the same as what obtains in other countries. When it appeared to us that trafficking in mandrax and other serious habit-forming drugs was getting out of hand we decided to impose a minimum punishment of 10 years and P 15,000 or 3 more years for dealing in these substances. As a result and fortunately for us cases of possession of habit forming drugs dropped dramatically such that it is now rare to have more than three cases of possession of mandrax and the like in a year. It can happen that a drop in the number of cases is a result of poor detection, or criminals adopting more sophisticated methods of transporting the drugs. I do not believe that in our case the drop was due to any of these reasons but rather the severity of the punishment and better detection methods which clearly discouraged the traffickers.

Stiff penalties in one country and lax laws in a neighbouring state cannot deal effectively with the problem. So that although we may not have uniform penal laws it is necessary that generally the laws must be severe in the whole region.

In compliance with the 1988 Treaty we have set a number of measures which we believe will go a long way towards thwarting the activities of drug traffickers. We have in place a law providing for the forfeiture of proceeds of serious crimes. Possession of or dealing in habit-forming drugs is a serious offence. Under this Proceeds of Serious Crimes Act it is possible to investigate a drug trafficker, locate the proceeds of the trafficking and apply to court for a forfeiture order.

In an attempt to close as many loopholes as possible we also recently passed another law cited as Corruption and Economic Crime Act No. 13 of 1994. Under this law we can require anyone who appears to live beyond his known sources of income to explain his wealth and if he cannot, he will be found guilty of an offence.

I firmly believe that everything ought to be done to strip criminals of all property acquired through any criminal activity.

The result of drug trafficking is not just the acquisition of lots of money by the traffickers. There are two other consequences which call for serious attention from each State. When the trafficker has been arrested, prosecuted and sent to prison, he cannot just be locked up until the last day of his sentence. It is necessary to take measures that can help reintegrate the criminal into the open society. Consequently, our prison system is designed to offer the inmates certain skills like carpentry, bricklaying, tailoring, welding etc. There must be a follow-up of those who have served their imprisonment to help them secure employment or help set themselves up with some cottage industry. Because of lack of resources we have not as yet set up programmes specifically tailored for ex-prisoners. There is however, a general programme of financial assistance under which anyone who wants to set up any industry gets assistance. For example, if one wanted to engage in tailoring, that person would be helped with money to buy sewing machines. Indeed, the government helps further by paying part of the wages of the unskilled labour. We have a long way to go but we have made a modest start.

Fortunately for us we do not have a big problem of drug abusers. Presently we only have small boys who sniff glue and ultimately become street children. This is a new phenomenon for which programmes are being worked out through non-governmental organizations.

It is generally believed that the greater the rate of unemployment, the greater the chances of people engaging in illegal activities. Idle minds will in most cases turn wayward. The majority of small-time and first-time criminals do it to make ends meet, to earn some income which means that if they had been gainfully employed they would not have been tempted to engage in criminal activities.

Many States unfortunately are unable to provide jobs or work opportunities for their ever-swelling populations. Hence, there is a great need for the more developed countries to help the less developed countries in their endeavours to create viable economies. The world has become a global village so that apart from humanitarian considerations, neighbours must help each other. If you do not help those States whose development lags so far behind that their people cannot but illegally produce and/or traffic in dangerous drugs, you are in the long run going to be the victim as the drugs will soon reach the more affluent societies who are the big consumers. One only hopes the United Nations will produce a comprehensive development plan for the world. For our part in our region we are trying out our hand at SADC, that is, the Southern African Development Community, of Angola, Botswana, Lesotho, Malawi, Mauritius, Mozambique, Namibia, South Africa, Swaziland, Tanzania, Zambia and Zimbabwe. We are thankful for the help we receive from all our friends and we look forward to greater cooperation in future.

It is in this field of cooperation that I think the world should help those countries that produce crops or plants from which dangerous drugs are produced to embark on crop substitution. Instead of the poppy fields we should see more and more coffee plantations and the like.

Cash crops which are in world-wide demand will be a good base for sustainable development. Whenever any country can achieve sustainable development, it is necessary that the country should also strive for an equitable system of income distribution. A skewed income distribution can only lead to instability in the end. Although I am not an economist, it is my view that each country must guard against marked income disparities. By 'income' I do not mean cash as in end of month take-home pay. No. In my view income distribution means ensuring that society as a whole has a certain acceptable minimum standard of living. Thus in my view a properly run economy is a mixture of capitalism and socialism. This can be achieved by the State providing certain basic necessities, for example, health facilities, education, pensions for the aged and destitute allowances which will ensure that all groups can afford the minimum living standard. We call it social mutual responsibility. We must encourage production of wealth by ensuring fair returns for capital that has been invested. We must ensure that labour is fairly rewarded. We must make it the responsibility of everyone to ensure that any disadvantaged member of our society is looked after. Simply put, we must contribute to a common pool from which the basic needs of all of us can be met.

I look at the system of justice as the justice that obtains in any society. That system may include the use of the court system but it need not. The justice system is a system that deals with the rights of the individual from birth to the very last day in the form in which we are today.

M.D.M.A. ('ECSTASY') IN ITALY: EPIDEMIOLOGY, POLICY AND LEGAL ASPECTS

Angelo Zaglio

On the basis of figures regarding the amounts of drugs and psychotropic substances intercepted and seized annually, the number of deaths related to illicit drug use, the number of drug users turning to public and private rehabilitation organizations etc., a significant change in drug consumption patterns in Italy is evident. A decline in the demand for opiates and anxiolytics is accompanied by an increasing market for stimulants, substances which can exalt an individual's personality. Accordingly, M.D.A (methil-dioxi-amphetamine) and M.D.E.A (methil-dioxi-ethil-amphetamine) are slowly disappearing from the Italian market, while M.D.M.A. (2-4 metil endiossi metamphetamine, or Ecstasy) consumption is progressively expanding, especially in environments frequented by young people for group recreation such as discos, large music concerts, rave parties etc. According to statistics on subjects involved in anti-drug operations, although heroin continued to be the most abused drug during 1995, M.D.M.A. registered an increase of 70% for the age group 18-24, a rate of increase higher than that of either hashish or marijuana which would normally be more popular among young people. This boom is the consequence of the creation of a market for Ecstasy over a three year period by certain national criminal organizations. M.D.M.A. abuse is thus clearly on the rise.

In Italy the National Committee for Co-ordination of Anti-Drug Actions formulates general policy and issues guidelines for action against the illegal production and distribution of narcotics and psychotropic substances nationally and internationally. In 1995 the police force and other agencies under the supervision of the Central Direction for Anti-Drug Action for Public Security (D.C.S.A) achieved considerable results. The volume of drugs and psychotropic substances intercepted and seized by the Police Force was at significant levels in both absolute (20 tons) and relative terms (with reference to M.D.M.A. - 155,000 tablets). However, preventive action by the police force is becoming increasingly difficult due to the peculiarities of stimulant drugs like M.D.M.A, such as the ease of production of such substances and the clandestine nature of marketing and distribution. Italian law also provides for the rehabilitation and treatment of drug dependence by registered agencies monitored by the Public Drug Dependence Service.

While non-therapeutic personal use of drugs and psychotropic substances is discouraged by Italian law through the imposition of criminal penalties, legal interventions concerning drug trafficking and sale need more attention, particularly because there is serious cause for concern over the increasing demand for Ecstasy.

DRUG POLICY AND DRUG CULTURE: NATIONAL EXPERIENCES FROM THE UNITED STATES AND MICRONESIA

Marke E. Wojcik[1]

The problems facing the world today, and our apparent inability to solve them, make for sobering reflection. But the fact is that we do possess the ability to eradicate poverty, guarantee health care for all, and curtail the flow of arms. What we lack is only the will—and the leadership—to address these troubles that affect our world.[2]

In crafting a global drugs law to address drug trafficking and drug use throughout the world, it will be important to consider the drug policies and drug cultures of many nations, large and small.[3] In the United States, politicians are claiming that domestic use of illegal narcotic drugs is on the decline and that crime rates attributable to drug use have also declined.[4] Public perceptions, however, often appear to be at odds with those state-

[1]The author thanks Messrs. Joseph E. Stauffer and David W. Austin for their assistance with research for this article, and Professors Ralph Ruebner and Nobert Gilmore for helpful suggestions concerning the intersections of civil rights and drug policies. The author also thanks Professor R.K. Nayak and the Indian Law Institute for the opportunity to participate in the Conference on Global Drugs Law, held in New Delhi, India. Finally, the author thanks Deans R. Gilbert Johnston and Susan Brody of The John Marshall Law School for their continuing support of his research.

[2]Oscar Arias, (Former President of Costa Rica, Nobel Peace Prize, 1987), *Of Arms Dealers and Dope Peddlers*, World Press Review, Feb. 1997, at 48 (reprinting an October 21, 1996 article from the English newspaper, *The Guardian*).

[3]See, e.g. Jean-Paul C. Grund, Drug Use as a Social Ritual: Functionality Symbolism and Determinants of Self-Regulation 257 (1993).

[4]President William J. Clinton, Message to the Congress of the United States Transmitting the National Drug Control Strategy (Apr. 29, 1996), reprinted in 32 Weekly Comp. Press. Docs. 757 (1996).

ments; people who see drug sales or who experience crimes related to drug use refuse to believe that drug use and crime are on the decline in the United States. This public attitude may in turn affect judicial attitudes in criminal cases related to drug use. Some judges may countenance infringements or outright violations of constitutional rights to protect the greater public good from the scourge of drugs.[5] This quandary poses a major public policy problem for the United States, as the nation will decide whether to abandon fundamental rights and liberties enshrined in federal and state constitutions in the name of a (perceived) greater social good, or to find a way to wage its war on drugs without sacrificing its own national values.

Small nations face similar issues. One of the states of the Western Caroline Islands is the Republic of Palau, a nation with a population of only 15,122. An increase in drug trafficking in Palau seems to have produced relatively severe judicial attitudes similar to those in the United States, and the court systems may tolerate infringements of civil rights to protect the public from drug traffickers.

National Experiences from the United States

Overview: Before his re-election in 1996, U.S. President Bill Clinton told the U.S. Congress that in the last few years the United States had made 'significant progress against drug use and related crime.'[6] President Clinton claimed that since 1992, the number of Americans who used cocaine decreased by 30 per cent.[7] He stated that the amount of money spent on illegal narcotic drugs also decreased by approximately 23 per cent from an estimated $64 billion dollars in 1991 to an estimated $49 billion U.S. dol-

[5]See, e.g. Todd Witten, Note, *Wilson* v. *Arkansas*; Thirty Years after Ker the Supreme Court Addresses the Knock and Announce Issue, 29 Akron L. Rev. 447 (1996).

[6]President William J. Clinton, Message to the Congress of the United States Transmitting the National Drug Control Strategy (Apr. 29, 1996), reprinted in 32 weekly Comp. Pres. Docs. 757 (1996).

[7]Id. The use of 1992 as a benchmark figure is no surprising in a document with important political implications within the United States. That was the year in which William J. Clinton was elected as President of the United States. The year 1996, in which the report was published, was the year in which he ran for re-election. The political implications are shaded by the knowledge that President Clinton had been challenged as being "soft on drugs" because of his admission that he had experimented with drugs in earlier years.

lars in 1993.[8] He announced that the number of murders within the United States related to the drug industry declined by 12 per cent since 1989 and that robberies declined by 10 per cent since 1991.[9]

President Clinton also proclaimed 'major success' in the arrest, prosecution, and dismantling of criminal drug networks within the United States. For example, the operational task forces of a 'High Intensity Drug Trafficking Programme' in Miami resulted in indictments of more than 250 individuals for drug trafficking and other drug-related criminal activities.[10] Another federal tool to assist local authorities in drug enforcement, the U.S. Drug Enforcement Administration's Mobile Enforcement Teams (MET), resulted in the arrests of more than 1,500 persons across the United States who were charged with violent or predatory crimes.[11]

Beyond the domestic gains claimed within the United States, President Clinton also pointed to important international developments in the global war on drugs. These developments include the arrests of major drug traffickers from Colombia, a multinational 'air interdiction programme' that closed the main air routes for smugglers between Peru and Colombia, and close cooperation between the United States and the governments of Peru, Colombia, and other countries to destroy the economic incentives to produce cocaine.[12] He also claimed credit for taking 'the serious step of cutting off all non-humanitarian aid to certain drug producing and trafficking nations that have not cooperated with the United States in [international]

[8]Id. "In 1993, the year from which the most recent data is available, Americans spent an estimated $ 49 billion on illegal drugs, $ 31 billion on cocaine, $ 7 billion on heroin, $9 billion on marijuana, and $ 2 billion on other illegal drugs."Executive Office of the President of the United States, the National Drug Control Strategy 11 (1996).

[9]President William J. Clinton, Message to the Congress of the United States Transmitting the National Drug Control Strategy (Apr. 29, 1996), reprinted in 32 Weekly Comp. Pres. Docs. 757 (1996). Critical readers and political scientists may question why each of these figures use an anonymous source when everything can be proven by statistics except the truth. The use of varying years certainly calls into question whether there are underlying policy considerations in the report that would shift if the figures were to use the same year for each category.

[10]Id.

[11]Id.

[12]Id. See also Linda Robinson, An Inferno Next Door; Mexico's Drug Gangs Buy the Officials they Can and Kill Those they can't I.S. News & World Rep. Feb. 24, 1997 at 36, 39.

narcotics.'[13] He also instructed U.S. government officials to block loan requests from the International Bank for Reconstruction and Development (the World Bank) and other multilateral development banks.[14] In President Clinton's words, these collective actions highlight 'the unwavering commitment of the United States to stand up against drug production and trafficking.'[15]

The emphasis on foreign action (rather than actions within the United States) is also reflected in the International Narcotics Control Strategy Report issued in 1996 by the Bureau of International Narcotics and Law Enforcement Affairs of the U.S. Department of State. In the transmittal letter for that document, President Clinton identified several countries—including India as "major illicit drug producing or drug transit countries.'[16] The nations or territories identified in the transmittal letter were Afghanistan, the Bahamas, Belize, Bolivia, Brazil, Burma, Cambodia, China, Colombia, the Dominican Republic, Ecuador, Guatemala, Haiti, Hong Kong, India, Iran, Jamaica, Laos, Lebanon, Malaysia, Mexico, Nigeria, Pakistan, Panama, Paraguay, Peru, Syria, Taiwan, Thailand, Venezuela, and Vietnam.[17] In the view of the United States government, foreign-based drug trafficking organizations are among other things, a 'direct and increasing threat to democracy and free market economies abroad, undermining U.S. efforts to make America more secure and competitive.'[18]

Social Reactions: In the United States there is a wide chasm between the successes claimed by President Clinton in the United States' war on illicit drugs and the public perceptions about drug use and its devastating effects. It would be inappropriate, however, to claim that there is any national consensus on drug policies in the United States. Instead, there is a

[13]See President William J. Clinton, Message to the Congress of the United States Transmitting the National Drug Control Strategy (Apr. 29, 1996), reprinted in 32 Weekly Comp. Pres. Docs. 757 (1996).

[14]Id.

[15]Id.

[16]Office of the White House Press Secretary. Text of a Letter from the President to the Chairmen and Ranking Members of the Senate Committee on Foreign Relations, the Senate Committee on Appropriations, the House Committee on Appropriations, and the House Committee on International Relations (Feb. 23, 1996), reprinted in United States Department of State Bureau for International Narcotics and Law Enforcement Affairs, International Narcotics Strategy Report vii (1996).

[17]Id

[18]Executive Office of President of the United States, the National Drug Control Strategy 41 (1996). Additionally, "[t]raffickers continue to corrupt governments at the highest levels, further thwarting international narcotics efforts." Id.

spectrum of private opinion that includes persons who abhor all drugs for personal or religious reasons,[19] persons who tolerate 'social' or 'recreational' use of drugs (and, in effect, treating most non-injection drug use on a level roughly comparable to social tolerance of alcohol[20] and tobacco[21] use), persons who promote expanded medical uses of drugs such as marijuana to alleviate some adverse symptoms of diseases and to increase appetites (factors important, for example, for persons living with HIV), and persons who support decriminalization[22] of most or even all drugs.

Having acknowledged that there is a spectrum of private opinion within the United States, it may be fair to say that for many persons in the United States, drugs are directly seen as a major scourge on society. Drugs are seen as the root cause of criminal activity that is often related to the habits of drug users whose personal financial resources are inadequate to support their consumption.[23] Indeed, drug cases are flooding the criminal courts of America's major cities and overcrowding prisons all across the country.[24] Drugs are seen to cause severe urban blight and the general decline of neighbourhoods. Drugs also cause severe social problems including homelessness. Intravenous drugs are also blamed for the spread of HIV

[19]See also M.K. Gandhi, Key to Health 17 (1948) ("There is a school who favour limited and regulated consumption of alcohol and believe it to be useful. I have not found any weight in their argument. Even if we were to accept their view for a moment, we have still to face the fact that innumerable human beings cannot be kept under discipline. Therefore, it becomes our duty to prohibit alcoholic drinks even if it were only for the sake of this vast majority.")

[20]But see M.K. Gandhi, Key to Health 17 (1948) ("Alcohol makes a man forget himself and while its effects last, he becomes utterly incapable of doing any thing useful. Those who take to drinking, ruin themselves and ruin their people. They lose all sense of decency and propriety.")

[21]But see M.K. Gandhi, Key to Health 21 (1948) ("Tobacco has simply worked havoc among mankind. Once caught in its tangle, it is rare to find anyone get out again. The use of tobacco is prevalent all over the world in one form or another. Tolstoy has called it the worst of all intoxicants. This verdict of that great man should command our attention and respect ... I can certainly say that I am not aware of a single advantage accruing from the use of Tobacco.")

[22]To some attorney and legislators, "decriminalization" may simply be an euphemism for "legalization."

[23]"Each year over one million persons are arrested on drug-related charges." Executive Office of The President of The United States, The National Drug Control Strategy 12 (1996).

[24]See, e.g., Editorial, A Court for Addicts, N.Y. Times, Feb 19, 1997 at A18.

through the sharing of contaminated needles.[25] Drugs are even blamed for the corruption of some domestic[26] and foreign[27] law enforcement officials who might be lured by huge payments of money in return for their silence. Thus, for many persons, a culture that seems to have accepted drugs has destroyed the trust that citizens should otherwise have in the abilities and integrity of their governments to cope with issues related (directly or indirectly) to drug use. The perceived inabilities of governments to deal effectively with these issues can lead to a sense of urban despair.

Some of these public perceptions about drugs ignore the fact that drugs are hardly a problem of only the inner cities of the United States. For example, a Gallup poll discovered that 45 per cent of Americans can report that they, or a close friend or family member, have used illegal drugs.[28]

On the other hand, many other persons, and particularly young persons, continue to be relatively ignorant or complacent about the real dangers of involvement with drugs or drug trafficking.[29] This ignorance or complacence may be related to diminished attention to the drug problem by national and local media, or it may be due to the entertainment and sports industries' fascination with drugs, which some would argue leads to the social legitimization of illicit drug use.[30]

[25] See, e.g. Norbert Gilmore, Public Health, AIDS, Drug Use, and Human Rights, in 3 Indian Law Institute, AIDS-Law Humanity 11, 36 (1995); Lawrence O. Gostin, Public Health and Human Rights in the AIDS Pandemic in 1 Indian Law Institute, AIDS-Law and Humanity 20, 24 (1995), Eric R. Ram, Children Made Orphans by AIDS, in 1 Indian Law Institute, AIDS-Law and Humanity 99, 103-04, 110 (1995).

[26] See, eg. Dan McGraw. The American Connection, U.S. News & World Rep., Feb. 24, 1997, at 40.

[27] See, e.g., Julia Preston, A General in Mexico's Drug War is Dismissed on Narcotics Charges, N.Y. Times, Feb. 19, 1997, at A1 (reporting that General Jesus Gutierrez Rebollo, [t] the army general" who headed Mexico's national drug agency has been dismissed from the armed forces and is being detained pending arrest on charges that he protected and accepted huge payments from one of Mexico's most notorious drug barons".)

[28] Executive Office of the President of the United States, The National Drug Control Strategy 11 (1996)

[29] See, e.g. Stephen Franklin, Peru Prison 'Nightmare in Hell' For Illinois Teen, Chicago Trib., Feb. 2, 1997, at 1 (relating the story of Jennifer Davis, an Illiniois teenager who agreed to smuggle cocaine out of Peru for $ 5,000 and who is now currently in prison in Peru).

[30] See President William J. Clinton, Message to the Congress of the United States Transmitting the National Drug Control Strategy (Apr. 29, 1996), reprinted in 32 Weekly Comp. Pres. Docs. 757 (1996).

Young people may see criticism of drug use as hypocrisy that is essentially indistinguishable from their parents' use of alcohol and tobacco. Young people may see only the relatively 'positive' aspects of life related to drugs. For inner city youth in Chicago, for example, a life related to the trafficking of drugs might bring social prestige and significant material rewards including flamboyant jewellery, expensive cars, and sexual opportunities. It is not uncommon to see young men or women, alone or in groups, with large rolls of dollars which onlookers understand to be the products of illegal drug trafficking or some related activity. The feelings of onlookers may be mixed. For some young people, the lure of instant and easy money may present a temptation too great to resist. Additionally, in places such as Dade County Florida for example, the large investments of drug traffickers reportedly contribute to increases in the value of local real estate.[31]

Thus despite American government pronouncements that the domestic use of certain drugs has declined in recent years, there is a public perception that general drug use is actually on the increase. For example, people may hear a report that cocaine use in the United States is decreasing but understand it to mean instead that heroin use is on the rise. There is concern about the rise in the 'popularity' among young people of crystalline methamphetamine.[32] Previously this drug was characterized by its use in certain areas of the United States or by only certain groups, such as motorcycle gangs.[33] Still other concerns are raised with the emergence of the drug Rohypnol, a drug manufactured in Colombia, Mexico, and Switzerland but not marketed lawfully within the United States.[34] The drug is reportedly seven to ten times more potent that Valium, and chronic use leads to physical dependence and the need for medically supervised withdrawal.[35] Because the drug is frequently used with alcohol, marijuana, and cocaine, it is popularly known as a 'date rape' drug because of its effects on memory loss when the drug is taken with alcohol.[36] In March of 1996,

[31]See Nora v. Demleitner, Organized Crime and Prohibition: What Difference Does Legalization Make?, 15 Whittier L. Rev. 613, 632 (1994).

[32]Executive Office of the President of the United States, The National Drug Control Strategy 12 (1996).

[33]Id. See also O'Brien, Chicago Trib., Feb. 17, 1997, sec. 2, at 1.

[34]Executive Office of the President of the United States, The National Drug Control Strategy 12 (1996).

[35]Id. Rohypnol is available by prescription in Europe and many other parts of the world. Id.

[36]Id.

the U.S. Customs Service began seizing Rohypnol at U.S. borders upon the advice of the U.S. Drug Enforcement Agency and U.S. Food and Drug Administration.[37]

In the context of debates on drug policies, the rights of drug users themselves are usually overlooked. Dr. Norbert Gilmore, a Professor of Medicine at the McGill Centre for Medicine, Ethics, and Law, is one of the few voices to speak out for the human rights of drug users.[38] Professor Gilmore laments that there is almost no discourse about the human rights of drug users,[39] although there is a growing appreciation generally of the important relationships between the protection of human rights and the promotion of public health.[40] Indeed, at the 1995 Conference on Global AIDS Law sponsored by the Indian Law Institute, Professor Gilmore reminded the distinguished members of the audience that:

> Public health stands at the interface between the state and the public, so that there is, naturally, tension between public health and the State on the one hand, and between public health and the public, on the other hand. This is illustrated by its responses to the threats presented by HIV infection and by drug use. With regard to drug use, there is growing awareness that many of the harms from drug use are health problems; that drug use can be a public health crisis as shown by the spread of HIV infection through the sharing of injection equipment; that drug use can be responsive to public health prevention strategies, in particular harm reduction ones; that harm reduction and public health approaches are complementary and, at times, indistinguishable; that promoting and

[37]Id.

[38]See, e.g. Norbert Gilmore, Public Health, AIDS, Drug Use, and Human Rights, in 3 India Law Institute, AIDS—Law and Humanity 11 (1995).

[39]See, e.g., Norbert Gilmore, Drug Use and Human Rights: Privacy Vulnerability, Disability, and Human Rights Infringements, 12 J. Contemp. Health L. & Pol'y 355 (1996).

[40]See, e.g., 41st World Health Assembly Resolution WHA 41.2.4, Avoidance of Discrimination in Relation to HIV-Infected People and People with AIDS (May 13, 1988), reprinted in Arthur S. Leonard et al., AIDS Law and Policy 527 (2d ed. 1995); United Nations Commission on Human Rights, Resolution on HIV/AIDS, Res. 1995/44, adopted Mar. 3, 1995, reprinted in United Nations Development Project on HIV and Development, *HIV Law, Ethics, and Human Rights* 376 (D.C. Jayasuriya, ed. 1995); Res. 1995/21, adopted Aug. 24, 1995, reprinted in United Nations Development Project on HIV and Development, *HIV Law, Ethics, and Human Rights* 372, 374 (D.C. Jayasuriya, ed. 1995).

protecting human rights is an essential component of efforts to respond to public health problems, even though the promotion and protection of public health is one of the interests which, sometimes, may justify the restriction of human rights. The overwhelming conclusion is that drug use is a public health concern, and that public health responses to it are essential. Responding to the challenge presented by drug use, however, places public health in conflict with the States, since almost every country has made the 'production, manufacture, export, import, distribution of, trade in, use, and possession' of many drugs illegal, and interventions such as teaching drug users how to inject their drugs safely and providing them with sterile needles and syringes to do so obviously conflicts with laws which are aimed at prohibiting the possession, and so the use, of proscribed drugs.[41]

Should America Tolerate Civil Rights Violations for the Greater Good?

More and more, America's War on Drugs seems to require the sacrifice of political and civil rights otherwise guaranteed by the federal and state constitutions.[42] There are also likely infringements of certain provisions of international human rights instruments including the Universal Declaration on Human Rights,[43] the International Covenant on Civil and Political Rights[44] and its optional protocol,[45] the International Covenant on Economic,

[41]Norbert Gilmore, Public Health, AIDS, Drug Use, and Human Rights, in 3 Indian Law Institute, AIDS-Law and Humanity 11, 35-36 (1995).

[42]See, Nora V. Demleitner, Organized Crime and Prohibition: What Difference Does Legalization Make?, 15 Whittier L. Rev. 613, 633 (1994).

[43]Universal Declaration of Human Rights, G.a. Res. 217A, U.N. GAOR, 3d Sess., U.N. Doc. A/810, at 71 (1948).

[44]International Covenant on Civil and Political Rights, G.A. Res. 2,200, U.N. GAOR, 21st sess., Supp. No. 16, at 52, U.N. Doc. A/6316 (1967) (adopted Dec. 16, 1996 and entered into force Mar. 23, 1976).

[45]G.A. Res. 2,200, U.N. GAOR, 21st sess., Supp. No. 16, at 59, U.N. Doc. A/ 6316 (1967) (adopted Dec. 16, 1966, entered into force Mar. 23, 1976). Under the Optional Protocol, 'individuals who claim that any of their rights enumerated in the Covenant [on Civil and Political Rights] have been violated and who have exhausted all available domestic remedies may submit written communications to the [United Nations] Human Rights Committee for consideration.' Report of the Human Rights Committee, 39 U.N. GAOR Supp. (No. 40) at 110, U.N. Doc. A/ 39/40 (1994). A State that ratifies the optional protocol thus subjects itself to the jurisdiction of the U.N. Human Rights Committee, and the State may not invoke

Social, and Cultural Rights,[46] or regional instruments such as the American Declaration on the Rights and Duties of Man.[47] It would be naive, however, to suggest that there might be immediate and universal agreement on the applicability of international human rights norms to issues relating to socially unacceptable drug use.[48]

Because American society finds itself torn on many issues related to drug policy, issues often turn on whether violations of civil rights should be tolerated in the perceived name of a greater social good. Often the public debate must overcome the standard political rhetoric, such as that introduced by President Richard Nixon in the 1970s when he declared a 'war on drugs.'[49] In the 1980s Nancy Reagan, the wife of President Ronald Reagan, used a widely publicized campaign to urge young people to 'just say no' to drugs.

In the civil rights realm, however, it is not only the young people who should be saying 'no.' Judges, who are installed under the federal and

'considerations of domestic policy ... to prevent the Committee from considering claims from individuals subject to the State party's jurisdiction.' Views of the Human Rights Committee under Article 5, paragraph 4, of the Optional Protocol to the International Covenant on Civil and Political Rights (51st Sess.) concerning Communication No.414/1900, at 2-6, U.N. Doc. CCPR/C/51/D/414/1990 (1994).

[46]International Covenant of Economic, Social and Cultural Rights, adopted Dec. 19, 1966, entered into force Jan. 3, 1976, 999 U.N.T.S. 3, reprinted in Richard B. Lillich and Hurst Hannum, International Human Rights—Documentary Supplement 23, 24 (1995).

[47]American Declaration on the Rights and Duties of Man, O.A.S. Res. XXX, adopted by the Ninth International Conference of American States, Bogota, Colombia, Mar. 30-May 2, 1948, OEA/Ser. L./V/II.23/doc. 2 rev. 6, reprinted in Richard B. Lillich, International Human Right Instruments 430.1 (2d ed. 1990).

[48]Other objections have been raised in many contexts. For example, in considering objections from the Islamic Republic of Iran that international human rights norms were incompatible with Islamic law, a Special Representative of the United Nations Commission on Human Rights states: 'States of all political, economic, social, cultural, and religious persuasions participated in the drafting of the Charter [of the United Nations], the Universal Declaration of Human Rights and the International Covenant on Human Rights. The Universal Declaration of Human Rights and the International Covenants thus contain norms which, distilled from the collective experience and the common heritage of the world's peoples, represent universal standards of conduct for all peoples and all nations.' Preliminary Report by the Special Representative of the Commission on Human Rights on the Human Rights Situation in the Islamic Republic of Iran, at 3-9, U.N. Doc. E/CN.4/1985/20 (1985).

[49]See, E.g., Todd Witten, Note, *Wilson* v. *Arkansas*: Thirty Years after Ker the Supreme Court Addresses the Knock and Announce Issue, 29 Akron L. Rev. 447, 456 (1996).

state constitutions to uphold rights guaranteed in those documents, must also say 'no' when they are asked to ignore constitutional mandates. For example, one commentator notes: 'Faced regularly with the grim results of the illegal drug trade, the judiciary may be tempted to offer aid to the Government in its War on Drugs. But no matter how pressing the perceived need, the judiciary is simply without authority to trim back the Fourth Amendment [to the U.S. Constitution].'[50] The Fourth Amendment provides that '[t]he right of the people to be secured in their persons, houses, papers, and effects, against unreasonable searches and seizures, shall not be violated, and no Warrants shall issue, but upon probable cause supported by Oath or affirmation, and particularly describing the place to be searched, and persons or things to be seized.'[51]

Several court decisions can be read to suggest that courts have, from time to time, sacrificed individual civil rights for the sake of the greater good. The U.S. Supreme Court found in cases such as *Arizona* v. *Evans*[52] and *Murray* v. *United States*[53] that the Fourth Amendment to the U.S. Constitution does not expressly exclude the use of evidence that is obtained in violation of the Fourth Amendment. Civil rights advocates have questioned what incentives a narcotics officer might have to observe its requirements.[54] The U.S. Supreme Court also found that a police officer need not inform a person that he or she is free to go before asking for consent to a search for narcotic drugs and other contraband.[55] On the international level, the U.S. Supreme Court has also countenanced Mexico.[56]

Thus, although it may be uniformly acknowledged that the problems faced by the United States are serious, they can justify neither the violation of civil rights nor the abandonment of constitutional principles. Accordingly, efforts by the courts and prosecutors to bring the guilty to punishment must not sacrifice 'those great principles established by years of endeavor and suffering which have resulted in their embodiment in the fundamental law of the land.'[57]

[50]Id. at 456 n.12 (citing Charles P. Garcia, Note, The Knock and Announce Rule: A New Approach to the Destruction of Evidence Exception, 93 Colum. L. Rev. 685, 685 (1993)).

[51]U.S. Const. art. IV.

[52]*Arrona v. Evans*, 115 S. Ct. 1185 (1995).

[53]*Murray v. United* States, 487 U.S. 533 (1988).

[54]See, e.g., Murray, 487 U.S. at 544-47 (Marshall, J., dissenting).

[55]*Ohio v. Robinette*, 117 S. Ct. 417, 421 (1996). In that case, a police officer discovered a small amount of marijuana and, in a film container, a pill later determined to be methylenedioxymethamphetamine. Id. at 419.

[56]*United States v. Alvarez-Machain*, 504 U.S. 655 (1992).

[57]*Murray v. United States,s* 487 U.S. 533, 551 (1988) (Stevens, J., dissenting (quoting *Weeks v. United States*, 232 U.S. 383 (1914).

National Experiences from the Republic of Palau

Overview: The Republic of Palau is the world's newest nation. As the last Trust Territory under the United Nations Trusteeship system,[58] the Palau islands and other parts of Micronesia had been administered by the United States since the end of World War II. Before that time the Micronesian territories had been administered by Japan under a Mandate from the League of Nations. Most of the territory became the Federated States of Micronesia. The most westward group of islands—the islands of Palau-became an independent country on October 1, 1994[59] and a member of the United Nations on December 15, 1994.[60] Although the country has diplomatic ties with many countries,[61] Palau is a country in Free Association with the United States, meaning that it still has several important contacts and privileges with the United States. Palau is also near the Philippines, and there are several flights each week from Manila to Koror and frequent visits from shipping vessels.

The Philippines is known as a transit point for heroin and crystal methamphetamine; it is also an exporter of locally grown marijuana and hashish produced for export to the Pacific, East Asia, Europe, Australia, and the United States.[62] Heroin seizures at the Philippines' international airports declined in 1995, suggesting that drug traffickers may have shifted their use of the Philippines as a transhipment point for drugs.[63] One possibility is that some of that trafficking may have shifted quietly to the Republic of Palau.[64]

Cases involving illegal drugs increased in the Republic of Palau from 1991 to 1993.[65] Although the overall levels of drug trafficking are small, they must be viewed in the context of Palau itself; the nation has only 15,122 persons (as of the 1992 census). Cases frequently involve highly

[58]The Trust Territory of the Pacific Islands (TTPI) was designated as a Strategic Trust Territory under Article 83 of the U.N. Charter. As a Strategic Trust Territory, ultimate authority over the territory resided with the U.N. Trusteeship Council. See Mark E. Wojcik, T*he Quest for Harmony: A Pictorial History of Law and Justice in the Republic of Palau* 62 (1995).

[59]See, e.g., Palau Is Free, Tia Belau, Oct. 1, 1994, at 1.

[60]See, e.g., Palau Admitted to UN, Tia Belau, Dec., 17, 1994, at 1.

[61]See, e.g., Palau and India Tie Diplomatically, Tia Belau, Apr. 22, 1995, at 9.

[62]See, e.g., United States Department of State Bureau for International Narcotics and Law Enforcement Affairs, International Narcotics Strategy Report 292 (1996).

[63]Id. at 292-93.

[64]See, e.g., Filipino Busted for "Ice" Smuggling, Tia Belau, Feb. 11, 1995.

[65]See Tia Belau, Aug. 27, 1994, at 9.

respected citizens and others implicated in connection with attempted drug trafficking.[66]

An Illustrative Case: One case from the Republic of Palau illustrates some of the problems faced in that country. Felix Minor was convicted of attempted trafficking in crystalline methamphetamine, a controlled substance commonly known in Palau (and other countries) as 'ice.'[67] He was convicted of attempted trafficking in connection with the shipment to Palau of a carton that contained a cooler of prawns that were sent from the Philippines in 1993.[68] A Palauan customs officer inspecting the cooler found a suspicious soft spot in the lid of the cooler.[69] Using a knife, the customs officer removed a portion of the cooler lid and found that some of the foam insulation had been cut out to create a 'secret compartment' in the lid of the cooler.[70] Inside the secret compartment the customs officer found two plastic bags containing a substance similar in appearance to crushed ice.[71] Subsequent laboratory tests showed that the substance was approximately 125 grams of crystalline methamphetamine ('ice').[72] Experts testified before the trial court that persons in possession of more than three grams of ice usually intend to distribute the drug.[73]

The customs officer and the local police contacted Felix Minor the following morning to ask him to pick up the carton that was addressed to him.[74] Minor refused to collect the package, stating that he was not ex-

[66]See, e.g., Sungino Charged With 'Ice' Conspiracy, Tia Belau, Oct. 29, 1994, at 3; Peleliu Bust Scores $ Million in Weeds, Tia Belau, Oct. 29, 1994, Police Under Investigation for Peleliu Raid, Tias Belau, Nov. 12, 1994, at 3; Japanese to be Tried for Peleliu Marijuana Bust, Tia Belau, May 20, 1995; Sungino Found Guilty in "Ice" Conspiracy, Tia Belau, May 21, 1995, at 1; Japanese Guilty of Marijuana Trafficking and Possession, Tia Belau, June 4 1995, at 1; Airline Employee Nabbed for 'Ice' Trafficking, Tia Belau, July 1, 1995, at 3.

[67]*Minor v. Republic* of Palau, 5 ROP Interm. 1, 1 (1994).

[67]Id. at 1.

[68]Id. at 1.

[69]Id.

[70]Id.

[71]Id. at 1-2,

[72]Id. at 2.

[73]Id.

[74]Id.

pecting any shipment from the Philippines.[75] He refused to claim the shipment or to pick up the cooler.[76]

The following week the police officers executed a search warrant of Minor's house.[77] In his basement they found a cooler with a lid that had a secret compartment formed by cutting out part of the styrofoam lid, similar to the cooler that was found with the ice.[78] Minor admitted that the cooler in his basement was his property, and that it had been used for a shipment from the Philippines.[79] The police also found shipping documents related to several other shipments from the Philippines and certain cash transactions.[80]

Based on this evidence, the trial division of the Palau Supreme Court[81] found Minor guilty of attempting to traffic a controlled substance.[82] Minor was sentenced to ten years' imprisonment, although the execution of his sentence was suspended except for the first year of imprisonment.[83] The appellate division of the Palau Supreme Court found sufficient evidence to support the trial court's determination of guilt.[84] The cooler containing the ice was addressed to Minor, as was the outside carton in which the cooler was shipped.[85] Shipping documents accompanying the shipment were also addressed to him, and there were payment records between him and the shipper in the Philippines.[86] Finally, and most likely decidedly, the discov-

[75]Id. Minor denied that the shipment was his and stated that he would only accept the shipment if it were first opened by a customs agent. Minor was likely suspicious for the additional reason that there were no flights from the Philippines on the day when he was called to collect a shipment from the Philippines. Because Palau is such a small country, the flight schedules are commonly known by people who do regular business at the airport. Furthermore, Minor had been stopped three months earlier on a charge of attempting to import 'ice', but this charge was later dismissed because one of the law enforcement officers admitted to committing perjury in connection with obtaining a search warrant.

[76]Id.

[77]Id.

[78]Id.

[79]Id.

[80]Id.

[81]The Palau Supreme Court consists of a trial division and appellate division. See Palau Const. art. X, $ 2.

[82]Minor, 5 ROP Interm. at 2. Under the Palau National Code, the offence of trafficking includes possession of a controlled substance with the intent to distribute it. 34 P.N.C. $ 3301(a) (1).

[83]*Minor v. Republic* of Palau, 5 ROP Intrm. 1, 3 (1994).

[84]Id.

[85]Id. at 3-4.

[86]Id. at 4.

ery of a similar cooler in Minor's basement with a similar 'secret compartment' suggested to the court that Minor should be found guilty of attempted trafficking.[87]

Although Minor's conviction was affirmed, the court found that the sentence imposed exceeded the maximum punishment prescribed for drug trafficking.[88] The court undertook a review of the sentencing issue even though it had not been raised by the defense attorney or attorney general.[89] Under the version of the Palau Controlled Substances Act then in effect, methamphetamine was classified as a Schedule II controlled substance.[90] Trafficking in a 'narcotic drug' classified in Schedule II was punishable by ten years' imprisonment.[91] Trafficking in other substances, however, was punishable only by five years' imprisonment.[92]

Palau's Controlled Substances Act had not been revised in several years. It defined a 'narcotic drug' as 'opium, opiates and any extracts, derivatives, or chemical equivalent thereof and coca leaves and any derivative or chemical equivalent.'[93] The Appellate Division of the Supreme Court accordingly found that the trial court had exceeded its sentencing authority, as the maximum imprisonment for attempted trafficking of ice was only five years.[94]

The Minor case illustrates at least two important principles. First, the desire to convict someone of attempted trafficking in narcotic drugs may overshadow an individual's connection with drugs. Minor was convicted for the attempted trafficking of a carton that he never claimed, never expected, and never opened. Many would wonder whether someone who never claims an article could intend to distribute it. Second, the sentencing of a criminal defendant beyond the statutory limits can suggest a judicial desire to lock drug traffickers away for as long as possible. If people are to be locked up and thrown away, it should at least be done in accordance with the limits expressed by statute.

[87]Id.

[88]Id. (citing 34 P.N.C. $ 3305 (Palau National Code).

[89]Id. (citing Republic of Palau Criminal Procedure Rule 52(b) and *United States v. Green*, 735 F.2d 1203, 1205 (9th Cir. 1984).

[90]Id. citing 34 P.N.C. $ 3301(b)(1)).

[91]Id. (citing 34 P.N.C. $ 3301(b)(1)).

[92]Id. (citing 34 P.N.C. $ 3301(b)(2)).

[93]Id. (citing 34 P.N.C. $ 3301(q)).

[94]Id. (citing 34 P.N.C. $ 3301(b)(2)).

Conclusion

Drugs present a serious problem in both the United States and the Republic of Palau. While politicians in the United States claim that domestic use of illegal narcotic drugs is decreasing,[95] the general public still sees drug sales and still experiences crimes related to drug use. The public attitude that refuses to believe that drug use and crime are on the decline in the United States—and in Palau—may adversely affect judicial attitudes in criminal cases so that some judges may sacrifice constitutional rights in the course of hearing criminal cases.[96]

Oscar Arias, a former President of Costa Rica and a recipient of the Nobel Peace Prize in 1987, noted that although the world faces serious problems, 'the fact is that we do possess the ability to eradicate poverty, guarantee health care for all, and curtail the flow of arms. What we lack is only the will and the leadership to address these troubles that affect our world.'[97] He made these observations in response to U.S. President Bill Clinton's statement to the U.N. General Assembly that 'in the post cold war era, the world's most pressing threats are drug trafficking and terrorism.'[98] President Arias admits that these are issues of great magnitude, but states that 'they are only manifestations of other, more fundamental issues.'[99] His words point out that the debate is far from over, and that many issues need to be considered in the context of terrorism and drug trafficking.

The growth of poverty and inequality, the continued denial of democratic freedoms and basic human rights, environmental degradation, slow progress in health and education, the social impact of technological change, the external debt in developing countries, and corruption are the sources of conflict that can lead to terrorism and drug trafficking. These are the fundamental issues that the international community must address.[100]

[95]President William J. Clinton, Message to the Congress of the United States Transmitting the National Drug Control Strategy (Apr. 29, 1996), reprinted in 32 Weekly Comp. Pres. Docs. 757 (1996).

[96]See, e.g., Todd Witten, Note, *Wilson* v. *Arkansas*: Thirty Years after Ker the Supreme Court Addresses the Knock and Announce Issue, 29 Akron L. Rev. 447 (1996).

[97]Oscar Arias, *Of Arms Dealers and Dope Peddlers*, World Press Review, Feb. 1997, at 48 (reprinting an October 21, 1996 article from the English newspaper,

PART IV

SPECIFIC ISSUES

THE CRIMINAL JUSTICE SYSTEM AND THE TREATMENT OF DRUG MISUSE

Hamid Ghodse

The relationships between drug misuse and crime are well known and can take different forms. For example, there is a small group who, as a result of drug taking, have changed their behaviour from non-delinquent to delinquent; another group consists of those who commit crime, out of economic necessity, to pay for their expensive habit; and there is also a group for whom drug-taking is jut an extension of their criminal way of life. These models may be helpful in considering the relationship between treatment and the criminal justice system. Thus, if misusers are committing crime to feed an expensive habit, that is if an economic model predominates, there is perhaps an argument for doctors to prescribe for addicts, to avoid the commission of crime. However, if crime precedes drug taking, it could be argued that there should be greater attention paid to stopping criminality; although in one UK study, where 50 per cent of subjects were found to have committed a crime before being arrested for drugs, most also continued to take drugs after being caught, implying that contact with the criminal justice system had no impact on their drug-taking. In this complex arena it is important that the different systems work together effectively, but inevitably there are tensions in this approach.

I would firstly like to examine, very briefly, how treatment programs can impact on crime and, secondly to explore how the criminal justice system can interact with treatment programs.

Treatment, of course, is important, because of its effect in reducing demand for drugs. A *cured* addict/ drug misuser doesn't seek drugs and, in addition, will not introduce others to drugs; and although health care professionals may argue vigorously about the comparative effectiveness of different treatment approaches, one fact is rarely discussed—that the very existence of treatment programs, whatever their nature, offers hope to drug misusers that their condition is treatable. This encourages people to try giving up rather than continuing to misuse drugs for ever and this, I believe, probably has a major, if intangible effect on drug related crime and the criminal justice system.

Obviously if drug misusers are to be treated they have to be attracted into treatment programs, preferably at an early stage of their drug-taking career. For this reason, there has been an explosion over the last few years of community based, outreach programs aimed at making services easily accessible. To attract dependent opiate-users into treatment, and to retain them in treatment while individualized care plans are prepared and agreed upon it is often necessary to prescribe for them, at least in the short-term, before drug withdrawal can be started—and this poses a dilemma. Prescribing liberally risks making a non-dependent user into a *legal* addict; having stringent criteria before prescribing risks alienating the very people you are trying to help. Furthermore, if low threshold community based treatment centres become too popular, they may encourage the congregation of large numbers of drug misusers and facilitate drug dealing.

Drug withdrawal—detoxification—is clearly only the first stage of treatment. Some would say that coming off is easy, and that it is the longer term problem of staying off that is more difficult. Certainly, relapse prevention is a crucially important element of all treatment programs and encompasses a variety of therapeutic interventions, such as counselling, group work, vocational therapy etc. But the important point is that it is long-term and that it may not be immediately successful. Substance dependence, like many other medical conditions (such as leukaemia or multiple sclerosis) is a relapsing condition and resumption of drug taking should be interpreted as evidence of the severity of dependence rather than the *fault* of the individual, reflecting *weak will* and lack of motivation. Indeed, physiological evidence of opiate dependence persists for months after drug withdrawal has been completed, so that punitive responses to relapse from the criminal justice system are inappropriate.

An alternative approach to drug withdrawal is the provision of long-term maintenance treatment. This is appropriate only for those who are dependent on opiates who may be prescribed methadone or another opioid as a substitute for the illicit heroin which they have been taking. While the legal provision of a drug of dependence can hardly be considered treatment, because the user continues to be dependent, in theory it should reduce involvement in illegal activities. However, it requires the prescription of just the *right* amount of methadone, so that the patient has to take all of it personally to prevent the onset of withdrawal, and has no surplus to produce euphoria or to sell. Even so, some may continue to be involved in the illicit drug market, using their maintenance prescription as just one of several sources of supply.

Because of the potential benefits of treating drug misusers, there has been a trend amongst law enforcement agencies of dealing with the problem in this way, rather than by only using a punitive approach. For example, there is a growing number of arrest referral schemes, whereby those arrested for drug-related offences are advised about access to local treatment programs, and some police forces work closely with these programs and their specialist workers. It is worth noting that the time of arrest often offers a window of opportunity when a drug misuser, who has previously rejected treatment intervention, may be particularly receptive to advice and treatment, not least because of the belief that it may be advantageous in a forthcoming court case. However, drug workers should be used in addition to, and not as a substitute for, qualified legal advice.

The treatment of drug misuse may also be one component of a community penalty for a drug-related offence, typically as part of a probation order. In this situation, the probation service itself may provide treatment programs, often in partnership with specialist agencies, such as community drug teams, drug dependency units, self-help organizations such as Narcotics Anonymous, or residential therapeutic communities. In the United States, compulsory drug testing may also be required, providing evidence of compliance, or non-compliance with treatment programs, but posing new legal and ethical dilemmas. In all of these programs, the element of coercion, whether formal or informal, impacts on the therapeutic process, changing the therapeutic relationship between the health care professional and the drug misuser. It also has implications for issues such as client confidentiality. However, evidence from the United States suggests that this sort of coercion is an effective way of getting drug misusers into treatment, and keeping them there, and that they seem to do as well as those entering treatment entirely voluntarily.

Finally, it is important to consider the treatment and the management of drug misuse within prisons, because many drug misusers pass through the prison system at some stage in their career, and for some it may be the first time that their dependent state has been formally identified. The wide availability of drugs within prisons, their importance within the prison economy, and the concentration of drug misusers all contribute to the difficulty of managing the problem. Nevertheless, in theory prisons could offer important opportunities for initiating treatment with detoxification and reduction prescribing, although it is essential that this is followed up with treatment strategies aimed at preventing relapse after discharge into an external environment that is completely different from that in prison.

Maintenance prescribing is uncommon in prison, although some argue that prisoners on short term remand who have been receiving opiate maintenance before admission should continue to do so. Most people would agree however, that it is not possible to provide sterile injection equipment in prison because this would constitute overt support for an illegal activity—although, given the risks posed by HIV/AIDS in prison, this sort of approach cannot be ignored.

Given the magnitude of the drug problem within the prison system, it is essential that more people working there are trained in the management of drug misuse—its prevention, detection and treatment—and that treatment approaches that are appropriate for the prison environment are developed. There has been little evaluation of these so far although evidence from the United States suggests that prison-based therapeutic communities, *drug-free wings* and cognitive-behavioural programs may all be promising.

The examples that I have outlined suggest that it is possible for the criminal justice system and treatment services to work together, although the underlying philosophical difference between the two should not be underestimated. For example, the only goal for law enforcement agencies may be to achieve abstinence whereas many treatment services first seek to improve the health of substance misusers, seeing this as a necessary first step on the road to abstinence.

The difference in approach can be illustrated by some practical experiences: for example, the introduction of compulsory urine-testing in prison, intended to prevent substance misuse through the deterrent effect of detection, may have the unintended effect of increasing opiate abuse, as inmates learn that opiates are less likely to be detected than cannabis because of their shorter half-life. Similarly, the single-minded focus on abstinence results in less emphasis being placed on the longer-term goal of rehabilitation, whereas a combination of both approaches is most likely to benefit the individual.

However, in practice, many law enforcement systems are overwhelmed by the dimensions of today's world-wide drug abuse epidemic with the expansion of production, trafficking and abuse into regions not previously affected. This results in police agencies and courts being flooded with cases, particularly involving low-level offenders, leaving few resources for authorities to go after the higher echelon traffickers, whereas countries could and should set a higher priority on apprehending and punishing high-level drug criminals. In contrast, alternatives to prison sentences should be considered for those convicted of possessing small amounts of illicit drugs. Incidentally, both the high number of drug-related convictions and an increasing length of prison sentences can adversely affect prison conditions.

The increased availability of drugs in prisons, the related risk of HIV and other infections, and the exposure of young offenders to a school of crime within the prison, can be cited as side effects of law enforcement and criminal justice policies that require close consideration. This makes it all the more important to consider psychological and social treatment programs for some addicts as a cost-effective alternative to imprisonment.

In addition, an arrest and/or conviction may be sufficient to motivate a drug abuser to undergo treatment and not become more deeply involved in criminality. For example, in France, completion of a prescribed course of treatment can provide grounds for not prosecuting a drug offence; alternatively, addicts may present themselves anonymously for treatment. In Malaysia, if an arrestee yields a positive result on a urine test, a magistrate may order him/her to attend a rehabilitation centre under strict conditions. In Portugal, when drug-dependent offenders sentenced for certain drug crimes voluntarily seek treatment, the court may suspend the punishment, although if the addict fails to take the required treatment, the suspended punishment may be imposed.

In the United States of America, in some states, special drug courts have been established to cope with the large number of minor drug offenders entering the criminal justice system. The special courts, while retaining the power to deal with offenders, send those charged with relatively minor offences to education, treatment or vocational assistance programs. At the end of the program a person could have the charge dismissed or be placed on probation. In Venezuela, a person possessing a small quantity of an illicit drug for personal use but not having been arrested for any crime, is tested in a prevention centre; if found to be an addict, he or she must undergo compulsory treatment.

The above examples demonstrate a variety of ways in which the criminal justice system is working closely with treatment services. However, it must be clarified and emphasized that this approach does not imply the decriminalization of drug related offences.

The way forward, towards achieving the *best of both worlds* for addicts, surely lies in increased collaboration between the criminal justice and health care systems, beginning with improved staff training as well as inter and intra-agency liaison and resulting in more people entering treatment, hopefully at an earlier stage.

Opportunities for greater collaborative working include court referral and diversion schemes, greater use of bail hostels, and pre-sentence reports containing clear treatment proposals. Counselling services working in prisons could be very useful, although aftercare following release is of comparable importance.

Treatment, rehabilitation and social re-integration involve much more than simply supplying licit drugs as a substitute of illicit drug abuse. Ideally, treatment and care should be mult-disiciplinary and multi-agency, while law enforcement agencies and the judiciary can contribute a great deal to demand reduction strategies and together with other sectors, both statutory and non-statutory, governmental and non-governmental, undermine the activities of drug traffickers and criminals. Demand reduction including treatment, rehabilitation, social integration, education and prevention are very socio-culturally sensitive and provision for them must therefore be responsive to the norms of the community to ensure their success.

In contrast, supply reduction, which is also of the utmost importance, has international dimensions in almost every respect and requires the full coordination of all communities in the world and hence the existence of the International Conventions. Universal ratification of the Conventions and implementation of their provisions by all parties with their full cooperation and collaboration in all areas covered by the three conventions provide opportunities for demand reduction activities to be both culturally responsive and successful. The hope for the future is that there will be universal commitment to the fulfillment of the aims and objectives of the Conventions.

ACCESSIBILITY TO PAIN KILLERS AND INTERNATIONAL DRUG CONTROL TREATIES

D.C. Jayasuriya

In the mid-1980s it was estimated by the World Health Organization that some 3.5 million patients with cancer were needlessly suffering from pain due to difficulties in having access to pain killers.[1] The attention of the international community to this situation was also drawn by the International Narcotics Control Board (Board), the International Union Against Cancer and the International Federation of Pharmaceutical Manufacturers Associations.

Responding to the above concerns, the United Nations Economic and Social Council adopted a resolution in 1988[2] requesting the Board to review the demand for and supply of opiates for medical and scientific purposes and to enter into a dialogue with interested governments and other parties. By a subsequent resolution adopted in 1989[3], the Council requested the Board to assess legitimate needs for opiates in various countries in the world hitherto unmet because of insufficient health care, difficult economic situations or other conditions.

Pursuant to the above resolutions, the Board published in 1989 a report entitled 'Demand for and Supply of Opiates for Medical and Scientific Needs'[4] based on studies done in selected countries to ascertain the availability of opiates for medical purposes. The Board pointed out that: 'Evidence available suggests that medical needs for opiates, particularly that related to the treatment of cancer pain, is not being satisfied'.[5] The impediments to medical availability of opiates were documented in relation to the follow-

[1] W.H.O. *Cancer Pain Relief*, Geneva, 1986.

[2] Economic and Social Council Resolution 1988/10.

[3] Economic and Social Council Resolution 1989/15.

[4] United Nations. International Narcotics Control Board. *Demand for and Supply of Opiates for Medical and Scientific Needs*. New York, 1989 (E/INCB/1989/1/Supp.)

[5] *Ibid*, p 17.

ing three problems areas: (a) impediments in health care system; (b) impediments in legislation and administration; and (c) impediments associated with professional practices.

Based on the findings, the Board formulated a series of recommendations addressed to Governments, World Health Organization, and professional associations and medical instructors.

The above recommendations were accorded wide publicity by the Secretariat of the Board, the World Health Organization and others.[6] In 1995 the Board conducted a study[7] to evaluate the extent to which the recommendations made in the 1989 report had been implemented by various countries. The questionnaire prepared for the purpose was transmitted to the Governments of 209 countries and territories and approximately one-third responded to it.

While over sixty countries around the world had established or were in the process of establishing national cancer control programs with emphasis on pain management, many countries noted that there were still factors that impeded the medical use of opiates. While some of the impediments were common to a large number of reporting governments, others were of concern only to a few governments. The impediments noted, the number of reporting governments and the response rate are given below in Table 1:

Table 1
Factors that Impede the Medical Use of Opiates

Number of reporting governments	*Response rate (percentage)*	*Impediment*
23	72	Concerns about addiction to opiates
19	59	Insufficient training of health-care professionals about opiates
19	59	Laws or regulations that restrict opiate manufacture, distribution, prescription or dispensing
15	47	Reluctance to prescribe or stock opiates because of concerns about legal sanctions
12	38	Reluctance to stock opiates because of concerns about theft or robbery

...contd.

[6] See, for instance, Jayasuriya, D.C. 'Analgesics and Cancer Patients: Legal and Policy Impediments', *Health Action*, March 1991, 27-28.

[7] United Nations, International Narcotics Control Board. *Availability of Opiates for Medical Needs*, New York 1996.

Table 1 (contd.)

Number of reporting governments	*Response rate (percentage)*	*Impediment*
12	38	Administrative burden of regulatory requirements for opiates
11	34	Insufficient import or ı.ıanufacture of needed opiates
11	34	Potential for opiate diversion
10	31	Cost of opiate medications
7	22	Insufficient health-care resources, personnel and facilities
6	19	Administrative burden of import-export requirements
5	16	Problems in the opiate distribution system
4	13	Absence of national policy or guidelines

Source: United Nations. International Narcotics Control Board. *Availability of Opiates for Medical Needs*', New York, 1996, p 5.

The principal international drug control treaties are structured on the premise that certain drugs of abuse with proven therapeutic value must be readily available but under controlled conditions to prevent their abuse or misuse.

In translating the treaty objectives into national legislation, countries have adopted different approaches. These have, to varying degrees, impacted on the availability of drugs for medical purposes. The main problems areas encountered by countries can be summarized as follows:

Problem Areas

(1) Having out-dated and/or strict laws that do not provide for a proper balance as envisaged by the two Conventions. The 1961 Single Convention on Narcotic Drugs and the 1971 Convention on Psychotropic Substances contain four schedules each providing for different levels of control. In translating the treaty provisions into national legislation, not all countries have adopted the same approach.

(2) Some countries have stringent prescription requirements that serve as a disincentive for medical practitioners to prescribe and/or pharmacists to dispense. There are countries that require prescriptions for scheduled drugs to be completed in triplicate with the prescribing practitioner being under an obligation to preserve the counterfoil

for a specific period of time. The special prescription pads required for the purpose can only be obtained from the regulatory body. If the practitioner is unable to produce the counterfoil within the stipulated time period, the person is liable to be imprisoned. As a result of this stringent requirement, it was found that more than 50 per cent of physicians in the capital city of one country with this requirement did not use the special prescription pads, with the consequence that cancer patients with pain did not have access to pain killers.[8] Other problems areas associated with stringent prescription requirements are dosage limitations (having a ceiling per prescription) and not allowing repeat prescriptions, making it difficult for cancer patients in pain to seek consultations and replenish their stock of drugs.

(3) More and more countries are affected by the cost of medicines. Cost implications have a bearing on the availability of cancer pain relief drugs. In several countries the available drugs are over-priced, making it difficult for patients to obtain them. One country reported that the prohibitive cost of opiates is compounded by new structural adjustment programs of the World Bank and the International Monetary Fund.[9] Another country noted that the prices of drugs had escalated with the privatization of the Government Medical Stores.[10]

(4) Attitudes of pharmacists and pharmacy-related practices have a bearing on the availability of drugs. Due to stringent record-keeping and security problems, both medical practitioners and pharmacists in some countries do not stock opiates. In some others, opiates are not available in adequate quantity, particularly during the weekends, because of storage and security problems.

(5) Unfounded fears among medical practitioners and pharmacists that opiate availability might lead to problems of dependency among non-cancer patients have resulted in reluctance to prescribe and/or dispense them to genuine cancer patients with pain. There are also various cultural beliefs which affect the use of strong medications; in some cases it has been noted that, even though opiates are available and have been prescribed, patients and/or their families are reluctant to use them.

[8] Jayasuriya, D.C. 'The Impact of Scheduling Drugs on the Practice of Medicine: a Pilot Study Based on Visits to the Philippines, Sri Lanka and Thailand' (Geneva, World Health Organization, 1984). Paper presented at WHO Program and Planning Working Group Meeting, Geneva, 1985.

[9] See, for instance, the reply from Kenya in United Nations. International Narcotics Control Board. *Availability of Opiates for Medical Needs*, New York, 1996. p 24.

[10] See, for instance, the reply from Malaysia in United Nations. International Narcotics Control Board. *Availability of Opiates for Medical Needs*, New York, 1996, p 25.

Positive Changes

Despite the problem areas enumerated above, several countries have reported positive and encouraging changes.

There have been policy, legislative and/or administrative reforms introduced to facilitate access to drugs and to improve their availability. This has been possible mostly in those countries that have formulated national policies on cancer control[11] or have introduced pain relief initiatives.[12]

Drug regulatory authorities in several countries have closely monitored the situation to ascertain whether there are diversions from licit supplies. Evidence seems to suggest that facilitating access to opiates for the genuine community of patients with pain does not lead to their abuse or misuse by persons who are otherwise dependent on various drugs.[13] Some countries have introduced special requirements relating to the use of opiates for the treatment of addiction, so as to minimize even the minimal chances of diversion.

Several developed countries have introduced continuous professional education programs for medical practitioners, pharmacists and other health care workers on pain relief and rational drug use.[14] These programs have been particularly helpful in sensitizing the medical community to the applicable legal requirements and the need to make pain killers available to those who have a medical need.

The economic dimensions of the problem of availability have been addressed by some countries by providing opiates free of charge to cancer patients or by requiring health insurance schemes to cover their costs.

The creation of acute pain control teams within hospitals has been a particularity useful innovation that has led to increased usage and pain relief among a large number of patients. The continuous dialogue involving medical practitioners, pharmacists and hospital administrators has facilitated a realistic assessment of the medical need for opiates.[15]

[11] World Health Organization. *Cancer Pain Relief: A Guide to Opioid Availability*, Geneva, 1996.

[12] Stjernswärd, J., et al. 'Opioid Availability in Latin America: the Declaration of Florianopolis'. *Journal of Pain and Symptom Management 10(3)*, 1995, 233-236.

[13] Joransen, D.E. 'Availability of Opioids for Cancer Pain: Recent Trends, Assessment of System Barriers, New World Health Organization Guidelines, and the Risk of Diversion'. *Journal of Pain and Symptom Management*, 8(6) 1993, p 353-360.

[14] Yoshida, T. 'Regulatory Control and the Rational Use of Drugs', *World Health*, No. 4, 1995, 6-7.

[15] Jayasuriya, D.C. and I. Khan 'Scheduling Drugs and National Legal Controls: The Need for Research', *Pakistan Journal of Pharmaceutical Sciences*, 7(2), 1994, 79-84.

Conclusions

The international drug control treaties envisage a balance being maintained between supply of opiates for licit medical purposes on the one hand, and preventing their abuse or misuse on the other. Problems of accessibility to opiates have arisen not due to treaty requirements, but due to other reasons mentioned above.

'Freedom from Pain' is a slogan that is used by cancer control programs and patient associations throughout the world. 'Freedom from Pain' is also an important dimension of the 'Right to Health'. In order to make the 'Right to Health' a reality, countries need to review existing laws, regulations and practices that may impede access to pain killers. Based on an assessment of current problem areas, countries need to develop appropriate solutions so that cancer patients can live with dignity and without needlessly suffering from pain.

THE SECOND OBJECTIVE OF DRUG CONTROL LAWS

Tokuo Yoshida

Support by the general public is one of the requirements for drug control laws to be effective. The law has to be well understood and supported by a broad range of individuals in society. Support from specialist policy-makers, government offices and medical experts is not enough. This is because the criminal justice system, without the full support of the general public, will find it difficult to enforce the law with vigour. Thus, the effect of the law on civil life indirectly affects the efficiency with which the law is enforced by the criminal justice system.

Ideally, the general public should be able to feel good effects of the law in their civil life. At least, they should not feel any bad effects of the law. It is for this reason that we stress the importance of the second objective of the international drug control conventions. Both the 1961 and 1971 Conventions aim at restricting the manufacture, distribution and use of controlled drugs strictly to medical and scientific purposes. While it is necessary to prevent their diversion for non-medical use, it is equally important to ensure the availability of narcotic drugs and psychotropic substances for legitimate medical use. However, the second objective of the conventions is not adequately realized both at the national and international levels. Two examples of this problem are outlined below:

1. Availability of opioid analgesics for the relief of severe pain

Opioid analgesics are indispensable to medicine for relieving severe pain, such as cancer pain, of patients. These drugs are subject to international and national control. A recent survey published by the International Narcotics Control Board (INCB) has shown that their availability for medical use is inadequate in many countries, and that the national control authorities have identified a number of impediments, including regulatory ones.

2. Availability of controlled medicines for the relief of disaster-stricken peoples

The time-consuming export-import control procedure applicable to the international movement of controlled drugs makes timely international donations of controlled medicines for the relief of disaster-stricken peoples virtually impossible. Through continued dialogue with the INCB, we have convinced the international drug control policy-making body, the UN Commission on Narcotic Drugs, to endorse a new, flexible way of interpreting the conventions to allow the timely international provision of controlled medicines in emergency situations.

WHO'S ROLE IN INTERNATIONAL HARMONIZATION OF PHARMACEUTICAL LEGISLATION AND REGULATIONS

Agathe Wehrli

WHO is a specialized agency of the UN system created in 1948, and according to its Constitution it acts as the directing and co-ordinating authority on international health work. WHO's overall objective is the attainment by all people of the highest possible level of health, defined as a state of complete physical, mental and social well-being and not merely the absence of disease or infirmity. There are thus close links between the objectives of WHO and of this Conference on Global Drugs Law.

WHO's concerns relate not only to the trafficking and abuse of internationally scheduled substances, but also to the availability and rational use of some of them in medicine in the form of pharmaceutical products. While such pharmaceutical products are, of course, still subject to international conventional requirements, they are also subject to general pharmaceutical legislation. Close cooperation is consequently required at the international and national levels between people involved in implementing international drug control conventions and regulators of medicinal products, commonly referred to as 'drug regulators'.

Until 20 years ago WHO's activities relating to pharmaceutical products consisted mostly of recommendations concerning standards with respect to safety, purity and potency of biological, pharmaceutical and similar products moving in international commerce. Since then it has been increasingly recognized that what developing countries—and more recently the newly independent states of the former Soviet Union—need is not just technical standards, but also policy, administrative and legal guidance. The urgency for strengthening national drug regulatory capacities has been compounded by the increase in the number of reports about trade in counterfeit and/or substandard pharmaceutical products which threaten to erode confidence in the health-care system because such products may be inefficacious or toxic. The issue has been addressed in several resolutions adopted by the World Health Assembly requesting the Director-General of WHO to initiate programs for the prevention and detection of the export, import and smuggling of falsely labelled, spurious, counterfeited or substandard pharmaceutical preparations, and to cooperate with the Secretary-General of the United Nations in such cases when the provision of international treaties are violated.

It was against this background that WHO formulated guidelines for developing national drug policies in which legislation and regulation have been identified as first components of a drug policy. This was followed by the publication of a set of Guiding Principles for Small Drug Regulatory Authorities, and two sets of guidelines that address specifically international trade issues. These are the Guidelines on the Implementation of the WHO Certification Scheme on the Quality of Pharmaceutical Products Moving in International Commerce, and the Guidelines on Import Procedures for Pharmaceutical Products. The next text to be issued will be the Guiding Principles for National Drug Legislation. This text is at an advanced stage and is expected to become available later this year.

MONEY LAUNDERING: INTERNATIONAL EFFORTS AND RECENT DEVELOPMENTS IN THE MOVEMENT OF DRUG-RELATED MONEY

Nara Srinivasan and Roderic Underwood

'A billion here and a billion there. Pretty soon you are talking about real money'. Everett Dirkson (1896-1969)

In light of recent international money laundering regulations, drug traffickers and organized criminals are discovering new money laundering techniques in order to avoid detection and criminal sanctions. Some of these techniques are sophisticated; however many are extremely simple. Nevertheless, the days of putting money into Swiss bank accounts are disappearing. Even high profile people such as former South Korean President Roh Tae Woo and former Mexican President Carlos Salinas are finding out that their positions and financial networks are not enough to keep their dishonest earnings from being found.[1]

This paper will outline some of the reasons why criminals are finding it more difficult to launder their dishonest earnings from drugs by giving a brief overview of international anti-money laundering initiatives, describe recent trends in the movement of drug monies and suggest ways to help combat these trends.

What is money laundering?

The concept of money laundering has been variously defined. Many definitions have been asserted to explain money laundering as a concept. For example, the Australian Bureau of Criminal Intelligence has defined money laundering as: 'The use of physical and/or financial processes in order to obscure the links between a person or organization, and income or assets acquired legally or illegally by that person or organization for the purpose

[1] Office of International Criminal Justice (1996), Money Laundering Tactics Changing.

of avoiding prosecution, payment of government charges and to legitimize the income or assets'.[2]

Powis (1992) asserts that money laundering is the use of money derived from illegal activies by concealing the identity of the individual who obtained the money and converting it to assets that appear to have been derived from a legitimate source.[3] However, probably, the simplest definition is the washing of dirty money to make it appear legitimate.[4]

International Efforts to Combat Money Laundering

In recent years there has been a growing awareness in the fight against the laundering of money which has been derived from criminal activity, especially those monies derived from drug trafficking. In the past, traditional law enforcement methods concentrated on establishing evidence to link a suspect to a crime. This practice resulted in investigators concentrating solely on recovery of stolen property and paying little or no attention to the wider proceeds of the crimes such as large bank accounts, expensive houses, expensive education for children and other items of value which a successful criminal could flaunt or conceal. This is not a criticism of any investigator or police service. The real truth of the matter is that the international legislators did not provide for such powers within their legal systems. However, this situation has changed and is continually changing as a result of international initiatives.[5] Many countries around the world are already engaged in a concerted effort to combat international money laundering. Through the enactment of counter-money laundering laws, bilateral and multilateral agreements, nations have joined together to cultivate an international awareness of the seriousness of money laundering. The following is a broad overview of international efforts which have been established to deal with this phenomenon.

The United Nations Convention against Illicit Traffic in Narcotic Drugs and Psychotropic Substances

The United Nations (UN) Convention against Illicit Traffic in Narcotic Drugs

[2] Detective Sergeant Leon Smith, Proceeds of Crime Unit, Western Australia. Money Laundering Seminar Friday, 9th August, 1996, Perth, Western Australia.

[3] Powis, R.E. (1992), *The Money launderers. Lessons from the drug wars*. USA: Probis Publishing.

[4] Graham Pinner, Deputy Director Austrac, Money Laundering Seminar Friday, 9th August 1996, Perth, Western Australia.

[5] Detective Sergeant Gerand Giblin, Bureau of Fraud Investigation, Garda Siochana, Ireland. Personal Communication, January 23, 1997.

and Psychotropic Substances, which was adopted in Vienna, Austria on 20th December 1988 was one of the first international efforts to criminalize the proceeds of drug trafficking and to provide for confiscation of these monies and for extradition of offenders. In addition, the representatives also agreed to the following:

* mutual legal assistance;
* the transfer of criminal prosecutions from one signatory to another;
* that traditional secrecy and confidentiality between bank and customer should be disregarded during criminal investigations; and
* that member states take appropriate measures to facilitate the confiscation of assets which were believed to be the proceeds of money laundering.[6]

Basle Committee on Banking Regulations and Supervisory Practices

The Vienna Convention was followed in December 1989 by the Basle Committee on Banking Regulations and Supervisory Practices. The committee consisted of representatives of the central banks of the G-10 Nations.[7] The Basle Committee argued that banks and other financial institutions may, unwittingly, be used as intermediaries for the transfer of illegally obtained money. It was further argued that banking supervisors and management should treat these practices as a matter of urgency. The main causes for concern asserted by the committee was '(that) public confidence in banks, and hence their stability, can be undermined by adverse publicity as a result of inadvertent association by banks with criminals'.[8] The Basle Committee adopted the 'Statement of Principles' on the prevention of criminal use of the banking system for the purpose of money laundering. In order to reduce the possibility of banks being used in money laundering schemes, they formulated the two following measures:

(1) the requirement that customers be clearly identified,
(2) greater cooperation between banks and law enforcement services.

[6] Gilmore, W.C. (1992) (Ed.) *International efforts to combat money laundering*, Cambridge: Grotious Publications Ltd.

[7] The members of the G-10 Nations are United States of America, United Kingdom, Belgium, Canada, France, Italy, Japan, the Netherlands, Sweden, Switzerland, and Luxembourg.

[8] Gilmore, W.C. (1992) (Ed.) *International efforts to combat money laundering*, Cambridge: Grotious Publications Ltd. Chapter V, document pg. 274.

Financial Action Task Force

The Financial Action Task Force (FATF), which is one of the key organizations that addresses the global problems of money laundering, was established following the 15th Economic Summit of the seven major industrial nations (G-7).[9] This Summit was held in Paris on 16th July 1989. In addition to the summit participants eight other countries (Sweden, Netherlands, Belgium, Luxembourg, Switzerland, Austria, Spain and Australia), joined the Task Force in order to increase its expertise and reflect the views of other countries concerned in the fight against national and international money laundering. The FATF consists of 26 countries, the European Commission and the Gulf Cooperation Council, and was established to promote the development of effective anti-money laundering controls and to encourage cooperation to counter-money laundering efforts among its membership around the world.[10] The FATF's mandate was 'to assess the results of cooperation already undertaken in order to prevent the utilisation of the banking system and financial institutions for the purpose of money laundering, and to consider additional preventive efforts in this field, including the adaptation of legal and regulatory systems so as to enhance multilateral judicial assistance'.[11] The first report of the FATF was published in 1990. This report contained 40 recommendations to counter money laundering and has been regarded as the most influential report to date in the fight against money laundering.[12] The recommendations included:

* that the United Nations Covention be adopted and ratified by the countries;

* that bank secrecy should be curtailed for investigation purposes;

* that money laundering should be criminalized by means of national criminal laws;

* that not only the proceeds of drug trafficking be considered but also the illegal proceeds of other crimes;

* that all bank transactions over a certain level be registered and that all suspicious transactions be reported;

* that bank employees be trained to recognize suspicious transactions;

[9] Members of the G-7 Group: United States of America, Japan, Germany, France, United Kingdom, Italy and Canada. Also at this meeting was the Commission of the European Communities.

[10] Gilmore, W.C. (1992) (Ed.) *International efforts to combat money laundering*, Cambridge: Grotious Publications Ltd. p. 33.

[11] *Ibid.*

[12] Detective Sergeant Gerand Giblin, Bureau of Fraud Investigation, Garda Siochana, Ireland. Personal Communication, January 23, 1997.

* that international cooperation should be strengthened, and that extradition of persons suspected of involvement in money laundering should be facilitated.

In July 1990, at the Houston Summit of the Heads of State of Government of the seven major industrialized countries (G-7), it was agreed that all members of the Organization of Economic Cooperation and Development (OECD)[13] and financial centre countries would implement the recommendations of the Task Force. Representatives from Denmark, Finland, Greece, Ireland, New Zealand, Norway, Portugal, Turkey, Hong Kong and the Gulf Cooperation Council also participated in many of the meetings. Consequently, most of these countries endorsed the report and subsequently qualified for membership of FATF.

The efforts of the FATF have resulted in the establishment of Financial Intelligence Units (FIUs) in various countries around the world to detect criminal abuse of financial systems and to ensure adherence to financial laws.[14] Perhaps the most significant qualities of FIUs is that many operate separate from the Justice Ministries in their respective countries. They maintain independent relationships with financial institutions and law enforcment services. These relationships help to bridge the private and governmental sectors in an effort to focus attention on the problem of money laundering. The establishment of FIUs has led to the creation of an organization, known as the Egmont Group of nations that have implemented FIUs. The Group held its initial meeting at the papais d'Egmont in June 1995. A consensus was reached that improved interaction and communication among FIUs would serve a broad range of common goals in the areas of sharing information, coordinating training and addressing legal issues unique to money laundering.[15] As part of the FATF's external relations program, it has encouraged the development of sister organizations such as the Caribbean Financial Action Task Force (CFATF).

[13] OECD members: Australia, Austria, Belgium, Canada, Czech Republic, Denmark, Finland, France, Germany, Greece, Hungary, Iceland, Ireland, Italy, Japan, Luxembourg, Mexico and Netherlands.

[14] The following is a list of FIUs which have been established as a result of the efforts of the FATF. Australian Transaction Reports and Analysis Centre (AUSTRAC); Celule do Traitementdes Informations Financiers (CITF, Belgium); Financial Crimes Enforcement Network (FinCEN, USA); National Criminal Intelligence Service (NCIS, UK); Traitement Du Renseignement et Action Contre Les Circuits Financiers Clandestines (TRACFIN; France).

[15] Information relating to Financial Intelligence Units can be accessed on internet-http;//www.ustreas.gov/treasury/bureaus/fincen.

Council Directive 91/308/EEC

On 10th June 1991 a primary legal obligation was imposed on member states of the European Union by Concil Directive 91/308/EC, 'Prevention of the Use of the Financial System for the Purpose of Money Laundring'.[16] The view expressed in this document was that financial institutions and confidence in the financial markets as a whole could be jeopardized, leading to a fall in public trust and confidence. These assertions were particularly important with regard to the provision of Council Directive 89/646/EEC which established the concept of a single banking licence which could be granted to any bank which would then entitle the grantee to operate throughout the European Union (EU). The provisions of the 1991 Council Directive imposes an obligation on member states to ensure that credit and financial institutions conduct business in a manner which facilitates investigations into money laundering activities. Some of these provisions include identifying customers in certain circumstances and maintaining the identification documents for at least five years, the keeping of adequate records of suspicious transactions, paying special attention to transactions with third countries which do not apply comparable anti-money laundering standards to those established by the EU and the lifting of bank secrecy for cases under investigation.

On 19th September 1996 the Organization of Economic Cooperation and Development (OECD) issued a press release which asserted that the Financial Action Task Force was concerned that 'more than six years after the establishment of the FATF in 1989, Turkey is regrettably the only FATF member which has not passed anti-money laundering legislation and whose compliance with FATF recommendations is seriously deficient.'[17]

Recent Trends in the Movement of Drug Related Monies

Law enforcement services, especially those in the United States of America, believe that recent international money laundering legislation has been successful in curtailing money laundering activities.[18] However, this suc-

[16] Gilmore, W.C. (1992) (Ed.) *International efforts to combat money laundering*, Cambridge: Grotious Publications Ltd.

[17] OECD News Release, Paris, 19th September 1996. Financial Action Task Force on money laundering issues a statement about the lack of anti-money laundering laws in Turkey.

[18] Statement by Harold D. Wankel, DEA Chief of Operations, United States Department of Justice, to the Housing and Banking Committee, Money Laundering by Drug Trafficking Organizations. 28 February, 1996.

cess has forced criminals to adopt other methods to disguise and move their illicit cash. When international legislation caused deposits over a certain amount (usually $10,000) to be reported by financial authorities structuring became the method of choice for many launderers. One form of structuring is smurfing, in which individuals recruited by the traffickers run from bank to bank and deposit just under the legal reporting requirement. However, this method is cumbersome and not without substantial risk.[19] Therefore, to solve this problem currency smuggling has become a preferred option for money laundering.[20] Although currency smuggling is not a new phenomenon, the practice has increased because of the minimal risk involved. For instance, monies derived from the proceeds of drug trafficking can be smuggled from a regulated country to an unregulated country. The cash can then be deposited into the formal financial system of that country and can then be returned through wire transfers to selected regulated countries. Wire transfers have caused many problems for investigators trying to follow money trails. The fact that more than 700,000 mostly legitimate wire transfers occur daily in the United States, moving well over $2 trillion[21], highlights the difficulty faced by investigators. When drug cash has been repatriated, after smuggling it abroad, its origin is extremely difficult to detect. Even if detected, differences in national laws, regulations and enforcement practices seriously impair the investigations of law enforcement services.

Currency Smuggling Typologies?

Drug trafficking generates an enormous amount of cash. It is estimated that the sale of illegal drugs, in the USA, generates more than $100 billion annually.[22] Because most drug transactions are small, drugs traffickers must contend with a large volume of small-denomination bills. This leaves the traffickers with the problem of concealing large amounts of cash. For example, about 450 paper bills weigh 1lb., so that $1 billion in $100 dollar bills weighs over 11 imperial tons. It is estimated that more than $15 billion of the $50 to $75 billion earned in illegal drug money each year is

[19] US Custom Service, Chapter Report, 03/09/94: Money Laundering. US efforts to fight it are threatened by currency smuggling.

[20] *Ibid.*

[21] US Congress, Office of Technology Assessment, (1995). Information technologies for the control of money laundering. Washington DC: US Government Printing Office.

[22] US Custom Service, Chapter Report, 03/09/94: Money Laundering. US efforts to fight it are threatened by currency smuggling. p.7.

thought to be transported in the form of currency, with the remainder being wired abroad after having been deposited in the US banking system.[23] This equates to over 75 imperial tons being smuggled each year out of the United States, which suggests that placement of cash is a major problem faced by those who do not want to operate through the national banking networks.

The FATF has noted that many features can be found in the states of the former Soviet Union and Eastern Block which make the countries very attractive to money launderers. It maintains that much of the banking system is corrupt or corruptible, and many countries possess no money laundering legislation. It further maintains that law enforcement structures are ill-equipped to curtail the movement of drug related monies, that there is a high propensity for official corruption and there exists a desperate need for capital.[24] The former UN Secretary General, Boutros Boutros-Ghali argues that 'the collapse of communism and the disintegration of the Soviet Union have led to a weakening of institutional structures and a loss of social and ideological benchmarks in Eastern Europe'.[25] These issues coupled with the suggestion that more than 50 per cent of all newly created banks in Russia have been acquired by the so-called 'Russian Mafia'[26], establishes Eastern Europe as a major money laundering centre in the proceeds of crime in the foreseeable future. Other major laundering centres are: Columbia, Mexico, Nigeria, Middle East and Southeast Asia. The main centres in Southeast Asia are Thailand, Singapore and Hong Kong[27], where money laundering is conducted through a complicated maze of trusted confidants who engage in underground banking known as 'hawallah', 'hundi' or chiti banking.[28]

[23] *Ibid. p.11.*

[24] FATF-vii Money Laundering Typologies. Public report of the experts. 4th June 1996.

[25] Speech of UN Secretary-General, Boutros Boutros-Ghali, at the opening session of the World Ministerial Conference on Organized and Transnational Crime, 22nd November, 1994, Naples, Italy.

[26] Pinner, G. (1996) Money Laundering; The state of play. In A. Graycar and P Grabosky (Eds.) *Money Laundering in the 21st Century: Risks and Countermeasures.* Australian Institute of Criminology.

[27] Statement by Harold D. Wankel, DEA Chief of Operations, United States Department of Justice, to the Housing and Banking Committee, Money Laundering by Drug Trafficking Organizations. 28 February, 1996.

[28] South , N. (1995) On cooling hot money: Translantic trends in drug-related money laundering and its facilitation. Dr. South is a senior lecturer in Criminology at the University of Essex, England. This paper can be accessed on the internet: http://www.acsp.uic.edu/iasoc/south.htm.

Currency smugglers use a variety of techniques to take money out of the country. However, four main avenues have been identified as being most favoured by the smugglers viz- air, sea, land and mail.[29]

Air

Airlines are used for currency smuggling because (1) the smugglers can stay close to their money during the transportation process; (2) destinations can be reached quickly and easily; and (3) preplanning is kept to a minimum.

Passengers can smuggle currency concealed on their person, in hand luggage or in unaccompanied baggage. The US Drug Enforcement Administration (DEA)[30] and US Customs services have provided the following examples of how currency has been smuggled out of the country on commercial airlines.[31]

According to the DEA, the Cali Mafia is one of the primary recipients of drug proceeds from the United States. Until recently they were responsible for 90 per cent of the cocaine sold in the US. Colombian economists conservatively estimate that about US $4.5 billion is repatriated annually to Columbia by drug traffickers. It is also known that Columbian traffickers have purchased a fleet of large planes, such as Boeing 727s, Caravelles and the Turboprop Lockheed Electras. They use these planes to transport tonnes of cocaine to Mexico, Canada, Portugal and West Africa for sale in the United States and Europe. Once they have off-loaded the cocaine they reload the planes with US cash, sometimes as much as $20 to $30 million in drug profits to return to Columbia.

In November 1988 customs officers seized $1,017,832 being transported in checked baggage from Miami to Columbia. The currency consisted primarily of $20 bills stacked in groups of 100 and bound by rubber bands. The currency was packed among the wiring in electric space heaters and in suitcases. A follow-up investigation resulted in the seizure of an additional $2,40,000 from a garage at the residence of one of the violators. This currency was wrapped in foil and concealed in microwave ovens and heaters awaiting shipment.

In January 1991, a Chicago O'Hare airport security guard at an x-ray security point observed a large amount of currency hidden in a false-bot-

[29] US Custom service, Chapter Report, 03/09/94: Money Laundering. US efforts to fight it are threatened by currency smuggling.

[30] *Ibid.*, p.5

[31] US Custom service, Chapter Report, 03/09/94: Money Laundering. US efforts to fight it are threatened by currency smuggling. p.12.

tom briefcase. Customs officials responded by performing a search of passengers boarding a flight to Paris, which had a connection to Hong Kong. The CMIR requirement (report of international transportation of currency) was announced over the intercom prior to passengers boarding the flight. The suspected violator approached an inspector and declared $9,650. He was informed that he only had to declare money if the amount exceeded $10,000. While boarding the aircraft the suspect was stopped in the jetway and advised again of the currency reporting requirement. He verbally declared $100,000 but then completed a CMIR for $105,000. He was again afforded the opportunity to amend his declaration, which he did for $170,000. Customs' inspections disclosed the suspect was carrying $184,000, which was subsequently seized.

In September 1992 federal and states authorities performed an outbound currency search of a commercial carrier's crew members departing from New York, inbound to Colombia. A flight attendant was stopped and informed of the currency reporting requirement. She declared a total of $1000. Upon examination of her hand-carried crew bag, a custom inspector found $2,600 in a roll of toilet paper $12,400 in an envelope. $20,000 in a wooden box, $1,627 in her wallet, $5,000 in a carry-on garment bag, $40,000 in a box of laundry detergent, and $13,300 in her jacket pocket. In total she was carrying $95,541. In October 1996, Mexican authorities found $12 million inside suitcases taken from a private plane that is believed to belong to the Carrillo-Fuentes drugs organisation.[32]

Another technique is the concealment of money inside the body itself. For example, in one case, at New York's JFK airport, a woman swallowed $7,500 in fifteen condoms in a body cavity, and concealed $47,894 in her baggage.

Currency smuggling by air can also include air cargo. In one of the largest detected cases inspectors at New York (JFK) found $6,469,024 in 26 sealed metal containers. In another case, inspectors found $ 1,752,106 in cash and money orders in a water heater. In still another case employees accidentally pierced the support railing on a pallet containing empty fruit boxes, eventually leading to the discovery $989,915 hidden in hollowed out portions of the wood.

Land

Smuggling currency across land, although lacking in speed and the ability to reach many international destinations, is still a relatively easy way to

[32] Statement by Harold D. Wankel, DEA Chief of Operations, United States Department of Justice, to the Housing and Banking Committee, Money Laundering by Drug Trafficking Organizations. 28 February 1996.

transport cash. Border crossings offer advantages for smugglers because customs presence tends to be infrequent and in many cases, especially in Europe, may be non-existent. Though the United States of America borders only two countries, US customs assert that currency smuggling is on the increase.[33] US customs presence tend to be less at outbound stations, inspections tend to be infrequent as they interfere with the flow of traffic and at times cause massive traffic congestion. Another advantage of land border crossings is that vehicles in which to conceal the currency are easy to obtain.

Customs official have found currency in obvious locations such as seats, trunks, false compartments, dashboards and door panels. But unless custom officials have some evidence that concealment methods are being used, they are not likely to perform the detailed searches necessary to disclose hidden funds during routine inspections.

In one example of currency being smuggled across a land border, US customs stopped an individual crossing into Mexico at Otay Mesa, California and asked if he had currency to declare. The individual told the agents that he was carrying US$9,000. A search of the individual disclosed $14,010 in a portfolio, $2,216 in his pocket, and $200 in his wallet.

A second example given by US customs refers to four individuals who were crossing the border at Hidalgo, Texas, in a van. When asked if they had currency to declare, they responded that they did not. A search located two suspicious envelopes; they were asked again and repeated that they had nothing to declare. A search of the envelopes led to the seizure of $18,657 and the arrest of two occupants.

In another recent incident, US customs inspectors and border patrol agents located US $1,290,700 in Holland, Vermont which was destined for Canada. The perpetrators were arrested for attempting to transport currency out of the United States. They were travelling off road, using heavy duty all-terrain vehicles.

In Mexico, between April and October 1995, Mexican authorities made three seizures of US currency which totalled nearly $20 million. Last April $6.2 million was discovered in a cargo of air conditioners.

Sea

Although smuggling by sea can have the advantage of reaching many destinations, it can, at times, be a cumbersome exercise. For example, it may require the use of other parties such as exporters or ship personnel and

[33] US Custom Service, Chapter Report, 03/09/94: Money Laundering, US efforts to fight it are threatened by currency smuggling.

the smuggler may be physically separated from the currency for long periods. At the same time, however, smuggling by sea offers certain advantages. The main advantage is that ship cargo typically involves large containers within which currency is very easy to conceal and difficult to detect.

Recently US customs has begun to target outbound sea shipments, netting several large seizures. In one inspection inspectors at Newark seaport seized $763,240 that had been concealed beneath the floor of a refrigeration unit in a ship bound for Colombia. They also seized $7,1785,161 from two 20-foot containers loaded with dried peas, again on a vessel destined for Colombia. In this case the packing and shipping company had freshly painted each container in order to conceal the front walls. A subsequent investigation led to the seizure of a further $4,00,00 bringing the total to over $11 million. According to US customs this seizure represented approximately one month's drug profits.[34] In March 1992, Panamanian authorities seized $7.1 million from two containers on a ship inbound from Miami. It can be seen from these few examples that currency smuggling by sea allows for vast sums of monies to be smuggled at one time. Because the risk involved in the use of commercial shipping is minimal, it is likely that smugglers will continue with this method.

Mail

The US postal service and FinCEN (Financial Crimes Enforcement Network) maintain that although the extent of mail smuggling cannot be measured, the US mail and private couriers are being used to send currency illegally out the country. Because of the volume of mail and packages that leave countries daily it is fair to assume that this is the case internationally. Specific data on the number and dollar amount of seizures is unavailable. However, the US postal inspection service estimates that as many as 25 separate criminal organizations are involved in sending unreported currency out of the country by air mail, through one major airport on the east coast alone.[35] The DEA has also seen an increase in the shipment of large quantities of postal money orders. These money orders are shipped directly to Colombia and Panama. The names on the money orders are left blank. The funds are sold to *casas de cambios* or money changing houses for cash that will be deposited into a trafficker's account. The money orders are then sold and resold through the network and are finally redeemed outside of Colombia.[36]

Cyberpayments

In addition to the increase in currency smuggling the emergence of new payment technologies has presented new challenges. For many years the banking and financial services industry has been developing new methods of cash payments. One of these methods is generally referred to as 'cyberpayments.' A significant feature of the new cyberpayments is that they include a new form of currency. Cyberpayments also comprise other payment components which emulate current payment systems. For example, already in use are cybercheques, cybercredit and cyberdebit. Cybercurrency therefore includes the attributes of conventional currency which are: a store of value, a medium of exchange, and ease of use. However it has one very important added feature—almost instant electronic transfers from point to point.[37]

Cybercurrency is still in the experimental stage. The cash is loaded on to a card containing a chip, which can be filled via telephone or bank machines which can be moved from card to card and can be used for purchases of any amount. However, the problem for government and law enforcement services, is that there is no way to track the card's transactions because, unlike Visa and Mastercard, there is no registration of the transaction.[38] The inability to trace such funds presents an opportunity for the movement of illicit funds.

Even though Cyberpayments are still in a 'first generation' form a large number of countries have made the move to smart card payments.[39] It is argued that within the next few years Cyberpayments will, to some degree, substitute and supplement all current means of payment and a variety of monetary instruments.

Many issues are raised by this technology, including whether such payments constitute legal tender and whether they are liable to the same currency reporting and supervision measures as paper currency. Will report-

[36] Statement by Harold D. Wankel, DEA Chief of Operations, United States Department of Justice, to the Housing and Banking Committee, Money Laundering by Drug Trafficking Organizations. 28 February, 1996.

[37] Cybercurrency, USIS, American Embassy, Stockholm (1996) webmaster @ usis.usemb.se

[38] Office of International Criminal Justice, (1996). Money laundering tactics changing. This paper can be accessed on the internet-http://www.acsp.uic.edu/OICJ/Pubs/CJI/202091.HTM.

ing regulations have to be completely redesigned to include the reporting of currency in cyber form moving to other countries via the internet or smart cards?[40]

Potential steps in digital cash transactions

D'Alelio and Collins (1966)[41] espouse that there are many possible approaches for transactions involving cyber payment via smart cards or the internet. One possible structure would involve the following steps:

(1) The customer establishes an account with Issuer (Virtual Bank) by depositing funds with the issuer. (2) The issuer holds the customer's funds for future use. (3) When the customer requires to make a purchase over the internet, the customer sends an encrypted electronic e-mail message to the Virtual Bank requesting funding. The message contains a unique digital signature. (4) Virtual Bank debits the customer's account and sends the customer digital cash via the phone line to the customer's computer. (5) The customer transmits the digital cash to the vendor, who can verify its authenticity and have it credited to the vendor's account with Virtual Bank, or can have the cash-e-mailed to another person or bank account.

Digital cash systems may create a trail of transactions, but they may also be anonymous depending on the particular system. In an anonymous system, Virtual Bank adds a private signature that only it can create. In order to verify that digital cash was issued by Virtual Bank, the computer user can decode a public version of the private signature using a key provided by Virtual Bank.

While it is not clear who the major cyberpayment players will be in the next five or ten years, it is inevitable that cybermoney will originate outside the purview of international central banks, which are largely responsible for traditional monetary regulation. If this situation holds true, it will result in major implications for Governments and law enforcement services.

In relation to money laundering the regulatory gaps are sizeable. Stanley E. Morris, Director of the Financial Crimes Enforcement Network (FinCEN), points out that there are no laws that limit the balance of electronic currency that can be loaded onto a smart card. This may create a major op-

[39] Wahlert, G. (1996). Implications for law enforcement of the move to a cashless society. In A. Graycar and P. Grabosky (Eds.) *Money Laundering in the 21st Century: Risks and Countermeasures*. Australian Institute of Criminology. p.22.

[40] Also known as a 'chip stored value card'. This card, similar to a credit card, has an embedded integrated circuit or microchip. Smart cards can be recognized by their distinctive contacts, which resemble something like a gold coloured flower at one corner of the card.

portunity for money launderers. In addition it has not been determined whose tax laws apply to transactions in cyberspace.[42]

The FATF maintains that experts have no data to indicate the extent of cyberpayments nor evidence to suggest that cyberpayment technologies are being used by criminal organizations to launder money. However, there is general agreement that the issue must be addressed immediately. As mentioned earlier, the cyberpayment industry is still in a developmental stage; nevertheless, having regard to the speed with which the use of electronic money is growing, governments cannot afford to wait unit the launderers have exploited the cybersystem. FATF experts are adamant that governments must be proactive in their efforts to safeguard the system and work with vendors and users of cyberpayment technology to identify vulnerabilities, and build appropriate safeguards into system design and operations.[43]

What can we do?

Over the years governments and law enforcement agencies have discovered the power of the illegal drug industry. Nevertheless, the same governments and law enforcement agencies have begun to realize the power of financial investigations.[44] Drug trafficking is ultimately a cash business and drug traffickers must find ways to legitimize such cash. Money laundering is the only way that they can do that. Attacking the financial base of any organization will have a direct impact on its ability to do business; this principle also holds true for the illegal drug industry.

No single public or private organization has the expertise and resources to understand and respond to the ever increasing movement of illegal drug monies. If legislation and enforcement is to be effective, agencies must continue to strengthen international partnerships and maintain strong ties with counterparts in the financial centres of the world. Unregulated countries must be urged to pass effective counter-money laundering and forfeiture laws.

[41] D'Alelio, E & Collins, J.T. (1966) *The internet and business: A lawyer's guide.* USA Computer Law Association. Chap.8.

[42] Information relating to FinCEN and access to publications can be accessed on internet—http:/ www.ustreas.gov/treasury/bureaus/fincen.

[43] FATF-vii Money Laundering Typologies. Public report of the experts. 4th June 1996.

[44] Two major international financial operations carried out recently were: Operation Green Ice (1992) where over $50 million in cash was seized and over 200 people arrested world-wide, and Operation Dinero (1994), a two-and-a-half year operation involving Italy, Spain, Canada and the UK. This operation led to the penetration of the Cali cocaine organizations.

In relation to currency smuggling, customs services must place more emphasis on inspecting the flow of cargo leaving the country. Special efforts must be made to inspect outgoing passengers and cargo to intercept and curtail currency being smuggled out of regulated countries. However, a problem arises in relation to bulk cargo, which is difficult to inspect without the use of large and sophisticated equipment. In general, customs services have a shortage of such equipment and whatever equipment they have tends to be devoted to inbound inspections. To ameliorate this problem, international customs agencies need to make a concerted effort to train personnel who will specialize in inspecting outbound passengers and currency. Coupled with training, the use of especially trained dogs to detect concealed currency and the use of specialized X-ray vans may be some of the immediate changes needed to combat currency smuggling.

In the area of cyberpayments, there is an ongoing debate on how to define a bank. Governments need to introduce laws which will include depository and non-depository institutions and all providers of financial services so that all currency operators, whether paper or cyber, will be bound by national and international currency reporting laws.

There is also a great need for governments, law enforcement services and financial investigators to understand this new and emerging system. Financial regulators must respond to the advent of E-cash. The technology is complex, but to the user, E-cash is as easy as pushing a button. It must be remembered that the internet knows no boundaries nor does it have an off switch, and no amount of wishing by regulators will change that fact.

BLACK HAWALA, FINANCIAL CRIMES AND THE WORLD DRUG TRADE

Patrick Jost

The term *hawala*[1] (also spelled *havala, hawallah* or *hawalah*) is often used interchangeably with the term *hundi*[2]. Both refer to an alternative remittance system used extensively in India and Pakistan.

In current usage in Hindi and Urdu, the word 'hawala' has the meanings 'trust' and 'reference'. It is also used colloquially for 'money' (hawala is a means of transferring money, and it is based on trust or an appropriate reference). In some contexts (particularly journalism), it may be used to refer to payments made in connection with bribery and money laundering. The term *hawaladar* refers to a hawala broker or dealer.

The term and spelling *hawala* will be used throughout this paper for consistency.[3] In addition, we will use the term *black hawala*, following usage 'black money' and 'black market' to refer to illegal hawala activities.

Hawala predates 'traditional' or 'western' banking (the first 'western bank' in India was the Bank of Hindustan, established in Calcutta around 1770).[4] Prior to this, the operations of *sarafs* and *potedars*[5], who were primarily moneychangers (and essentially the predecessors of the hawaladars discussed in this paper) were a fundamental component of the commercial and financial infrastructures. Today, hawala and 'traditional' banking exist as parallel, but intertwined, economic systems in India and Pakistan.

[1] The world 'hawala' comes from the Arabic root for 'transfer.'

[2] The word 'hundi' also has the meanings 'cheque' or 'bill of exchange' in Hindi and Urdu.

[3] The common usage 'hawala/hundi system' is correct but redundant.

[4] Dwijendra Tripathi and Prithi Misra, *Towards a New Frontier: History of the Bank of Baroda*, 6, 1985.

[5] The word 'saraf' comes from the Arabic root for 'to exchange money'; the word 'potedar' is the Hindi word for 'treasurer.'

Hawala consists of several distinct but interacting schemes that form the overall 'hawala system'; three will be discussed in detail in this paper. The first is the transfer of money through a hawaladar. This is the most common 'type' of hawala transaction or hawala scheme, and it is often erroneously assumed that these transfers are the entire hawala system. The second scheme is the manipulation of invoices to hide the movement of money in shipments of goods. The third scheme involves smuggling gold, often using Dubai as a starting point, to India and Pakistan.

*The following scenarios show the operation and interaction of the schemes that constitute hawala**

In this scenario, an expatriate Indian working in New York wants to send one lakh[6] of rupees to his sister in Delhi.[7] He explores several means of doing this: the bank, a bureau de change and two hawaladars.

The Bank

The bank gives the official exchange rate for rupees (for the purposes of this paper, that is assumed to be 31 Rs/$) and charges $25 for the exchange. The cost of the 100,000 rupees would be $3225; adding the $25 fee brings the total cost of this transaction to $3250.

The bank option, however, requires filling out various forms. The expatriate Indian may not want any paperwork, such as transfer records; even if documenting the transaction is not a problem, language problems may make it difficult or impossible for him to do so.

The Bureau de Change

The bureau de change offers a rate even less attractive than the bank and charges a higher fee. Also, even though not as much paperwork is required, the process is still somewhat cumbersome.

[6]A lakh is 100,000; this term is part of the numbering system used in India and Pakistan, frequently used when discussing money.

[7]This is a very common 'transaction size' and is colloquially referred to as a 'peti' (suitcase/box/chest in Hindi).

* The Hawala Transfer scheme

The Hawaladars

In conversations with two local hawaladars[8], he encounters slightly different pricing schemes. The first hawaladar will give him a slightly better rate (this would be the 'black market' rate—assumed to be 35 Rs/$) than the bank or bureau de change and will charge a 'fee' of ten percent of the amount to be sent. The 100,000 rupees will cost $2857, he fee adds $288 for a total of $3145—a much better deal than the bank or bureau de change!

The second hawaladar offers the same rate of exchange but a different pricing scheme—one rupee per dollar.[9] The price for the 100,000 rupees is the same, $2857, and the fee adds another $81 for a total of $2938—the 'best deal' of all!

The Indian decides to make use of the services of the second ('one rupee per dollar') hawaladar. He gives $2938 to this hawaladar. The New York hawaladar contacts an associate in Delhi, and tells him of the requirement to deliver 100,000 rupees. The Delhi hawaladar sends someone out with the money, and the transfer is complete. Since, as was mentioned before, there is no need for receipts or other paperwork. The expatriate trusts the system, and is confident that the money will be delivered to his sister.

The Under-Invoicing Scheme

The hawaladar in New York facilitates many transfers to India and Pakistan through his network of connections there. Eventually, it is necessary for him to balance accounts with them. A common way to move money illicitly into a country with strict currency import controls (details of the relevant Indian legislation will be discussed later in this paper) is to under invoice the value of goods shipped there.

If the New York hawaladar owes the Delhi hawaladar $200,000, he might purchase $250,000 worth of computer equipment (or something else which can be sold in India). He will then ship this equipment to Delhi, along with an invoice for $50,000. The Delhi hawaladar remits this—establishing enough of a paper trail to satisfy casual scrutiny and to provide the appearance of compliance with currency controls.

[8] Hawaladars often place advertisements in Indian community newspapers offering 'quick delivery' and 'good rates.'

[9] This pricing scheme was observed in the case *US v Ismail*, discussed later in this paper. Even though the case involved Pakistani, not Indian, rupees, this is still a typical hawala pricing scheme.

The Delhi hawaladar sells the computer equipment for at least $250,000—he recovers the $50,000 he 'paid' for the equipment as well as the $200,000 that he was owed by the New York hawaladar.

The Over-Invoicing Scheme

Here, the Delhi-based hawala broker needs to send $200,000 to his associate in New York.

Once again, this invoice manipulation scheme begins with the New York hawaladar's purchase of $250,000 worth of computer equipment, and its subsequent shipment to Delhi.

This time, however, he inflates the value to $450,000 and invoices appropriately (bribery or a free trade zone are often used to avoid excessive duty payments, or merchandise that is not subject to duty can be used). The broker in Delhi remits $450,000. This reimburses the New York broker for the $250,000 that was paid for the computer equipment and also provides him with $200,000 that he was owed by the Delhi broker. Once again, enough of a paper trail has been established to provide an appearance of compliance with currency control regulations.

In brief, however, there is* a large demand for gold in India for cultural and economic reasons; India, which is not a producer of gold, is arguably the world's largest consumer of gold.[10] Hawaladars exploit this situation; gold can almost always be sold at a profit in India. The details of the 'gold situation' in India will be discussed later in this paper.

A Typical Gold Smuggling Scheme

Several hawaladars have decided to pool some money and purchase a large quantity of gold in Dubai. They will arrange to have this gold smuggled from Dubai to India through various means, such as small ships sailing between Dubai and Mumbai[11] or through an informal network of couriers (often Indians or Pakistanis working in the Gulf) who make extra money smuggling gold bars into India.

Once the gold has reached India, the smugglers deliver the gold to a designated person (usually another hawaladar or a jeweller who does business with hawaladars) who pays them for their services; this payment can be money or a share of the gold that was smuggled.

[10] Jennifer Morrow, 'In Depth: Gold Obsession' *Media Web India/Indian Economy Overview*, October 1996.

[11] Formerly and internationally known as 'Bombay'.

*Gold smuggling—Overview

The members of this informal 'hawala gold syndicate' now have several options. They can sell all of the gold, and move the profits out of India (using the invoice manipulation schemes described above), they can sell some of the gold to obtain money needed to satisfy clients' money delivery requirements or they can deliver gold to recipients in India.

Black Hawala in India and Pakistan

This section will attempt to summarize the criminal nature of certain hawala transactions (i.e. 'black hawala') in India and Pakistan.

One aspect of hawala that lends itself to criminal activity is its anonymity. Records of individual hawala transactions are not usually kept, making tracing them almost impossible (an important exception to this will be discussed later). Hawaladars maintain records indicating money owed and money due, but little more than that, and records are not necessarily maintained after accounts have been settled.

Black Hawala in India

The ability to conduct anonymous transactions makes it possible to violate various provisions of India's Foreign Exchange Regulation Act (FERA). Some of the objectives of this Act were the establishment of controls over foreign exchange, the prevention of capital flight and the maintenance of external solvency.

This Act regulates foreign exchange and the transfer of money into and out of the country. Foreign exchange must be conducted at authorized rates by authorized dealers. Remittances to foreign countries are permitted to satisfy payments for imports and specified personal transactions. All other remittances must be approved by the Reserve Bank of India.[12]

The hawala transfer and invoice manipulation schemes discussed above are clear violations of the FERA and Indian customs regulations. The favourable prices available to expatriates and others in the hawala transfers depend on the rupee/dollar exchange rate on the black market. The same transaction would not be cost effective to the customer if the official exchange rate were used.

The misrepresentation of the value of a shipment constitutes a violation in both India and the exporting country of customs regulations. Over invoicing facilitates the transfer of money out of India in violation of the FERA. The appearance of a 'payment for imports' provides an illusion of compliance with the FERA, but the law is being broken nonetheless.

[12]M.L. Tannan, *Tannan's Banking Law and Practice*, India 1996, 594-596.

The manipulation of invoices is not limited to the settlement of accounts between hawaladars. It is a major means of facilitating capital flight out of India. In a study done of trade between the United States and India[13], it was determined that these techniques were used to move between $1065 and $370 out of India illegally in 1993.

This paper would not be complete without some mention of the current 'Jain Hawala Case'. Since this case has received substantial international press coverage and is the topic of at least one book[14], only a brief summary will be provided here. S.K., N.K. and B.R. Jain, brothers and partners in various construction-related businesses, are accused of having paid bribes to numerous politicians.[15] These bribes were allegedly paid through hawaladars working with the Jains or through hawala-related operations of the Jains themselves.

There are two things that make this case interesting. First, it is documented, which is rare in hawala cases. Diaries seized from the Jains document the payments that were made.[16] Second, it is a testimony to the effectiveness of hawala at moving money without being detected.

These diaries document payments of approximately $18 million to about 100 people over a two year period. The smallest payment was about $800, the largest $3 million.

Even though India is not a major producer of gold, the demand for gold is very high. Gold has religious and cultural significance in India and is also seen as a hedge against inflation; almost every Indian family of any means maintains a small stock of gold.

Indian law regulates the import of gold, which is also subject to duty. Indian residents returning to India may only bring in gold jewellery (no bullion); NRIs (non-resident Indians) are only allowed to bring in 10 kilograms every six months. Couriers coming to India are not allowed to bring in any gold at all.

The demand for gold is greater than the supply. Smuggling of gold is a profitable enterprise, as described in the 'gold scenario' above. In January 1997, Indian authorities doubled the amount of gold that NRIs could bring in to the country from 5 to 10 kilograms.[17] This change was done to

[13]John Zdanowicz, William W. Welch and Simon J. Pak, Capital Flight from India to the United States Through Abnormal Pricing in International Trade, *Finance India*, X3, 1995.

[14]Sanjay Kapoor, *Bad Money, Bad Politics: The Untold Hawala Story*, 1996.

[15]Narayanan Madhavan, "Indian Police Charge 14 More in Corruption Scandal' *Reuters World Service* (New Delhi), 22 February 1996.

[16]Charu Lata Joshi, 'Hawala Case: Crucial Clues', *India Today*, 15 March 1996.

[17]Dev Varam, 'Low Gold Prices to Fuel India Sub-Continent Demand', *The Reuter Asia-Pacific Business Report*, 6 January 1997.

recoup at least some of the duty that is lost through gold smuggling; it is not clear what overall effect this will have on the gold smuggling situation in India.

Black Hawala in Pakistan

In Pakistan, some circumstances are similar or identical to those in India, specifically:

* Use of hawala by expatriate workers to remit money;
* Manipulation of invoices to remit money;
* Black market currency speculation;
* Gold smuggling.

Pakistan has a significant internal heroin abuse problem, and it is a major trans-shipment point for drugs produced in Afghanistan. The proceeds from the domestic heroin trade must be laundered, as must the monies associated with the 'export' drug trade.

Hawala is particularly attractive to drug traffickers (in Pakistan and elsewhere) for several reasons.[18]

* Anonymity: hawala transactions are usually impossible to trace;
* Speed: hawaladars can move money with a phone call or fax;
* Economy: black market speculation is cost effective.

These circumstances, combined with the availability of foreign currency and accounts and the deregulation of foreign exchange in Pakistan[19] have created an environment conducive to black hawala, which facilitates drug trafficking and other crimes in Pakistan.

Black Hawala Elsewhere

Black hawala facilitates crimes such as capital flight, currency transfer violations and gold smuggling in India and Pakistan. It is also undoubtedly a facilitator of criminal activity elsewhere. In this section, examples from the United States and United Kingdom will be used.

It is often difficult to locate 'hawala' cases because they are usually not recognized as such. In the US and UK, indicators of hawala might be found in cases involving customs offences, tax evasion and drug trafficking.

[18]Saud Ahmad Mirza, 'Report submitted by Mr. Saud Ahmad Mirza, SSP/Joint Director at 2nd Asian Money Laundering Workshop'; Proceedings of a workshop held at Hong Kong (14-15 November 1996) by the Financial Action Task Force.

[19]Peter Montagnon and Farhan Bokhar, 'Prospects for Pakistan/Decade of Uncertainty', *The Financial Times*, 12 December 1996.

In one US case (*US v Ismail*[20]) a Pakistani living in the Washington, DC area was doing hawala transfers for other expatriates. Large cash transactions at the bank used by some of the defendants were brought to the attention of customs and tax authorities. Their subsequent investigation uncovered a scheme in which surgical instruments were being imported at inflated prices (over-invoicing) to facilitate the illegal transfer of money from the US to Pakistan. Convictions were obtained for customs violations, making false statements and filing tax fraud.

This case typifies one of the problems encountered with hawala: what is illegal in one jurisdiction is not illegal in another. Providing an alternative remittance service is not illegal in the United States; if there had not been tax and customs violations, there would not have been a case.

A United Kingdom case from 1985[21] is also worth discussing. In this case, Choraria was convicted of 'being knowingly concerned in the fraudulent evasion of the prohibition of importation of a Class A controlled drug, namely heroin'. Choraria is described as the 'banker who knowingly enabled payment for heroin imported into this country illegally to be transferred to India from whence the heroin had been sent.'

Choraria operated two legitimate businesses, a confirming house[22] and a remittance service, both of which were appropriately licensed (given the facts of the case, it is likely that at least part of the remittance business was hawala-based). In this case, Choraria facilitated the transfer of money from parties in Karachi and Mumbai as part of heroin smuggling.

What is interesting about this case is the fact that hawala, 'a term unknown to the bankers from Hambros' (Choraria's bankers), had to be explained at length by Choraria and his nephew, an accountant, during the course of the trial. It also appears that even some of the criminals in the United Kingdom did not understand the means by which money was being moved!

[20]The full citation is UNITED STATES OF AMERICA, Plaintiff-Appellee, *v. ISMAIL*, Defendant-Appellant. UNITED STATES OF AMERICA, Plaintiff-Appellee, *v. SHAKEEL AHMAD*, a/k/a Javed Iqbal, Defendant-Appellant. UNITED STATES OF AMERICA Plaintiff-Appellee, *v. MIAN TAUQIR AHMED*, a/k/a Tauqir Ahmed, Defendant-Appellant. UNITED STATES OF AMERICA, Plaintiff-Appellee, *v. MOHAMMAD BASHIR*, Defendant-Appellant. No. 95-5299, No. 95-5324, No. 95-5325, No. 95-5326, 97 F.3d 50; 1996 U.S.App. LEXIS 25229; 96-2 U.S. Tax Cas.

[21]*R v Choraria* Court of Appeal (Criminal Division) 27 March 1985.

[22]In the import/export business, a confirming house acts on behalf of the buyer by dealing directly with the exporter to complete the contract. There is no overseas credit risk or financial burden for the exporter because the confirming house provides short term credit to the overseas buyer, who pays a commission for this service.

Finally, in early 1997 it is anticipated that principals in MGM Marwex International, the United States subsidiary of Frankfurt-based MGM Marwex Geldwechsel, will go on trial for laundering drug money.[23] The defendants are accused of using Marwex as well as hawala techniques to facilitate the laundering of money for an international drug trafficking organization.

Black Hawala's Criminal Connections

We will now broaden the scope of our discussion and develop several general models that show the role that black hawala plays in a wide range of criminal activities.

Drug Trafficking

The operations of drug trafficking operations are well documented elsewhere[24]; we shall confine our discussion to the fact that they are profit making operations. Unlike most other businesses, however, their profits are derived from illegal activities. The illegal profits have to be laundered in order for the criminal activity to continue. All but the smallest drug operations depend on money laundering to survive.[25]

Money Laundering and Hawala

Money laundering is the process of converting the proceeds of a criminal activity into funds with an apparently legal source. Money laundering may be further divided into three subprocesses or stages: placement, layering and integration.

Placement and Hawala

In the placement stage, the money launderer disposes of the proceeds of a criminal activity (which are often in the form of cash). At this stage, financial institutions can be a 'chokepoint' in the money laundering cycle, and it is also at this stage that laundered money is particularly vulnerable to detection. Many countries have enacted anti-money laundering counter-

[23]Nicholas Riccardi, 'Businessman Indicted in Money Laundering', *The Los Angeles Times*, 9 November 1995.

[24]Dorn et al. (1992:3-59) is a good overview of the evolution and operation of drug markets; Ruggiero and South (1995:67-108;109-144;145-189) addresses Europe and includes detailed case studies of London and Turin.

[25]FinCEN (1992:3-6) provides a high level summary of the relationship between drug trafficking and money laundering.

measures that exploit this vulnerability. In the United States, the Bank Secrecy Act[26] calls for several types of reporting to the United States Department of the Treasury.[27] First, all cash transactions over $10,000 (this includes bank transactions, transactions at casinos and physical shipments of cash into or out of the United States) must be reported. Second, any shipments or receipts of monetary instruments with a value greater than $10,000 must be reported. Third, any person with a financial interest or signatory authority over bank, securities or other financial accounts outside the United States with a value greater than $10,000 must report this.

Effective April 1, 1996, the United States implemented a requirement for financial institutions to report suspicious transactions.[28] A Suspicious Activity Report (SAR) must be filed following the discovery of insider abuse involving any amount, violations aggregating $5,000 or more where a suspect can be identified; violations aggregating $25,000 or more regardless of a potential suspect, or transactions aggregating $5,000 or more that involve potential money laundering or violations of the Bank Secrecy Act.

Since many hawala transactions are not conducted in the banking system, the regulatory requirements associated with banks do not exist. If we recall the 'hawala transfer scheme' discussed earlier, money was paid to a hawaladar, not a bank, and therefore no report would have been filed, even if the amount of the transaction exceeded the reporting threshold. Since many hawaladars also operate legitimate (or legitimate-appearing) businesses, they can take the aggregate cash payments received from their hawala customers, mix them with the profits from their other business activities, and deposit them in a bank. If the deposit exceeds a reporting threshold, the report will most likely represent the deposit as the proceeds from a legitimate business and it is unlikely that the transaction will be reported as suspicious.

[26]31 USC 5311-5328.

[27]The forms used for filing these reports (Form 4789, Currency Transaction Report [CTR]; Form 8362, Currency Transaction Report for Casinos [CTRC]; Form 4790, Report of International Transportation of Currency or Monetary Instruments [CMIR], TD F 90-22.1, Report of Foreign Bank and Financial Accounts [FBAR] and TD F 90-22.47, Suspicious Activity Report [SAR]) and descriptions of the circumstances under which they must be filed can be obtained from FinCEN's World Wide Web Internet site: http://www.ustreas.gov/treasury/bureaus/fincen.forms.html; the Adobe Acrobat Reader needed to view and print the forms is also available at this site. If you have problems with this site, please contact webmaster@fincen.treas.gov.

[28]In many countries, suspicious transaction reporting is the only reporting that is required. In the United Kingdom, for example, suspicious transactions must be reported to the National Criminal Intelligence Service. Gold and Levi (1994) describes this system in detail.

Layering and Hawala

In the layering stage, the money launderer manipulates the illicit funds to make them appear as though they were derived from a legitimate source. A component of many layering schemes has been seen to be the transfer of money from one account to another. Even though this is done as carefully as possible, when it is done through the 'traditional' banking system it presents two problems to the money launderer. First, there is the possibility that a transaction could be considered to be suspicious and reported as such. Related to this is the paper trail created by these transactions. If any portion of the laundering network is examined, the related paper trails could lead a diligent investigator directly to the source of the criminal proceeds and unravel the money laundering network.

Hawala transfers, as seen above, leave what is at best a sparse or confusing paper trail. Even when invoice manipulation is used, the mixture of legal goods and illegal money, confusion about 'valid' prices and a possibly complex international shipping network create a trail much more complicated than a simple wire transfer. Hawala's formidable ability to convert money into gold is another consideration. Gold is as good as money (money is as good as gold?), can always be sold at a good price and is traded on markets world-wide. Gold is also untraceable.

It should be mentioned that hawala transfers are not limited in size to small remittances from expatriates. Evidence suggests that BCCI used hawala techniques in conjunction with its global network to facilitate arms deals, tariff evasion and other crimes.[29]

Integration and Hawala

In the integration stage, the launderer invests in other assets, uses the funds to enjoy a luxurious lifestyle or reinvests his profits into criminal activities.

The same characteristics of hawala that make it a potential tool for the layering of money also make it ideal for the integration of money. This is when money seems to become legitimate, and, as we have seen, hawala techniques are capable of transforming money into almost any form, offering many possibilities for establishing an appearance of legitimacy.

[29] V.K. Banker, 'L' Affaire BCCI' 1991, 47-50.

Hawala and Other Systems (Comparison with the US-Mexico Border Situation)

There are some interesting parallels between drug trafficking and related money laundering along the border between the United States and Mexico[30] and hawala.

The size of this border makes it impossible to patrol effectively. Drugs are transported using light aircraft, couriers (often illegal aliens doing this as a means of earning money) or concealed in the millions of vehicles that cross the border each day. These smuggling activities are believed to be controlled by Mexican crime 'families' operating in conjunction with Colombian cartels.

Some of the components in the money laundering operations associated with this drug market are:

bureaux de change[31] and remittance houses[32];
Mexican bank drafts; and
car dealers.

Along the US-Mexico border, bureaux de change provide various financial services such as wire transfers and exchange between US dollars and Mexican pesos. Remittance houses are similar operations, and may also provide services such as cellular telephones and pagers.

Mexican bank drafts, which are bearer instruments, (i.e. payable to the bearer) were developed by Mexican banks to assist in the facilitation of trade between the United States and Mexico. They have come to be used as a money laundering instrument because of their liquidity and lack of a paper trail. Typically, money launderers will transport bulk currency from the United States into Mexico and deposit it into a Mexican bank. They will then ask for a draft in dollars, which is then transported back into the United States and deposited into a bank there, effectively laundering the cash that was transported into Mexico.

Auto dealers (along with other businesses such as jewellers) are required to report cash transactions in excess of $10,000.[33] This law is difficult to

[30]FinCEN (1993) discusses the Southwest Border situation in detail.

[31]These are referred to as *casas de cambio* (Spanish for 'exchange houses') along the US-Mexico border; they often specialize in the conversion of dollars and pesos.

[32]A giro is an instrument allowing a direct transfer of money from one account to another. Remittance houses along the US-Mexico border often use giro transfers, hence the name giro house.

[33]These reports are filed on the Internal Revenue Service's Form 8300 (Report of Cash Payments Over $10,000 Received In a Trade or Business); this reporting is not part of the Bank Secrecy Act.

enforce, and money launderers exploit this, using the automobile as an instrument to facilitate the laundering of money.[34] A money launderer can visit a dealership and purchase a car for cash. In large US cities, there is a large market for automobiles (especially 'luxury' or 'sport' models), so the launderer can easily resell the car. The launderer will insist on a certified cheque (or some similar instrument) for payment. This, like the Mexican bank draft can then be deposited into a bank, circumventing cash transaction reporting requirements.

The bureaux de change and remittance houses along the US-Mexico border perform some of the same 'informal' financial services offered by hawaladars. Even though different means are used, both provide a means of disposing of large quantities without using traditional financial institutions, bypassing any reporting or disclosure requirements. Both also provide means of moving and transforming money, making them effective participants in layering and integration.

Mexican bank drafts and automobiles serve as alternative instruments in money laundering along the US-Mexico border. In hawala, gold is often the alternative monetary instrument of choice. Even though automobiles are bulkier than gold, the market for them may be larger and is certainly much less regulated.

We have presented this analysis of the similarities between hawala and money laundering along the US-Mexico border to establish and validate a more general framework for addressing the problems caused by money laundering and their potential solutions.

Some Consequences of Black Hawala

When hawala is used, for example, to facilitate the financing of heroin smuggling from India to the United Kingdom, problems associated with hawala, such as capital flight in India (or any other country, such as Pakistan, with a hawala-based parallel economy) are most likely exacerbated.

Bank fraud occurs in many forms in India and includes phenomena familiar to western bankers such as robbery and corruption and others such as loan mela[35] which are unique to India. It should come as no surprise

[34]This is not unique to the Southwest Border; Hall (1995) describes but one of several 'auto-laundries' that have been identified in the Washington, DC area.

[35]Ghosh (1991:117-134,155-165); the term 'mela' is the Hindi word for a camp or fair. 'Loan melas' or 'loan camps' were established by the Government of India to assist economically weak persons obtain loans. Unfortunately, the counterfeiting of the eligibility paperwork for the loans often leads to widespread abuse of the system.

that hawala techniques play a major role in the laundering of the proceeds associated with these frauds. The inherent global nature of hawala, acquired through its interaction with the drug trade and other criminal activities, provides a wide variety of options for the disposal of fraudulently obtained money.

What has happened is that a bad situation has become worse. Due to the involvement of so many factors outside India's borders, internal measures are most likely inadequate. These problems, which have become global in scope[36], will require similarly global solutions.

Fighting Black Hawala

The majority of this paper has been concerned with the discussion and examination of problems; the remainder will attempt to address some solutions.

The components of an effective anti-money laundering programme are anti-money laundering legislation, training of law enforcement, judicial and financial sector personnel on the nature and implementation of this legislation and agreements to facilitate international co-operation on the investigation and prosecution of financial crime cases.

Anti-money laundering legislation is the foundation of an anti-money laundering programme; without it, money laundering is not a crime. Training increases awareness of the problems associated with money laundering and allows money laundering legislation to be used effectively. International agreements and co-operation minimize issues of jurisdiction and allow for interdiction of complex, border-crossing money laundering operations.

Financial Action Tast Force (FATF) Recommendations Applicable to Hawala

FATF has developed a set of 40 recommendations[37] that establish a basic framework for anti-money laundering efforts. They address the criminal justice, law enforcement and financial systems with respect to regulation and international co-operation. Given the diversity of the world's legal systems,

[36]It is not coincidental that Morris-Cotterill (1996:31-66), addressing the situation in the United Kingdom, and Minn (1996:1-3), addressing the situation in India, have compiled very similar lists of problems, such as corruption, welfare fraud, tax evasion and drug trafficking, that are facilitated or exacerbated by money laundering and related financial crimes.

[37]These citations reflect the revised recommendations that were issued in June 1996.

the recommendations are principles for action, rather than detailed prescriptions. The recommendations are not particularly complex or difficult; the main 'prerequisite' is that a country has the political will to act against money laundering. Additionally, the recommendations contain no proposals that would compromise the freedom to engage in legitimate transactions or threaten economic development.

Several of the FATF 40 Recommendations are particularly relevant to hawala-facilitated money laundering:

Recommendations 4 and 5 call for countries to criminalize money laundering. The predicate offences should be extended beyond drug trafficking to include all serious offences. A country should determine which crimes would constitute the predicate offences for money laundering. Additionally, the offence of money laundering should apply when the perpetrator knowingly participates in the activity.

Recommendation 6 suggests that countries allow corporations, and not just their employees to be held liable for criminal liability with respect to money laundering.

These recommendations would cause certain aspects of hawala to be recognized as criminal money laundering and establish standards of liability and culpability for corporations as well as persons. It has also been observed that anti-money laundering laws in many countries are restricted to drug-related money laundering. Since not all money laundering is drug related (e.g. the proceeds of bank fraud or arms dealing), legislation with a broader scope is needed, as it is often impossible to distinguish one type of money laundering from another. As the discussion above has shown, it is often the case that hawala operates either beyond or at the boundary of existing laws, making prosecution difficult or impossible.

Recommendation 14 calls for financial institutions to pay attention to all complex, unusual and large transactions and all unusual patterns of transactions that have no apparent economic or apparent lawful purpose. The background and purpose of such transactions should be examined and documented, and these findings should be made available to assist appropriate regulatory and enforcement personnel.

Even though it is unlikely that hawaladars will ever be subject to any sort of formal scrutiny, it is often necessary for them to make use of the banking system, and this can be scrutinized. Scrutiny of the banking system creates a 'choke point' that could impede the effectiveness of hawala-based money laundering.[38]

[38]Neil Darbyshire, 'Criminal Money Route Traced' *The Daily Telegraph*, 22 September 1988.

Recommendation 15 calls for financial institutions suspecting that funds stem from a criminal activity to report this suspicion to a designated authority. This recommendation seeks to establish a suspicious or unusual activity reporting system as an anti-money laundering resource. It is an extension of the idea introduced in Recommendation 14.

The 'designated authority' for the receipt of suspicious activity reports is often referred to as a Financial Intelligence Unit (FIU). FIUs and their role within individual national anit-money laundering programmes are the result of a natural evolution of these efforts. In some countries, the difficulty of retrofitting anti-money laundering measures into already existing law enforcement structures led to the designation of a central point for co-ordinating the efforts of several different law enforcement and/or judicial authorities. In other countries, officials identified from the beginning that a comprehensive anti-money laundering program -including a system for disclosure of suspect financial transactions- requires a central office or agency in order to assess and process these reports.

On 9 June 1995, representatives of 24 nations and 8 international organizations met for the first time at the Palais d'Egmont-Arenberg in Brussels. The purpose of this gathering was to examine the phenomenon of FIUs. Created by an ever-growing number of countries as part of their anti-money laundering efforts, these organizations numbered just over a dozen at this first Brussels meeting. Less than a year later, at the third meeting of the Egmont Group in San Francisco, there were 18 such units present.[39]

Although differing in size, structure, and individual responsibilities, all FIUs share a common purpose -the fight against money laundering. The goal of Egmont, therefore, has been to seek ways to develop among participants a more effective and practical co-operation, especially in the areas of information exchange and sharing expertise.

In addition to the adoption of the FATF 40 Recommendations, FinCEN also encourages the establishment of an FIU and participation in the Egmont Group.

[39]As of the writing of this paper (February, 1997) FIUs had been established in Aruba, Australia, Austria, Belgium, Chile, the Czech Republic, France, Hungary, Iceland, Ireland, Luxembourg, Monaco, Netherlands, the Netherlands Antilles, New Zealand, Norway, Panama, Portugal, Slovakia, Slovenia, Spain, Sweden, the United Kingdom and the United States. FIUs are being planned or are under development in Argentina, Antigua, Bolivia, Brazil, Bulgaria, Canada, Colombia, Croatia, Cyprus, Estonia, Finland, Greece, Italy, Latvia, Lithuania, Mexico, Poland, Switzerland, South Africa and Turkey.

Understanding is the Nemesis of Black Hawala

If nothing else, this paper has attempted to raise the level of understanding of hawala and its relationship to money laundering, drug trafficking and other criminal activities.

For readers already familiar with hawala, we hope to have shown how hawala contributes to drug abuse and other crimes in the Americas and Europe. For readers already familiar with the drug trade and money laundering, we hope to have shown that these activities may facilitate capital flight and other economic problems in countries such as India and Pakistan.

On a somewhat formal level, FATF recommendations 30-40 call for the strengthening of international co-operation through the exchange of information, co-operation in confiscation, mutual assistance and extradition. These recommendations, along with the others (those discussed above as well as those remaining) establish a basic and effective framework for fighting money laundering.

This formality, however, must be combined with a general, possibly informal understanding of what is going on. We have but to recall the confusion of policemen, prosecutors, bankers and criminals in *R. v Choraria* to see that a lack of understanding of Hawala's role is as problematic as the lack of an effective anti-money laundering infrastructure.

FinCEN has taken some preliminary steps to document the workings of hawala and to make this information available to the law enforcement, regulatory, legislative and financial communities. It is hoped that at some point some of this information can be formally integrated into anti-money laundering training programmes.

In the same vein, this same research was used to develop the findings presented here. It is anticipated that as nations such as India and Pakistan undertake to implement more rigorous anti-money laundering disciplines, training and technical assistance will be required. Part of this training might consist of a combination of a look at the 'big picture' of drug trafficking and money laundering as well as a regional analysis, which will help to understand not only the role that hawala plays but also what can be done about the problem.

Finally, if nothing else, it is hoped that this paper will serve as the catalyst for some discussions on the topics of hawala, money laundering, drug trafficking and financial crimes.

Glossary

This glossary contains certain terms used in this paper as well as others that the reader may encounter while researching hawala and related topics.

confirming house: in the import/export business, a confirming house acts on behalf of the buyer by dealing directly with the exporter to complete the contract. There is no overseas credit risk or financial burden for the exporter because the confirming house provides short term credit to the overseas buyer, who pays a commission for this service.

crore: 10,000,000 [ten million]; part of the Indian/Pakistani numbering system, frequently used when discussing money. A crore is 100 *lakhs*.

FinCEN: the Financial Crimes Enforcement Network, part of the United States Department of the Treasury; it is concerned with money laundering and other financial crimes.

hawala (also spelled *havala, hawallah or hawalah*) refers to an alternative remittance system used extensively in India and Pakistan. It is often used interchangeably with the world *hundi*. The word 'hawala' comes from the Arabic root for transfer. In business usage, it has the meanings 'trust' and 'reference' in Hindu and Urdu and is also used colloquially for 'money' (hawala is a means of transferring money, and it is based on trust or an appropriate reference). In some contexts, it refers to payments made in connection with bribery and money laundering.

hawaladar: a hawala broker or dealer.

hundi: another term for *hawala*; the word also has the meanings 'cheque' or 'bill of exchange' in Hindi and Urdu.

integration: the third and final stage of money laundering In this stage, the launderer invests in other assets, uses the funds to enjoy a luxurious lifestyle or reinvests his profits into criminal activities.

lakh: (also spelled *lack*: 100,000 [one hundred thousand]; part of the Indian/Pakistani numbering system, frequently used when discussing money.

layering: the second stage of money laundering. In this stage, the money launderer manipulates the illicit funds to make them appear as though they were derived from a legitimate source.

mechanism: in money laundering, a business or financial enterprise that facilitates money laundering; includes traditional and non-traditional financial institutions as well as retail outlets.

mela: from the Hindi word for a camp, fair or association. 'Loan melas' or 'loan camps' were established by the Government of India to assist economically weak persons obtain loans. Unfortunately, the counterfeiting of the eligibility paperwork for the loans often leads to widespread abuse of the system.

money laundering: the process of converting the proceeds of a criminal activity into funds with an apparently legal source. Money laundering may be further divided into three subprocesses or stages: *placement, layering* and *integration.*

placement: the first stage of money laundering. In this stage, the money launderer disposes of the proceeds of a criminal activity (which are often in the form of cash).

process: in money laundering, the generic model describing how criminally derived proceeds are transformed into legitimate appearing funds; includes the three stages: *placement, layering* and *integration*.

scheme: in money laundering, a series of money laundering techniques whereby proceeds from a particular operation are transformed into legitimate appearing funds.

technique: in money laundering, an individual process or step in the money laundering process.

tola: approximately 11.7 grams (the weight of a silver rupee); this is a common unit used in the precious metals and jewellery businesses in India, Pakistan and Persian Gulf.

Bibliography

Banker, V.K. (1991), *L'Affaire BCCI*. Delhi: Konark.

Darbyshire, Neil (1988), 'Criminal Money Route Traced' *The Daily Telegraph*, September 22, 1988.

Das, Biswajyoti (1996) 'India Plans to Recover Huge Amounts of Black Money' *Reuter Textline/Reuter News Service-India* November 12, 1996.

Deloitte Touche Tohmatsu International/C.C. Chokshi & Co. (1995) *India: International Tax and Business Guide*. New York: Deloittee Touche Tohmatsu International.

Dorn, Nicholas; Murji, Karim and South, Nigel (1992), *Traffickers: Drug Markets and Law Enforcement*. London: Routledge.

Fitch, Thomas (1993), *Dictionary of Banking Terms*. Happauge, New York: Barron's Educational.

Ghosh, S.K. (1991), *Indian Banking: Crime and Security in Indian Banks*. New Delhi: Ashish Publishing House.

Gold, Michael and Levi, Michael (1994), *Money-Laundering in the UK: an appraisal of suspicion-based reporting*. London: The Police Foundation.

Gupta, Suraj B. (1992), *Black Income in India*. New Delhi: Sage Publications.

Hall, Charles W. (1995), 'Keeping Tabs on Cash Car Deals; Paper Trail Ties Drug Money to Auto Firms, FBI Says,' *The Washington Post*, December 15, 1995.

Hongkong and Shanghai Banking Corporation (1994) *India* (Business Profile Series). Hong Kong: Hongkong and Shanghai Banking Corporation.

Joshi, Charu Lata (1996), 'Hawala Case: Crucial Clues,' *India Today*, March 15, 1996.

Kapoor, Sanjay (1996), *Bad Money, Bad Politics: The Untold Hawala Story*. New Delhi: Har-Anand Publication (Alka Paperbacks).

Madhavan, Narayanan (1996), 'Indian Police Charge 14 More in Corruption Scandal', *Reuters World Service (New Delhi)*, February 22, 1996.

Malhotra, Angelian (1995), 'India's Underground Bankers' *Asia, Inc. Online/Asia, Inc*. August 1995.

Meenai, S.A. (1984), *Money and Banking in Pakistan*, Karachi: Oxford University Press.

Mirza, Saud Ahmad (1996) *Report Submitted by Mr. Saud Ahmad Mirza, SSP/ Joint Director at 2nd Asian Money Laundering Workshop Hong Kong 14/ 15 November 1996*. Paris: OECD/FATF.

Montagnon, Peter and Bokhar, Farhan (1996), 'Prospects for Pakistan/Decade of Uncertainty', *The Financial Times* December 12, 1996.

Morris-Cotterill, Nigel (1996), *How Not to be a Money Launderer*. Brentwood, Essex: Silkscreen Publications.

Morrow, Jennifer (1996), 'In Depth: Gold Obession' *Media Web India/Indian Economy Overview*, October 1996. New Delhi: Media Web India.

Pathak, R.C. [compiler] (1995), *Bhargava's Standard Illustrated Dictionary Hindi-English*. Varanasi: Bhargava Book Depot.

Quereshi, Bashir Ahman [compiler] (1992), *Standard Twentieth Century Dictionary Urdu into English*. Delhi: Educational Publishing House.

Riccardi, Nicholas (1995), 'Businessman Indicted in Money Laundering', *The Los Angeles Times*, November 9, 1995.

Ruggiero, Vincenzo and South, Nigel (1995), *Eurodrugs: Drug Use, Markets and Trafficking in Europe*. London: UCL Press.

Sinha, D.K. (1996), *Report of Indian Delegate Shri D.K. Sinha, IPS, DIG, CBI Calcutta at Second Asia Workshop on Disposal of Proceeds of Crime Money Laundering Methods Held in Hong Kong on 14-15 November, 1996*. Paris: OECD/FATF.

Tannan, M.L. (1996), *Tannan's Banking Law and Practice in India*. New Delhi: India Law House.

Thakur, Sushila (1990), *Two Decades of Indian Banking: The Service Sector Scenario*. Delhi: Chanakya Publications.

Tripathi, Dwijendra and Misra, Prithi (1985), *Towards a New Frontier: History of the Bank of Baroda*. New Delhi: Manohar.

U.S. Department of Justice, Drug Enforcement Administration [DEA] (1993) *Money Laundering in Southwest Asia*. Washington, DC: Department of Justice, DEA Publication DEA-930001.

U.S. Library of Congress (1996), *India: A Country Study*. Washington, DC: Government Printing Office.

U.S. Library of Congress (1995a), *Pakistan: A Country Study*. Washington, DC: Government Printing Office.

U.S. Library of Congress (1995b), *Persian Gulf States: Country Studies*. Washington, DC: Government Printing Office.

U.S. Department of the Treasury, Financial Crimes Enforcement Network [FinCEN] (1993), *Southwest Border Threats Assessment: Overview*. Vienna, VA: Financial Crimes Enforcement Network.

U.S. Department of the Treasury, Financial Crimes Enforcement Network [FinCEN] (1992), *An Assessment of Narcotics Related Money Laundering*. Vienna. VA: Financial Crimes Enforcement Network.

Varam, Dev (1996), 'Low Gold Prices to Fuel India Sub-Continent Demand', *The Reuter Asia-Pacific Business Report*, January 6, 1997.

Zdanowicz, John S., Welch, William W. and Pak, Simon J. (1995) 'Capital Flight From India to the United States Through Abnormal Pricing in International Trade' *Finance India*, Vol.X, No.3, September 1995.

THE FORTY RECOMMENDATIONS OF THE FINANCIAL ACTION TASK FORCE ON MONEY LAUNDERING

Introduction

(1) The Financial Action Task Force on Money Laundering (FATF) is an inter-governmental body whose purpose is the development and promotion of policies to combat money laundering—the processing of criminal proceeds in order to disguise their illegal origin. These policies aim to prevent such proceeds from being utilized in future criminal activities and from affecting legitimate economic activities.

(2) The FATF currently consists of 26 countries[1] and two international organizations[2]. Its membership includes the major financial centre countries of Europe, North America and Asia. It is a multi-disciplinary body—as is essential in dealing with money laundering—bringing together the policy-making power of legal, financial and law enforcement experts.

(3) This need to cover all relevant aspects of the fight against money laundering is reflected in the scope of the forty FATF Recommendations—the measures which the Task Force have agreed to implement and which all countries are encouraged to adopt. The Recommendations were originally drawn up in 1990. In 1996 the forty Recommendations were revised to take into account the experience gained over the last six years and to reflect the changes which have occurred in the money laundering problem.[3]

[1] Reference in this document to 'countries' should be taken to apply equally to 'territories' or 'jurisdictions'. The twenty six FATF member countries and governments are: Australia, Austria, Belgium, Canada, Denmark, Finland, France, Germany, Greece, Hong Kong, Iceland, Ireland, Italy, Japan, Luxembourg, the Kingdom of the Netherlands, New Zealand, Norway, Portugal, Singapore, Spain, Sweden, Switzerland, Turkey, United Kingdom, and the United States.

[2] The two international organizations are: the European Commission and the Gulf Cooperation Council.

[3] During the period 1990 to 1995, the FATF also elaborated various Interpretative Notes which are designed to clarify the application of specific Recommendations. Some of these Interpretative Notes have been updated in the Stocktaking Review to reflect changes in the Recommendations.

(4) These forty Recommendations set out the basic framework for anti-money laundering efforts and they are designed to be of universal application. They cover the criminal justice system and law enforcement; the financial system and its regulation; and international cooperation.

(5) It was recognised from the outset of the FATF that countries have diverse legal and financial systems and so all cannot take identical measures. The Recommendations are therefore the principles for action in this field, for countries to implement according to their particular circumstances and constitutional frameworks allowing countries a measure of flexibility rather than prescribing every detail. The measures are not particularly complex or difficult, provided there is the political will to act. Nor do they compromise the freedom to engage in legitimate transactions or threaten economic development.

(6) FATF countries are clearly committed to accept the discipline of being subjected to multilateral surveillance and peer review. All member countries have their implementation of the forty Recommendations monitored through a two-pronged approach: an annual self-assessment exercise and the more detailed mutual evaluation process under which each member country is subject to an on-site examination. In addition, the FATF carries out cross-country reviews of measures taken to implement particular Recommendations.

(7) These measures are essential for the creation of an effective anti-money laundering framework.

THE FORTY RECOMMENDATIONS OF THE FINANCIAL ACTION TASK FORCE ON MONEY LAUNDERING

A. General Framework of the Recommendations

(1) Each country should take immediate steps to ratify and to implement fully, the 1988 United Nations Convention against Illicit Traffic in Narcotic Drugs and Psychotropic Substances (the Vienna Convention).

(2) Financial institution secrecy laws should be conceived so as not to inhibit implementation of these recommendations.

(3) An effective money laundering enforcement program should include increased multilateral co-operation and mutual legal assistance in money laundering investigations and prosecutions and extradition in money laundering cases, where possible.

B. Role of National Legal Systems in Combating Money Laundering

Scope of the Criminal Offence of Money Laundering

(4) Each country should take such measures as may be necessary, including legislative ones, to enable it to criminalize money laundering as set forth in the Vienna Convention. Each country should extend the offence of drug money laundering to one based on serious offences. Each country would determine which serious crimes would be designated as money laundering predicate offences.

(5) As provided in the Vienna Convention, the offence of money laundering should apply at least to knowing money laundering activity, including the concept that knowledge may be inferred from objective factual circumstances.

(6) Where possible, corporations themselves, not only their employees, should be subject to criminal liability.

Provisional Measures and Confiscation

(7) Countries should adopt measures similar to those set forth in the Vienna Convention, as may be necessary, including legislative ones, to enable their competent authorities to confiscate property laundered, proceeds from, instrumentalities used in or intended for use in the commission of any money laundering offence, or property of corresponding value, without prejudicing the rights of bona fide third parties.

Such measures should include the authority to: (1) identify, trace and evaluate property which is subject to confiscation; (2) carry out provisional measures, such as freezing and seizing, to prevent any dealing, transfer or disposal of such property; and (3) take any appropriate investigative measures.

In addition to confiscation and criminal sanctions, countries also should consider monetary and civil penalties, and/or proceedings including civil proceedings, to void contracts entered into by parties, where parties knew or should have known that as a result of the contract, the State would be prejudiced in its ability to recover financial claims, e.g. through confiscation or collection of fines and penalties.

C. Role of the Financial System in Combating Money Laundering

(8) Recommendations 10 to 29 should apply not only to banks, but also to non-bank financial institutions. Even for those non-bank financial institutions which are not subject to a formal prudential supervisory regime in all countries, for example bureaux de change, governments should ensure

that these institutions are subject to the same anti-money laundering laws or regulations as all other financial institutions and that these laws or regulations are implemented effectively.

(9) The appropriate national authorities should consider applying Recommendations 10 to 21 and 23 to the conduct of financial activities as a commercial undertaking by businesses or professions which are not financial institutions, where such conduct is allowed or not prohibited. Financial activities include, but are not limited to, those listed in the attached annex. It is left to each country to decide whether special situations should be defined where the application of anti-money laundering measures is not necessary, for example, when a financial activity is carried out on an occasional or limited basis.

Customer Identification and Record-keeping Rules

(10) Financial institutions should not keep anonymous accounts or accounts in obviously fictitious names: they should be required (by law, by regulations, by agreements between supervisory authorities and financial institutions or by self-regulatory agreements among financial institutions) to identify, on the basis of an official or other reliable identifying document, and record the identity of their clients, either occasional or usual, when establishing business relations or conducting transactions (in particular opening of accounts or passbooks, entering into fiduciary transactions, renting of safe deposit boxes, performing large cash transactions).

In order to fulfil identification requirements concerning legal entities, financial institutions should, when necessary, take measures:

(i) to verify the legal existence and structure of the customer by obtaining either from a public register or from the customer or both, proof of incorporation, including information concerning the customer's name, legal form, address, directors and provisions regulating the power to bind the entity.

(ii) to verify that any person purporting to act on behalf of the customer is so authorized and identify that person.

(11) Financial institutions should take reasonable measures to obtain information about the true identity of the persons on whose behalf an account is opened or a transaction conducted if there are any doubts as to whether these clients or customers are acting on their own behalf, for example, in the case of domiciliary companies (i.e. institutions, corporations, foundations, trusts, etc. that do not conduct any commercial or manufacturing business or any other form of commercial operation in the country where their registered office is located).

(12) Financial institutions should maintain, for at least five years, all necessary records on transactions, both domestic or international, to enable them to comply swiftly with information requests from the competent authorities. Such records must be sufficient to permit reconstruction of individual transactions (including the amounts and types of currency involved if any) so as to provide, if necessary, evidence for prosecution of criminal behaviour.

Financial institutions should keep records on customer identification (e.g. copies or records of official identification documents like passports, identity cards, driving licences or similar documents), account files and business correspondence for at least five years after the account is closed.

These documents should be available to domestic competent authorities in the context of relevant criminal prosecutions and investigations.

(13) Countries should pay special attention to money laundering threats inherent in new or developing technologies that might favour anonymity, and take measures, if needed, to prevent their use in money laundering schemes.

Increased Diligence of Financial Institutions

(14) Financial institutions should pay special attention to all complex, unusual large transactions, and all unusual patterns of transactions, which have no apparent economic or visible lawful purpose. The background and purpose of such transactions should, as far as possible, be examined, the findings established in writing, and be available to help supervisors, auditors and law enforcement agencies.

(15) If financial institutions suspect that funds stem from a criminal activity, they should be required to report promptly their suspicions to the competent authorities.

(16) Financial institutions, their directors, officers and employees should be protected by legal provisions from criminal or civil liability for breach of any restriction on disclosure of information imposed by contract or by any legislative, regulatory or administrative provision, if they report their suspicions in good faith to the competent authorities, even if they did not know precisely what the underlying criminal activity was, and regardless of whether illegal activity actually occurred.

(17) Financial institutions, their directors, officers and employees, should not, or, where appropriate, should not be allowed to, warn their customers when information relating to them is being reported to the competent authorities.

(18) Financial institutions reporting their suspicions should comply with instructions from the competent authorities.

(19) Financial institutions should develop programs against money laundering. These programmes should include, as a minimum:

(i) the development of internal policies, procedures and controls, including the designation of compliance officers at management level, and adequate screening procedures to ensure high standards when hiring employees;

(ii) an ongoing employee training programme;

(iii) an audit function to test the system.

Measures to Cope with the Problem of Countries with No or Insufficient Anti-Money Laundering Measures

(20) Financial institutions should ensure that the principles mentioned above are also applied to branches and majority owned subsidiaries located abroad, especially in countries which do not or insufficiently apply these Recommendations, to the extent that local applicable laws and regulations permit. When local applicable laws and regulations prohibit this implementation, competent authorities in the country of the mother institution should be informed by the financial institutions that they cannot apply these Recommendations.

(21) Financial institutions should give special attention to business relations and transactions with persons, including companies and financial institutions, from countries which do not or insufficiently apply these Recommendations. Whenever these transactions have no apparent economic or visible lawful purpose, their background and purpose should, as far as possible, be examined, the findings established in writing, and be available to help supervisors, auditors and law enforcement agencies.

Other Measures to Avoid Money Laundering

(22) Countries should consider implementing feasible measures to detect or monitor the physical cross-border transportation of cash and bearer negotiable instruments, subject to strict safeguards to ensure proper use of information and without impeding in any way the freedom of capital movements.

(23) Countries should consider the feasibility and utility of a system where banks and other financial institutions and intermediaries would report all domestic and international currency transactions above a fixed amount, to a national central agency with a computerized data base, available to competent authorities for use in money laundering cases, subject to strict safeguards to ensure proper use of the information.

(24) Countries should further encourage in general the development of modern and secure techniques of money management, including increased

modern and secure techniques of money management, including increased use of cheques, payment cards, direct deposit of salary cheques, and book entry record of securities, as a means to encourage the replacement of cash transfers.

(25) Countries should take notice of the potential for abuse of shell corporations by money launderers and should consider whether additional measures are required to prevent unlawful use of such entities.

Implementation, and Role of Regulatory and other Administrative Authorities

(26) The competent authorities supervizing banks or other financial institutions or intermediaries, or other competent authorities, should ensure that the supervized institutions have adequate programs to guard against money laundering. These authorities should co-operate and lend expertise spontaneously or on request with other domestic judicial or law enforcement authorities in money laundering investigations and prosecutions.

(27) Competent authorities should be designated to ensure an effective implementation of all these Recommendations, through administrative supervision and regulation, in other professions dealing with cash as defined by each country.

(28) The competent authorities should establish guidelines which will assist financial institutions in detecting suspicious patterns of behaviour by their customers. It is understood that such guidelines must develop over time, and will never be exhaustive. It is further understood that such guidelines will primarily serve as an educational tool for financial institutions' personnel.

(29) The competent authorities regulating or supervising financial institutions should take the necessary legal or regulatory measures to guard against control or acquisition of a significant participation in financial institutions by criminals or their confederates.

D. Strengthening of International Co-operation

Administrative Co-operation

Exchange of general information

(30) National administrations should consider recording, at least in the aggregate, international flows of cash in whatever currency, so that estimates can be made of cash flows and reflows from various sources abroad, when this is combined with central bank information. Such information should be made available to the International Monetary Fund and the Bank for International Settlements to facilitate international studies.

(31) International competent authorities, perhaps Interpol and the World Customs Organization, should be given responsibility for gathering and disseminating information to competent authorities about the latest developments in money laundering and money laundering techniques. Central banks and bank regulators could do the same on their network. National authorities in various spheres, in consultation with trade associations, could then disseminate this to financial institutions in individual countries.

(32) Each country should make efforts to improve a spontaneous or 'upon request' international information exchange relating to suspicious transactions, persons and corporations involved in those transactions between competent authorities. Strict safeguards should be established to ensure that this exchange of information is consistent with national and international provisions on privacy and data protection.

Other forms of Co-operation

Basis and means for co-operation in confiscation, mutual assistance and extradition

(33) Countries should try to ensure, on a bilateral or multilateral basis, that different knowledge standards in national definitions i.e. different standards concerning the intentional element of the infraction—do not affect the ability or willingness of countries to provide each other with mutual legal assistance.

(34) International co-operation should be supported by a network of bilateral and multilateral agreements and arrangements based on generally shared legal concepts with the aim of providing practical measures to affect the widest possible range of mutual assistance.

(35) Countries should be encouraged to ratify and implement relevant international conventions on money laundering such as the 1990 Council of Europe Convention on Laundering, Search, Seizure and Confiscation of the Proceeds from Crime.

Focus of improved mutual assistance on money laundering issues

(36) Co-operative investigations among countries' appropriate competent authorities should be encouraged. One valid and effective investigative technique in this respect is controlled delivery related to assets known or suspected to be the proceeds of crime. Countries are encouraged to support this technique, where possible.

(37) There should be procedures for mutual assistance in criminal matters regarding the use of compulsory measures including the production of records by financial institutions and other persons, the search of persons

and premises, seizure and obtaining of evidence for use in money laundering investigations and prosecutions and in related actions in foreign jurisdictions.

(38) There should be authority to take expeditious action in response to requests by foreign countries to identify, freeze, seize and confiscate proceeds or other property of corresponding value to such proceeds, based on money laundering or the crimes underlying the laundering activity. There should also be arrangements for coordinating seizure and confiscation proceedings which may include the sharing of confiscated assets.

(39) To avoid conflicts of jurisdiction, consideration should be given to devising and applying mechanisms for determining the best venue for prosecution of defendants in the interests of justice in cases that are subject to prosecution in more than one country. Similarly, there should be arrangements for coordinating seizure and confiscation proceedings which may include the sharing of confiscated assets.

(40) Countries should have procedures in place to extradite, where possible, individuals charged with a money laundering offence or related offences. With respect to its national legal system, each country should recognize money laundering as an extraditable offence. Subject to their legal frameworks, countries may consider simplifying extradition by allowing direct transmission of extradition requests between appropriate ministries, extraditing persons based only on warrants of arrests or judgements, extraditing their nationals, and/or introducing a simplified extradition of consenting persons who waive formal extradition proceedings.

Annex to Recommendation 9: List of financial activities undertaken by businesses or professions which are not financial institutions

(1) Acceptance of deposits and other repayable funds from the public.

(2) Lending.[1]

(3) Financial leasing.

(4) Money transmission services.

(5) Issuing and managing means of payment (e.g. credit and debit cards, cheques, traveller's cheques and bankers' drafts...).

(6) Financial guarantees and commitments.

(7) Trading for account of customers (spot, forward, swaps, futures, options...) in:

(a) money market instruments (cheques, bills, CDs, etc.);

[1]Including *inter-alia* consumer credit; mortgage credit; factoring, with or without recourse; and finance of commercial transactions (including forfeiting).

(b) foreign exchange;

(c) exchange, interest rate and index instruments;

(d) transferable securities;

(e) commodity futures trading.

(8) Participation in securities issues and the provision of financial services related to such issues.

(9) Individual and collective portfolio management.

(10) Safekeeping and administration of cash or liquid securities on behalf of clients.

(11) Life insurance and other investment related insurance.

(12) Money changing.

AN OVERVIEW OF THE GLOBAL MONEY LAUNDERING PROBLEM, INTERNATIONAL ANTI-MONEY LAUNDERING STANDARDS AND THE WORK OF THE FINANCIAL ACTION TASK FORCE

Rick McDonell

There are many definitions of money laundering. In order to understand the problem and the international counter-measures it is useful to have a workable definition.

Perhaps the simplest definition is that money laundering is *the process of converting cash, or other property which is derived from criminal activity, so as to give it the appearance of having been obtained from a legitimate source.* In other words, it is making dirty money appear clean.

An example of a more formal definition is *the concealment or disguise of the true nature, source, location, disposition, movement or ownership of property knowing that such property is derived from criminal activity.*[1]

The Money Laundering Problem[2]

I doubt that anyone could disagree with the proposition that one of the most important economic developments of recent years has been the increasing level of globalization, in terms of the world economy and its capital markets. Economies are more open than they have ever been, allowing individuals and entities to transfer funds with minimal difficulty. As a result, on a daily basis, we see huge sums of money being shifted freely

[1]*Money Laundering in Australia,* FATF Asia Money Laundering Workshop Report, Hong Kong, October 1995.

[2]Drawn in part from *Money Laundering and the International Financial System.* International Monetary Fund—Fiscal Affairs Department, IMF Working Paper, V. Tanzi, may 1996.

from country to country in search of the most favourable economic conditions with the highest rate of return.

Whilst this globalization has in many ways been very beneficial (allowing capital to flow towards countries where productivity is high, facilitating the recycling of capital from countries with current account surpluses and assisting the integration into the international economic system of economies in transition), it has also had its costs (large sudden movements of capital promoted by speculators in search of quick gains allows countries with structural fiscal deficits to postpone needed corrections because of easy access to foreign borrowings and the increasing ease with which drug dealers and weapons smugglers are now able to shift their products throughout the world). A cost of particular relevance to the paper I am presenting today, is the opportunity that this globalization has provided to persons engaging in criminal activities, to launder in an international arena funds illicitly obtained.

There is much evidence available of the large amount of money to be made by organized crime groups engaging in illicit activities, such as the production and distribution of illegal drugs, smuggling, fraud, embezzlement, corruption, prostitution and large-scale tax evasion to name but a few. By engaging in these sorts of activities criminal groups find themselves in receipt of significant sums of money, often much greater than they are able to dispose of conveniently in the immediate or short term. To enjoy the benefits in the longer term, the funds need to be stored in such a way that their value is preserved and they don't attract the attention of the authorities, i.e. the funds need to be laundered.

Estimates of the annual magnitude of the global money laundering problem range from $U.S. 500 billion (from narcotic sales alone) to more than U.S. dollars one trillion (when non-drug proceeds are added). The globalization of the capital markets has, in some ways, provided more opportunities for money laundering activities. The much larger volume of legitimate capital moving at any one time in the world, and the relatively limited controls on that movement, have made it possible for illicit funds to enter the system largely invisibly.

Available information indicates that while the activities which produce the illicit funds tend to be country-specific, the actual laundering occurs on a more international level. Globalization allows professional money launderers to exploit differences in controls and regulations very efficiently. The movement of illicit funds is not influenced so much by possible rates of return as by the differences in controls and regulations which make it safer to launder money in some countries rather than in others. Such money may, for this reason, move in directions quite contrary to those that would be expected on the basis of economic fundamentals. This sort of behaviour can have a number of ramifications. Capital is invested less optimally and the world growth rates can be reduced, not only because of the effects of the criminal activities on resource allocation, but also because of the allocation of the proceeds of that activity. It may also confuse policy makers in countries where there continues to be a high rate of capital inflow in the face of factors such as high inflation and an overvalued exchange rate.

A large stock of laundered proceeds may also bring some inherent instability to the world economy. For example, the movement of very large sums at any one time can create macroeconomic difficulties for the countries that lose or receive this money and, at least in theory, could have a significant impact on the world economy. At the national level these large flows of capital could influence variables including the interest rate, exchange rate and asset prices.

Often domestic money laundering can be fought on the national level, through the introduction of appropriate policies. An effective solution to the international problem can only be found at the international level. This is because international money laundering activities are, partly, the result of different controls and regulations which exist in various countries and jurisdictions. The more effective controls become in one country, the more the criminal element will shift its funds to take advantage of a less regulated environment. International coordination of economic policy, in this respect, cannot be fully effective as long as the controls and regulations imposed by individual jurisdictions differ and as long as there is a large pool of unstable money in search of a friendly environment from a regulatory point of view.

Financial Action Task Force

At the G7 Summit in Paris in 1989 the leaders determined that an international Task Force was required to deal with the international problem of money laundering. They established the Financial Action Task Force (FATF) which was mandated to examine measures that could be adopted in each country to combat money laundering. Soon afterwards all members of the OECD joined the Task Force.

There is a separate Task Force in the Caribbean (CFATF) and regional efforts are underway in Asia and Africa.

What Does FATF Do?

The primary purpose of the FATF is the development and promotion of policies to combat money laundering. Because anti-money laundering action requires input from various arms of government, the Task Force comprises senior officials from the legal, financial and law enforcement ministries.

The FATF's 40 Recommendations

The first task of the FATF was to develop a set of policy guidelines for governments. This resulted in the publication of 40 recommendations, now know universally as '*the FATF's 40 Recommendations.*' These 40 Recommendations set out the basic framework for anti-money laundering efforts and are designed to be of universal application. Recognizing the diversity of the legal and financial systems of countries throughout the world, the Recommendations are in fact principles for action which countries can implement according to their particular circumstances and constitutional framework. Put simply they are flexible in application and their introduction does not restrict legitimate transactions, or deter economic development.

The Recommendations were initially drawn up in 1990. They were revised in early 1996 taking into account experience gained over the last six years and reflecting the changes and trends in money laundering methods which have been identified in recent years including technological changes.

In brief the 40 Recommendations address three areas:

* Legal
* Financial and Regulatory
* Law Enforcement

Legal: This area of the Recommendations recognizes that the first step in the process is to ensure that money laundering is a criminal offence and that there are legal measures available to enable the confiscation of laundered property.

These principles encourage countries to take such measures as may be necessary, including the making of laws, to enable the criminalization of:

(a) the laundering of monies derived from narcotic trafficking; and

(b) the laundering of monies derived from all serious offences.

Measures should also be adopted as necessary, including legislative ones, to enable competent authorities to confiscate laundered property, the proceeds of laundering, instruments used or intended to be used in the commission of a money laundering offence or property of corresponding value.

These measures should include the authority to:

(1) identify, trace and evaluate property which is subject to confiscation; (2) carry out provisional measures, such as freezing and seizing, to prevent any dealing, transfer or disposal of such property; and (3) take appropriate investigative measures.

Law Enforcement: In this respect the Recommendations are directed towards ensuring that there be the widest range of mutual assistance between countries when conducting money laundering investigations and prosecutions. In other words they are about having the tools necessary to police the legislation.

Cooperative investigations between the appropriate competent authorities of different countries are to be encouraged and there should be procedures in place for the provision of mutual assistance in criminal matters.

Countries should also have procedures in place to extradite individuals charged with money laundering or related offences. Each country should recognise money laundering as being an extraditable offence and consideration should be given to the simplification of the process.

Financial and Regulatory: These Recommendations emphasize the need to prohibit the holding of anonymous accounts and to introduce procedures within financial institutions to identify and report suspicious transactions. They also ensure an ability to detect and then investigate suspicious transactions.

It should be noted that the Recommendations extend not only to traditional banks but also to non-bank financial institutions such as bureaux de change. A number of measures in this part of the Recommendations are worthy of mention.

For example, the Recommendations encourage the introduction of customer identification and record-keeping rules. Financial institutions should not keep anonymous accounts or accounts in obviously fictitious names. They should be required to identify clients, on the basis of reliable documents, and record their identity when establishing business relations or conducting transactions. Financial institutions should maintain, for at least five years, all necessary records of transactions.

There should be increased diligence on the part of financial institutions. This involves paying attention to all complex, unusually large transactions, and all unusual patterns of transactions, which have no apparent economic or obvious lawful purpose. If financial institutions suspect that funds stem from a criminal activity then they should be required to report their suspicions promptly to the competent authorities.

Financial institutions should develop anti-money laundering programmes. Such programmes would include, as a minimum:

(1) The development of internal policies, procedures and controls including the designation of compliance officers at management level, and adequate screening procedures to ensure high standards when hiring employees; (2) An ongoing employee training programme; and (3) An audit function to test the system.

Financial institutions also need to introduce measures to cope with the problem of countries with no or insufficient anti-money laundering measures. All the principles mentioned above should be applied to branches located abroad, especially in countries that don't apply the Recommendations, insofar as local laws and regulations permit. Financial institutions should also pay special attention to business relations and transactions with persons, countries and financial institutions from countries which do not apply the Recommendations.

Countries should consider implementing measures to detect or monitor the physical cross-border transportation of cash and install a system whereby financial institutions report all domestic and international currency transactions above a fixed amount to a national central agency. Countries should encourage the development of modern and secure techniques of money management and take notice of potential areas for abuse.

Finally, the competent authorities responsible for the supervision of financial institutions should work to ensure that those institutions have adequate programmes to guard against money laundering and take necessary legal or regulatory measures to prohibit their control or acquisition by criminal elements.

Onwards From the 40 Recommendations

The 40 Recommendations have now been implemented in almost all of the FATF member countries and they have been internationally accepted as the policy standard for anti-money laundering measures.

In recent years the FATF began to look beyond its member countries, adopting an 'external relations strategy' aimed at having the 40 Recommendations accepted and implemented throughout the world. In pursuance of this goal in 1992 a Caribbean FATF was established followed by the FATF Asia Secretariat in December 1994.

The FATF Asia Secretariat

The Asia Secretariat aims to promote the adoption of the 40 Recommendations in the Asia/Pacific region and to coordinate and in some instances provide, anti-money laundering training and technical assistance. Part of this work involves the establishment of a regional group so that efforts can be focused.

Political commitment is essential if policies and laws are to be implemented. In Asia this commitment is growing. The second APEC Finance Ministers Meeting held in Bali, Indonesia, on 16 April 1995 included in its Joint Ministerial Statement an expression of support for anti-money laundering work. The Statement referred to money laundering in the following terms:

> 'It is important, in the context of strengthening capital markets, that we support international anti-money laundering efforts in the region and encourage adherence to the international standards and recommendations which have been developed in this area. We refer this issue to the next Deputies meeting for further discussion.'

At APEC's Seventh Ministerial meeting in Osaka, Japan, 16 and 17 November 1995, the Joint Ministerial Statement of Foreign Ministers noted that the Second APEC Finance Minister's Meeting was held in Indonesia in 1995 and that the meeting had discussed various issues such as capital flows, exchange rate movements and funding for infrastructure development and, amongst other issues, anti-money laundering efforts.

At the Third Meeting of APEC Finance Ministers, on 17 March 1996, Kyoto, Japan, the Joint Ministerial Statement included the following:

> 'We continue to recognize money laundering as a priority concern and one which could threaten legitimate institutions and economic policies. We endorse established international cooperative work and encourage adherence to international standards in the anti-money laundering field as well as on-going regional efforts including the one in the context of Financial Action Task Force towards enhanced cooperation in this area. We will be briefed regularly on the progress made toward improved international and regional cooperation.'

The Asia/Pacific Group on Money Laundering

In order to progress anti-money laundering efforts in the region it has been proposed that a regional Steering Group be established, comprising as many countries as wish to join. It is hoped that this mechanism will provide a forum for action against money laundering in the region and ensure that regional factors are taken into account when policies and laws are being developed and implemented. The first meeting of the Steering Group in fact took place just days ago on 24 February in Bangkok.

The FATF Typology Exercise

The work of FATF is not, however, restricted to encouraging the world-wide adoption of the 40 Recommendations. FATF continues to monitor and discuss other relevant issues associated with money laundering and to formulate appropriate policy responses. In trying to understand the problem presented by money laundering, its size, nature and international scope FATF is required to conduct ongoing analytical work reassessing old and current trends and watching for future developments. This is called a typologies exercise and is completed annually.

At the most recent exercise the main topics for discussion were:

(1) Monetary or percentage estimates of the money laundering that can be quantified, and if this is not possible, rough estimates of the size of money laundering activities relative to the amount of legitimate activities; (2) The principal sources of illegal proceeds laundered; (3) The principal money laundering methods detected in the following sectors: banking, non-bank institutions and non-financial businesses; (4) Electronic funds transfers and whether there are difficulties in identifying the ordering customer in an electronic funds transfer transaction; (5) new (and/or proposed) money laundering counter-measures (legislative, regulatory, policy etc); and (6) Non-FATF members—key money laundering centres/regions including details relevant to the matters outlined above.

Keeping these topics in mind, member delegations were invited to provide an analytical overview of their money laundering situation, including case studies where possible.

Asia/Pacific Region Disposal of Proceeds of Crime—Money Laundering Methods Workshop

In the Asia/Pacific region a similar exercise is conducted. The first *Asia/Pacific Regional Disposal of Proceeds of Crime—Money Laundering Methods Workshop* was held in Hong Kong on 17 and 18 October 1995. A second was held more recently on 14 and 15 November 1996. It was jointly sponsored by FATF and ICPO-Interpol and was attended by qualified law enforcement officers from the following jurisdictions:

> Australia, Hong Kong, India, Indonesia, Japan, Malaysia, New Zealand, Pakistan, Peoples Republic of China, Republic of Korea, Singapore, The Philippines, Sri Lanka, Thailand, United Kingdom, United States of America and Vietnam.

The following international organizations were also in attendance: Interpol, General Secretariat, United Nations Drug Control Programme, TRACFIN (France), National Criminal Intelligence Service (UK).

The Workshop was focused towards developing a better understanding of how money laundering occurs in this region—that is, what methods are being used. By adopting this approach we can ensure that the policy makers as well as law enforcement agencies have a better understanding of the problem.

The aim of the workshop was to:

> Bring together knowledgeable law enforcement officers from the Asia/Pacific region in order to identify the current ways in which proceeds of crime are used or laundered, to determine any emerging trends or patterns within or between countries in the region and to consider practised ways to improve detection and seizure of those proceeds especially when they are transmitted to another country.[3]

Prior to the workshop, delegations were requested to prepare reports addressing the following criteria:

(1) Identification of the source of proceeds of crime. (2) Overview of how proceeds of crime are disposed of in the delegation's jurisdiction. (3) Case examples of the above and comment on the principal money laundering methods identified. (4) Estimation of the size of the problem in the delegation's jurisdiction. (5) Case examples of proceeds and laundering between jurisdictions in the region. (6) Ways in which law enforcement co-operation might be strengthened.

As you might conclude from the range of jurisdictions represented, the experience of the different delegations was quite diverse. Some of the jurisdictions had not yet enacted anti-money laundering legislation, whilst others had done so and in fact had some experience in the enforcement of these laws. However, all jurisdictions had experience of financial crime or confiscation of illegal proceeds.

Findings and Case Examples

The workshop found that drug and financial crimes continued to be the most frequently reported sources of illegal proceeds. Other sources reported included corruption, smuggling (electronics, vehicles, machinery, gold etc.), prostitution, gambling and arms trafficking. A new source identified in the region was organized illegal immigration.

The Asia region is a cash-orientated area where the flow of cash across borders is an everyday occurrence. In the majority of cases there are no mechanisms in place to track large cash transactions. Further, the issue of

[3] *Asia/Pacific Region: Disposal of proceeds of crime—Money laundering methods workshop*, Report of the Expert Group, Hong Kong, 14 and 15 November 1996.

non-regulated remittance services is a long-standing tradition in Asia, where they are frequently cheaper than the services provided by regulated financial institutions. Hence, it is difficult to distinguish what cash originates from the proceeds of crime and what is legitimate earnings, and the amount of cash actually being moved between jurisdictions.

Methods for disposing of illegal proceeds range from the simple to the increasingly complex. The workshop was unable to construct a finite list, but there were some notable recurring methods evident through the jurisdictions. Examples include:

The Smuggling or Couriering of Currency Across National Borders

This simple method involves the illicit carrying or sending of currency across a national border to another jurisdiction. Some jurisdictions limit the amount of money that can be legally brought into the jurisdiction. Others, while enunciating no limit, require the movement to be reported to government authorities once the currency exceeds a certain stipulated amount.[4] Most jurisdictions in the Asia/Pacific region have no restrictions or reporting requirements.

Case Example—Australia: An investigation into a fraud against the revenue of one of the states of Australia, involving a sum of AUD $14 million, identified a method of money laundering concerning the illegal transfer of funds overseas.

A travel agency and duty free shop in another Australian state was used to channel approximately AUD $ 8 million in illegal fraud proceeds overseas. The person who operated the business, purchased 'travellers cheques/drafts' payable to third parties. The drafts were then posted to persons in middle eastern countries including Lebanon and Israel, where the drafts were banked. A simple but effective way of contravening the anti smuggling laws of the country.

The Use of Bearer Instruments

This method involves the utilization of financial instruments which are exchanged for currency upon presentation at the relevant financial institution. Bearer instruments can include bank drafts, stock certificates, bonds and insurance certificates.

[4]An example of this is Australia where the legislature places an obligation on persons to report to the Government all physical transportations of cash into or out of Australia of AU$5,000 or more.

Case Example: United States: A recently filed Suspicious Activity Report (SAR) indicated a potential money laundering scheme involving approximately US 1 million in travellers cheques. Most of the travellers cheques were purchased in the amount of US$ 2,000. There were 486 separate purchase documents, however there were six different counter signatures, none of which matched the original signature. The total US$ one million in travellers cheques was deposited into one bank account in Miami.

The Use of Telegraphic Transfer to Send Money Internationally

Funds are moved between jurisdictions utilizing the international electronic banking system, mainly the Society for World-wide Interbank Financial Telecommunications system (SWIFT).

Case Example: Australia: The investigation of a national and international narcotics distribution network, and the subsequent arrest of the principals, led to the seizure of millions of dollars worth of cash and assets including jewellery, property and motor vehicles. The modus operandi of this syndicate was to place cash into the financial system in non reportable amounts (less than AUD $10,000) and then transfer the funds to a financial centre in Asia via telegraphic transfer. Over a 28 month period approximately AUD $16 million was found to have been transferred from Australia.

Alternative Remittance Services

This includes any method which remits funds to or from a jurisdiction without involving the mainstream banking system. Dedicated money remittance agencies exist, their sole business being the forwarding and receiving of funds between jurisdictions.[5] Often such agencies are not regulated and hence not covered by anti-money laundering programmes.

Case Example—Pakistan: A Pakistan heroin dealer in Oslo wanted to have his profits sent home to Pakistan. He approached an *Hawala* banker who contacted a colleague in Karachi. The latter knew a local factory owner who wanted to purchase machinery in New York but who, because of currency restrictions, could not get his Pakistani rupees exchanged. The proceeds from the sale of heroin were sent to New York to pay for the machinery. The factory owner deposited his money in rupees with the *Hawala* banker in Karachi, who paid it into the heroin dealers local account.

[5] Western Union Financial Services is one such agency with approximately 18,000 agents within the United States of America and 6,000 in jurisdictions outside the United States. Western Union estimates it conducts some 18 million remittance transactions each year of an approximate total value of $5 billion.

This method of laundering illicit proceeds also involves the use of alternative banking—an unofficial or parallel banking system, originally designed to circumvent currency controls, which enables fund movements between jurisdictions without producing a paper trail. At the Hong Kong Workshop much of the presentation given by the Indian delegation related to the prevalent form of alternative banking in that country, the *Hawala* system, including a large amount of gold smuggling.[6]

Case Example—India: Indian officials received information that a person staying in a hotel room in Madras was likely to receive or distribute large amounts of foreign currency. Surveillance was instituted and searches made at the premises of the person. At that time Rs. 8 million was recovered from the premises and forfeited to the Indian Government. According to the person occupying the premises the amount seized was intended for distribution in India and was the sale proceeds of smuggled gold belonging to a well known gold smuggler based in Dubai. Further investigation revealed that the person had so far received and made payments totalling US$3 million under instructions from the gold smuggler in Dubai.

Purchase of Assets

This method involves the simple conversion of illegal proceeds into a new or different asset. That asset can be virtually anything, but more commonly includes real estate, jewellery, antiques and luxury motor cars and boats.

Case Example—Pakistan: In June 1996 the Anti Narcotics Force Pakistan (ANF) received a request from a Dutch law enforcement authority to assist in the investigation of a Dutch drug trafficking organization. The organization had allegedly transported hashish to North America, Canada and Europe, and apparently 270,000 kgs were transported from Pakistan to North America and Europe between 1988 and 1991.

The Dutch organization used a middle-man for the transfer of payments to the suppliers in Pakistan. This was done through different accounts held with banks in Belgium and the Netherlands. Money was transferred from these accounts to bank accounts held in Karachi. ANF found that these accounts were actually operated by a money-changer. On questioning, the money changer stated that these accounts were operated as foreign exchange accounts, and were opened in the name of an expatriate Pakistani in com-

[6] Gold smuggling in India is mainly done by Dubai syndicates with connections to Hong Kong and Singapore—the smuggling is indicated by the large gold arrivals in Dubai which are far in excess of local gold demand. The smuggled gold has to be paid for in an acceptable foreign currency and *Hawala* is used as a convenient medium to convert the sale process of gold in the Indian market into foreign currency for payment offshore.

pliance with the strict foreign exchange regulations which existed prior to 1992 (these regulations made it illegal for money changers to deal in foreign exchange or keep foreign exchange accounts). The money-changer further stated that the amounts received into the accounts were so received on the express instructions of a co-conspirator and that when funds were withdrawn they were handed over to representatives of the co-conspirator. Investigators were unable to link the co-conspirator with the suppliers of the hashish, however it is believed that the funds were either invested into real estate or smuggled out of the country.

The Use of False Invoicing

This is the process of issuing an invoice for an article that is not related to its true value or worth, creating a fraudulent audit trail for proceeds laundered in the transactions.

Case Example—United States: US authorities investigated a Chinese heroin smuggling operation based in New York. This organization controlled a multi state food supply business for hundreds of small Chinese restaurants. The deliveries to these restaurants usually included cash. An inflated invoice was provided to the restaurant which included the value of the supplies plus the cash. The cash was then added to the restaurant takings and banked accordingly. The owners of the restaurant then wrote a cheque for the inflated invoice amount to the supplier. The inflated total invoices were then used as their cost of supplies. The cash was deposited in banks, and bank money orders, postal money orders and cash cheques were purchased and sent to Hong Kong.

Conclusions and Recommendations from the Workshop

The workshop was the second its kind in the region. Participants recognized the need to take account of regional factors, especially the widespread use of cash in everyday commerce and the contribution this makes to the problems of money laundering. It was also noted that there is a need for close cooperation with the banking and financial sector if a successful law enforcement effort is to be maintained against money laundering. Participants also recognized the need to identify and advance training needs because the absence of trained investigators impedes the successful advancement of money laundering investigations.

The Workshop Made the Following Recommendations:

(a) All jurisdictions accept the need for an annual collection and collation of methods of money laundering occurring within their jurisdiction. (b) All jurisdictions accept the need for regular periodical review of methods of money laundering occurring within the Asia/Pacific region as a whole. (c) The FATF Asia Secretariat be tasked with ensuring that such regular periodical review does occur. (d) That all jurisdictions recognize the importance of the financial sector in identifying money laundering methods and trends and the need to actively involve the financial sector in this task.

Concluding Remarks

I hope that this presentation has served to increase your awareness of the anti-money laundering effort globally and in the Asia/Pacific region.

Also I hope it has helped to increase your understanding of some methods criminals use in laundering their money. It is important that you be aware of the magnitude, complexity and potential of the problem and its ability to cross borders.

Finally I hope this presentation has encouraged you to add to our pool of knowledge and the need to continue sharing that knowledge. The money laundering problem is a dynamic one which requires that we work together to achieve solutions.

DRUG TRAFFICKING: CONFISCATION, FORFEITURE OF ASSETS AND MONEY LAUNDERING

M. Zakaria Siddiqi

Trafficking in narcotic drugs is regarded as a most pernicious illegal activity, generating organized criminality and drug abuse. Those involved in this activity have amassed wealth. In many cases their proximity to those high up in government has insulated them against their apprehension. The drug trafficker causes a most devastating impact on social, moral, economic and political system. Drug trafficking is a world-wide phenomenon. It is a multi billion dollar illegal industry. The Group of Seven Financial Action Task Force in its 1990 report estimated US $300 billion to be the gross proceeds of world-wide drug trafficking in 1987.[1] The figure must have gone up by now.

An effective strategy in this war against the trafficker requires a multi-pronged attack on all fronts requiring innovation, new weapons and tactics. They should be attacked where it hurts most. They should be deprived of the glee that holds the whole thing together, namely 'money', and measures should be need in a way that their trade becomes an economically unviable occupation. The weapons gaining recognition are asset seizure, restraint order, forfeiture, money laundering offences and international cooperation for mutual assistance.

This paper addresses the following:

* Confiscation of drugs and instruments of trafficking.
* Foreiture of assets (illegally acquired property or proceeds of crime).
* Tracing and identifying assets.
* Seizure, freezing and restraint order.
* Money Laundering.
* International cooperation on a mutual basis in asset tracing and foreiture.

[1] Report of the *Financial Action Task Force on Money Laundering* p. 1-3 (1990).

The Legal Regime: Response to International Conventions

The oldest drug law in India related to the control of opium and the regulation of poppy cultivation. It was the Opium Act of 1857 which was followed by the Opium Act of 1978. India has always been responsive to the international concern for drug related problems. It participated in the Second International Opium Conference held in Geneva in 1924 called by the League of Nations.[2] India adopted the Convention and enacted the Dangerous Drugs Act, 1930. India was also a signatory to the Single Convention on Narcotic Drugs, 1961, the Protocol of 1972 amending the said Convention, as well as Convention on Psychotropic Substances, 1971. To give effect to these international conventions India enacted the Narcotic Drugs and Psychotropic Substances Act in 1985 (hereafter referred to as NDPS Act) repealing the earlier legislation. India became a signatory to the UN Convention against Narcotic Drugs and Psychotropic Substances, 1988. Various provisions of the 1988 UN Convention have been incorporated into the NDPS Act by amendments to the Act in 1989.[3]

The NDPS Act, 1985 as amended in 1989, provides for regulation of the cultivation, manufacture of drugs and psychotropic substances, distribution and export-import both nationally and internationally. The NDPS Act contains deterrent penal provisions in the form of imprisonment from 10 to 20 years and heavy fines from one to two lakh rupees for drug trafficking, and death penalty for repeaters. Besides the penal measures, the Act provides for the search, seizure, attachment, confiscation of drugs and its instrumentalities and forfeiture of assets (illegally acquired property). Export and import of drugs is also prohibited under the Customs Act, 1962, and any currency involved in drug trafficking is subject to confiscation under the Foreign Exchange Regulation Act, 1973 (hereafter referred to as FERA).

Considering the magnitude of clandestinely organized drug trafficking activities Indian legislators thought it necessary to provide for the *detention without trial* of drug traffickers whether Indian or foreigner for a certain period under the Prevention of Illicit Traffic in Narcotic and Psychotropic Substances Act, 1988 (Act No. 46 of 1988). The expression 'illicit traffic' under Act No. 46 of 1988 covers:

[2] S.K. Ghosh, *The Traffic in Narcotic and Drug Addition*, 92 (1987).

[3] Section 2 of the NDPS (Amendment) Act, 1988 amends the long title of the Principal Act by inserting, inter alia, the following: "to implement the provisions of the International Conventions on Narcotic Drugs and Psychotropic Substances".

the cultivation of drug producing plants, manufacture, production, possession, sale, purchase, transportation, export, import of drugs and also financing, abetting or conspiring in drug related activities as well as harbouring persons engaged in illicit drug trafficking.

Confiscation of Drugs and Instrumentalities of Crime Harbouring

As a part of the strategy to combat the evil of drug related offences the NDPS Act confers power upon the Court to order the confiscation of drugs and the instrumentalities (things) used in the commission of the offence.[4] They may include drugs, substances, plant, and material by means of which offence is committed or any package or receptacle[5] or any animal or conveyance used in carrying the drug[6], or any good used in concealment of the drug.[7] The order of confiscation operates against the thing irrespective of the fact whether the accused is convicted or acquitted or discharged[8] or when the offender is not known or has absconded.[9] Even the sale proceeds of narcotic drugs in the hand of any person are subject to confiscation.[10]

Under the Custom Act,[11] and under FERA[12], both the Court and the adjudicating authorities are competent to pass a confiscation order, in respect of the drug or currency involved in drug trafficking under certain circumstances.

A confiscation order under the NDPS Act is similar to foreiture *in rem* under which a felon forfeited his goods and chattel to the Crown upon commission of an offence. Forfeiture arose from the concept of 'deoband'. After deoband was abolished in 1846, English law continued to provide for statutory foreiture of offending objects used in violation of customs and revenue laws; statutory forfeiture was enforced under *in rem* procedure, that is against the thing which has been declared unlawful or which has been used for an unlawful purpose. It is precisely this meaning in terms of confiscation that is prescribed under the NDPS Act, 1985.

The Problem of Terminology

The term 'confiscation' is linked to that of 'foreiture.' Both terms are used loosely and interchangeably. Each describes the deprivation, alienation and

[4] Section 60 (1) NDPS Act, 1988.
[5] Section 60 (2) NDPS Act.
[6] Section 60 (3) NDPS Act.
[7] Section 61, NDPS Act.
[8] Section 63, (1) NDPS Act.
[9] Section 63 (2) NDPS Act.
[10] Section 62, NDPS Act.
[11] Section 122 Customs Act, 1962.
[12] Section 63 Foreign Exchange Regulation Act, 1973.

withdrawal of certain legal rights. In both disinvestment of proprietary interest is ordinarily for the benefit of State. Foreiture under Common Law refers to the eschewing by the State of specific property immediately connected with crime. Confiscation is a relatively recent term used to denote deprivation of assets that are the illegal gains and proceeds of crime.[13] The term confiscation has been used in UK, USA and Australian legislations to refer to foreiture *in personam*.[14] This is probably due to an aversion to the old form of forfeiture of felon's property both in England and the USA.[15] Confiscation is widely used in several European countries.[16] The difference between foreiture and confiscation is blurred in the Indian legislations. Foreiture under NDPS (Amendment) Act, 1988 (Act II of 1989) embraces what in other places is regarded as confiscation. Further, where illegally acquired property is converted into foreign currency either in India or abroad such currency is liable to confiscation under FERA, 1973 and if the same money is attempted to be taken out of the country it is liable to be confiscated under the Customs Act, 1962.

Forfeiture of Assets

Article 5 of the 1988 UN Convention directs the signatory Parties to adopt measures to confiscate the proceeds and the instrumentalities of the offences covered by the Convention. Consequent to the ratification of the 1988 UN Convention Indian legislators introduced the system of foreiture of property by amending the NDPS Act in 1989.

Even before the amendment s. 62 of the NDPS Act allowed confiscation of proceeds of the drug sale. As long as such proceeds remained in the form of money they could be confiscated. But if the money was laundered out and lost its original form by conversion into assets (gold, shares or real estate), it could not be subject to confiscation.

The amending Act II of 1989 provides for a special foreiture procedure which fills the significant gap by depriving the drug trafficker of all gains of criminal activity after a thorough investigation into all assets belonging to him whatever mode of transfer he has adopted to convert them.

[13] Hodgson, *Profits of Crime and their Recovery*, p 5 (1984).
[14] The Drug Trafficking Act, 1994 (U.K.); The Continuing Criminal Enterprise Act, 1970 (USA); and The Proceeds of Crime Act, 1987 (Australia).
[15] Maxeiner, 'Bane of American Forfeiture Law: Banished at last", (1977) 62 *Connell L. Rev*. 768.
[16] *Belgian Penal Code*, Art. 42; *French Penal Code*, Art. 470; *German Penal Code*, Act 93-74; *Italian Penal Code*, Art. 40.

Illegally Acquired Property (Forfeitable Assets)

Unlike other countries the Indian legislation NDPS Act 1985 uses the expression 'illegally acquired property' to denote forfeitable assets (or proceeds of crime). This expression has been borrowed from the Smugglers and Foreign Exchange Manipulators (Forfeiture of Property) *Act*, 1976. Under the NDPS Act the expression means any property acquired wholly or partly out of or by means of by means of any *income, earning* or *assets* drived or obtained from (a) sale of illicit (drug) traffic or (b) wholly or partly *traceable* to such property, whether such property is in the hands of the drug trafficker or in the hands of any holder of such property, except a transfer in good faith for adequate consideration.[17]

Any property shall be deemed to be 'illegally acquired property' if it was acquired by the drug trafficker within a period of *six years* from the date of charge for specified offences under the NDPS Act.

In this paper the terms forfeitable assets or drug proceeds have been liberally used for the expression 'illegally acquired property'.

Applicability of Forfeiture Proceedings

Under the NDPS Act a forfeiture order can be passed in respect of 'illegally acquired property' against (a) *any person* who has been convicted of a serious drug offence (punishable with five years imprisonment or more) in India (b) or convicted of like offence abroad or (c) or has been detained[18] under applicable detention law[19] in India.

A forfeiture order is an order *in personam.* If the person referred to above transfers the forfeitable assets to his *relative*, *associate* or to *a trust* such property can be subject of forefeiture. The rights of a holder of such property in good faith for adequate consideration are however protected.[20]

Procedure of Forfeiture

The Forum: Unlike the confiscation of drugs and intrumentalities of drug offence which fall within the competence of Criminal Courts, the forfeiture proceedings under NDPS Act are undertaken by an administrative officer appointed by the Central Government. He may be a Collector of Customs or Collector of Central Excise or Commissioner of Income Tax or any

[17] Section 68 B (g) NDPS Act, 1985.
[18] Section 68 A(2), NDPS Act.
[19] *The Prevention of Illicit Traffic in Narcotic Drugs and Psychotropic Substances*, Act, 1988.
[20] Section 68 A(2) (d) (c) and (f) NDPS Act.

equivalent officer of the Central Government. Such administrative officer is designated under the Act as Competent Authority. This authority is clothed with all the powers of a Civil Court including the power to issue process, to call witnesses and to require discovery and production of documents.[21]

The Proceedings: The forfeiture proceedings commence with the serving of a show cause notice to a person who has illegally acquired property (from drug trafficking). He is required to show cause as to why such property should not be forfeited to the Central Government. Where any other person holds the property on behalf of a trafficker a copy of the notice is served also on him.[22]

The Competent Authority, after considering the explanation, material on record and hearing the affected person (named in the notice), by an order record the finding that the whole or any part of such property stands forfeited.[23] Where such forfeitable assets consist of shares in any company they shall stand forfeited and the company shall forthwith register the Central Government the transfer of such shares.[24]

Where any property held in a trust is wholly illegally acquired property or where any contribution is made to the trust out of such property, the author of the trust or the contributor has to satisfy the Competent Authority about the source of money or assets out of which and the means by which he acquired the property.[25]

Where the trust is created out of drug assets, such assets are liable to forfiture. In case of contribution to a trust the money or assets liable to forfeiture must not be less than 20 per cent of the value of the trust.[26]

The offener or the person affected has to furnish evidence regarding the source of income, earnings or assets and prove that they are not illegally acquired property. Under s. 68 J the *burden of proof* lies on the affected person.

Fine In Lieu of Forfeiture: Section 68 K of the NDPS Act permits a person to opt for a fine in lieu of forfeiture. This is allowed where the affected person is able to account for the money or assets but unable to account for only a part of it; the Competent Authority may permit such person in lieu of forfeiture to pay a fine equal to the market of such part of the property.

[21] Section 68 R NDPS Act.
[22] Section 68 H NDPS Act.
[23] Section 68 I NDPS Act.
[24] Section 68 I (4), NDPS Act.
[25] Section 68 L NDPS Act.
[26] Section 68 L read with Section 68 B(b) (vi) (2).

Appeal: Against an order of forefiture an affected person has the right to appeal before an appellate tribunal whose decision shall be final.[27] Neither any order passed by the Competent Authority nor that of the appellate tribunal can be challanged before a Court.[28]

Receiver of Forfeited Assets

Under section 68 G the Central Government may appoint one or more *receivers* (Administrators) from amongst its officers to receive, manage or disposed of property seized or forfeited under the Act. Such Officer has all the powers to enforce a forfeiture order even by taking possession forcibly of such property with the help of police, if necessary.[29]

Observations

The 1988 UN Convention does not prescribe uniform legislative measures in view of wide variations in legal systems of the signatory Parties. Indian forfeiture provisions do not reflect the global trend. In a number of common law countries forfeiture/confiscation orders are passed by the courts both in respect of drugs, instrumentalities of drug trafficking as well as proceeds or assets drived from drugs. The Indian law on the other hand prescribes two different adjudication processes. One by the convicting Court in respect of drugs and instrumentalities of drug offence and the other by an administrative officer in respect of forfeiture of assets illegally acquired.

In order to comply with the 1988 Convention India did not borrow any legislative model from outside, rather it adopted a domestic model. The forfeiture provisions and other ancillary provisions have been literally picked up from the Smugglers and Foreign Exchange Manipulation (Forfeiture of Property) Act, 1976 (Act 13 of 1976).

In may be noted that the property acquired from drug trafficking was also liable to be forfeited under Act 13 of 1976. The application of that Act has now been abolished by s. 22 of NDPS Amendment Act 1988. Conferment of powers on two different agencies may involve duplication of proceedings. As discussed earlier, sale proceeds of drugs are liable to confiscation by an order of the Court under section 61 of the NDPS Act while the same may constitute 'money derived' from drug trafficking and liable to forfeiture by an order of an administrative authority under the Act.

[27] Section 68 O NDPS Act.
[28] Section 68 Q NDPS Act.
[29] Section 68 U(2) and (3) NDPS Act.

Tracking the Forfeitable Assets

Tracing the proceeds of crime for the purposes of forfeiture proceedings is a new concept in the fight against drug trafficking. The dubious means by which the identity of property is concealed requires an extensive money trail. The purpose of tracing and identifying the 'illegally acquired property' of the drug trafficker is to uncover the location of such property which has been concealed or has undergone the process of money laundering to disguise the nature and original source of such property. It may be converted either by electronic transmission or by any other means.

The 1988 Convention places considerable importance to tracing the proceeds of trafficking for its eventual confiscation, notwithstanding commercial secrecy the bank of. The Convention favoured extensive investigatory powers with a view to depriving the trafficker of their profits wherever held.

Section 68 N of the NDPS Act introduced for the first time the concepts of *t*racing (which include determining the nature, source, disposition, movement, title or ownership of property) and identifying (which means establishing the proof that such property was drived from illegal drug traffic). The investigatory powers parallel to those of an officer in charge of a police station may be conferred on any Gazetted Officer of the departments of central excise, narcotics, customs, revenue intelligence or Boarder Security Force to conduct investigations into forfeitable assets of drug traffickers.

For the purposes of tracing and identifying any illegally acquired property the NDPS Act confers powers on the investigating officer to conduct inquiry, investigation or survey in respect of any person, place, property, assets, document or book of accounts in any bank or financial institution.[31]

Restraint Order: Freezing and Attachment

Freezing of forfeitable assets has been recommended in the 1988 Convention. It forms part of the strategy to combat drug trafficking in the legislation of many countries. Indian legislation (NDPS Act) contains comprehensive provision for freezing the assets by temporarily prohibiting all forms of transfer of property. This is done through a restraint order made by an investigating officer. Such order is to be confirmed by the Competent Authority.

The power of freezing the assets is similar to the provisions contained in Civil Procedure Code. The Code contains provision to prohibit transfer

[30] Section 68E read with Section 53 NDPS Act.

[31] Section 68E (2) NDPS Act.

where a defendant, with intent to obstruct or delay execution of any decree that may be passed, is about to dispose of or remove wholly or any part of that property. The Civil Court may even order the attachment of such property pending the decision.[32]

A restraint order under the NDPS Act is an extension of civil process. It may prohibit any form of disposition of property by conveyance, delivery, payment or other alienation including creation of trust, lease, mortgage, charge or any transaction to diminish or increase the value of property. The NDPS Act penaliszed knowingly acquirng by above mode of transfers any property regarding which proceedings have commenced under the Act.[33]

The investigating officer making a restraint order is authorised to seize illegally acquired property when such property is likely to be transferred or concealed by the trafficker with a view to frustrating the forefeiture proceedings under the Act.[34] The property so seized may be placed under the custody of receiver (or Administrator) appointed under the Act.[35]

Flow of Information

For the purposes of tracing the proceeds of drug traffickers, inter-agency communication of information will go a long way in effective enforcement of the law. The NDPS Act requires a host of officers of Central and State Governments to assist in forfeiture proceedings and furnish necessary information when required. They can *suo motu* furnish such information that may be useful in forfeiture proceedings.[36] Section 68S of the Act confers wide powers upon the Competent Authority to secure information that may be useful for various actions under the Act from any officer or authority of Central Government. State Government, or local bodies.

Any information that comes to the knowledge of income tax officers, custom officers and personnel of enforcement directorate raising suspicions about transactions connected with drug trafficking may be helpful even before investigation is undertaken under the Act. Even the expenditure statement of an individual with newly acquired wealth if properly investigated may lead to fruitful results. It was through such study of expenditure behaviour, telephone calls, hotel accommodation, house furnishing that the Internal Revenue Service of the United States was able to dismantle the empire of a gang leader.[37]

[32] R. 5 Order 38 Code of Civil Procedure 1908.
[33] Section 68Y NDPS Act.
[34] Section 68F NDPS Act.
[35] Section 68G NDPS Act.
[36] *Ibid.*
[37] Short, *Crime Inc, The Story of Organised Crime* pp. 100-107 (1984).

For exchange of inte-ragency information the Vohra Committee has recommended the creation of a nodal body.[38] The suggestion deserves due consideration. This body will be a depository of information to be exchanged domestically as well as internationally.

In drug trafficking financial transactions constitute one of the important segments of activity. More powers are desirable which will make it possible to obtain material at an early stage of investigation or even before the commencement of investigation. The banks or other financial institutions are under no obligation to report suspected transactions. The issue has been discussed in a later part of this paper.

The 1988 UN Convention recommends reconsideration of 'bank secrecy' legislation. It is desirable that investigating Officers should have access to confidential banking and other material at a very early stage of investigations, so that they may obtain a restraint order for freezing the account of a drug trafficker.

Money Laundering

Linked with the problem of asset forfeiture and confiscation proceedings is the clandestine system of money laundering. The whole process of forefeiture can be frustrated by a cunning, manipulative drug trafficker who successfully converts either himself or through his associates and helpers, the drug money into assets that snap the latter's linkage with the former.

Anti-money laundering law is a necessary concommitant of forfeiture law. There is global concern for an effective money laundering law due to the wide sweep of money laundering activities both nationally and internationally. The concern is reflected in various Conventions and bilateral treaties. The 1988 UN Convention to which 138 countries are signatory directs the Parties to incorporate into their domestic legislation anti-money laundering measures into their domestic legislations. Article 3 (1) (b) (i) and (ii) of the 1988 Convention relates solely to drug money laundering. Likewise, G-7 countries in 1989 constituted the Financial Action Task Force (FATF) to deal with money laundering through banking and other financial institution. The FATF has made significant recommendations on money laundering. Some of the recommendations relate exclusively to drug-related money laundering. These recommendations have been incorporated into the legislation of G-7 countries and many other countries. India is also a member of the FATF but it has yet to enact an anti-money laundering law.

Money Laundering: What is it?

Money laundering is an illegal activity devised to convert illegally obtained property for legitimate uses by concealment or disguising the true nature and source. The expression 'money laundering' was used by Unites States enforcement Officers during 1920-30 with reference to Mafia ownership of laundromats where illicit money from bootlegging, gambling and prostitution was cleaned. The mafia bosses bought laundromats from small Italian families and used them as financial and tax alibi for illicit income.[39] Money laundering as understood today is 'the process by which one conceals or disguises the true nature, source, disposition, movement or ownership of money for whatever reason.'

The common devices of money laundering include investment in property dealings (real estate), investment in silver, gold or gems, investment in shares, bonds or Indira Vikas Patras. Money laundering through offshore transactions involves puting the money in a local bank, then using the facilities of transfer to a banks in tax haven countries.[40] Involvement of bank in money laundering business has led to more regulatory mechanisms in many countries world over. The discovery of illegal money laundering of drug money for Panama leader by the Bank of Credit & Commerce International S.A. led to closure of the bank's branch in Florida (USA).[41] Two junior offices of the bank pleaded guilty and received prison sentence of two years.[42]

Money laundering through financial institutions may be adopted by several techniques. But a generic model described by a US Senate Subcommittee's Report on Foreign Relation (1989) is as follows:

According to this model, money laundering consists of three distinct stages namely: (a) placement (b) layering and (c) integration. *Placement* is disposal of ill-gotten cash along with legitimate cash drawn from some shady or cover business into a deposit of a bank or financial institution or intermediary. *Layering* is the processing of funds among various accounts both nationally and internationally through a review of complex transactions designed to disguise the trail of illicit proceeds. The final stage *integration* is the process of shifting the laundered funds to legitimate organizations with no apparent link to organized crime. Once the funds are integrated, they can be managed by sophisticated investment managers. It is,

[38] Vohra Committee Report, 1993, reprinted in *Souvenir, XXIV Criminological Congress*, India Society of Criminology, Bangalore, 1996.

[39] D.A. Chaiken, 'Investigating Criminal and Corporate Money Trails' in Brent Fisse, et. al. (Ed) *The Money Trail*, 258, (1992).

[40] Bahamas, Bermuda, British Channel Island, Cayman Island Cook Island, Gibralter, Hong Kong, Liberia, Luxembourg, Panama, Switzerland are some of tax haven countries.

[41] *Ex parte Bank of Credit and Commerce International*, (1989) 3 W.L.R. 1054.

[42] M. Levi, 'Regulating Money Laundering,' *British Journal of Criminology* p 119 (1991).

therefore, necessary that illicit money is identified by the bank and the investigating agencies at the placement stage.

The United States, the U.K., Australia[43] and a host of other countries have enacted legislation by introducing a system of 'Cash Transactions Report' or 'Suspect Transaction Report.' Under this system any amount in excess of $10,000 deposited in the bank has to be reported to the Central Regulatory Authority. Interestingly many offenders started depositing amounts little less than $10,000 to avoid detection. To meet such situations, the system of 'Structured Transaction Report' has been introduced under which the bank is obliged to report when a single depositor has made split deposits in a short period. There is nothing in *Indian Banking Companies Regulation Act*, 1949 of any bulk cash reporting requirement. Introduction of both 'Cash Transaction Report' as well as 'Structured Transaction Report' systems in India are desirable.

Money Laundering Outside the Banking System

Apart from money laundering through banks and financial institutions there are several other means and methods of money laundering. Some of them have no paper trail making the task of discovery and proof highly improbable. These methods include investment in smuggling of gold and foreign local currency, and the use of bureaux de change. However in all these cases the risk of interception by the custom officers and other enforcement officers is always present.

Yet another most elusive method of money laundering is *Hawala* transaction. It is a widely used technique of transmission of money from one country to another outside normal banking through reference of private operators.

Hawala: For years expatriates working abroad from India and Pakistan have been using hawala transactions for remittances back home at a more favourable rate of exchange than the official rates in the normal banking channel. Under this system money is paid abroad by an expatriate to a hawala operator who directs his reference man in the home country to deliver money in local currency to a receipient of the expatriate's choice.

Recent trends in hawala transactions have been causing concern globally. Some of the recommendations of FATF also refer to the hawala method of money laundering. Under Indian Law (the Foreign Exchange Regulation Act 1973) this activity constitutes an offence. There are wide spread undisclosed breaches of this law by smugglers, gun runners, terrorists and corrupt officials who receive or send money to or from India through hawala transactions. It is one of the popular methods of transfer of money by the drug mafia in Pakistan. Hawala transactions have recently caused turmoil in the Indian political system by the discovery (through chance information from a militant) of 'infamous Jain Diaries. These diaries contain references to payment of money by Jain brothers, Delhi industrialists, to the tune of Rupees 1.8 crore to no less than 100 persons, many of them noted political figures.

Internationally this method offers a good alternative for drug money laundering outside the banking system. Movement of money through hawala leaves no paper trail making it difficult if not impossible for the investigators to trace laundered money.

How to Deal with Money Laundering?

You cannot fight money laundering activity unless there is an effective anti-money laundering law. Such legislation should be the top priority of the agenda to fight drug trafficking. The countries which have enacted anti money laundering law have made not only the activity itself a crime but have brought within its ambit those who help, assist and conspire with the drug trafficker in siphoning his illegal money. Any person who with knowledge allows money laundering through an organization for which he works is also liable to punishment. Failure to report suspicious transactions knowingly should also be made an offence.

India is committed to enacting an anti-money laundering law, being signatory to the 1988 UN Convention and as a member of FATF 1989. The Ministry of Finance, as reported in newspapers, is working on a draft Bill on money laundering with a view to bring within its coverage laundering of illegal proceeds from smuggling, contraband arms sale, bribery, corruption, bank fraud, manipulation of foreign exchange, over and under invoicing and also the proceeds of drug trafficking.

It is hoped that the proposed law will effect suitable changes in the NDPS Act to harmonize it with the former. Further additional investigatory powers need to be given to the enforcement officers under the NDPS Act for an effective enforcement of money laundering law. Needless to say the proposed law will bring within its sweep money obtained from drug traffickers by the corrupt drug enforcement officers.

International Cooperation: Mutual Assistance Schemes

Drug trafficking has global ramifications. The trafficker knows no boundaries. Narcotic drugs and pasychotropic substances move from one country to another country in search of a lucrative market. They change hands in several transit countries. Likewise drug sale proceeds move from consumer country to processing country, and furthers to producing country. Unless there is international cooperation among nations the illegal drug industry will continue to florish. The concept of mutual assistance in criminal matters on a reciprocal basis is catching upto fight transnational criminality. Nations are coming closer in cooperating with each other in matters such as extradition, transfer of prisoners, transfer of proceedings, investigations into local illegal money, restraint and attachment orders, freezing assets, confiscation and forfeiture of illegal proceeds of crime.

Beside the 1988 UN Convention there are several regional treaties on mutual assistance programs. These include European Convention on Mutual Assistance in Criminal Matters, 1959; Inter-American Convention on Mutual Legal Assistance in Criminal Matters; bilateral treaties between United States and Switzerland 1977 and non-treaty schemes for Mutual Assistance in Criminal Matters within the Commonwealth (Zimbabwe, 1986).[44]

Article 7 of the 1988 UN Convention is exclusively devoted to stamping out drug trafficking through mutual assistance schemes by signatory Parties. It mandates domestic legislation for:

* tracing and identifying illegal drug assets,
* seizure and restraint orders,
* confiscation/forfeiture of drug assets, and
* sharing of assets.

The 1988 Convention recommends more liberal laws of extradition. The domestic legislation must provide for reception of a request from a requesting State for restraint and/or confiscation order. The requested State must comply with the request within the parameters of constitutional and procedural safeguards. In view of important differences between Common Law countries and Civil Law jurisdictions the domestic law should contain flexible provisions for reception of requests from judicial authority or other central authority, modified rules of evidence and practicable investigative measures.

As discussed earlier India follows a dual system of confiscation and foreiture. Domestica asset forfeiture of drug trafficker is adjudcated by an administrative authority. But mutual assistance requests from foreign States emanating either from a judicial authority or other prescribed authority are attended to by the courts in India through central bovernment.

[43] *Bank Secretary Act*, (U.S.) 31 U.S.C.S. 5313; *Drug Trafficking Act*, 1994 (UK) 50; *Cash Transaction Report Act*, 1988 (Australia).

[44] Mc Lean, *Mutual Assistance in Criminal Matters: The Commonwealth Perspective* (1988) 37 I.C.L.Q. p.177.

Mutual Assistance Law

With a view to providing mutual assistance in criminal matters the Code of Criminal Procedure 1973 was amended in 1993 to incorporate a new chapter V.A. entitled as 'Reciprocal Arrangements in Certain Matters and Procedure for Attachment and Forefeiture of Property.' The reciprocal assistance under this Chapter between India and Contracting State includes the following areas: (a) Serving the executing summons or warrants on or against a person to attend court or produce documents; (b) Transfer of prisoners involved in illegal acquisition; (c) Tracing and identifying illegally acquired property including bank account. (d) Seizure and freezing proceeds of crime; (e) Forfeiture of illegally acquired property (or proceeds of crime).

Requests for above matters can be made or accepted in such form as the central government may prescribe for transmission or receipt of such request by a Court in India or a court or other authority outside India. The provisions relating to forfeiture are identical with chapter V. A. of the N.D.P.S. Act 1985 and the Smugglers and Foreign Exchange Manipulators (Forfeiture of Property) Act, 1976.

Letter Rogatory: With a view to procuring evidence from abroad and permitting such exercise in India by foreign investigators a system of Letter Rogatory has been incorporated into section 166 A of Criminal procedure Code under which a criminal court in India upon request of an investigating Officer issue a letter of request addressed to a court or authority outside India to allow:

* to examine any witness,
* to record his statement,
* to produce any document or thing,
* to send such statements or documents or authenticated copies thereof.

A corresponding provision is contained in section 166 B of that Code for receipt of a similar letter of request on reciprocal basis from a court or an authority of that country in respect of crimes committed by their citizens in India. Such requests are transmitted through the central government in India.

These useful provisions are not allowed to operate effectively on principles of soveringnity and due to the reluctance of Courts to expose them to foreign jurisdictions.

India has entered into mutual assistance treaties with a number of countries including the UK, the USA and Switzerland. After much hesitation Switzerland agreed to open up its door to investigate banks accounts. Despite mutual bilateral agreements much of the desired information is not available. Many commonwealth countries have not enacted mutual cooperation laws or have not entered into agreement with India for such assistance. They may thwart an effective monitoring of money laundering activities and other drug related activities.

Extradition: The 1988 Convention calls upon the signatory Parties to re-examine their legislation to facilitate more flexible systems of extradition law. Countries bound by extradition treaties take an extremely technical view in extradition proceedings which impede the transfer of the required person. India has entered into extradition treaties with a number of countries but the cumbersome procedure and technicalities have affected the interests of requesting and requested States. This has happened recenttly in two instances. A request from Singapore to extradite a business tycoon, Rajan Pillai, was frustrated due to judicial technicalities and his untimely death in judicial custody; on the other hand, the Hong Kong Court insisted on a formal charge against Amir Bhai who was supposed to be one of the key figures in the Jain Hawala Case, thereby allowing him to escape to a safe haven. It is imperative that a liberal view should be adopted in extradition proceedings by the requested State. To this end domestic legislation should be reviewed to make it consistent with the 1988 UN Convention and other international treaty obligations.

Conclusion

The review of procedures regarding confiscation, forfeiture of property and money laundering leads us to conclude, on account of the multiplicity of agencies involved in combating drug trafficking, that they are not functioning in a coordinated manner. Proper delineation of jurisdiction of criminal courts and adjudicating authorities in respect of confiscation and forfeiture is lacking. There are many loopholes in the statutes through which drug traffickers may escape detection. The problem of corruption at lower levels has made the drug traffic lucarative even for enforcement officers.

The slow process by which our judicial system moves seriously hampers the effective functioning of enforcement agencies. Absence of money laundering legislation (money laundering as such is no offence) has helped in generating funds for anti-national terrorist activities in the country. The sooner we address to these problems the better it will be. The drug traffickers should not be allowed to take advantage of the liberalization of the Indian economy.

MONEY LAUNDERING

Bishwajit Bhattacharyya

Dirty and crumpled linen looks respectable after laundering. So does black money generated by not quite legitimate means. Money laundering is menace hurting the economies of most developing countries. India is no exception.

By the time this paper is read, the Union Budget, 1997 would have already been presented by the Indian Finance Minister. It is widely believed that some proposal will be made to bring about legislation with respect to money laundering. Whether or not any such proposal is actually made, it is important to gauge the extent, ramifications and implications of money laundering in India, so that remedial measures can be initiated on a war footing. This paper attempts only to analyse the situation from the Indian perspective.

What is international money laundering? Simply stated, it means unaccounted cross-border transfer of funds. The twin aspects of money laundering are generation of unaccounted funds, and cross-border transfer thereof in circumvention of monetary control legislation. That such ill-gotten funds are often used for subversive and other unlawful activities is hardly in dispute. It is not my intention in this paper to deal in detail with such activities. My attempt here shall be limited only to the extent of analysing the situation with respect to the monetary control legislation in India, called the Foreign Exchange Regulation Act, 1973 (hereafter referred to as FERA).

It is estimated that funds worth over US $100 billion have been generated and/or stashed abroad by resident Indians in defiance of FERA. It is almost an accepted fact that every businessman in India, if he is worth his salt, has a hidden account overseas. Many Indian businessmen on their return journey to India halt at Zurich, ostensibly to change flights, but for what purpose really the world knows! And the latest development of real estate transactions in India has seen the emergence of an ingenious additional component apart from 'black' and 'white', namely 'green.' Obviously, 'green' implies money received abroad, and this now constitutes the most preferred category. Little wonder that official ('white') prices of real estate in India are on the decline! The situation presents a grim picture.

What is the way to check all these contraventions? Has FERA achieved its objective, to wit, 'conserve foreign exchange resources of the country,' and thereby to prevent leakage thereof? Section-14 of FERA empowers the Central Government to issue notification in the Official Gazette, ordering every person in or resident of India to surrender to the Reserve Bank of India (through an authorized dealer in foreign exchange) all foreign exchange that such person 'owns or holds.'

Indeed the Central Government has issued notifications under this provision. Therefore, 'owning' and 'holding' foreign exchange or foreign assets by a person in or resident in India are prohibited barring specific exemptions that have been carved out. Despite this, unlawful overseas accounts and assets maintained by residents continue to flourish. The enforcement of Section-14 of FERA has thus been dismal. The Central Government has not created any machinery that can identify violators of the law as aforesaid. On the contrary, by a notification dated 17.7.1992 in the Official Gazette, the Central Government, exercising powers conferred under Section-14 of FERA, has given a carte blanche from the rigors of Sections-8, 9, 24 and 25 of FERA, to all those persons who have been resident outside India for a continuous period of not less than one year, and have returned to India on or after 18.4.1992. The notification has far reaching ramifications.

It should be noticed that the aforesaid categories of persons, even after becoming residents under the FERA from the cut-off date of 18.4.1992 would not be required to surrender their forex assets in India. They would further be eligible to maintain and operate foreign currency accounts abroad. Even immovable properties and other securities abroad may be freely held by them for the rest of their lives without being required to obtain the permission of the Reserve Bank of India (RBI) as had been the requirement earlier. The scheme can be taken advantage of by resident Indians by temporarily changing their residential status to NRI (Non Resident Indian) for a year.

Whilst from the viewpoint of deregulation, the scheme is a landmark, it has created a fertile ground for laundering money lawfully. How? The notification clearly stipulates that these foreign assets should have been acquired by the person 'lawfully' while resident outside India. And the word 'lawfully', as the notification clarifies, means 'otherwise than in contravention of FERA 1973'. This is an extremely unfortunate clarification. If a person is non-resident under the FERA, then there is absolutely no bar under the FERA to acquire forex whatever be the source of such funds. There may be a bar under many other laws, but not under FERA. FERA fails to distinguish between clean income and ill-gotten laundered income and is concerned only with exchange control and regulation. So a person can theoretically swindle money overseas as a non-resident and still take advantage of the scheme. FERA alone is not enough to punish such a person.

The authorities in India should have clarified the term 'lawfully' as 'not in contravention of any extant law', and should thereby have broadened the scope of ineligible funds. Regretfully, the conclusion that one is forced to draw is that the generation of ill-gotten laundered funds has been encouraged by the deregulation.

It is against the aforesaid background that the proposed reported move by the Ministry of Finance, Government of India, to make it a crime to launder proceeds from any criminal acts including bank frauds, smuggling, terrorism, bribes and other acts of corruption has to be lauded. It is equally heartening to note that the Government of India is considering a proposal to confiscate assets from the proceeds of any criminal act including under-invoicing, hawala transactions and manipulation of NRI deposits. It is, therefore, necessary that a Money Laundering Act should be brought about in India on the pattern of money laundering Acts in USA, UK, Singapore and Australia. India has been committed to bringing about money laundering legislation since she became a signatory to the 1988 UN Convention on Illicit Traffic and Narcotics, and subsequently a member of the 1989 Financial Act on Task Force.

In this context, I cannot but express surprise that some of those provisions in FERA that had the effect of checking money laundering had been repealed on 8.1.1993. For example, Section-23 of FERA stands repealed. This section had earlier empowered the Central Government by issuing notification in the Official Gazette, to acquire foreign securities. Similarly, Section-25(3) of FERA stands repealed. This provision had earlier empowered the Central Government to direct any person holding any immovable property outside India to sell the whole or any part thereof and further required the proceeds of such sale to be received in India through an authorized dealer. It is common knowledge that laundered funds have allotropic modifications. Prime among these are foreign securities and immovable properties abroad. By switching off its powers to confiscate properties abroad generated out of laundered funds, the Central Government has possibly attempted to give an encouraging signal to foreign investors. But the tragedy is, this move may possibly have encouraged money launderers as well. The need of the hour is to arrive at some kind of a judicious blend of the carrot and stick policy, so that the message goes out loud and clear that in India violators of the law have no place.

One paradoxical situation that has emerged in this context is that while under Section-33(1) of FERA the Central Government is fully empowered to call for information and ask for returns from any person with regard to his foreign securities and immovable properties abroad, after receiving such information, the Central Government can do little beyond gazing at such information in silent appreciation, since by the aforesaid repeal of Sections-23 and 25(3), the Central Government has disabled itself from confiscating such assets, even if these have been unlawfully acquired by means of laundered funds.

These steps have been retrograde from the viewpoint of checking the menace of laundered money and the consequent assets generated. One hopes that these anomalies will be duly corrected by the authorities in India.

Another point that needs serious consideration is that of amnesty schemes. Amnesty schemes have invariably failed in the past. Amounts realized from such schemes have been insignificant. Besides, such schemes have sent wrong signals to offenders of the law, while making honest law-abiding citizens a disgruntled lot. It has put a premium on dishonesty and in one masterstroke managed to induce a number of law abiding citizens to commit offences.

No developing country can afford such luxuries. Indeed, India cannot afford them either. Even the beneficiaries of the scheme have been deceived. Some of those who have availed themselves of the amnesty schemes in the past have had to bear the brunt of investigating agencies. It is all too well known that cases have been opened against some, contrary to the representations made while launching such amnesty schemes. I know of specific instances of such cases, but am refraining from commenting further in order to maintain professional ethics. No one really trusts the contents of such schemes which themselves are ill-conceived and ought not to be resorted to.

In the end, I must add that the role of commercial banks and financial institutions should henceforth come under closer scrutiny. It has to be recognized that money laundering has two facets. First, transfer of unaccounted funds from India to abroad and second, channelling unaccounted funds from abroad to India through the banking channel or otherwise. The source of the money laundered is always unaccounted, dubious and illegal. Banks must be made accountable for accepting or transferring such funds. It is just not enough for banks to plead ignorance about the source of funds and to take shelter behind customer's instructions. Whilst it is true that banks should not be made to institute any roving enquiry before accepting funds, yet if any glaring instance is brought to light where it is established that the bank has knowingly allowed funds of dubious source to be transacted, then it must be held guilty of abetting the crime, and must be tried for criminal conspiracy under Section-10 of the Indian Evidence Act 1872.

Therefore, there seems no alternative to bringing about stringent money laundering legislation in India. The message has to go out loud and clear that economic offenders are traitors to humanity at large. It is not enough to confiscate properties of such offenders. Punishment awarded should be stringent. If only society ceased to be so utterly insensitive to the fatal blows to the country's economy and boycotted the uncaring offenders, much of the stringency could be dispensed with.

CONTROLLED DELIVERY

Nihal Jayasinghe

Controlled Delivery is a concept relating to the enforcement of law pertaining to criminal offences, wherein law enforcement officers (Police officers) permit offenders (suspects) to commit criminal offences, under their (Police officers) close surveillance, with the view to identifying all connected offenders, and the exact modus-operandi (method of committing) of the offence.

This investigative technique is of immense practical value in the identification and apprehension of all directly and indirectly connected suspects involved in organized crime, wherein offences are committed across and through boundries of nations, in particular, in investigations into illicit trafficking of arms and narcotics. In the larger interests of justice, it could be very useful to facilitate Controlled Delivery, rather than to apprehend a few suspects within a nation, no sooner they are detected having committed an offence. It is in the global interest to permit the commission of an offence in the nature of trafficking a consignment of narcotics from one country to another, and then simultaneously apprehend all the suspects involved in the exportation of the illegal consignment from the first country, and those responsible for the importation of the consignment into the second country.

More specifically, Controlled Delivery in relation to narcotics means, the technique of allowing illicit or suspect consignments of narcotic drugs and psychotropic substances, to pass out of, through or into the territory of one or more countries, with the knowledge and under the supervision of their competent authorities, with a view to identifying persons involved in the commission of offences established by law.

This investigative concept relating to narcotics received international recognition in 1988, with the incorporation of this technique into the United Nations Convention against Illicit Traffic in Narcotic Drugs and Psychotropic Substances. According to Article 11 of this Convention, 'parties (to the Convention) shall take necessary measures, within their possibilities, to allow for appropriate use of Controlled Delivery at the international level, on the basis of agreements or arrangements mutually consented to, with a view to identifying persons involved in offences established in accordance with article 3, paragraph 1 (of the Convention), and to taking legal action against them.

Sri Lanka ratified this Convention in 1991. Even though Sri Lanka has ratified the Convention, we have not yet enacted legislation enabling the official execution of Controlled Delivery.

According to the relevant laws of Sri Lanka (The Police Ordinance and the Act of Criminal procedure), Police Officers are primarily "Preventive Officers". Therefore, Police officers are bound to prevent the commissioning of an offence, no sooner they observe the preparation for the commissioning of an offence. This becomes more important since unlike under the normal penal law of Sri Lanka, under the Poisons, Opium and Dangerous Drugs Ordinance, even an act committed in preparation to commit an offence under the Ordinance, is an offence. On the other hand, if Police officers were to adopt the technique of Controlled Delivery as a mechanism in a particular investigation, they would have to violate this legal duty, and turn a 'temporary watchful eye' to offenders' activities in the preparation to commit offences, and even to offenders committing certain offences. Of course, this is in good faith, and in the larger interests of justice.

It is anticipated that Controlled Delivery would be 'legally recognized' in Sri Lanka in the near future. Even prior to the introduction of new legislation relating to Controlled Delivery, Sri Lanka and the United Kingdom acting in cooperation with each other carried out a Controlled Delivery in 1992-93, with great success. The Police Narcotics Bureau of the Sri Lanka Police learnt of a group of person making preparations for the illicit trafficking of a consignment of cannabis (locally known as ganja) from Sri Lanka to the United Kingdom. Their modus-operandi was to conceal the cannabis in coir bales. As the Sri Lankan authorities were about to arrest the local suspects, the UK police and their customs requested the Sri Lankan Police to permit the consignment to leave Sri Lanka, enabling them to identify those persons who were involved in the importation of the consignment of cannabis into the UK.

Accordingly, the first ever Controlled Delivery took place. Under the close surveillance of the Sri Lankan Police, a container load of 64 coir bales in which 600 kgs of cannabis was concealed left Sri Lanka by ship. The Sri Lankan suspects were kept under close surveillance. After the ship reached UK, and after the suspects in UK took custody of the consignment of cannabis, the suspects in both countries were arrested simultaneously.

I am informed that the suspects arrested in the UK have been convicted after trial and sentenced. The trial against the Sri Lankan suspects is pending. If the Sri Lankan and the UK authorities had not adopted the Controlled Delivery technique, no sooner had the suspects in Sri Lanka been apprehended, those in the UK would have gone underground, and hence the UK police would not have been able to identify and apprehend them, and also identify the modus-operandi they adopted to bring cannabis into UK without being detected.

We would all agree that, in order to eradicate the narcotics problem, law enforcement has to be dealt with at an international level. In this regard, Controlled Delivery is a very important and useful investigative tool. Nevertheless, this tool has to be used carefully and efficiently. There should also be no room for misuse and/or corruption.

In Sri Lanka, the following guidelines were laid down for the Police, in the earlier mentioned case:

* Obtain a detailed and specific request from the foreign law enforcement Agency. This request for mutual assistance should be properly authenticated by the head of the relevant law enforcement authority in the requesting State.
* The requesting State should be a signatory to the 1988 UN Convention.
* The request should be accompanied by a Guarantee of Reciprocity.
* Prepare an action plan to which the requesting State agrees.
* If there is a risk of the relevant consignment falling into unwanted hands or getting lost, do not go ahead with the plan.
* Arrive at an agreement with the requesting State regarding the meeting of high operational costs. Inform Police Headquarters.
* File a Report with the judicial authority (Magistrates Court), indicating the relevant action plan.
* Set-up a strong and close surveillance on the local suspects.
* Give effect to Controlled Delivery.

Law enforcement authorities should be warned not to adopt Controlled Delivery in cases where there are reasonable grounds to believe that there could be a threat of bodily harm to persons or damage to property. Furthermore, even in the course of Controlled Delivery, if there is a threat of bodily harm to persons or damage to property, Controlled Delivery should be immediately stopped, and the available suspects should be arrested.

THE DRUG TRADE AND POLICE CORRUPTION

B S J O'Keefe

One of the areas of strategic interest to the Independent Commission Against Corruption is the impact the illegal drugs market, with the huge amounts of cash it generates, has on police and other public officials involved in the justice system. Criminals involved in the drug trade have a strong incentive to undermine the effective policing of drug laws both within nations and internationally. In most countries we have seen attempts, often effective, by criminals to undermine effective action by police, prison officers, custom officials and other law enforcement agencies. We have also seen criminals try to undermine the judges and magistrates charged with administrating justice; for example, the assaults on the judiciary in Italy have captured world attention.

My perspective is that of the head of a specialist organization, the Independent Commission Against Corruption, established to deal with corrupt conduct by public officials, including police, in the state of New South Wales in Australia. This paper outlines the steps taken in NSW to deal with police corruption, much of which has its origins in the responsibility given to police for controlling the illicit drug trade. In addition, it will refer to the influence that the drug trade has had on the system of justice in NSW.

The NSW Independent Commission Against Corruption

Two consistent themes affect government and its use of power in Australia. The first is that power is divided vertically between the national (federal) government, state governments and local or regional governments. The second is that at the national and state levels, power is divided horizontally between Parliament, the government of the day (Executive) and an independent Judiciary which is, and is vigilant to remain, independent.

The vertical power sharing arrangements are based on the Australian Constitution and the Constitution of each State.

The Commonwealth of Australia is a federation in which the Federal Parliament has specific, designated powers conferred on it by the Australian Constitution. These specific, designated powers cover such matters as trade and commerce, currency, banking, taxation, foreign affairs, defence, customs and excise, post and telegraph, migration, industrial relations and a number of other matters. The states (6) and territories (2) have the residual powers but they also have powers in respect of matters over which the Federal Parliament has power, except in relation to duties of customs and excise, which is an exclusive federal domain. Provision is made in the Constitution for the resolution of conflict between laws of the Federal Parliament and laws made by the Parliaments of the states and territories. Federal law prevails in the case of conflict (s.119). The Federal Parliament has effective ultimate control over Federal Territories and has established an Australian Federal Police Force which operates Australia-wide and also carries out conventional policing functions in Federal Territories.

The final arbiter of the law-making power of the Federal Parliament and of the respective powers of the Commonwealth and States is the High Court of Australia. It is the Australian equivalent of the Supreme Court of India or of the United States and in recent years has adopted an expansionary view in relation to Commonwealth powers. Subject to the Federal Constitution, each state has plenary powers to make laws for the peace, order and good government of the state and since 1984, these powers have had extra territorial operation. Prior to that time, the powers of a state were limited to the geographic area of the state. That was changed by the Australia Act 1984. The powers of the states can be and are exercised in respect of industrial relations, land controls and taxes, *police*, transport, energy, education, public works, health and hospitals. General taxation powers are also available but, as the result of an agreement between the states and Federal Government, the power is not exercised by the states and territories in respect of personal or company incomes.

There are three major political parties in Australia, both in the Federal and state spheres. They are the Labor Party, the Liberal Party and the National Party. There are other minor parties which have representation in some of the Parliaments, for example the Australian Democrat Party. The Liberal and National Parties are in coalition in the Federal Parliament and in a number of states, including New South Wales. They can best be described as the conservative parties. The name of the Labor Party accurately suggests its origins and its policies. Whilst in a number of areas its policies are not different in essence from those of the conservative parties, they frequently have a different emphasis. At the present time the majority party in the Legislative Assembly of New South Wales is the Labor Party and, as a consequence, it forms the Government of New South Wales.

All this is by way of background for those who may not be conversant with the governmental situation in Australia.

New South Wales

In New South Wales, at both state and local government levels, there is a collection of checks and balances between the elected representatives of the people in Parliament and in Councils, the executive government and the courts. All citizens have access to the courts whenever their legitimate interests and legal rights are affected by the actions of the government of the day (Executive). However, within New South Wales there is a further dimension to the system of accountability.

There is a commitment on the part of each of the major political parties in New South Wales to ensure that the public sector, including the Police Service, is honest and impartial. The desire for integrity in the public sector crosses party lines. In 988 the then government (a Liberal/National Party coalition government) established the Independent Commission Against Corruption. It did so with the support of all political parties. The Commission (or ICAC as it is commonly referred to), thus had broad based political support and continues to have it.

New South Wales is at the forefront of providing a secure, corruption free environment in which business can deal with government, secure in the knowledge that government decision-making is open and accountable to its citizens and to Parliament. The Independent Commission Against Corruption is a major force in ensuring this accountability. More recently a special Royal Commission has been looking at corrupt conduct in the Police Service and the Police Integrity Commission will carry on the kind of work undertaken by the Royal Commission when it concludes its task.

The Independent Commission Against Corruption

At both state and local government levels in New South Wales, the ICAC is the premier body for ensuring the private sector can have confidence in the probity of public officials in their decision making. It is a unique organization in Australia. It operates as a standing Commission of Inquiry into corruption and has done so now for more than seven years.

The mission of the Independent Commission Against Corruption is to expose and minimize corrupt conduct within, and affecting, the public sector in NSW. 'Corrupt conduct' is defined broadly. In general terms it includes any conduct involving the dishonest, partial or like improper exercise of public power by a public official and includes various types of specific criminal conduct, one of which is illegal drug dealing [s.8(2)].

The Act of Parliament under which it is set up (the Independent Commission Against Corruption Act 1988) establishes a charter which can be summarized as requiring the elimination or minimization of corruption through investigation, prevention and education. The ICAC is independent of the government of the day. The government cannot direct its operations nor can it direct which matters will be investigated or the outcome of ICAC investigations.

However, the ICAC is accountable. That accountability is not to the government. It is to the Parliament, as the representative of the people. Accountability is achieved primarily through two committees but also more generally through the press and the public because much of our work is done in public and is thus subject to scrutiny. One committee consists of eleven Parliamentarians drawn from the two Houses of our state Parliament, namely the Legislative Assembly and Legislative Council. The selection is on a cross-party basis and so amongst its eleven members there are six Government members, four coalition party members (Opposition) and one independent member. That Committee is known as the Parliamentary Joint Committee (PJC) on the ICAC. The PJC is charged with monitoring and reviewing the exercise by the Commission of its functions, examining each report (whether annual or otherwise) which the commission issues It also look at trends and changes in conduct and practices which relate to or may touch upon corruption. However, the PJC cannot deal with operational matters. Its powers are those of inquiry and examination and of report to Parliament.

The other accountability mechanism built into the ICAC is a committee known as the Operations Review Committee (ORC). The ORC consists of up to eight members of whom the Commissioner of the ICAC is one, the Commissioner of Police another, a representative of the Attorney-General a third, and there are also four community representatives. The function of this committee is to advise the Commissioner whether the Commission should investigate any complaint or discontinue the investigation of any complaint and to advise the Commissioner on any matters which the Commissioner may refer to the ORC for advice. As the Commissioner I am not bound to accept any advice which is tendered to me by the ORC, but as a matter of practice I do. However, at times there may be reasons known to me, but not known to the ORC, which could lead to its advice in a particular matter not being accepted.

The Independent Commission Against Corruption receives its work in a number of ways. First, individuals (members of the public) may complain to the Commission about what they perceive to be corrupt conduct. Second, the heads of government departments and governmental agencies (including the Police Commissioner) *are under a duty* to report to the Commission any matter they suspect on reasonable grounds concerns or may concern corrupt conduct. Third, the Parliament may refer a matter to the Commission for inquiry and report. Fourth, the Commission may of its own motion undertake investigations in relation to any particular matter or area of operation in the public sector.

The Commission has discretion in relation to the first two categories. Generally it is concerned to follow up only those matters which are significant, relatively recent and are either indicative of systematic problems or likely to be of more general application than the instant case. The effect of organized illegal drug dealing on the public sector is most serious. It is often associated with a systems failure in the public sector (revenue evasion, currency violations, vice, illegal gambling, violence etc.) or attempts to pervert the course of justice.

There is no discretion in relation to matters referred by the Parliament. All such matters *must* be investigated and reported to the Parliament.

An investigation which involves a public hearing must be the subject of a report to Parliament; at times reports are made on the results of private hearings. When completed each report is transmitted to the Speaker of the Legislative Assembly and the President of the Legislative Council and is generally widely publicized.

A finding by the Commission that an individual has engaged in corrupt conduct may have repercussions for the individual at a departmental level; it certainly has repercussions at a personal level or, where relevant, at a professional level. However, such a finding is not a finding of a conviction of a criminal offence and the Commission does not itself undertake a prosecutorial role, but may, in appropriate cases, prepare briefs of evidence for reference to the Director of Public Prosecutions and may recommend that consideration be given to prosecuting a particular individual or individuals or may recommend the granting of immunity to a particular individual or individuals. However the decision-making power in relation to such matters resides outside the Commission.

The jurisdiction of the Commission is wide-ranging; its powers great. It has jurisdiction over all public officials, including

(i) the Governor (as the Queen's representative); (ii) all Ministers of the Crown; (iii) all Members of Parliament; (iv) all Judges, Magistrates and holders of other like offices; (v) all heads of departments and other public servants; (vi) members of the Police Service—in respect of some aspects of their conduct and in relation to anti-corruption systems and education; and (vii) officials of local government, including elected members of Councils.

Its jurisdiction also extends to those in the private sector who deal with the public sector. Thus dealings between the public and private sectors are an area in which the Commission has a role. Ensuring that honesty, integrity and impartiality are the touchstones of this public/private sector relationship is an important part of the work of the Commission.

The Commission's powers include a power of investigation. In furtherance of this power the Commission may summon witnesses, interrogate them either in public or private, search premises, take possession of relevant papers and other materials. It can require members of the Public Service to make written statements and can also require people who are called before it to answer questions whether or not the answers to such questions may incriminate them or tend to incriminate them. This is a major departure from the long established common law which enables persons to refuse to answer questions on the grounds that the answers may incriminate or tend to incriminate them. However, the Parliament has provided that answers which are given to the Commission, after objection has been taken, may not subsequently be used in any proceedings against the witness giving the answer, whether those proceedings be civil, criminal or disciplinary in nature.

Whilst investigations form an important part of the Commission's role and dominated the early life of the Commission, I have taken the view since my appointment as Commissioner on 14 November 1994, that in the long term there is a great deal to be gained from placing increased emphasis on the prevention of corruption and on education, whilst at the same time maintaining a strong, effective investigative function.

In the field of medicine it is axiomatic that prevention is better than cure. It is my belief that this axiom can properly be transposed into the field of corruption. This does not mean that the exposure of corruption should be abandoned or that the investigative processes of the Commission should be put on hold or downgraded, any more than the axiom, when applied to the field of medicine, means that people who are sick should not be treated and cured. The Commission maintains a strong investigations program and continues to hold public and private hearings as part of the process of detection and exposure of corrupt conduct.

However, detection and exposure are not *per se* sufficient to prevent corruption. Most people and organizations would prefer to have active prevention strategies in place rather than face the pain and damage which public exposure can bring. To contribute to long term minimization of corruption, the ICAC has become more collaborative and works more with public sector agencies and other organizations to provide advice about overcoming systemic weaknesses that allow corruption to occur. It seeks to build sound relationships and to help motivate public sector organizations to minimize corruption themselves.

In February 1995 I announced a shift in the way in which the Commission would work in 1995 and beyond. The essence of the shift was that the Commission increased its emphasis on collaboration, advice and education. This shift was based on two guiding principles: (i) unity of purpose with the public sector; and (ii) the adoption of a strategic orientation to drive the Commission's work agenda.

The first principle involves the Commission undertaking a proactive role and working in collaboration with the various public sector agencies in order to define the best ways in which systems may be introduced or existing systems modified, so that those who wish to do the right thing will know what to do, whilst those who do not, will more readily and quickly come under attention.

This approach enables the Commission to tap into the budgets and other resources of larger government departments and agencies, thereby expanding our outreach and enhancing our effectiveness, on much the same conceptual model as that which underlay the success of Hercules in his labours.

The second principle is based upon the concept that the community of New South Wales should get best value out of the Commission's budget (approximately $ 14m) and from the work of its staff (145) by choosing our work on the basis of strategic analysis of data and an understanding of the opportunities for corruption in the systems which are in operation in the public sector.

Corrupt conduct is, at least to an extent, a cultural matter. What is popularly regarded as corrupt may vary from country to country, from time to time. Some things may be regarded as innocent, even though they result in decisions being made on the basis of favouritism or other grounds of partiality. However, the drug trade is not regarded as innocent, nor are its effects on the criminal justice system tolerated in any country which has a system of government which seeks to improve the situation or condition of its citizens.

With this in mind the ICAC works to educate the public sector and the community about probity standards and makes information available so that ethics and corruption prevention remain current issues in the public domain. This work extends to those parts of the private sector which deal with the public sector. This is an area in which new opportunities for corruption can arise, and is thus a focus of attention for the ICAC.

Integrity in a system of government tends to promote efficiency, whereas a public administration which is corrupt is likely to be inefficient. Such a system is almost certain to be a wasteful system. The World Bank has recently acknowledged this and reflects that in its lending criteria. A corrupt system of public administration is certain to be a frustrating system for the bulk of those whom it is supposed to serve. It is certain to be a system in which there is little confidence in the community which it exists to serve and in those who might be considering investing in the state or place in which that system of public administration operates. A system of public administration which is inefficient is likely not only to be wasteful but also to create opportunities for corruption. Thus from whatever direction one approaches a system of public administration, inefficiency and waste can be expected to go hand in hand with corruption and lack of public and investor confidence. Eliminating corruption can be expected to reduce inefficiency and waste. It can also be expected to improve community confidence, as well as confidence in prospective investors. In short, honesty and integrity in government are good for the economy.

Recent community attitude research demonstrates that the community in New South Wales demands an ethical public service and can recognize instances of corruption. That same research shows that there is also strong support (91 per cent) for the work of the ICAC. Power tends to corrupt and absolute power corrupts absolutely (Lord Acton 1887).

ICAC Investigation into Police

In 1991, the ICAC commenced an investigation into the relationship between police and criminals. It was focused on specific areas of criminality, particularly armed robberies and illegal gambling, since it had received specific allegations that police officers were involved in giving permission—the green light—for armed robberies to be carried out. There were also allegations that illegal gambling was being protected by police officers.

In line with the corruption prevention approach I have already outlined, the ICAC also undertook two corruption prevention projects which paralleled the investigation. The first dealt with the manner in which police handled informants; the second looked at the corruption risks in the management of criminal investigations—an area identified as being under 'high risk' of corruption.

Public hearings were held over a period of 12 months and involved 147 witnesses and 625 exhibits.

As a direct result of evidence of corrupt conduct and mismanagement in the Police Service Gaming Squad revealed at the hearings, the Squad was disbanded and its responsibilities handed over to local police patrols.

The ICAC released two reports at the end of this investigation (Milloo I and Milloo II): the first dealt with the evidence gathered during the investigation about corrupt conduct by individuals; the second focused on the systems weaknesses which had been identified. Sixteen recommendations for improvement were made. They covered:

- — the relationship between police and informants;
- — the management of criminal investigations, using computerized case management systems;
- — the role of managers in providing effective supervision;
- — record management by the Police Service;
- — the conduct of prosecutors;
- — systems for dealing with misconduct and complaints against Police officers.

In February 1997, the ICAC issued a third report in relation to this investigation (Milloo III). It is a progress report on the performance of the NSW Police Service since April 1994 in implementing our recommendations for change. One of the benefits of having a standing anti-corruption body such as the ICAC is that it is there to monitor and assist the implementation of its recommendations. I am happy to report that overall our recommendations have led to substantial change and improvement, although there is still a distance to go.

Royal Commission into the NSW Police Service

Since May 1994 Justice James Wood of the New South Wales Supreme Court has been conducting a Royal Commission into the NSW Police Service because our Parliament decided that the number of allegations of corruption and criminal conduct by NSW Police warranted a Royal Commission being established to examine the Police Service.

The Royal Commission was given substantial resources (resources far in excess of those available to the Independent Commission Against Corruption) to focus on corruption within the Police Service. The ICAC provided the Royal Commission with substantial amounts of information on corrupt police and handed over a number of ongoing investigations which we had commenced. The Royal Commission thus had an excellent base for its work.

The Royal Commission held public hearings throughout 1995 and 1996, and is due to issue a final report at the end of March 1997.

During 1996, the Royal Commission issued two interim reports which recommended a number of reforms to the way in which allegations against police should be dealt with. In August 1996, a new Police Commissioner, Peter Ryan QPM, was appointed. Commissioner Ryan comes from the United Kingdom with impressive credentials. Since his appointment he has set about implementing substantial reform in the NSW Police Service. He is providing excellent leadership in this regard and I am confident that he will be successful in his efforts.

A major recommendation by the Royal Commission was for the establishment of a new body, the Police Integrity Commission (PIC), to investigate the most serious allegations of misconduct by Police officers. The government accepted this recommendation and the new body commenced operations on 1 January 1997. Its Commissioner, a District Court Judge, has been appointed for a period of two years.

Drugs and Police Corruption in NSW

The relationship between drugs and police corruption has been clearly revealed in the evidence made public in the Royal Commission into the NSW Police Service. That evidence shows a clear connection between drugs and police corruption at a number of levels, including the local level in both metropolitan and non-metropolitan areas, and at higher levels involving both state and federal police.

One scenario which is fairly typical in large cities is the concentration of the drug trade in those central city locations which attract high levels of tourism, are centres of entertainment and have a substantial transient population. Those of you who have been to Sydney may be familiar with one such place, an area known as Kings Cross. It is geographically small and located adjacent to the central business district of the city. It is an area in which vice, gaming and drug distribution have been centred for many years and which has long attracted the criminal element.

Our investigations, as later augmented by the work of the Royal Commission, unearthed evidence of wide spread interdependence between police on the one hand and drug dealers and other criminals on the other. The key to the interdependence was money, the primary source of which was drugs and those forms of criminality so frequently associated with drugs—vice and gambling.

The investigation showed that many police had abused their positions and powers in return for corrupt payments, often very substantial and usually over a protracted period. Whilst in some cases nothing was offered in return, the payments were frequently made following a direct or indirect threat of heavy police attention. However, in most cases police accepted payments as part of an informal partnership with criminals and even if payment did not achieve positive police assistance, it at least contributed to apathy and inertia on the part of police.

The Kings Cross and adjacent police stations have very high workloads and therefore the system made it easy for corrupt police to avoid targetting those enterprises which made payments to them. Inadequate, or deliberately lax, supervision compounded the problem. There was also evidence that criminals used this situation to advantage by supplying information to corrupt police about the activities of their competitors. This allowed the police officers in question to achieve high arrest rates and substantial drug seizures, thus giving them the appearance of successful, hard working police officers. However, this appearance cloaked the evil that continued to fester and spread.

The Royal Commission's first interim report offered the following comment about the drug trade in Kings Cross:

> There is also compelling evidence that the nature of the drug trade over recent years has changed in Kings Cross. There was a shift away from small unorganised one person drug dealing operations. These were displaced by drug dealing entrepreneurs who, with the tacit assistance of those senior police prepared to accept regular corrupt payments, established significant drug dealing enterprises. This led to the evolvement of a "code of practice" whereby high levels of drug dealing were tolerated by police, in return for an acceptance by these entrepreneurs, of a code directed to ensuring a peaceful coexistence between police and drug dealers who abided by the code. The code eschewed gang warfare and violence which was a threat to the general public, but was permissive of large scale drug dealing. Although providing a form of regulation of prohibited substances, the suppression of which was effectively impossible, its evolution was a distortion of policing. Other measures are required for the regulation of conduct or substances, where there is a market demand and a lack of uniform support for the laws dealing with them (p 37).

In addition to this highly organized corruption, opportunistic corruption was also found, such as the division of spoils following drug arrests, searches and confiscations. Most often this occurred in circumstances in which it was not in the interests of the person searched or arrested to complain. In those cases in which the property stolen was drugs, they then became available for resale, supply to informers, or for use in 'loading' suspects, who were not involved in the partnership between criminals and police.

Evidence of assault and robbery and other forms of stand-over tactics by certain police was also unearthed. In some cases, the police officers known for this type of activity, particularly the shaking down of drug users and street dealers, were ostracized—not because of the criminality involved, but because this type of behaviour made it difficult for other corrupt activities to pass without notice.

This type of activity by police was found to occur not only in highly urbanized areas but also in a large residential area about one hour's drive north of Sydney, an area noted for its beaches and waterways. It was the subject of persistent rumours that police attached to the local drug unit had been acting corruptly. Direct and compelling evidence of this (eg. video tapes of police involvement in drug dealing, association with prostitutes and other related activities) was obtained. Evidence of bribery, extortion, dealing in drugs, sharing in rewards paid to informants, and illegal activities designed to gain prosecutions of particular individuals was also found.

The corruption uncovered was not dissimilar to that uncovered by the Mollen Commission in New York. It is a form of corruption which combines drug law enforcement with serious abuse of police powers so as to extort monies, steal cash and drugs and recycle those drugs. Such behaviour is not only aberrant, but also undermines community confidence in law enforcement at the primary, indeed crucial, level and tends to create a climate of suspicion about other elements in the criminal justice system.

A Joint Commonwealth State Task Force on Drug Trafficking (JTF) was set up by Commonwealth and state authorities to address the problem of high level drug trafficking. The JTF was located in NSW and staffed by officers from the Australian Federal Police and the NSW Police Service. The JTF was an elite group and appointment to it was regarded as a credit to one's career. The conviction rate achieved by the JTF was extremely high and they were amply supported with resources and advice. However, corruption infiltrated the JTF.

This corruption took various forms, such as:

— bribery in exchange for an offer of favourable treatment;
— 'stings' upon persons of interest, where offers of assistance were made and money paid in exchange for assistance, but none was forthcoming;
— people being convicted on the basis of evidence which was improperly obtained or just fabricated;
— opportunistic larceny of money and property (including drugs) located during the course of searches;
— collusion to thwart investigation by outside agencies or to assist those under investigation.

It is Australia's experience that the relationship between drugs and police corruption is not limited by either state or national boundaries. For example investigation by an anti-corruption agency in Queensland, a neighbouring state of NSW, has recently exposed police involvement in the drug trade in a popular tropical tourist resort.

Early in February 1997, a former NSW Police Officer, who spent 10 months in jail for contempt of the Wood Royal Commission, was arrested in Canada as a major figure in an international drug smuggling cartel. The individual involved, Charles Staunton, served in the NSW Police Service from 1978 to 1987 and reached the rank of Constable Ist Class. He was arrested in a restaurant in Montreal, Canada where it was alleged he had been involved in the distribution of 3.6 tonnes of hashish.

All in all, more than 200 current and former police officers have been named by the Royal Commission. The corruption alleged in respect of a substantial proportion of these was related to the illegal drug trade. To keep this figure in perspective however, it must be remembered that at the present time there are just under 14,000 sworn police officers in the New South Wales Police Service, that the officers and former officers named were named in respect of activities which were said to extend back over a substantial period (back to the 1970's) and that the percentage of the Service at one time involved was not high in absolute terms, but far too high in absolute terms, far too high for a law enforcement body. Nonetheless there have been some areas of operations in the Police Service in which the effects of corruption and allegations of corruption have been very impactive. To use the words of the present Commissioner:

> "Our detective force overall has been decimated by the Royal Commission and resignations and retirements that stem from the Royal Commission."

There can be no doubt that the relationship between police and criminals, whether it be in armed robberies and gambling as examined by the ICAC or drugs and corruption as highlighted by the Royal Commission, is a fertile ground for police corruption and that the illegal drug trade itself generates a great number of criminal offences, both against the person and against property. Offences against the person not unusually arise out of internecine disputes between rival importing or distribution groups, or are offences committed by persons who are under the influence of drugs. Many offences against property (ranging from armed hold-ups of banks and other places where money may be kept, to breaking, entering and stealing from dwelling houses) are committed by people who are addicted to drugs and need money to feed their drug habit. The cost of attempting to deal with these offences is high, the effort often unrewarding and the effect such as to withdraw police officers from other duties.

Such considerations have led some to call for the decriminalization of drugs, including hard drugs such as heroin. Although suggestions along these lines have been made in a number if parts of the world (including New South Wales) there is no evidence which would inspire confidence that any such experiment would succeed. The experience in Holland and in Switzerland rather suggests the contrary. In addition, at least in Australia, community response to such suggestions is adverse and the political response mirrors that of the community. Interestingly, in New South Wales such suggestions have met with bipartisan opposition.

But the problem does not rest with the police. As I mentioned earlier, the ICAC has responsibility for all public officials in NSW, including the judiciary. In relatively recent times, NSW has had allegations that a District Court Judge was an associate of known drug dealers. While he was acquitted on criminal charges, he resigned from the bench soon after his acquittal. Investigation also revealed an association between the then Chief Magistrate in NSW and individuals later convicted of major drug deals. The Chief Magistrate concerned was later convicted of perverting the course of justice; however, this related to matters not directly related to drug dealing.

Although, thankfully, the judges in Australia have not been tainted by suggestions of corruption, whether arising out of the illicit drug trade or otherwise, the same cannot be said of the system as a whole. There is evidence to suggest that there has been manipulation of the listing system so as to delay the dates of trials and to ensure that matters come before judges who are less severe than some of their brethren. In addition, a high percentage of the trials that related to importation or distribution of drugs are lengthy. Their length is generated in part by the complexity of the legal system, the restrictions on admissibility of evidence and the well-founded desire of the community to ensure that its judicial system does not give rise to innocent people being convicted, and partly by the fact that drug importers and distributors have access to large sums of money to fund their defence and to raise every conceivable (and inconceivable) technicality. As the OJ Simpson trial in the United States clearly establishes, the more money available, the longer, more complex and less satisfactory the trial process.

Thus, even for those police officers, judges and other persons involved in the criminal justice system who are not tainted by any hint of corruption, there is an impact by the illicit drug trade and the cost to the community of that impact alone, whilst not calculable, must be high.

There are effects within the community that go beyond money: (i) the effect on the users, their spouses and children—which in turn impacts on the cost of the social security system; (ii) the decline in the confidence of the community in the law enforcement and criminal justice system; (iii) a sense of failure of our institutions and our society; (iv) an anger that people of lower moral worth can become so powerful whilst good people become the victims; etcetera, etcetera, etcetera. The litany is almost endless.

Dealing with Police Corruption

Success in dealing with police corruption does not come easily or immediately. The work of the Independent Commission Against Corruption, the evidence before the NSW Royal Commission and the experience of police services like that of New York City (which I visited last year) suggest that a number of elements are needed in combination and over time. They are:

— a strong Police Commissioner who is committed to rooting out corruption and who leads by example;
— an external agency to investigate the most serious forms of misconduct and corrupt activity by police, and monitor internal investigations (i.e. by the police themselves);
— an on-going commitment to and effective implementation of corruption prevention and education to recreate a culture of ethical behaviour throughout the Police Service;
— external monitoring of the reform effort to ensure that vigilance and performance do not wane.

In NSW we have achieved the appointment of a new Commissioner, who is showing all the signs of meeting the above requirements. We have established a new external agency focussed solely on investigating serious police misconduct. The ICAC will be assisting in the corruption prevention and education work of the Police Service; and we at the ICAC are currently working on a new model for external scrutiny of the reform process.

In focusing on the adverse effects of the illicit drug trade on the criminal justice system (from detection through to punishment) one must be careful not to make the assumption that the illicit drug trade is the only source of corrupting influences or that it and its effects are restricted to the Police Service. In an age of materialism money can speak the language of many a bureaucrat and it is important that all attention not be focused on the Police Service. For example, even in the field of illicit drugs, it is necessary to keep in mind that importation may involve customs officials or immigration officials and that even after a drug importer, distributor or user has been sentenced, the effects of illicit drugs may continue into the prison system. In that system control of drugs gives power within the prison to those who exercise that control. That power may extend not merely to other prisoners, but may, and not infrequently does, involve officials within the prison administration. That is a matter at which the ICAC is presently looking.

We must also remember that the illegal drug trade is not about to give up and go away. The money and power associated with that trade are too great for that to occur.

Some argue that the criminals are winning the war and that new strategies for combating illegal drugs must be found.

As law enforcement techniques become more sophisticated, and hopefully more successful, the organization of the drug trade is likely to change so as to meet the threat which that sophistication and success pose. So too will the attempts to undermine our criminal justice system change. New forms of police corruption and corruption of the criminal justice system will emerge to replace the corruption we are now successfully exposing and preventing. Agencies such as the Independent Commission Against Corruption will have to be more resourceful and work 'smarter' to ensure that we outpace the changes in the face of corruption, both that related to the illicit drug trade and otherwise. Careful, lengthy, expensive and technically sophisticated investigations will be part of our armoury. So too, for the longer term, will be the corruption prevention and educational weapons.

We need to learn from each other. I hope that my address gives you a better understanding of the problems which we confront in Australia, our response to those problems, the success which we are having in dealing with those problems and the commitment of the Government of New South Wales to an honest, open, transparent public sector.

THE SCOURGE OF DRUGS

Frank Elbe

Drugs have become a menace to mankind. We are in fact dealing with a security problem of global dimensions. It is not only a threat that affects affluent societies, but also developing countries. Those who produce drugs or deal with them unscrupulously launch an aggression against mankind, against human life and political environment. At the end of the 20th Century there are many other dangers threatening mankind on this planet Earth. The nuclear arsenal might destroy everything that we have constructed and developed for millennia and our natural environment is in greater danger than ever before. Obviously, in those issues we have clearly recognized the problem and we have already started to take steps to minimize them. The problem of drugs, however, has been growing and in spite of a lot of goodwill of the entire world this threat has not become smaller.

Greedy and ruthless mafia organizations turn people into addicts destroying them both physically and morally. Age is no reason when it comes to profit. Drugs are sold worldwide to twelve-year-old children in the vicinity of schools. Drugs harm those children in a manifold sense. The poison not only destroys their health but above all young people are deprived of a meaningful perspective for their future life. Many of them become thieves, burglars, prostitutes-prositutes to procure drugs for themselves. Having become dependent on narcotics their energies are absorbed by the painful processes of rehabilitation and de-addiction. These energies are lost for their education and formation, and that at the most important phase of human life. The costs for medical treatment and social rehabilitation have become a growing burden on the finances of our society. Nobody knows how to assess the mental and emotional losses of families at all social levels that are plunged into unimaginable tragedies. I think that it is appropriate to first address the human damage that drugs do. In our daily life unfortunately we have ourselves become witnesses of what happens to our friends, our relatives and our neighbourhood. Worldwide human lives are wrecked by drugs, families are destroyed and societies change their structures due to drug consumption and in the meantime huge profits are amassed which damage our national economies. We speak about 'One World' and herein we try to express our wish and need to keep this 'One Planet' alive. At the same time we have to find out that soon this might become a 'drug planet.'

We know about the immediate effects of drugs but do we fully comrpehend the harm that organized crime does to the global political environment, to the political and social order of societies, to the economic development of Third World countries, to the hope that all people share, namely to life in a world of peace, stability, justice and prosperity? Have we visualized the full scope of the criminal energies that drug producers and criminal organizations unfold in the aggression against the peace of the world? The criminal energy of drugs reaches so far as to force the addicts to commit crimes in order to satisfy their obsession. For a young person the drug addiction may start as a fun game in which the domino theory comes into play. The knock-on effect of this popular game becomes a life threatening chain reaction if the dominoes are replaced by drugs. Once the drugs have got hold of just one person, the chain of disasters has started to move. The production of cocaine has nearly tripled from 1987 to 1994 and opium production has risen more than 100 per cent the same time. In 1994 the production of opium amounted to 7,900 tons. About 2/3rd of opium and heroin production originates from neighbouring countries, Afghanistan and Myanmar. The commercial value of drug consumption worldwide amounts up to US $ 600 billion, that is almost 10 per cent of the GNP of the USA.

Given the giant commercial dimension of the business in drugs it does not require any great power of imagination to understand the magnitude of the threat to global security. Those who produce drugs need an environment of chaos and disorder, and if this is so, they will add to the creation of chaos, because an environment lacking political stability and order is conducive to the undisturbed production of drugs, and to their commercial interests. In other words, many of the conflicts that stem from social or economic disparties or religious fundamentalism are already usurped by the interest of the drug barons. These conflicts loose their authenticity. They become tools for the provision of a smoke-screen behind which organized crime is conducting its business. Under such circumstances the classical regions for drug production are doomed to fail in their political and economic development, since drug production requires the opposite of political stability and economic prosperity. Their instability then radiates into other parts of the world.

Thousands of miles away from the areas of drug production another threat looms. The enormous profits from the business with drugs must be turned clean. Money laundering by organized crime has thus become a serious threat to the societies of Europe and the USA. It presents an assault on their democratic and economic stability. It is only a question of time as to when this phenomenon will extend to other parts of the world, if it has not already done so.

In the world of today we cannot run away from the threats to our common security. We are all sitting in the same boat, so let us fight drugs to protect our children, our democratic institutions and above all the peace of the world.

Since drug consumption is a global problem, we need global answers to this threat. Countries and all international organizations have to work together to eliminate this danger. This is about the implementation of existing laws against drug abuse and illegal trade and about international legal co-operation. Special programs for elimination of drug abuse must be developed and implemented. It is also quite important to amend the existing projects to include drug problems. Those who for example work as social workers in the slums or with street children will have to include the drug issue on their agenda be it preventive work or action against already ongoing drug abuse. If we finally manage to combine all the various and different activities against drugs into a functioning network the justified hope of eliminating the drug problem worldwide may exist.

DRUG USE AND HUMAN RIGHTS

Norbert Gilmore

Drug use[1] is a complex social phenomenon involving a bewildering diversity of drugs, the people who use them, the situations in which they are used, including public and government responses to drug use. It is a popular, costly and controversial behaviour that raises a vast array of human rights concerns.[2]

Most drugs are forcefully prohibited, their use is vigorously condemned, and those who use them are deeply stigmatized—a combination that, all too often, trumps human rights. So often, in fact, that Justice Thurgood Marshall had to remind the U.S. Supreme Court that there is 'no drug exception' to the protection provided by the Constitution.[3] Yet, little is known about drug-related human rights concerns, in particular infringements.[4] Few of them have been documented or analyzed,[5] and they are rarely mentioned in the literature on drug use and on human rights.[6]

[1] Drug use is used as a neutral, generic term that includes the use, misuse or abuse of all illicit and prescription drugs or substances. See, for example, Byck, R. Cocaine, marijuana, and the meanings of addiction. In *Dealing with Drugs. Consequences of Government Control* (Edited by Hamowy R.), pp.221-245. DC Heath and Co, Toronto, 1987.

[2] Gilmore, N. Drug use and human rights: privacy, vulnerability, disability and human rights infringements. *J Contemp Health Law Policy* 12, 355-447, 1996.

[3] Wisotsky, S. 'A society of suspects: The war on drugs and civil liberties'. *USA Today Magazine*, p. 17-21, at p.17, July 1993.

[4] A foundation has been established recently in Amsterdam to address the issue of human rights and drug use. *The International Foundation for Drug Policy and Human Rights* can be contacted via its internet home page at URL=http://www.drugtext.nl or URL = http://www.drugtext.org.

[5] Silvis, J., Hendriks, A. and Gilmore, N. (Eds). *Drug Use and Human Rights in Europe. Report for the European Commission.* p3-4. Willem Pompe Institute for Criminal Law, Faculty of Law, Utrecht University, Utrecht NL, 1992; Husak, D.N. *Drugs and Rights*, Cambridge University Press, New York, 1992.

[6] Silvis, J., Hendriks, A. and Gilmore, N. (Eds) *Drug Use and Human Rights in Europe. Report for the European Commission.* Willem Pompe Institute for Criminal Law, Faculty of Law, Utrecht University, Utrecht NL, 1992.

International legal and policy responses to drug use, including the international drug conventions and treaties on which they are based, rarely address human rights issues. Nor do they appear to have been scrutinized for their compliance with human rights standards.[7] The only express reference to drug use in international human rights conventions and treaties is in the European Convention on Human Rights,[8] and the only express reference to drug use in international legal instruments addressing drug control is a single statement in the United Nations Convention against Illicit Traffic in Narcotic Drugs and Psychotropic Substances.[9] There is also no reference to drug use in the 1988 publication *United Nations Action in the Field of Human Rights*, nor in the Vienna Declaration and Programme for Action adopted at the 1993 World Conference on Human Rights.[10] Much more worrying is the suppression of an attempt by the World Health Organisation's Expert Committee on Drug Dependence in 1993 to address drug-related human rights concerns.[11] The only exception to this poverty

[7] Fluss, S.S. *Human Rights and Responsibilities*. Unpublished paper presented at a World Health Organization Advisory Group Meeting on Policies, Legislation and Programmes on Dependence and Harmful Use of Drugs and Alcohol, Cambridge MA, 31 Jan-2 Feb 1994. Programme on Health Legislation, World Health Organization, Geneva, 1994.

[8] *European Convention on Human Rights,* Art 5.1.e. In Council of Europe. *European Convention on Human Rights. Collected Texts,* p 13-36 at p. 15-16. Council of Europe Press, Strasbourg, 1994.

[9] *United Nations Convention against Illicit Traffic in Narcotic Drugs and Psychotropic Substances*. Sec. 14, Par. 2, as discussed in Silvis, J. The history of drug control with regard to human rights. In *Drug Use and Human Rights in Europe. Report for the European Commission* (Edited by Silvis, J., Hendriks, A. and Gilmore, N.) p. 33-52, at p. 47-48. Willem Pompe Institute for Criminal Law, Faculty of Law, Utrecht University, Utrecht NL, 1992.

[10] Fluss, S.S.: *Human Rights and Responsibilities*. Unpublished paper presented at a World Health Organization Advisory Group Meeting on Policies, Legislation and Programmes on Dependence and Harmful Use of Drugs and Alcohol, Cambridge MA, 31 Jan-2 Feb. 1994.

[11] Room, R. Drug policy flashpoint: WHO balks at declaring drug users' human rights. *The Journal* [of the Addiction Research Foundation, Toronto] 23(3), 12, 1994.

of discourse about drug-related human rights concerns appears to be data on drug-related domestic civil rights issues in the U.S.A.[12]

Drug-related infringements are, for practical purposes, also undocumented and unanalyzed, but most people who are familiar with drug use and efforts to control it would acknowledge that infringements occur, although they are likely to disagree about the details of particular infringements such as their frequency, the particular rights involved and the situations in which they occur. Attempting to identify and catalogue drug-related situations or circumstances that are likely to jeopardize or infringe rights is problematic in the absence of data on threats and infringements. It is made even more difficult because of diversity of drugs, the people using them and the situations in which they are used. Nevertheless, particular infringements that could and are likely to occur can be catalogued, at least provisionally, on the basis of current laws, policies, and practices that address drug use. Among them, and the categories to which they belong, are the following:

Detection of drug users which can include breaches of privacy; absent or diminished data protection and protection against self-incrimination; mandatory or compulsory medical examination or drug testing; and, the compatibility of registers of drug users with human rights protection;

Integrity of persons which can include absent or diminished due process; arbitrary searches, seizure, arrest or detention; and, mandatory or compulsory treatment;

Criminal justice procedures which can include interference with the presumption of innocence and rules of evidence; absent or diminished protection against self-incrimination; and, use of special rules and practices relating to offences committed while intoxicated

Detention which can include arbitrary arrest, detention or imprisonment; absent or reduced access to medical and social assistance, and treatment when in detention; absent or diminished protection against cruel, inhuman and degrading treatment; arbitrary or excessive sentencing policies and practices;

[12] See, for example, Grinspoon, L. and Bakalar, J.B. The war on drugs—a peace proposal. *N Engl J Med* 330, 357-360, 1994; Wisotsky, S. A society of suspects: The war on drugs and civil liberties. *USA Today* p17-21, July 1993; Gostin, L.O. Waging a war on drug users: an alternative public health vision. *Law Med. Health Care.* 18, 385-394, 1990; Schwartz, R.L. Implications of the constitutional right of privacy for the control of drugs: and introduction. In *Feeling Good and Doing Better. Ethics and Nontherapeutic Drug Use.*, pp.129-155. Edited by T.H. Murray, W. Gaylin and R. Macklin. Human Press, Clifton NJ, 1984; Richards, D.A.J. *Sex, Drugs, Death and the Law: An Essay on Human Rights and Overcriminalization*, p157-212. Rowman & Littlefield, Totowa NJ, 1982; Richards, D.A.J. Drug use and rights of the person: a moral argument for decriminalization of certain forms of drug use. *Rutgers L. Rev.* 33, 607, 1981.

Health care which can include absent or reduced availability of and access to care and treatment, including methadone maintenance, as well as rehabilitation and social reintegration; and, absent or reduced availability of access to preventive measures such as clean needles and syringes, methadone maintenance, counselling and education;

Employment which can include arbitrary or discriminatory drug testing policies, absent or reduced work or promotion opportunities; and, unjustifiable dismissal; absent or reduced accommodation of disabled or handicapped persons who use drugs;

Housing which can include absent or reduced housing opportunities; eviction; and, insecure tenure;

Education which can include absent or reduced opportunities for public, private, technical or professional education;

Mobility which can include arbitrary or discriminatory exclusion from immigration and travel; border searches and enquiries;

Insurance which can include absent or reduced eligibility for life, disability or health insurance.

While agreement about the nature, scope and prevalence of particular infringements related to drug use may be unlikely, there would probably be agreement that the most pervasive means whereby human rights are infringed in the context of drug use is wrongful discrimination against drug users.[13] Again, drug related discrimination is, for practical purposes, undocumented and unanalyzed, so that its frequency and seriousness are unknown. A notorious example of the discrimination against drug users is the Americans with Disabilities Act of 1990 which expressly excludes anyone presently using drugs from its protection.[14]

[13] McCarthy, G. Drug use and discrimination. *National AIDS Bull* (Australia), 1994; 8: 32-33.

[14] *Americans with Disabilities Act of 1990*. Sec. 510(a). In contrast, Sec.25 of the *Canadian Human Rights Act* recognizes previous or existing dependence on a drug or alcohol to be a disability. Drug users were not the only groups expressly excluded from the protection of the *Americans with Disabilities Act*. As Parmet comments: Recognizing the breadth of the definition [of disability in the Act], and bowing to the political fear that it might include "politically undesirables", 'Congress explicitly excluded homosexuality[17] and a whole array of specific sexual and behavioural traits which offend traditional morality.[18] The Act also excludes current users of illegal drugs.[19] Those who have stopped using illegal drugs and have either been successfully rehabilitated, or are currently in a rehabilitation program, are covered, as are those erroneously thought to use illegal drugs.[20] (Parmet, W.E. Discrimination and disability: the challenges of the ADA. *Law Med Health Care*. 18: 331-344, at p.332, 1990).

The Roots of Neglect

The neglect of drug-related human rights issues is not surprising when the plight of many drug users and impediments to respecting their rights are considered. Three impediments stand out as having a powerful, adverse impact on the awareness of and respect for human rights. These are: (1) the triad of stigmatization, scapegoating (or exclusion) and discrimination; (2) misperceptions about the benefits, risks and harms from using drugs; and (3) disregarding drug use as private behaviour.

First, the use of drugs is very stigmatizing behaviour, with drug users being among the most stigmatized people anywhere. To a large extent this is because the possession (and, hence, the use) of most drugs is prohibited, and the public generally sees their use as extremely dangerous ('addictive'). Those who use drugs, other than for the moderate use of alcohol or tobacco and the use of medically prescribed therapy, are widely perceived as blameworthy scapegoats who deserve exclusion and punishment—a situation that is very prone to discrimination against drug users. So strong is the stigma that claims to rights seem to evaporate before it.

Second, the use of prohibited drugs is widely perceived to be an inescapably harmful and costly behaviour without redeeming benefits for the user or the public. Suppressing it is widely considered necessary in order to protect those who would use drugs and the public, even if the measures trample rights.

Third, using prohibited drugs is commonly viewed to be a crime and a 'public' behaviour that jeopardizes the public's health, safety and security, as opposed to a 'private' one that is risky but innocuous for most users. It is a view made worse by the violence, crime and corruption that are associated with and attributed to drug use and drug users. As such, it necessitates strong counter-measures to control those who use drugs, especially those who make them available, even when those measures threaten or infringe rights. In other words, drug-related hazards are popularly seen to be a compelling public interest that justifies the infringement of rights. Unfortunately, these measures are not without their direct and opportunity costs, as Seigel of the American Civil Liberties Union has noted:

Conted. from pre page
Note 18 in this statement goes on to state that

[the] ADA, Sec 511(b) excludes "transvestism, transsexualism, paedophilia, exhibitionism, voyeurism, gender identity disorders not resulting from physical impairments, or other sexual behaviour disorders; (2) compulsive gambling, kleptomania, or pyromania; or (3) psychoactive substance use disorders from current illegal use of drugs." (*Ibid*, endnote 18, at p.341)

'{T}oday, inner-city residents and minorities are not only victims of even more dangerous drugs, introduced into their communities by callous profiteers; they are also, along with their civil liberties, the chief casualties of the war on drugs. [M]artial law has been declared in our inner cities, with police raids, curfews, and war relentless searches being the order of the day. At the same time, almost nothing is being done to ameliorate the grinding poverty and despair that are the causes of much of the drug abuse our government claims it wants to end.'[15]

It is not surprising, therefore, that limiting the autonomy of drug users and, sometimes, that of the public, invading their private lives, and discriminating against them occurs frequently, and is seen by the public, and by governments, to be a tiny price for ridding daily life of the menace of drug use. Working to promote and protect the rights of drug users in such a situation seems heretical. It is easily misinterpreted as betraying the public's health, safety and security, condoning drug use, if not promoting it, and impending efforts to suppress what is perceived to be a dangerous, criminal and generally harmful behaviour.

Drug use is a problem of excesses. The excesses are numerous: drug use itself and those who use drugs, direct costs, lost opportunities and a myriad of other harms including health ones, crime, violence and corruption associated with and attributed to drug use, along with social disruption and disrespect for laws and policies. They are excessive because they are potentially preventable or reducible. They are increasing, despite efforts to control them because of the limited efficacy and, sometimes failure of efforts to prevent or reduce them and the harms from those efforts, themselves. Increasingly, the public is becoming frustrated by and disillusioned with their persistence and growth. Many people believe that increased and stronger intrusive, coercive and punitive policies and practices are needed to rein in these excesses, even though they are sometimes ineffective, excessively costly and harmful for users and the public.[16] For others, ineffec-

[15] L Seigel of the American Civil Liberties Union quoted in Evans DG: How many liberties are we losing? *Human Rights* 1990 17(2): 14-17, at p15.

[16] A recent survey from the U.S.A. found that

> ... the public prefers a balanced approach, mixing law enforcement, prevention, and treatment. A majority of Americans want criminal sanctions focused on drug dealers, but intensive help for drug users, or those vulnerable to drug abuse.

When asked specifically if they wanted more spent on a range of overseas and border interdiction efforts, a remarkable 74 per cent of the respondents chose programs in (their) community for drug education, treatment, prevention, and law enforcement. When given the choice of what to do about drug users, respondents by almost a two-to-one ratio chose court-supervised treatment over prison.

(Anonymous: Drug use occupies emergency rooms, public opinion polls. *Public Health Rep.* 1994; 109: 586-587) tive, costly and harmful policies and practices need to be reined in, if the excesses are to be prevented or reduced. Recent referenda in Arizona, California[17] and Italy[18] illustrate this all too well. This is most evident in the emergence and growth of the harm reduction movement, and in the emerging public health responses to drug use. Until recently, public health responses had focused mostly on alcohol and tobacco use. This is changing, in large part, because of the growing awareness of the catastrophic health consequences of drug use, in particular diseases such as hepatitis and AIDS. It is also occurring at a time when there is increasing appreciation that promoting and protecting human rights is essential for responses to public health threats to be effective.[19] In many respects, harm reduction and new public health responses to drug use are similar, if not indistinguishable. While they are seldom formulated as explicit human rights initiatives, importantly, they are compatible with, if not indistinguishable from them.

The triad of stigmatization, scapegoating and discrimination

Stigmatization, scapegoating and discrimination have a powerful impact on the opportunities of drug users and, sometimes, the public, to enjoy and exercise their rights. The triad has contributed to and been reinforced by the historical, political and economic construction of drug use that has made the 'production, manufacture, export, import, distribution of, trade in, use and possession' of many drugs illegal internationally and domestically.[20] As a result, using drugs has become ruthlessly stigmatizing. Most drugs are widely thought to be 'evil,' 'enslaving' and inescapably harmful, ne-

[17] Kassirer, J.P.: Federal foolishness and marijuana. *N Engl J Med 1997* 336: 3366-367.

[18] Arnao, G. Italian referendum deletes sanctions for drug users. *J Drug Issues* 1994 24: 483-487.

[19] Mann, J.M., Gostin, L., Gruskin, S., Brennan, T., Lazzarini, Z., Finebery, H.V. Health and human rights. *Health Human Rights* 1994 1: 6-23.

[20] See, for example, Berridge, V. Drug policy: should the law take a back seat? *Lancet* 347, 301-305, 1996; Manderson, D. *From Mr Sin to Mr Big: A History of Australian Drug Laws*. Oxford University Press, Melbourne, 1993; Manderson, D. History of Australian Law. Conventional Wisdom. In *Drug Policy. Fact, and the Future*, p81-94. Edited by Fox, R. and Mathews, I. Federation Press, Annandale, NSW, 1992; Mitchell, C.N. *The Drug Solution*. Carleton University Press, Ottawa, 1990; Nadelmann, E.A. Drug prohibition in the United States: costs, consequences, and alternatives. *Science*. 249, 939-947, 1989; and, Musto, D.F. *The American Disease. Origins of Narcotic Control*. Expanded edition. Oxford University Press, New York, 1987.

cessitating their prohibition or very stringent control, including making their possession a crime. As a result, most drug users are viewed as different from 'us,' weak-willed, blameworthy, deserving of punishment, and unworthy of their rights.[21]

Discriminating against them is commonplace. Many are sacked, evicted, expelled from school, banned from sports, precluded from immigrating and from professions and, more and more, imprisoned. Their exclusion is so common that it seems a ubiquitous response to drug use. Abstinence, being drug-free, would seem to be the only protection or escape from it. For example, drug testing is being used increasingly, in numerous jurisdictions, to detect drug uses who are then excluded from work, school or sports until they are abstinent. Continued participation in most drug treatment programmes is conditional upon remaining drug-free.[22] And, methadone maintenance programmes are woefully inadequate because of reluctance to promote or implement what is widely perceived to be continuing drug use, rather than a harm-avoiding treatment. For some people, including many former drug users, abstinence is a pragmatic way of avoiding drug-related harm to themselves and others.[23] But, for many people, there is a moral tone and religious zeal to this either/or construction of drug use.[24] One cannot be half-innocent; one is either abstinent, that is 'clean', or is blamed, punished, and excluded from a wide variety of daily activities, including being expelled from treatment programmes. This is not far-fetched. The U.S. government's drug control policy, for example, is one of

[21] Gilmore, N. and Somerville, M.A. Stigmatization, scapegoating and discrimination in relation to sexually transmitted diseases: overcoming "them" and "us." *Soc Sci Med* 33, 1339-1359, 1994; Turner, C.F., Miller, H.G. and Moses, L.E. (Eds). *AIDS, Sexual Behaviour and Intravenous Drug Use*, p 388-399. National Academy Press, Washington DC, 1989.

[22] Hubbard, R.L., Marsden, M.E., Rachal, J.V., Harwood, H.J., Cavanaugh, E.R. and Ginzburg, H.M. *Drug Abuse Treatment. A National Study of Effectiveness.* University of North Carolina Press, Chapel Hill NC, 1989.

[23] Cook, C.C.H. The Minnesota model in the management of drug and alcohol dependency: miracle, method or myth? Part 1. The philosophy and the programme, *Br. J. Addiction* 83, 625-634, 1988; Makela, K. Social and cultural preconditions of Alcoholic Anonymous (AA) and factors associated with the strength of AA. *Br. J. Addiction* 86, 1405-1413, 1991.

[24] Blackwell, J. Sin, sickness, or social problem? The concept of drug dependence. In *Illicit Drugs in Canada*, p 158-174. Edited by Blackwell, J. and Erickson, P.G. Nelson Canada, Scarborough ON, 1988; Szasz, T. The morality of drug controls. In *Dealing with Drugs. Consequences of Government Control* (Edited by Hamowy R.) p 327-351. DC Heath and Co., Toronto ON, 1987; Szasz, T.S. The ethics of addiction. *Int J. Psychiatry*. 10, 51-61, 1972.

zero tolerance,[25] user accountability,[26] mandatory minimum prison sentences,[27] and denial of federal benefits.[28] In such a setting, promoting and protecting the human rights of drug users is easily overlooked, neglected or seen to be one more impediment to stopping drug-related excesses.

Cuio bono*: Benefits, Risks and Harms from Drug Use*

A deep misunderstanding of the benefits, risks and harms from using drugs further contributes to and compounds the neglect of drug-related human rights concerns. There are times when drug use puts some people out of work or school, and into hospital, prison or poverty and, sometimes, kills them. The toll is dismaying. One-sixth of the world's disabled population is disabled because of 'chronic alcoholism and drug abuse.'[29] Alcohol misuse costs UK industry $2 billion annually, with health care costing another $150 million.[30] The U.S. federal government is spending over $15 billion in 1996[31] in an effort to control drugs that are used illegally by over 72 million Americans—almost a third of the U.S. population.[32] Adding to

[25] Gostin, L.O. Waging a war on drug users: an alternative public health vision. *Law Med. Health Care* 18, 385-394, 1990.

[26] *Ibid.*

[27] Vincent, B.S. and Hofer, P.J. *The Consequences of Mandatory Minimum Prison Terms: A Summary of Recent Findings*. Federal Judicial Centre, Washington D.C., 1994 [accessed at URL=http://www.fjc.gov/docs/cons_mand_minim/cons_mand_minim.html].

[28] Bureau of Justice Assistance. *Denial of Federal Benefits Program and Clearinghouse. Bureau of Justice Assistance Fact Sheet.* U.S. Department of Justice, Washington, DC, November 1995 [Doc. FS000102].

[29] Despouy, L. *Human Rights and Disabled Persons. Study Series 6.*, at p. 15. United Nations Centre for Human Rights, Geneva, 1993. [U.N. Publication Sale No. E 92.XIV.4].

[30] Hall, C. Abuse of alcohol costing industry $2 billion a year. *Electronic Telegraph* (London), "Home News", at URL=http://telegraph.co.uk/et/1995/9/18/nalcoh18.html, 18 September 1995.

[31] Brown, L.P. *The 1995 National Drug Control Strategy*, pp 43-46. Office of the National Drug Control Programme, Wshington DC, 1995 (accessed at URL = http://www.ncjrs.org/pdffiles/ndc2.pdf].

[32] Office of National Drug Control Policy Drugs & Crime Clearinghouse. *Drugs and Crime Facts*, 1994, p. 30. Office of National Drug Control Policy Drugs & Crime Clearinghouse, Rockville MD, June 1995 [Publication NCJ]-154043].

these costs are crime,[33] violence,[34] corruption,[35] and even threats to national security,[36] which are often blamed on drug use. These examples point out how dangerous drug use can be for some people.

On the other hand, drug use can be beneficial. Moderate alcohol use, for example, can prolong life, although far more people are harmed by its use.[37] Opiates can relieve pain or be used detrimentally.[38] The same can be said for anxiolytics and sedatives. Obviously, using drugs is beneficial for many people who use them, otherwise many fewer people would be using them. And, the number of people using them is staggering: more than a billion people smoke tobacco,[39] in the United Kingdom, half a million people reportedly use ecstasy on any weekend,[40] more than one-third of 16-29 year olds have used cannabis, with slightly less than one-sixth having used amphetamines or LSD,[41] in France, 11 per cent of the population use psychotropic drugs for medical therapy,[42] in Canada, lifetime

[33] Abadinsky, H. *Drug Abuse. An Introduction*, p 14-22, Nelson Hall, Chicago IL, 1989.

[34] Collins, J.J. Summary thoughts about drugs and violence. In *Drugs and Violence: Causes, Correlates and Consequences* (Edited by De La Rosa, M., Lambert, E.Y. and Gropper, B.), p 265-275. U.S. Department of Health and Human Services, Rockville MD, 1990 [NIDA Research Monograph 103; DHHS Publication No (ADM) 90-1721)].

[35] Evans-Pritchard, A. The battle no one can win. *Electric Telegraph* (London), "World News," at URL = http://telegraph.co.uk/et/96/4/1wamb31.html, 1 April 1996.

[36] Marshall, J. Drugs and United States foreign policy. In *Dealing with Drugs. Consequences of Government Control* (Edited by Hamowy R.), p. 136-176. DC Health and Co., Toronto ON, 1987.

[37] Robson, L., Single, E. *Literatire Review of Studies on the Economic Costs of Substance Abuse. A Report of the Canadian Centre on Substance Abuse*. Ottawa, Canadian Centre on Substance Abuse, 1995 [accessed at URL = http://www.ccsa.ca/costslit.htm#estimates].

[38] Foley, K.M.: Misconceptions and controversies regarding the use of opioids in cancer pain. *Anti-Cancer Drugs* 1995; 6 (Suppl 3): 4-13.

[39] World Health Organization. *Tobacco Alert: Tobacco: The Twentieth Century's Epidemic*. Programme on Substance Abuse, World Health Organization, Geneva, January 1996 [accessed at URL = http://who.ch/programmes/psa/toh/Alert/Jan96/tajan4.htm].

[40] Bowditch, G. Drugs group urges resignation over 'safe Esctasy' row. *The Times* (London), "Britain", at URL = http://the-time.co.uk/news/pages/96/04/11/timnwsnws01026.html, 11 April 1996.

[41] Steele, J.: Young whites are biggest drug users. *Electronic Telegraph* (London), "Home News", 6 May 1996 (accessed at URL = http://www.telegraph.co.uk/et/96/5/6/home.html, 6 May 1996.

[42] Anonymous. La France sous les tranquillisants. *Le Monde* (Paris), p. 1, 20 March 1996.

drug use by 4 per cent of the population includes the use of LSD, methamphetamine or heroin, with a quarter of them, at some time, having injected their drugs,[43] and in the U.S.A., 20 per cent of high school seniors report using prohibited drugs regularly,[44] and 7 per cent of Americans report having used a prohibited drug in the past month.[45] It is difficult to believe that all of these people, or even most of them, have been seriously harmed by their drug use, other than for the illegality of using them.[46] And, non-users are seldom harmed by drug use, other than by the costs and other harms incurred by efforts to suppress it.[47] The end result of this situation is that the benefits from drug use such as pleasure,[48] altered sensation, perception, and performance,[49] and relief or escape from intolerable or insufferable situations,[50] are publicly undervalued, sometimes resented, rarely condoned and most condemned.

One consequence of undervaluing drug-related benefits and exaggerating its risks and harms is an overwhelming belief by the public that the use of most drugs is so dangerous and the harms are so expensive that

[43] Shah, C.P. *Public Health and Preventive Medicine in Canada*, p. 90. University of Toronto Press, Toronto, 1994.

[44] Brown, L.P. *The 1995 National Drug Control Strategy*, p. 1. Office of the National Drug Control Programme, Washington DC, 1995 [accessed at URL = http://www.ncjrs.org/pdffiles/ndc2.pdf].

[45] Newcomb, M.D. Substance abuse and control in the United States: ethical and legal issues. *Soc Sci Med* 35, 471-479, 1992.

[46] See, for example, Eisenhandler, J. and Drucker, E. Opiate dependency among the subscribers of a New York area private insurance plan. *J A Med Assoc* 269, 2890-2891, 1993; Husak, D.N. *Drugs and Rights*, footnote 108 at p. 128. Cambridge University Press, New York, 1992; Buckley, Jr., W.F. Economic impact of drugs on society. In *Drugs and Society to the Year 2000. Proceedings of the XIV World Conference of Therapeutic Communities, Montreal 22-27 September 1991* (Edited by Vamos P. and Corriveau, P.J.), p 196-199. Portage Program for Drug Dependencies Inc, Montreal, 1992.

[47] Maynard, A. The economics of drug use and abuse. In *Cocaine: Scientific and Social Dimension. Ciba Found Symposium No. 166*, p 242-251. Ciba Foundation, New York, 1992.

[48] Brock, D.W. The use of drugs for pleasure. Some philosophical issues. In *Feeling Good and Doing Better. Ethics and Nontherapeutic Drug Use* (Edited by Murray, T.H., Gaylin, W. and Macklin, R.), p 83-105. Humana Press, Clifton NJ, 1984.

[49] Murray, T.H. Drugs, sports and ethics. In *Feeling Good and Doing Better, Ethics and Nontherapeutic Drug Use* (Edited by Murray, T.H., Gaylin, W. and Macklin, R.), p 107-126. Humana Press, Clifton NJ, 1984.

[50] Gilmore, N. Drug use and human rights: privacy, vulnerability, disability and human rights infringements. *Contemp Health Law Policy* 12, 355-447, 1996.

Draconian measures are necessary to suppress it,[51] despite the cost and the harms these measures inflict, including respect for human rights. Reinforcing this belief is the arbitrary distinction between prohibited drugs and those which are marketed publicly such as tobacco, alcohol and codeine.[52] Prohibited drugs are not only seen as extremely dangerous and excessively harmful but their benefits are considered to be self-indulgent[53] or unmerited rewards that seldom benefit anyone other than those who use them. In contrast, the use of drugs that benefit others is often encouraged, or at least tolerated, such as when it relieves pain and anxiety, generates tax revenue and legitimate profits, and facilitates celebrations and other social interactions, even if the risks and harms from using these drugs are no less, and sometimes greater than those from the use of prohibited drugs. The end result of the misperception of drug related benefits, risks and harms is predictable: governments forcefully suppress the use of prohibited drugs in order to avoid what are perceived as excessive risks and harms without competing benefits, while permitting non-prohibited drugs to be commercialized, licensed and taxed.

Drug Use: *Private Behaviour* versus *Public Menace*

Governments and the public seldom recognize that using drugs is a private behaviour.[54] Rather, they see it as a criminal act whereby claims to privacy are forfeited by possessing drugs in most jurisdictions. No one would disagree that harms such as overdoses, infections, dependence and heedless, crime-prone drug-seeking need to be prevented or reduced but prohibiting everyone from using most drugs, and threatening or infringing their rights in the process, fails to recognize that, most of the time, drug use is a private behaviour when it is voluntary (as opposed to compulsive), and innocuous (or harmless to the user and other).[55] Some people will use drugs harmfully but this behaviour is not unique to drug use.

[51] Brown, L.P. *The 1995 National Drug Control Strategy*, pp. 43-46. Office of the National Drug Control Programme, Washington DC, 1995 [accessed at URL = http://www.ncjrs.org/pdffiles/ndc2.pdf].

[52] Goldstein, A. and Kalant, H. Drug policy: striking the right balance. *Science* 249, 1513-1521, 1990.

[53] United Nations. *The United Nations and Drug Abuse Control*, at p. 3. United Nations, New York NY, 1989 [United Nations Publication Saless No. E.90.1.3].

[54] Barnett, R.E. Bad trip: Drug prohibition and the weakness of public policy. *Yale LJ* 103, 2593-2630, 1994.

[55] Fry, S.A. Drug on the market. In *Paperweight*, p 316-318. Mandarin Paperback, London, 1992.

People act foolishly in many ways such as speeding, boxing, refusing to wear seatbelts and cycling or rollerblading without safety equipment, or they act dangerously such as when they autorace, skydive, and climb mountains. But, we do not blame or punish them with the same vehemence when they injure themselves or bystanders. Nor do we prohibit those activities like we prohibit drug use. Instead, we regulate them, requiring inspections, licenses, training, and the use of safety equipment such as helmets, lifejackets and seatbelts in order to prevent or reduce risks and harmful consequences.[56] Unlike those behaviours, drug use is subjected to privacy-invading state intervention to detect and suppress it.[57] It is perceived to be a 'public' menace from which people are to be protected by society and its institutions, rather than a 'private' behaviour insulated from such state interference.[58] Constructing drug use in this way not only jeopardizes the human rights of drug users but it removes their private behaviour from human rights discourse.

As a private behaviour, drug use is a particular situation of a more general one, namely that people use their bodies in a variety of ways for their own private, intimate and voluntary purposes, including pleasure, despite the risks inherent in this behaviour.[59] Many of these 'private' activities are prevalent and popular. Examples include such diverse activities as alpine skiing, rollerblading, playing soccer, sunbathing, racetrack betting, and drinking at social functions, receptions and sporting events. Some of them are hazardous and, indeed, some people engage in them because they are dangerous such as bungee-jumping, skydiving and whitewater rafting. Nevertheless, governments rarely prohibit them or interfere with them, other than to regulate them in order to prevent or reduce their risks and harms.

Becoming seriously dependent upon drugs, using them compulsively does not negate a *prima facie* presumption that drug use is a private behaviour. Dependence is an avoidable risk, not an inescapably harmful consequence of drug use. Many drug users can and do use drugs, often over a long

[56] Hibbs, J. Experts will check 'danger' activities. *Electronic Telegraph* (London), "Home News," at URL = http://telegraph.co.uk/et/96/3/27/npony27.html, 27 March 1996.

[57] Schwartz, R. Implications of the consstitutional right of privacy for the control of drugs. In *Feeling Good and Doing Better. Ethics and Nontherapeutic Drug Use* (Edited by Murray, T.H., Gaylin, W. and Macklin, R.), pp. 129-155. Humana Press, Clifton NJ, 1984.

[58] Friedelbaum, S.H. *Human Rights in the States. New Directionss in Constitutional Policy Making*., p. 77. Greenwood Press, New York NY. 1988.

[59] For a discussion of privacy, see Meyers DT: *Self, Society, and Personal Choice*. New York NY, Columbia University Press, 1989.

period, without necessarily becoming harmfully dependent upon them.[60] Compulsive drug use is a harm, like so many tragedies, injuries and other harms which can accompany other private, voluntary and pleasurable activities that are not prohibited. Instead, they are often strictly regulated in order to prevent or reduce those untoward outcomes. The use of tobacco and alcohol are examples of this approach.

Considering drug use to be a private behaviour has at least four implications for responses to drug use and, therefore, for promoting and protecting opportunities for people to enjoy and exercise their rights.

First, a *prima facie* presumption that drug use is a private activity would mean that legal and policy responses to drug use should not differ from those for similar private behaviours.[61] In other words, responses to drug use would have to be proportional and equal to other private ones.[62] Since rights-affirming-or, at least, less rights-infringing or less seriously infring-

[60] Nadelmann, E. Drug prohibition in the United States: costs, consequences, and alternatives. *Science* 1989, 249: 939-947; Gold, M.S., Schuchard, K. and Gleaton, T. Correspondence: LSD use among US high school students. *J. Am Med Assoc* 1994; 271: 426-427; and, Goldstein, A. and Kalant, H. Drug policy: striking the right balance. *Science* 1990; 249: 1513-1521.

[61] See Mitchell, C.N. A jsutice-based argument for the uniform regulation of psychoactive drugs. *McGill LJ* 1986, 31: 213-263. With regard to U.S. courts, it has been noted by Bakalar and Grinspoon that [t]he courts will not provide a judicial remedy for every dubious law, and they will rarely invalidate the legislature's classification of crimes. They would not overrule a state law that made picking pockets a more serious crime than shoplifting, or a law that required safety devices on chainsaws but not on power mowers. For similar reasons, they have not been willing to overrule penalties for marijuana possession and sale on the ground that they are too severe in relation to the penalties for other drugs or the dangers of marijuana itself. They have upheld state laws imposing a considerably longer maximum sentence for the sale of cocaine than for the sale of amphetamine, which are pharmacologically similar. And the special treatment of alcohol is not a constitutional problem because the Twenty-First Amendment, which repealed Prohibition, has been interpreted so that it supersedes other applicable constitutional provisions and gives the states full power over alcohol regulation. The problem of distinguishing the extent of harm ... may reduce the effectiveness of criminal laws on drug use and sale, but it has not been made into a constitutional obstacle.
(Bakalar, J.B., Grinspoon L. *Drug Control in a Free Society*. New York NY, Cambridge Univ Press, 1984, at p. 118-119).

[62] Proportionality is concerned about "whether the legislative response to illicit drug behaviour is appropriate relative to the state response to other particularly harmful behaviours ... Proportionality, like the efficient allocation of limited enforcement resources, includes comparison with other risk-producing conduct and the subsequent comparison of drug-related behaviours relative to one another."

ing-approaches are used in responding to those behaviours, drug-related human rights threats and infringements would be reduced. Rights are jeopardized far less by requiring seatbelts or bicycling helmets than by incarcerating someone who possesses, say, cannabis or cocaine.

Second, considering drug use to be a private behaviour would seriously question prohibiting the use of a drug when its use is voluntary and innocuous. It does not imply that people have a 'right' to use drugs.[63] Nor does it imply that governments cannot prohibit or limit the use of a drug when using it would have a serious but avoidable net harm for the user or for the public.[64] However, it would mean that whenever the use of a drug is prohibited or limited, this would be (1) the least intrusive and least restrictive measure reasonably available; (2) proportional to the benefits, risks and harms involved; and (3) not disproportionate to interventions that apply to similar private behaviours.

Third, considering drug use to be a private behaviour would shift the emphasis of government interventions from those primarily aimed at controlling the supply of drugs, and their use, to ones that would emphasize

Equality is concerned that like cases be treated alike, or 'that the legal definitions of offences correspond to meaningful categories of behaviour.' (Usprich, S.J. and Solomon, R.M. A critique of the proposed Psychoactive Drug Control Act. *Crim L.Q.* 35, 211-240. 1993, at p 216-217).

[63] As Husak has noted,

[o]ne reason to deny that adults have a moral right to use recreational drugs is that the principle of authonomy does not apply to or protect any recreational activity. According to thsi school of thought, no one has a right to play baseball, ski, or participate in any nonprofessional sport. Persons are morally permitted to engage in recrational pursuits only as long as consequentialist considerations allow them to do so. But as soon as a net balance of disutility is caused by a given recreational activity, the state would have the authority to prohibit it without infringing moral rights.

(Huask DN *Drugs and Rights*. Cambridge University Press, New York, 1992, at p. 142).

[64] Richards notes that

[a]t most, paternalistic concern for forms of irreparable harm might dictate appropriate forms of regulation to insure that drugs are available only to mature persons who understand, critically evaluate and voluntarily accept the risks. To minimize pointless risks, such regulations might insure that certain drugs, LSD, for example, are taken only under appropriate supervision. In general, however, there is no ground of just paternalism for an absolute prohibition of such drugs.

(Richards DAJ *Sex, Drugs, Death, and the Law: An Essay on Human Rights and Overcriminalization*. Rowman & Littlefield, Totowa NJ, 1982, at p 184 [footnote omitted]).

the prevention or reduction of risks and harms resulting from drug use. These would include implementing or strengthening interventions such as helping drug users, and people at risk of using drugs, to learn about drug use and its risks and harms, providing them with opportunities to avoid using drugs or, to use them in as harmless a manner as is possible, and helping to make available and accessible the care and treatment they may need, if they use drugs in a manner that is individually harmful to them. It is an approach that is consistent with other 'positive content' human rights obligations that aim to prevent diseases and protect people from them.[65] It is also an approach that is compatible with harm reduction, public health and human rights.[66] It would have the additional benefit to avoiding or reducing some of the situations in which rights are now jeopardized or infringed, in particular from activities aimed primarily at controlling the supply of drugs such as the drug testing, searches, and seizures.[67]

Fourth, considering drug use to be a private behaviour would help to ensure that the benefits, risks and harms associated with, or attributed to, the use of drugs would be assessed more accurately. This would include eroding the false dichotomy whereby the use of alcohol and that of tobacco are perceived to differ from that of other drugs. All drugs would be viewed as potentially harmful but able to be used in ways that can avoid or minimize these harms. This, in turn, would help to diminish the stigmatization and scapegoating of drug users and discrimination against them, thereby helping to decrease human rights threats and infringements.

[65] Such an approach is consistent with the positive content obligations pursuant to Art. 12 of the *International Covenant on Economic, Social and Cultural Rights*:
1. The States Parties to the present Covenant recognize the right of everyone to the enjoyment of the highest attainable standard of physical and mental health.
2. The steps to be taken by the States Parties to the present Convenant to achieve the full realization of this right include those necessary for:
(a) The provision for the reduction of the still birth-rate and of infant mortality and for the healthy development of the child;
(b) The improvement of all aspects of environmental and industrial hygiene;
(c) The prevention, treatment and control of epidemic, endemic, occupational and other diseases;
(d) The creation of conditions which would assure to all medical service and medical attention in the event of sickness.

[66] See, for example, Jonas, S. Dealing with the drug problem. *Preventive Med.* 23:539-544, 1994; and Gostin, L.O.: Compulsory treatment for drug-dependent persons: justifications for a public health approach to drug dependency. *Millbank Q 69* (suppl 1/2): 561-593, 1991.

[67] Wisotsky, S.: A society of suspects: the war on drugs and civil liberties. *USA Today*, July 1993, p 17-21.

Considering drug use to be a private activity is not a novel idea.[68] Governments already consider the use of some drugs to be a private matter despite the risks and harms involved. The most prominent example is government responses to tobacco and alcohol use. Almost everywhere, driving under the influence of drugs such as alcohol is forcefully prohibited.[69] Neither drinking alcohol nor driving when not under the influence of drugs is prohibited whereas driving when impaired is heavily penalized because of the risks to the driver and to other people. At the same time, governments educate people about the risks and harms from drinking alcohol, label bottles containing alcohol with health promoting messages, and they provide and, indeed, encourage treatment when alcohol use is compulsive. This response to alcohol use also illustrates the powerful impact of stigmatization. Alcohol abuse is strongly stigmatized whereas, in most cultures, its moderate use is, for practical purposes, unstigmatized—as alcohol advertising demonstrates. In contrast, the illicit use of most prohibited drugs is despised and severely penalized—even when the drugs are used with great moderation and at minimal risk to the user and to others.

Pragmatism and Prevention: Harm Reduction and Public Health

There is a triumvirate of dominant responses to drug use—the three "R"s of supply reduction, demand reduction and harm reduction. Between the polar extremes of efforts to reduce the supply of drugs and demand for them is the growth of efforts to prevent or reduce the risks and harms from using drugs.

Harm reduction is a pragmatic approach that aims to make drug use safer by preventing or reducing the health, economic and societal risks inherent in using drugs. It is an approach that applies to the use of all drugs, regardless of their legal status, whether prohibited, prescribed or marketed. It complements demand reduction but recognizes that as long as people use drugs, efforts are needed to prevent or reduce the harmful consequences from using them. It also recognizes that some efforts to control drug use, in particular supply reducing ones, can be counter-productive,

[68] See, for example, Richards, D.A.J. *Sex, Drugs and the Law: An Essay on Human Rights and Overcriminalization.* Rowman & Littlefield, Totowa JN, 1982, p 157-212; Mitchell, C.N. A justice-based argument for the uniform regulation of psychoactive drugs. *McGill LJ* 31: 213-263, 1986; and, Greenstein, H.M., DiBianco, P.E. Marijuana laws—a crime against humanity. *Notre Dome LJ 48*: 314-340, 1972.
[69] Alcohol is not the only drug involved, as shown by the recent report of driving under the influence of illicit drugs such as cannabis and cocaine (Brookoff, D., Cook, C.S., Williams, C. and Mann, C.S. Testing reckless drivers for cocaine and marijuana. *N Engl J Med* 335: 518-522, 1994).

adding to and, sometimes, compounding drug-related risks and harms. Discriminations limit people's autonomy; intrude into their private activities; impoverish them, drive users underground and away from education, counselling and health care; imprison them, leave them with criminal records, or unemployable; promote the adulteration of drugs and increase their prices, thereby promoting larceny and other crimes, as well as trafficking, in order to purchase drugs. One unwanted outcome of successful supply reduction is the vicious circle to which interdiction efforts are prone. When interdiction efforts are successful, and drugs become scarce, drug prices, profits, and production are likely to increase, unless demand for those drugs drops. One result is a shift to the use of more accessible but more dangerous drugs. Another is to drive buyers into poverty or crime in order to continue their drug use.[70] This, in turn, can lead to corresponding increases in police, court and prison interventions, thereby jeopardizing rights even more. Nowhere is this more evident than in the U.S. 'war on drugs', with its ever increasing budgets, arrests, assets confiscation, crime, violence, and threats to human rights.[71] This vicious circle becomes self-defeating as long as the demand for drugs is sustained. Hence, the growing momentum to decrease efforts aimed at reducing the supply of drugs and of suppressing their use while increasing those aimed at demand and harm reduction.[72]

Criminal justice approaches can prompt or force drug users to become 'invisible', self-excluding themselves from society, in order to hide from further stigmatization, blame, exclusion, discrimination, and punishment.[73] Many drug users are vulnerable to human rights abuses before using drugs; their drug use worsens their vulnerability; and, this self-exclusion worsens

[70] Maynard, A. The economics of drug use and abuse. In *Cocaine: Scientific and Social Dimensions. Ciba Found Symposium* No. 166, pp. 242-251. Ciba Foundation, New York, 1992.

[71] See, for example, Schmoke, K.L. Medicalizing the war on drugs. *Academic Med* 70, 355-358, 1995; Grinspoon, L. and Bakalar, J.B. The war on drugs-a peace proposal. *N Engl J Med* 330, 357-360, 1994; Gostin, L.O. Waging a war on drug users: an alternative public health vision. *Law Med Health Care*. 18., 385-394, 1990.

[72] Cotton, P. 'Harm Reduction' approach may be middle ground. J. *Am Med Assoc* 271, 1641-1645, 1994.

[73] See, for example, Gilmore, N. and Somerville, M.A. Stigmatization, scapegoating and discrimination in relation to sexually transmitted diseases: overcoming "them" and "us." *Soc Sci Med* 33, 1339-1359, 1994; Aggleton, P. and Gilmore, N. Social, cultural and political aspects of AIDS: an overview. AIDS 7 (suppl 1), S241-S242, 1993; and, Silvis, J., Hendriks, A. and Gilmore, N. (Eds): *Drug Use and Human Rights in Europe. Report for the European Commission*, at p 3. Willem Pompe Institute for Criminal law, Faculty of Law, Utrecht Unviersity, Utrecht NL, 1992.

it even more.[74] It is a self-fulfilling prophecy. One result is a paucity of information about human rights abuses inflicted on drug users, and a paucity of human rights claims and case law.[75]

Harm reduction is consistent with 'positive content' human rights obligations.[76] It recognizes the importance of addressing the social context in which people live and use drugs. It involves reducing poverty, ignorance, illiteracy, disempowerment, and other conditions which can deprive people of realistic opportunities to not use drugs or to use them safely.[77] It is also consistent with emerging public health responses to drug use. Public health systems are responding increasingly to drug-related health problems. Among their responses, many of which have been successful, are the distribution of bleach, clean injection equipment and condoms, education and counselling programs, improved access to health care and treatment, advocacy, and community development.[78] These responses are indistinguishable from harm reduction ones and, importantly, they are ones that promote and protect human rights.

Policy as Dogma: *Ideology, Economics and Expediency*

Drug use provokes extreme, often emotional and, sometimes, incoherent or inconsistent public and governmental responses. Puritans clash with libertarians and moralists confront pragmatists over what to do about drug use. At the heart of the debate is the question of whether drug use merits the measures which are used to control it, including those with impact on human rights. Caught in the middle, governments persist in their efforts to prohibit drug use,[79] generally relying on intrusive, coercive and punitive

[74] Nurco, D.N., Balter, M.B. and Kinlock, T. Vulnerability to narcotic addiction: preliminary findings. *J Drug Issues* 24, 293-314, 1994; Glantz, M. and Pickens, R. (Eds). Vulnerability to Drug Abuse. American Psychological Association, Washington D.C., 1992; Pearson, G. Drugs, law enforcement and criminology. In *Drugs Research and Policy in Britain. A Review of the 1980s* (Edited by Berridge, V.) p 139-169, in particular pp. 145-148.Averbury, Aldershot UK, 1990.

[75] Gilmore, N. Drug use and human rights: privacy, vulnerability, disability and human rights infringements. *J Contemp Health Law Policy* 12, 355-447, 1996.

[76] Leary, V. The right to health in itnernational human rights law. *Health Human Rights*. 1, 24-56, 1994.

[77] Mosher, J.F. and Yangisako, K.L. Public health, not social warfare: a public health approach to illegal drug policy. *J Publ Health Policy* 12, 278-323, 1991.

[78] Van Ameijden, E.J.C., Watters, J, van den Hoek, J.A.R., Coutinho, R.A. Interventions among injecting drug users: do they work? AIDS 1995; 9 (suppl A): S75-S84.

[79] Anonymous. Editorial: Bring drugs within the law. *The Economist*, 327, p 13-14, 15 May 1993.

measures—measures that are prone to human rights threats and infringements. The threats and infringements can vary from mundane ones such as employment, breathalyser, and sports-related drug testing to catastrophic ones such as the execution of drug traffickers in some countries,[80] life imprisonment for trafficking in cannabis in the U.S.A.[81] and having a criminal record for possession of cannabis, as half a million Canadians have learned.[82] But, drug users are not the only people at risk. A poll in the U.S.A. found '62 per cent of the respondents said they would be willing to give up some of their constitutionally protected rights in order to stop illegal drug use'.[83]

No one would dispute that interfering with rights is, sometimes, necessary, justifiable and desirable. But, it is questionable if most rights-infringing responses aimed at controlling drug use are justifiable,[84] when using drugs would otherwise be harmless for most of those who use them, and other, less invasive less restrictive responses are available, in particular those aimed at reducing the demand for drugs and preventing or reducing harms when drugs are used. A choice between measures that limit autonomy, invade privacy and discriminate against people using drugs, on the one hand, and those that can enhance the autonomy of people to not use drugs, minimize the unsafe use of drugs, respect privacy, and conserve resources for education, counselling, care and treatment, on the other hand, would seem straightforward. All too often, however, the choice has been to rely upon and strengthen criminal justice approaches, thereby worsening drug-related risks and harms and increasing human rights infringements, at the expense of rights-affirming efforts that aim to reduce both the demand for drugs and their harmful use.

If there is any public agreement, at all, regarding drug use, it is that responses to drug use and its harms can be improved, and these improvements are needed urgently. Few people, however, are likely to agree on what would improve the efficacy of responses while reducing costs and harms and avoiding additional ones. Governments appear reluctant or in-

[80] Jayasuriya D.C. Penal measures for drug offences: Perspectives on some Asian countries. *Bull Narcotics*, 36, 9-13, 1984.

[81] Whittell, G. Small time drug crooks clog California prisons. *The Times*, "Americas," at URL = http://the-times.co.uk/news/pages/tim/96/03/09/timfgname01004.html, 9 March 1996.

[82] Solomon, R.M. and Usprich, S.J. Drug law: fatally flawed with a Miami Vice view. *The Globe and Mail* (Toronto), p A17, 27 May 1993.

[83] Quade, V. We've already lost the War on Drugs. *Human Rights*. 17(2), 18-23, 1990.

[84] Room, R. Alcohol control and public health. *Ann Rev Publ Health* 5, 293-317, 1984.

capable of changing their policies substantitively. There are almost 3 million 'hard-core' users of heroin and cocaine in the U.S.A. a figure that is unchanged appreciably since 1988. Crime and violence have reached intolerable levels for the public who are frightened, worried and demanding safety and security be restored to their homes, schools, workplaces and streets. More and more drug users are burdening the U.S. health care and welfare systems, clogging its courts and overcrowding its prisons. Adding to the crisis is a serious shortage of drug treatment services, rehabilitation programmes and prison cells. In response, drug control expenditures have tripled over the past decade. Still, there is growing public disillusionment with drug control policies. The federal government's response, this year, has been to increase funding aimed at reducing the supply of drugs (from 65 per cent to 67 per cent of its drug control allocations) while dropping that for demand reduction and drug treatment (from 35 per cent to 33 per cent).[85] In contrast, the Canadian government allocates 70 per cent of its federal drug control budget to demand and harm reduction. Despite this, the Canadian Parliament recently passed a new federal drug control act that strengthens criminal justice responses to drug use. It was enacted in order to comply with the 1988 United Nations Convention against Illicit Traffic in Narcotic Drugs and Psychotropic Substances, to rationalize earlier drug control laws, and to ensure that federal drug control statutes would comply with Canadian human rights standards. The Netherlands has had to scale back some of its successful, rights affirming responses to drug use, in particular its efforts to "normalize" cannabis use, because of relentless international resistance, particularly by the French government. Thus, it would appear that human rights, implicit in harm and demand reducing responses to drug use, remain neglected in the discourse about improving responses to drug use.

Repatriating Human Rights

Human rights issues, other than privacy, have not been a significant part of the debate over what to do about drug use. This is a tragic oversight, since human rights concepts and principles can be a powerful tool, informing this debate, helping to analyze and reformulate legal and policy responses, and providing standards whereby the resulting responses can be assessed. They would also help to stop the tragic triad of stigmatization,

[85] Office of the National Drug Control Policy: The National Drug Control Strategy: 1996, Table 3-1 at p. 59. Office of the National Drug Control Policy, Washington DC, 1996.

scapegoating and discrimination, help to erase some of the misperceptions about the benefits, risks and harms from using drugs, and help to restore or enhance the autonomy of people at risk of using drugs or at risk of using them harmfully. It would help them to have realistic opportunities to not use drugs or to use them safely. It would return them from hiding in a crime-prone, violent underground, and from prison, to their homes. From a human rights perspective, the objectives of drug control policies should be to help people to have the strength and resilience to resist using drugs or using them harmfully, rather than forcing them not to use them and punishing them when they do.

Ensuring that responses to drug use respect human rights is a formidable challenge. Opinions about drug use and what to do about it are deeply entrenched, and the debate over changing government responses is an extremely divisive and impassioned one. It is often simplified and reduced to decriminalization or legalization of drug use, on one side, and expanding and strengthening efforts to prohibit drug use, on the other. Framing the debate in this way, however, risks de-emphasizing or overlooking issues which contribute to and compound this need for change such as stigmatization, vulnerability to use drugs and to be harmed by using them, and the harmful impact of some government responses, including their harmful impact on human rights.

It is interesting to ask how history will judge our responses to drug use and the choices we make to improve those responses. It will look harshly on ideology that perpetuates harmful, ineffective responses, on expediency that impedes responding in less harmful, more effective ways, and on inertia and political timidity that maintains a self-serving, ineffective and costly status quo. Historians will ask why a generation that codified human rights, and promoted their respect, did not look to those rights to guide them. Why it did not implement, or implement sooner rights-affirming responses while not stopping, or stopping sooner, those that imperil everyone's opportunities to enjoy and exercise their rights, including people who use drugs. Indeed, the measure of our respect for human rights, and their value in our society, will be the extent to which we promote and protect the rights of people whose rights are in greatest jeopardy. Drug users are one such group.

HARM MINIMIZATION - ENGAGING POLICE

Steve Allsop and Roger Nicholas

'Society's tolerance for contradiction continues in ways which provide our police with uneasy and complex tasks. This is most obvious in the area of drug abuse. We license and allow a generally easy access to tobacco, alcohol, sleeping pills and mild antidepressants, while maintaining an opposite set of legal attitudes towards other forms of drug use. The result provides the modern policing service with its greatest challenge' (Bradley and Cioccarelli, 1989, p3).

'The National Drug Strategy's Plan clearly offers a rational model for the incorporation of drug law enforcement into the NCADA principles. Regrettably, however, it offers comparatively little guidance on just how drug law enforcement should work with and complement health sector activities. Exhortations to work together, and for law enforcement to be within a framework of harm minimization do little to overcome acknowledged difficulties' (James and Sutton, 1996, p160).

Why Should the Police Adopt Harm Minimization Principles and Strategies?

Many groups and organizations are stakeholders in health. Consequently health enhancement requires intersectoral collaboration. However, while the importance of this strategy is readily acknowledged, there are few examples occurring in practice. The drug field is no exception to these observations. There are clearly a number of key stakeholders in the reduction of drug-related harm. In recognition of this, intersectoral collaboration is a cornerstone of the National Drug Strategic Plan (1993) of Australia which emphasized that, in order to increase the effectiveness of drug strategies, there is a need to develop far greater collaboration and commonality of purpose among relevant interest groups. For example, it was argued that:

> ... alcohol and drug problems need to be addressed in an integrated way across a broad range of areas. The Plan needs to develop strong

intersectoral linkages between all relevant sectors, including health, education, community services and law enforcement. (National Drug Strategic Plan, 1993, p5).

Unfortunately, the various groups involved in responding to alcohol and other drug problems, such as those in education, health, and law enforcement have more often than not acted unilaterally with limited or no consultation with other stakeholders.

Historically, the policing and health sectors have been considered to have quite distinct roles in responding to alcohol and other drug problems and there have been few examples of strong intersectoral linkages or commonality of purpose or method. A focus on harm minimization by the health sector has occasionally met with criticism from some members of the law enforcement sector and similarly, emphasis on supply reduction has earned few accolades for the police from the health sector. As noted by James and Sutton (1996), while harm minimization has been embraced by many in the health sector, it is perceived by some in the police force as at best 'warm and fuzzy' and at worst a form of complicity with illicit drug users. Critically, although the National Drug Strategy includes an exhortation to ensure that control measures should address harm minimization principles, there is little guidance on how this might be achieved.

An example of the tension between the sectors can be found in response to Operation Noah. The aim of Operation Noah was to encourage members of the public to contact the police if they had information relating to illicit drug use. The short term campaign was established in Victoria in 1982, expanded to a national campaign in 1985 and conducted annually in all regions until 1993. While some in the health sector professed support for Operation Noah, the annual initiative attracted a substantial amount of criticism from many health and community organizations. In fact, some groups considered the operation to be inconsistent with harm minimization strategies, arguing that it resulted in criminal charges for individual drug users while doing little, if anything, to reduce the overall level of drug related harm within the community. This is a criticism voiced in relation to the broad drug law enforcement effort. Sutton and James (1996a) observed that $300-400 million are spent each year on drug law enforcement activities, the impact of which is largely unevaluated. Specifically, there has been little formal evaluation of what increases in harms have arisen as a result of this activity. Certainly, law enforcement to date has not appeared to have had a significant impact on the overall level of illicit drug related harm, and a number of indicators, such as increases in harm from blood borne diseases and deaths from overdose, illustrate a significant increase in adverse consequences.

In relation to illicit drugs, there is a misplaced focus on individual drug users, which may have a number of negative effects. Recent research by James and Sutton (1996) and Green and Purnell (1995) indicated that the vast majority of drug offenders appearing before Australian courts do so for simple possession offences. James and Sutton (1996) suggested that one factor contributing to this phenomenon is that most arrests are made by non-specialist police. For example, in 1993-1994, in Victoria, the drug squad accounted for less than 4 per cent of all drug offences detected (Sutton and James (1996b). While Wetherburn and Lind (1996) proposed that such action may encourage some users into treatment, it is also possible that it may induce changes to more risky drug use patterns (e.g. hurried and higher risk needle use).

In addition to these criticisms, a paradox of drug law enforcement is that while there is an official focus on illicit drugs, harm arising in association with illicit drug use actually consumes the greatest amount of police time. By their own account, police spend significantly more time responding to illicit drug related harm. For example, Ireland and Thommeny (1993) reported that 62 per cent of incidents were judged by police in attendance to be alcohol related —77 per cent of street offences and 73 per cent assault incidents were considered to be alcohol related. Similarly, a survey of 450 police in South Australia found that police estimated that 70 per cent of their time was expended in responding to alcohol and other drug related incidents and 80 per cent of these were related to alcohol use (Nicholas, 1994).

Many people, including police, may well resist embracing harm minimization because it appears exotic and alien to their role. Sutton and James (1996b) reported that some police personnel believed that their role was simply the identification and prosecution of drug criminals; other agencies should be responsible for prevention, treatment and harm minimization. One method to encourage adoption of harm minimization principles would be to identify strategies which are entirely consistent with the police role, are likely to be effective and have a positive impact on police. If we include the sale of tobacco to minors and problems related to alcohol intoxication as central to the police role, harm minimization strategies can be perceived to be entirely consistent with policing. Police have the responsibility to enforce alcohol licensing laws and drink driving laws and in most jurisdictions, tobacco supply laws. In addition, arguably in terms of overall impact on the level of drug related harm in the Australian community, the three most important targets for drug law enforcement are enforcement of licensing law, enforcement of tobacco legislation and enforcement of drink driving legislation.

Random breath testing has been demonstrated to have a significant impact on the level of harm arising from drink driving. Similarly, enforcing the law on responsible serving of alcohol has a significant impact on related crime. For example, in one study, a change in police focus on the laws regarding serving minors and intoxicated customers was associated with a 21 per cent decrease in all crime (Jeffs and Saunders, 1983). In WA, a focus on serving tobacco to minors resulted in a significant change in retailers' behaviour (Wood and Clarke, 1994).

Any strategy to encourage adoption of harm minimization by police should include a re-allocation of policing resources to the drugs which contribute to the greatest harm in the community and, in relation to illicit drugs, away from a focus on possession to activities which reduce drug related harm. This would include changing the emphasis in policing from simply quantitative supply reduction of illicit drugs, to a process of using policing and law enforcement powers to reshape the nature of the illicit drug market into a series of structures which are less harmful. For example, focusing attention on the drugs and drug use patterns that create the greatest harm, rather than focussing attention simply on the largest supplier; avoiding harassment of sites where individuals can inject in comparative safety, rather than engaging in activity which encourages hurried and unsafe injecting behaviour.

What Harm Reduction Roles can Police Adopt?

One simple and critical role that can be undertaken by police is to support, and avoid compromising, harm reduction strategies undertaken by other sectors. For example, Arachne (1996) reported a case study of police impact on a needle exchange programme in Melbourne. Despite an official police policy not to defeat the purpose of needle exchange programs, and the existence of good relations between the needle exchange and the local police division, over a period of three years individual officers were reported to have increased their activity around the needle exchange. This included an obvious physical presence and police interviewing clients attending the service. Arachne reported that associated service decreased by 58 per cent, return rates of used syringes dropped by 70 per cent and the number of people returning used syringes dropped by 54 per cent.

On the other hand, there are examples of police and health reducing the distance between their philosophies and action. In South Australia, health and police services have combined to ensure that all levels of police receive training to facilitate their role in harm reduction strategies. Funding from the National Drug Strategy was provided to South Australia to develop and implement a training program for police. This aimed to ensure that police were informed about the principles of harm minimization and were able to identify harm reduction strategies consistent with their role.

The project resulted in training programs being established for police during recruit, vocational and promotional training and a number of collaborative initiatives between police and health staff have been implemented (Nicholas, 1994). Three specific outcomes are worth noting.

The first was that the SA police co-located an officer in the education services of the Drug and Alcohol Services Council (DASC) and the National Centre for Education and Training on Addiction. In addition to developing and delivering training programs to police, this initiative resulted in a training needs analysis of operational police, which in turn will form the basis of discussions for future activities.

The second outcome followed the implementation of workshops which focussed on the police role in reducing alcohol related crime, particularly violence, in and around licensed premises. This involved presentations given by senior police officers, each of whom had been intimately involved in developing and delivering such initiatives. The first workshop was attended by approximately 100 police officers, many of whom were senior operational staff (including the Assistant Commissioner). The second workshop was convened by the Coalition Against Crime. This involved representatives of the alcohol retail industry, local government, community members, senior police who had attended the first workshop, health services and the State Attorney General.

Shortly after the workshops, the Assistant Commissioner of Police requested that all regional police commanders develop a strategic plan to reduce alcohol-related violence in their areas. In addition, legislative changes were made which specifically aimed to prevent alcohol being served in a high risk manner. There are now clear indications that there has been a substantial change in police practice in the enforcement of the relevant legislation. The National Drug Crime Prevention Fund has subsequently funded a national application of this initiative, and indeed, the WA component of this initiative was delivered immediately prior to this symposium.

Thirdly, the South Australian Police resolved not to participate in Operation Noah. They considered that this operation was not consistent with supply reduction strategies already employed and, importantly, they were embracing the principles of harm minimization. They determined to replace Operation Noah with strategies consistent with harm minimization. The alternative was a campaign which included the development and distribution of resources to parents who may be concerned about their teenagers' potential or actual drug use, and the training of key health staff, including school counsellors. In this program, it was emphasized that parents should neither panic nor immediately contact police if they were concerned about drug use. Rather, the counsel was that they should consider a range of strategies aimed at improving the relationship between parents and teenagers and a number of alternative responses to surmised drug use were suggested. In addition, while Operation Noah focussed exclusively on illicit drug use, it was emphasized throughout the alternative that alcohol and tobacco contributed to the greatest amount of drug-related harm in young people and the community as a whole (see Allsop, Nicholas, Hall and Edmonds 1996).

Other collaborative activities between the sectors have included police collaboration with DASC, NCETA, the Dance Music Industry Association (DMIA) to develop and implement standards for safer dance parties. DASC, police, NCETA, the South Australian Voice for Intravenous Education (SAVIVE) and other health services collaborated to develop and implement strategies to reduce opioid overdose deaths. This included the development of official guidelines and policy for police attending overdoses. Police, DASC and SAVIVE collaborated in the development and implementation of workshops on harm minimization.

How Should We Encourage Police To Adopt Harm Minimization?

Police are under enormous pressure from the community to pursue illicit drug users. In combination with the relatively low onus of proof of drug laws to prosecute individuals for drug possession offences, this is likely to encourage a focus on illicit drugs and contribute to the substantial number of possession charges for individual drug users. In addition, the use of discretion in not arresting a person for simple possession exposes police to charges of corruption, especially in the light of the New South Wales Royal Commission. Nevertheless, the police already use substantial discretion in a range of activities. This discretion is usually based on two factors: resourcing implications and the recognition that strict enforcement of some laws may have deleterious effects on the community. For example, although not always adhered to, police generally have a policy of not waiting outside needle exchanges to arrest people for possession.

Thus, we as a community need to make explicit our requirements of the policing role. A major reason why some police resisted harm minimization, as noted by Bradley and Cioccarelli (1989), is that as a community we give police a very impressive mandate about the responses we want. We have to define the drug related legislative frameworks within which we want police to operate and define the levels of discretion they will exercise in those frameworks. Police cannot be held responsible for unenforceable legislation or for not using discretion when the community or police structures do not support this course. This means that the police must have systems in place to record and justify the use of discretion. That is, structural changes, legislative frameworks and community support are needed if police are to embrace harm minimization more actively.

James and Sutton's (1996) major recommendation was to comprehensively restructure drug law enforcement, to make harm reduction as important an objective as targetting and arresting high level suppliers (In relation to this they also noted that drug retailing in Australia is not controlled in a hierarchical manner. This means that there are few major drug suppliers and many more low level suppliers). To achieve this end, they proposed that a major role of drug squads will be to work in collaboration with local non-specialist police, health and other key stakeholders to develop, implement and monitor harm reduction strategies:

> With each local plan, emphasis would be on ensuring that law enforcement was used to reshape, rather than trying to eliminate, illicit drug markets and associated health, crime and other harms were kept to a minimum. (James and Sutton, 1996)

That is, there should be a change from police using law enforcement powers to simply enforce illicit drug laws, to using policing practices in the broadest sense to reduce drug related harm. They suggested that this should be accompanied by a change in performance indicators from simply focussing on apprehensions, to include price, purity, associated health problems, such as overdose, and drug related crime and violence associated with drug selling and acquisition. To this end, their report recommended that the national initiative should include development and trials of community policing and crime prevention which aimed to reduce the harmful impact of drugs. Indeed, one outcome of the work by James and Sutton has been the establishment of the National Community Based Approach to Drug Law Enforcement (NCBADLE), a strategy which aims to develop and trial harm minimization strategies across Australia. There is a need for national and state level policy mechanisms to introduce and implement harm minimization strategies.

In attempting to engage police in harm minimization, a number of factors should guide our action. As noted by Stockwell (1996), in order to implement effective harm minimization strategies, we need to be more specific in the definition of the variety of harms and potential responses. This translates to policing. Clearer definition of the harms we are seeking to minimize will help identify the role of the police. This will include precision on what is and what is not the role of police (The process will need to recognize that the police are not an homogenous group and that they have a wide range of roles.)

In attempting to engage the police, we will need to identify the benefits of harm minimization and how they can adopt an effective role. People will change their behaviour if they believe they can do it and if there are positive consequences of so doing. Police involvement in diversionary programs and support for methadone are likely to be enhanced by the knowledge that they have a significant impact on acquisitive crime. Police involvement in responsible serving of alcohol will be enhanced if there is support from the community and a recognition that this will reduce the police workload and risk to individual officers. Support will be increased for needle exchanges with the recognition of their impact on blood borne disease and the reduction in risk of blood borne diseases for individual officers.

It will be important to demonstrate to police and other sectors the strategic value of collaboration. The health sector is able to assist police with one of the most substantial problems they face. Methadone maintenance treatment and other interventions have a demonstrable and significant impact on acquisitive crime. The police are able to assist the health sector with a wide range of alcohol related intoxication problems. For example, police who have the role competence, confidence and legitimacy to prevent drunkenness may reduce the demand for sobering up services.

Expecting police to change their role implies the need for training. It is relevant to note that when the National Drug Strategy commenced, it was recognized that substantial education and training effort would be required to support a change in role and practice. It seems logical that police would require similar education and training opportunities. In developing such training, we should respect and acknowledge the skill base of police and focus on how this can be adapted to reduce alcohol and other drug related harm. In addition, we should recognize that education and training are not sufficient in themselves. These strategies require supports and changes in structures, including changes in police performance measures.

The literature on innovation dissemination and utilization can act as a guide to these activities. Allsop (1995) noted that these strategies include:

- Using education methods consistent with adult learning principles;
- Employing experiential and participative learning strategies;
- Establishing links between course content and participants' previous experience, learning and skills. This will include ensuring the establishment of links between course content and the participants' usual work role;
- Using methods which encourage participants to take responsibility for their own learning and translation of new knowledge and skills into the workplace;
- Providing the opportunity for post training practice, support and supervision;

• Linking education and training to leadership/championship which supports and legitimizes the use of the course knowledge and skills within the participants' agencies.

Conclusion

There has been a consistent call to narrow the distance between the police and health sectors. While the task may at first seem arduous, we should note major advances made in the health sector in the last ten years and be encouraged by the indicators that many police are keen to embrace both the principles and the practice of harm minimization. Engaging police in harm minimization has the potential of significantly reducing drug related harm. If we do not succeed in this task the efforts of other sectors will be at best limited, at worst, compromised.

Acknowledgments

The authors acknowledge funding from the National Drug Strategy, which supported a number of the initiatives described in this paper. The first author was a Visiting Research Fellow at Edith Cowan University when this paper was prepared and presented. Thanks to Niki Vincent for comments on an earlier draft.

REFERENCES

Allsop, S. (1995) Addiction Studies: Developing quality practice. In Dillon, P.(ed) *The National Drug Strategy : The first ten years and beyond.* Proceedings from the Eighth NDARC Annual Symposium, Monograph No. 27: 107-115.

Allsop, S., Hall K.M., Nicholas, R. & D. Edmonds, (1996) Dispensing with the ark** an intersectoral alternative to policing drug use *Health Promotion Journal of Australia,* 6(1): 38-41.

Arachne, J. (1996) The potential for police impact on AIDS and Hepatitis prevention programmes, *Proceedings of the 7th International Conference on the Reduction of Drug Related Harm*, Melbourne, Australian Drug Foundation.

Bradley, D. & Cioccarelli, P. (1989) in Chappell, D. & Wilson, P. (Eds) *Australian Policing: Contemporary issues*, Sydney, Butterworths.

Ireland, C.S. & Thommeny, J.L. (1993) The Crime Cocktail: licensed premises, alcohol and street offences, *Drug and Alcohol Review* 12: 142-150.

James, S. & Sutton, A. (1996) Joining the war against drugs? Assessing law enforcement approaches to illicit drug control. In *Australian Policing: Contemporary Issues* 2nd Ed., Sydney, Butterworths.

Jeffs, B.W. & Saunders, W.M. (1983) Minimizing Alcohol Related Offences by Enforcement of the Existing Licensing Legislation. *British Journal of Addiction*, 79: 67-77.

National Drug Strategic Committee. *National Drug Strategic Plan* 1993-1997. Canberral Australian Government Publishing Service, 1993.

Nicholas, R. (1994) *SA Police Drug Intervention Strategies,* Adelaide, Drug and Alcohol Services Council, South Australia.

Stockwell,T. (1996) The search for winnable harm reduction policies: Science versus politics? In *Proceedings of 2nd Window of Opportunity Congress.* Alcohol and Drug Foundation of Queensland, Brisbane.

Sutton, A. & James, S. (1996a) *Evaluation of Australian drug anti-trafficking law enforcement*, Payneham S.A. National Police Research Unit.

Sutton, A. & James, S. (1996b) From evaluation to the future: Australian drug law enforcement paper, *Proceedings of the 7th International Conference on the Reduction of Drug Related Harm*, Melbourne, Australian Drug Foundation.

Wetherburn, D. & Lind, B. (1996). The efficacy of heroin law enforcement in Australia. In *Australian Illicit Drug Report 1995-96*. Canberra, Australian Bureau of Criminal Intelligence.

Wood, L. & Clarke, L. (1994) A comprehensive approach to reducing the supply of tobacco to children in Western Australia, Paper Presented at *Winter School in The Sun, National Drug and Alcohol Conference,* July 1994, Brisbane.

*PROMOTING HARM MINIMIZATION: THE ONGOING ANTIPODEAN DEBATE ABOUT DRUG LAW REFORM**

Duncan Chappell

Victorians are justifiably concerned about widespread misuse of drugs in our community. Experimentation among young people is widespread. Use of drugs such as cannabis and amphetamines is high by international standards, despite prohibitionist laws and a strong commitment to law enforcement.

Concerns have become apparent about increasing adolescent initiation into heroin, and the proliferation of intravenous administration of amphetamines and the use of derivatives of this group such as Ecstasy. Use of multiple drugs is common as the same criminal source may offer a variety of drugs. There has been an increase in the number of deaths directly attributable to illicit drug overdose in the past three years. These are all reasons for re-evaluation of policies and programs.[1]

This recent statement by an official inquiry into drug policies and programs in the Australian state of Victoria is indicative of an extensive, lively and ongoing debate within the Australian community at large about drug

*In preparing this paper, under very tight time constraints, the author has been greatly assisted by many people. Special thanks are extended to Gabrielle Bammer, David McDonald, Helen and Michael Moore, Rhonda Moore, John Myrtle, Jennifer Norberry and Maree Weikes, for their generous help and advice. The final product is, of course, entirely the responsibility of the author.

[1]Victoria Premier's Drug Advisory Council, *Drugs and our Community: Report of the Premier's Drug Advisory Council,* Victorian Government, Melbourne, 1996, p iii (hereafter *Victorian PDAC Report*).

related issues.[2] While this debate is by no means new, nor unique to Australia, it is suggested that the debate has now reached a pivotal point in the Antipodes at which the advocates of reform are beginning to be both heard by and influence those possessing the power to implement change.

Australia has been fortunate over the past decade in possessing a National Drug Strategy (NDS) which has given substantial prominence to a national policy to minimize the harmful effects of licit and illicit drugs and drug use in the community.[3] This policy has resulted, among other things, in the widespread acceptance of needle exchange programs and other community health initiatives designed to curb the spread of the HIV/AIDS infection.[4] It has also produced a multi-disciplinary approach to the handling of drug prevention and control policies which has mitigated, to a degree, the harsher excesses of legislative proscriptions and penalties relat-

[2]The *Victorian PDAC Report* is the latest of a long series of official inquiries into drug related issues in Australia. The report contains a list of these inquiries since 1970 (see pp 143-144) as well as a quite extensive bibliography documenting the extensive contemporary literature associated with the nation's drug debate. See also, in general, McAllister, I., Moore, R. and Makkai, T. *Drugs in Australian Society: Patterns, Attitudes and Policies* Longman Cheshire, Melbourne, 1991; Manderson, D. *From Mr. Sin to Mr. Big. A History of Australian Drug Law*, Oxford University Press, South Melbourne, 1993; Fox, R. and Mathews, I. *Drug Policy. Fact, Fiction and the Future* Federation Press, Sydney, 1992.

[3]The NDS, established in 1985, has been widely acclaimed, both in Australia and internationally, as a leading model in the field. The strategy involves a balance between action addressing the demand for and supply of drugs. The strategy also involves a partnership between government and non-government sectors, and addresses all drugs in use in the Australian community. See Ministerial Council on Drug Strategy *National Drug Strategic Plan 1993-97*, Australian Government Publishing Service (AGPS), Canberra, 1993.

[4]See, for example, the description of the needle syringe exchange programme (NSEP) in place in Victoria since 1987 in the *Victoria PDAC Report* at p 53. In 1995 over two million needles and syringes were distributed free to drug users in Victoria through a variety of settings including community health centres, alcohol and drug agencies, shopping centres, hospital, pharmacies, youth services, municipal councils and Aboriginal co-operatives. Success of the NSEP is measured in rates of intravenous drug users who succumb to HIV infection. The estimated sero prevalence rate for intravenous drug users has stabilized below two per cent in Australia which is a low rate in comparison with other nations.

ing to illicit drug use.[5] Yet beneficial though the general effects of the NDS may have been, the predominant philosophy which has continued to guide Australian illicit drug policy and practice, at least into the early 1990s, has been of prohibition.

This paper contends that this predominant philosophy is now under sustained and critical review, and that the pendulum has finally begun to swing decisively towards the predominance of drug harm minimization policies in Australia and away from the long maintained prohibitionist stance.[6] While continuing to emphasize the need for law enforcement efforts to curb the supply of illicit drugs, policy makers are showing an increasing awareness of the benefits which can flow from a series of proposals designed to reduce drug related harm and demand. It is intended to demonstrate the nature of this paradigm shift in the drug debate by examining two current reform initiatives which remain areas of contention and controversy in Australia, and further afield. The first of these initiatives, yet to be implemented, involves a proposal to trial a new treatment option for dependent heroin users. The second, which is in the process of implementation, consists of a range of modifications to the penalties and policies regarding the possession and use of cannabis.

Before considering each of these initiatives in turn, mention must be made of the broad social and related context in which the Australian drug debate has been grounded. What follows is derived largely from the *Australian Illicit Drug Report 1995-96* produced by the Australian Bureau of Criminal Intelligence (ABCI)[7]. The report is in itself one small measure

[5]A significant number of people with serious drug problems come into contact each year with the criminal justice system in Australia. Penalties prescribed by legislation for the possession, use, supply and distribution of various categories of illicit drugs vary widely between jurisdictions. In the absence of a national criminal code, or a united system of policing, prosecution, adjudication of offences may face very different sentences and treatment outcomes depending on the jurisdiction in which they are located. See, in general, Chappell, D. and Wilson, P.R. (eds) *The Australian Criminal Justice System. The Mid 1990's*, Butterworths, Sydney, 4th Ed. 1994; Australian Bureau of Criminal Intelligence *Australian Illicit Drug Report 1995-96*, ABCI, Canberra, 1996.

[6]A very recent and significant illustration of just how far the pendulum has begun to swing can be found in a statement by the newly appointed Commissioner of the New South Wales Service, Peter Ryan, in February of this year calling for drug law reform, including a test of the decriminalization of hard drugs such as heroin. Ryan, a former senior police commander in the United Kingdom, is now in charge of Australia's largest police agency. See Australian Associated Press "Police Chief Urges Drug Law Reform" *The Australian*, 22-23 February, 1997.

[7]Hereafter *ABCI Drug Report 1995-96*. See note 5 above.

of the way in which the nation's drug debate has shifted. Until the mid 1990s the ABCI prepared annual assessments of illicit drug activities within Australia almost exclusively for use by law enforcement agencies and officials.[8] Access to these annual reports was restricted, and they contained limited information about harm minimization policies or practices.

The latest and current report in the ABCI series is dramatically different from most of its predecessors in both form and content.[9] Now freely available to the general public the report provides a comprehensive and careful appraisal of trends in illicit drug use and abuse. The report also contains references to the reform initiatives considered in this paper as well as describing other drug research and evaluation projects including a major study commen·ed by the ABCI into the efficacy of heroin law enforcement in Australia.[10] The report has now become an essential and authoritative public reference point for anyone seeking contemporary information about illicit drug issues in Australia.[11]

Illicit Drugs: Contextual Information

An island continent approximating in size to the continental United States, Australia has a population of about 17.5 million people. Most of this population lives in cities and towns scattered along the eastern and southern seaboard. The nation, which is comparativ·ly rich and developed in inter-

[8]The principal client for the *ABCI Drug Report* was, and remains, the Australasian Police Ministers' Council (APMC). The APMC meets on a regular basis to discuss and formulate national policing strategies as well as to oversee a range of national police services which includes the ABCI.

[9]The ABCI reports that its own analysts now prepare the annual Drug Report drawing on the resources of various law enforcement agencies throughout the country as well as health authorities, research bodies and other government agencies. See *ABCI Drug Report 1995-96*, px.

[10]See Weatherburn, D. and Lind, B. *Drug Law Enforcement Policy and its Impact on the Heroin Market*, NSW Bureau of Crime Statistics and Research, Sydney, 1995; *ABCI Drug Report 1995-96*, p 191-196.

[11]Another essential reference source is the drug abuse statistical series produced by the Federal Department of Human Services and Health. The series, for use in association with the NDS, contains a summary of the most useful statistical data available about drug-abuse in Australia including trends over the period the NDS has been in place. The latest report available is for the year 1994. See Department of Human Services and Health *Statistics on Drug Abuse in Australia 1994,* AGPS, Canberra, 1994 (hereafter *Drug Abuse Statistics 1994*).

national terms,[12] possesses a federal system of government with common law traditions dating back to the period prior to colonization as a penal settlement by Britain more than two centuries ago.

Australia has high rates of licit and illicit drug use.[13] Among the latter category cannabis continues to be the most popular drug of choice and is used by a wide section of the Australian community.[14] Surveys consistently report that approximately one third of adults have used cannabis.[15] A National Drug and Alcohol Research Centre report issued in January of this year showed that almost 40 per cent of boys had tried cannabis by the time they were 15 years of age, while one in four girls who had experimented with the drug did so before the age of 13.[16] Based on a 1995 National Drug Strategy Household Survey (NDSHS) the study also revealed an increase in the numbers of young people claiming to have been exposed to cannabis with 43 per cent of the males surveyed indicating they had the opportunity to use cannabis within the past 12 months.[17]

[12]The United Nations Development Program (UNDP) Human Development Index ranks Australia in eleventh place among the world's nations. See UNDP *Human Development Report 1996*, Oxford University Press, New York, 1996, p 28-29.

[13]The *Victorian PDAC Report* contains some comparative prevalence rates for illicit drug use (see p 16-17) in Victoria (1995), Australia (1993), Amsterdam (1994), the United States (1991 and 1994) and the United Kingdom (1992). Acknowledging the difficulties of making such international comparisons the report concludes: 'Cannabis is by far the most widely used drug in all cases, although reported rates of prevalence in the United Kingdom are significantly lower than in other countries. Only 14 per cent of those surveyed in the United Kingdom in 1992 had ever used cannabis. Amphetamines are the second most used illegal drug in Victoria, Australia and the United Kingdom, and cocaine is the second most used drug in the USA and Amsterdam. As noted earlier, the apparent similarity in prevalence rates between cocaine and heroin use is likely to be a result of the nature of household surveys and under-representation of some members of the community' *Victorian PDAC Report*, p 16.

Tobacco and alcohol have by far the highest levels of licit drug use in Australia. These two drugs alone account for the vast majority of all drug-related deaths with over 72 per cent (approximately 19000) of such deaths being attributable to tobacco in 1992 and 25 per cent (approximately 6500) to alcohol in the same year. (*Drug Abuse Statistics 1994*, p 5-11). In 1992, 536 deaths were attributed to illicit drug use (*Drug Abuse Statistics* 1994, p 54).

[14]Drug Abuse Statistics 1994, p 5.

[15]See above.

[16]See Mifsud, C. 'More Teenagers Using Cannabis' *Sydney Morning Herald* 17 January 1997, p 3. At the time of the preparation of this paper the author did not have direct access to the just published 1995 National Drug Strategy Household Survey.

[17]See Above.

All Australian jurisdictions reported in 1995-96 that cannabis was readily available to users and that most of the demand for the drug was met by domestic production.[18] A similar situation prevailed in relation to amphetamines, the second most commonly used drug after cannabis.[19] The NDSHS 1995 results showed that six per cent of those surveyed had tried amphetamines within the past 12 months, a figure which had remained relatively stable over recent years.[20]

Heroin users make up only a small proportion of the illicit drug consuming population, with about 0.4 per cent of those surveyed in the 1995 NDSHS stating they had tried heroin during the past 12 months.[21] It has still been estimated that the number of regular heroin users in Australia almost doubled between 1986 and 1990, and that this upward trend has continued.[22] According to the ABCI, heroin continues to be readily available in Australia with the main source of supply coming from South East Asia.[23]

Within this general context the ABCI's own assessment of the impact of current drug prohibition policies is far from optimistic:

> However, it is quite apparent that formal controls are not as effective as society would hope, a fact which is clearly evidenced by the variety and quantity of illicit drugs available in the community. Despite billions of dollars spent worldwide on illicit drug law enforcement, the availability of the LEAS [Law Enforcement Agencies] continue to report increases in purity levels, stable or increasing availability, expanding user markets and intermittent price decreases. Weatherburn and Lind (1995) report that there is no correlation in the busy distribution centre of Cabramatta between the price, purity and perceived availability of heroin and the average amount of heroin seized across Australia. Wodak and Owens (1996) report that 'restricting established illicit drugs often results in new, more concentrated drugs becoming available' (Wodak & Owens 1996 p 21-22), suggesting that the restrictions on cannabis have resulted in the expansion of the amphetamine industry. Hunt (1996) reports that prohibition has not deterred existing users or suppliers, and

[18]*ABCI Drug Report 1995-96*, p 2.

[19]See Above.

[20]See Above, p 3. According to the last NDSHS results, users of other illicit drugs like cocaine and LSD still remain only a very small minority of the illicit drug consuming population.

[21]See Above, p 20.

[22]*Victorian PDAC Report*, p 16.

[23]*ABCI Drug Report 1995-96*, p 3

> that as law enforcement agencies become more effective, the greater are the profits realized by suppliers.
> While those comments are valid, prohibition should not be dismissed as totally ineffective, particularly when the alternatives are considered. It is widely acknowledged that prohibition is not the complete answer to the drug problem in Australia, but then it would be the pinnacle of optimism to expect a state of total prohibition with nil supply and nil demand. Alternative policies need to be examined very carefully before society is expected to accept a radical change based entirely on the perception that prohibition is ineffective.[24]

A New Approach to Heroin?

Given such official views about the efficacy of current law enforcement efforts in dealing with the supply of illicit drugs it is scarcely surprising that an influential and authoritative group like the Victorian Premier's Drug Advisory Council should so recently call for a re-evaluation of drug policies and programs.[25] The *Victorian PDAC Report* did advance proposals for quite far reaching changes to drug laws in that jurisdiction, including regulating rather than criminalizing the use of marijuana. More will be said below about this particular proposal but attention is focused here upon another recommendation the Council made concerning treatment alternatives for dependent heroin users.[26]

Perhaps no single issue in the contemporary debate about illicit drug policies and programs in Australia has received more intensive scientific and public scrutiny over the past five years than a proposal, emanating in the Australian Capital Territory (ACT), to trial a heroin maintenance scheme

[24]*ABCI Drug Report 1995-96*, p 16. The references contained in the quotation are to Weatherburn and Lind, note 10 above; Wodak, A. and Owens, R. *Drug Prohibition: A Call for Change* University of NSW Press, Sydney, 1996; and Hunt, D. *Drugs. Some Current Issues. A Considered Approach by Police* Unpublished paper, 1996.

[25]The Victorian PDAC was chaired by Professor David Pennington, a former Vice Chancellor of the University of Melbourne and Chair of the National AIDS Task Force. Other members of the Council included distinguished community workers, health care professionals, academics and lawyers. The Council's report in general represents a balanced and moderate approach to drug law reform, backed by careful attention to the existing research available in Australia and abroad on drug related issues.

[26]The *Victorian PDAC Report*, as will be indicated in more detail below, expressed its support for an experimental trial involving the prescription of heroin to dependent users of this drug.

for dependent users of this drug.[27] Feasibility research regarding the scheme commenced in 1991 in a collaborative arrangement between the Australian National University's National Centre of Epidemiology and Population Health (NCEPH) and the Australian Institute of Criminology (AIC).[28] Guided by an Advisory Committee with Australia-wide representation from policy-makers, the judiciary, treatment service providers, academics and advocates for illicit drug users, the researchers carefully considered the risks involved in prescribing diacetylmorphine (heroin) to dependent users. They concluded in June 1995 that:

> '...the risks would be minimised and that they are outweighed by the potential benefits. The careful design of the clinical service incorporates numerous crucial safeguards.
> We have thought carefully about the best form of evaluation for a trial and have concluded that the core should be a randomized controlled trial that will examine the following clinical question:
> "If maintenance treatment for opioid dependence is expanded so that both injectable diacetylmorphine (heroin) and oral methadone are available, is this more effective than current maintenance treatment which involves the provision of oral methadone only?"
>
> In addition to the clinical issues, the research must have a strong criminological component which examines the social impact of expanded maintenance treatment, particularly the effects on crime...
> There is now a need for wide community discussion of the issues raised by our recommendations. Our research reveals that both the ACT community and the broader Australian community are convinced that new approaches to the 'heroin problem' are required. The steps proposed here are designed to move cautiously and with scientific rigour in an

[27]For a brief description of the events which gave rise to the ACT proposal see Bammer, G. 'When Science Meets Politics: The Australian Heroin Trial Feasibility Study' *International Journal of Drug Policy* (1996) Vol. 7: 1, 46-51. The ACT is the seat of the Federal Parliament, and the location of many Federal government agencies, as well as housing the nation's capital, Canberra. Landlocked by the surrounding state of New South Wales (NSW), the ACT has a population of about 300,000 persons. An estimated 1,000 dependent heroin users are believed to reside in the ACT. The Territory became a largely self governing entity in 1989. The initiatives concerning the proposed heroin trial have all occurred since this event.

[28] At the time of the commencement of the feasibility research the author was Director of the AIC. Together with Professor Robert Douglas, the Director of NCEPH, he acted as co-chair of the National Advisory Commitee established to oversight the research until leaving the AIC in April 1994.

evaluation of alternatives. This is an area in which there is remarkably little hard evidence. Preliminary experience from trials of diacetylmorphine prescribing in Switzerland is, however, reassuring. We believe the proposals described here are practicable, explore new territory and would contribute substantially to sound policy and treatment development for Australia'.[29]

As this quotation suggests the proposal to prescribe heroin to dependent users is not unique to Australia. The Swiss have already conducted a trial of this type, utilizing many of the experimental design techniques proposed in the Australian feasibility research.[30] In the United Kingdom such prescription has long been possible but much conjecture and dispute exists about its effectiveness.[31] The proposed Australian heroin trial now offers a new possibility to conduct a rigorous evaluation of this alternative approach to the treatment of heroin dependency.

Public opinion surveys undertaken as part of the NCEPH/AIC feasibility research indicate significant community support for the heroin trial in the ACT.[32] The local government in that jurisdiction has also supported the trial in principle but its implementation is at present blocked by opposition from political quarters.[33] That opposition comes principally from three jurisdictions which have traditionally been viewed as being more conservative in their approach to social issues—Queensland, Tasmania and Western

[29]See Bammer, G. *Report and Recommendations of Stage 2 Feasibility Research into the Controlled Availability of Opioids*. NCEPH, Canberra, 1995, p ii. This report contains a full list of the numerous publications which have resulted from this feasibility research between 1991 and June 1995.

[30]See Ladewig, D. and Kury, P. 'Heroin Substitution Trials in Switzerland—Context, Preliminary Data and Findings from an Evaluation Perspective' in Bammer, G. (ed) *International Perspectives on the Prescription of Heroin to Dependent Users: A Collection of Papers from the United Kingdom, Switzerland, the Netherlands and Australia*, NCEPH Working Paper No. 52, Canberra, 1997, p 31-45. The Netherlands is also to conduct a heroin maintenance trial during 1997. See Sturmans, F. 'The Prescription of Heroin to Heroin Addicts: A proposal for the Netherlands' in G. Bammer, above, p 39-46.

[31]See Fleming, P. M. 'Prescription Heroin as Treatment for Dependence—Current UK Situation', and Spear, H.B. 'Heroin and the British System' in Bammer, G. above, p 1-8 and p 9-16 respectively.

[32]See Bammer, G., note 29 above, p 15-17.

[33]See Bammer, G., note 27 above.

Australia—and also from New South Wales.[34] The ACT government has indicated that it is unwilling to proceed with the trial unless it receives majority support from its state and territorial counterparts, and also financial support from the Federal government.[35]

Discussions continue to try and obtain some measure of agreement among these governments to the launching of a quite modest trial which its proponents are convinced would do much to alleviate the harm caused by current policies regarding heroin. The social costs of these policies are high in terms of lost lives and lost opportunities and the damaging effects of marginalizing and disadvantaging dependent users. The financial costs of heroin use in the Australian community are also significant.[36] The esti-

[34]Speaking at a recent public forum to review Australian drug policies the Chief Minister of the ACT made the following comments about her government's attitude towards this opposition:

'In June 1995, Dr Gabrielle Bammer and her team from the National Centre of Epidemiology and Population Health at the Australian National University presented their report about a proposed trial to me. The report recommended that a Task Force, representing a broad cross section of community views, be established to seek community input and to determine whether or not Stage One of the trial, involving forty participants, should go ahead.

As a new government, we knew that this would not occur without political pain. After extensive consultation, the Task Force, chaired by former NSW State Coroner Kevin Waller, recommended that Stage One should proceed. My government took the view that there was no point in going ahead with a limited trial without the support of a majority of states and financial support from the Commonwealth.

When I sought national support at the 1996 Ministerial Council on Drug Strategy, I was very disappointed at the lack of courage displayed, especially by those states that sat on the fence. I respected the views of the Tasmanian Health Minister who voiced his opposition based on his concern for the Tasmanian poppy industry. I may not agree with him, but he had the courage to stand up and state his views. Professor Pennington's report clearly influenced the Victorian government and I appreciated the support of my Victorian colleagues. South Australia was also supportive.

I would not have been so disappointed if the states that opposed the trial had put forward fresh ideas to address the problem of heroin related deaths, but they did not. They simply put the entire issue into the too-hard basket, where this problem has remained for far too long. I was pleased though, that the new Federal Minister for Health took up the challenge of progressing the outstanding issues that surround the trial and I look forward to again vigorously supporting the trial at next year's Ministerial Council on Drug Strategy'. See Carnell, K. 'Crime, Drugs and Society' *The Sydney Papers* (1996) vol 8: 4, p 79-87, at p 83-84.

[35]See above.

[36]See in particular, the cost figures presented in Bammer, G., note 30 above at p 11, and in the *Victorian PDAC Report*, note 1 above, at p 8-10.

mated annual cost of an untreated dependent heroin user, including that person's criminal activity is about USD 50,000; of sending a heroin user to jail USD 35,000 per year; of various treatment options available currently, per person, between USD 1,500-15,999; and the proposed cost of the heroin trial, per person, about USD 7,000.[37]

It remains a moot point whether or not the Australian heroin trial will overcome its political obstacles. Optimism does seem justified, not the least because of support given to the trial by the Victorian PDAC in its Report and by many influential persons in the medical and health care profession.[38] Even without the trial, community and political awareness of the harm minimization alternatives available to deal with the 'heroin problem' has been much enhanced by the well publicized discussion about the merits and demerits of the proposal. In later historical perspective commentators may well conclude that this discussion was one of the crucial catalysts for change in drug policies and programs in Australia.

Possession and Use of Cannabis

Council Recommends that:

Recommendation 7:	The Victorian Government amend the Drugs Poisons and Controlled Substances Act 1981 (Section 3.8). Cannabis use is relatively widespread in our community. Council believes that strategies to reduce use and misuse are most likely to be effective if use of cannabis is no longer a criminal offence but is regulated in a number of important respects. Education and treatment will be facilitated by this change and respect for the law may also increase.
Recommendation 7.1:	Use and possession of a small quantity of marijuana should no longer be an offence. 'Small quan-

[37]See Bammer, G. note 29 above at p 11. These estimated costs have been converted from AUD to USD.

[38]The *Victorian PDAC Report* expressed the view that the proposed ACT trial was an attempt to develop sound research based experience of the effect of offering heroin in a controlled manner to dependent users. The Council urged Commonwealth support for the trial to proceed. See *Victorian PDAC Report*, note 1 above, p 93. The heroin trial has also had strong editorial support in the nation's leading medical journal. See Wodak, A.D. 'When Medical Research is Beholden to Politics', *Medical Journal of Australia* (1996) Vol 164, p 649-650.

tity' should be defined as no more than 25 grams (half the amount currently specified in the Act) (Section 3.8).

Recommendation 7.2: Cultivation of up to five cannabis plants per household for personal use should no longer be an offence. 'Household' should be defined to exclude everything other than private residences (Section 3.8).

Recommendation 7.3: Sale of marijuana should remain an offence. Sale of small quantities by an adult to an adult should incur a caution delivered by Victoria Police for a first offence, with an adjourned bond the preferred penalty for a second offence. Maximum penalties for sale to young people should be maintained at present levels: up to 25 years jail and a $ 250,000 fine for quantities above 100 kilos, etc.

Recommendation 7.4: Provisions of the Summary Offences Act 1966 should be reviewed to ensure offensive behaviour under the influence of marijuana can be dealt with by Police. Similarly, local government should establish bylaws that restrict consumption in public places. Such bylaws would reflect current restrictions on alcohol consumption (Section 3.8).

Recommendation 7.5: Legislation should be introduced to expunge all recorded convictions for possession and use of small quantities of marijuana (Section 3.8). Council believes that all other currently illicit drugs should retain that status, however, enforcement should include greater emphasis on treatment and rehabilitation, particularly where drug use is the only offence.[39]

These recommendations of the *Victorian PDAC Report* concerning cannabis represent the latest in a series of contemporary Australian proposals to effect substantial changes in the legal and allied policies governing the

[39] *Victorian PDAC Report*, note 1 above, p 129-130.

possession and use of this most widely consumed illicit drug.[40] Three Australian jurisdictions—South Australia in 1987, the ACT in 1993 and the Northern Territory in 1996—have now enacted legislation which treats the possession and use of small quantities of cannabis in the general manner proposed by the *Victorian PDAC Report.*[41] The phrase 'general manner' is used deliberately for each of these three jurisdictions has opted for slightly different legal approaches to the issues. In essence each jurisdiction has maintained the overall prohibition against the possession and use of cannabis while allowing expiration of minor offences by the payment of a small financial penalty.[42] The *Victorian PDAC Report* proposal would take this approach further by removing any criminal liability for such minor offences, and expunging all past recorded convictions for possession and use of small quantities of the drug.

No set of recommendations contained in the *Victorian PDAC Report* caused more public debate and controversy than those dealing with cannabis.[43] Eventually the Premier of Victoria, who had initially commissioned the Report, referred these and certain other contentious recommendations to an all party committee of the Victorian Parliament for further consider-

[40]An extremely comprehensive review of the existing information regarding the health and psychological consequences of cannabis use; the legislative options for cannabis use; patterns of cannabis use; and public perceptions of cannabis use can be found in a series of reports commissioned by a NDS Task Force on Cannabis. This Task Force was established in May 1992 and reported its findings to the Ministerial Council on Drug Strategy in September 1994. The broad purpose of the Task Force was to provide the NDS with cost effective options available to Australian jurisdictions for the control of cannabis consumption and minimization of harm arising from its use, as well as identifying uniform legislative approaches required to give effect to these objectives. See, in general, NDS *Report of the National Task Force on Cannabis*, AGPS, Canberra, 1994. The author, in his former role as Director of the AIC, oversighted research relating to one of the Task Force's commissioned reports. See McDonald, D., Moore, R., Norberry, J., Wardlaw, G. and Ballenden, N., *Legislative Options for Cannabis in Australia*, NDS Monograph Series No. 26, AGPS, Canberra, 1994.

[41]For a description of the South Australian and ACT legislation see McDonald *et al* above. The changes to the Northern Territory's laws on cannabis were made by the Misuse of Drugs Act (NT) 1996.

[42]For a summary of the laws and penalties prevailing in October 1995 in regard to cannabis in each Australian jurisdiction see Atkinson, A. and McDonald, D. 'Cannabis, the Law and Social Impacts in Australia' *Trends and Issues* No. 48, AIC, Canberra, 1995.

[43]See Pennington, D. 'Crime, Drugs and Society—An Overview from Victoria' *The Sydney Papers* (1996), Vol 8:4 (Spring), p 69-78.

ation.[44] Reflecting on the resistance that had emerged to the Council's cannabis proposals, the chair of the Victorian PDAC said the following in October 1996:

> 'I knew that we would be dealing with a situation where many in the community have strong views that any use of illicit drugs is an immoral act, open and shut; that anything to do with illicit drugs is something wicked. These views are very closely aligned to religious views or such people's set of moral values. Many are not willing even to have questions raised to see whether or not arrangements, as they stand, are productive or counterproductive in terms of curbing drug use. To them, to even attempt to publicly analyse such issues was, in itself, a threat.
>
> A second, and much larger group are people who are very fearful of illicit drugs and their possible effects on children; this is particularly so of parents who have young or teenage children. They fear that their own children might get caught up in the scene of illicit drugs and that liberalization of the criminal law would lead to a greater use and promiscuity with drugs—regardless of evidence from elsewhere that this does not occur....
>
> We were told by the Police Association, who came out early in the debate, that to decriminalize marijuana would lead to 'carnage on the roads'. This statement was repeated again and again throughout the debate. This was despite the fact that a study in three different States in Australia in which the Victorian Police participated in the early 1990s, and similar studies on either side of the United States and a study in Europe, all came up with the same answer—that marijuana is not the cause of fatal road traffic accidents.'[45]

The fierce and at times vitriolic opposition which was mounted against the *Victorian PDAC Report's* cannabis recommendations has succeeded in bringing a rather abrupt halt, almost certainly temporarily, to the growing movement to liberalize Australia's policies and programs in regard to this particular illicit drug. However, the opposition does appear to be contrary

[44]See above, p 78.

[45]See above, p 75. It should be noted that resistance of this type resulted in the virtual shelving of the reform proposals contained in the National Task Force on Cannabis Report delivered to the NDS Ministerial Council in late 1994. This Task Force recommended that 'jurisdictions consider discontinuing the application of criminal penalties for the simple use or possession of cannabis': See *Report of the National Task Force on Cannabis*, note 40 above, p xii.

to the broad sway of public opinion in this area, and the predominant research evidence concerning the social and allied impacts of current liberalizing trends in some parts of the nation. Survey research conducted for the NDS indicates that a little over one half of the Australian community now favours making legal the possession and use of cannabis, while a substantial majority is in favour of removing the criminal sections which currently apply in at least some circumstances in all jurisdictions.[46] The changes which have been made to legislation in South Australia and the ACT appear to have had little impact on levels of cannabis consumption.[47] The health risks among occasional users of cannabis also appear to be minimal. Evidence regarding the adverse consequences of long term, heavy use suggests an elevation of the health risks but they appear insufficient to justify, by themselves, the total prohibition of the drug.[48]

The Future

The assertion was made at the outset of this paper that a paradigm shift had occurred in the debate about drug issues in Australia, with advocates of reform now gaining ascendancy after suffering many years of neglect and opprobrium within the corridors of power. The pace of change being achieved by these reform advocates may still be frustratingly slow but the arguments they make for an approach to drug policies and programs that is based principally on harm minimization and demand reduction are now under active consideration at all levels of government in Australia. The reform debate has been greatly assisted by vigorous analytical research relating to many key issues affecting legislative, social, health, economic and allied aspects of drug policies and programmes. The level of dialogue may at times have been acrimonious and ill informed but in general reason rather than rhetoric is now prevailing to an ever increasing degree. The re-evaluation of drug policies and programs within the Austraian community is now well advanced, and set on a course which should lead to significant change.

[46]See, in general, Sanson-Fisher, R. and Bowman, J. *Public Perceptions of Cannabis Legislation in Australia*. NDS Monograph Series No.28, AGPS, Canberra, 1994; Atkinson, L. and McDonald, D., note 42 above, p 2.

[47]An extensive evaluation of the social impacts of the legislative options for cannabis in Australia has been undertaken by the AIC. This research is summarized in Atkinson, L and McDonald, D., note 42 above. A full report of the research results is available on disc from the AIC.

[48]See in general, Hall, W., Solowij, N. and Lemon, J. *The Health and Psychological Consequences of Cannabis Use*, NDS Monograph Series No.25; AGPS, Canberra, 1994.

TOWARDS PROSECUTING THE ILLICIT DRUG TRAFFICKERS BEFORE THE PROPOSED INTERNATIONAL CRIMINAL COURT—A CHALLENGE BEYOND 2000

*Narayana Rao Rampilla**

It is estimated that the trade in international narcotics is worth $500 billion a year and is second only to the international arms trade in value.[1] At one time, drug abuse may have been prevalent in the higher socio-economic brackets, but it permeates through all societies all over the world now.[2] Given the alarming nature of this problem, it is proposed to study the feasibility of prosecuting the illicit drug traffickers before the proposed International Criminal Court.

Existing Treaty Regime

There are three treaties that are in force dealing with narcotic drugs and psychotropic substances. They are: (1) Single Convention on Narcotic Drugs, 1961 ('1961 Convention'); (2) Convention on Psychotropic substances, 1971 ('1971 Convention'); and (3) United Nations Convention Against Illicit Traffic in Narcotic Drugs and Psychotropic Substances, 1988 ('1988 Convention'). (hereafter referred to as 'Conventions'). The basic theme under these Conventions is that the drug-related offences are dealt with under the provisions of municipal law by the nation states. Extradition mechanisms are

*The views expressed herein are of the author and do not necessarily reflect those of the United Nations.

[1]See Anti-Drug Abuse Act of 1988, L, No.100-690, s 4102 (a)(2), (6), 102 State. 4818, 4265 for a 1988 estimate by the United States Congress.

[2]See Home Office, Tackling Drug Misuse: A Summary of the Government's Strategy 5-6 (H.M.S.O., London: 3rd ed., 1988). The United Nations and Drug Abuse Control, DPI/1015/Re. 1-92085—November 1992, at 3.

envisaged to extradite and punish the criminals that operate internationally crossing the boundaries of the nation states. The underlying theme of these Conventions is the slogan of international cooperation. Two significant bodies emerge through these Conventions, namely, the International Narcotics Control Board ('Board') and the Commission on Narcotic Drugs of the Economic and Social Council of the United Nations ('Commission').

Some measures are included in these Conventions to ensure execution of the provisions of these Conventions and international cooperation. For instance, reporting obligation under the 1961 Convention.[3] According to article 20, paragraph 1(e) of the 1961 Convention, governments have to furnish to the Board statistical data on 'seizures of drugs and disposal thereof.' These data, which are to be submitted annually to the Board, comprise the substance and quantity seized, the quantity destroyed and the quantity used for licit purposes.[4]

International trade in substances in the Schedules of the 1971 Convention is controlled by the system of import and export authorizations.[5] International trade in substances in Schedule I is restricted to small quantities needed for scientific and very limited medical use.[6] With respect to substances in Schedule II, the simplified estimate system has been in place since the early 1980s, providing the competent authorities of exporting countries with information on the legitimate requirements for those substances in importing countries.[7]

Moreover, the Board urges the governments to ensure that licences for the manufacture of or trade in psychotropic substances are only granted to persons who are adequately qualified for the effective and faithful execution of the provisions of laws and regulations enacted in pursuance of the 1971 Convention, as required under Article 8, paragraph 4, of that Convention.[8]

The 1988 Convention goes further and specifically deals with illicit traffic in narcotic drugs and psychotropic substances. It incorporates a reporting requirement by the member states to the Board on licit trade in substances

[3]Article 20 of 1961 Convention.

[4]In 1991, the Board reminded Governments that had not provided seizure data during that year of their treaty obligations in that regard. In 1995, the Board conducted a review of seizure data for 1993 and the Board compared the seizure data submitted to it with data to ICPO/Interpol and to the Secretary-General. See Report of the International Narcotics Control Board for 1995, at para 57.

[5]See note 4, at para 95.

[6]Article 7 of the 1971 Convention.

[7]See note 4, at para 87.

[8]See note 4, at para 105.

in Table I and Table II[9]. Members are required to report to the Board the amounts seized of the substances in Table I and Table II and the method of diversion and illicit traffic.[10]

The Charter Structure Reflected in the 1988 Convention

Article 2, paragraph 4 of the Charter of the United Nations provides:

> 'All members shall refrain in their international relations from the threat or use of force against the territorial integrity or political independence of any state, or in any other manner inconsistent with the purposes of the United Nations.'

Article 2, paragraph 7 of the Charter of the United Nations further provides:

> 'Nothing contained in the present Charter shall authorize the United Nations to intervene in matters which are essentially within the domestic jurisdiction of any state or shall require the members to submit such matters to settlement under the present Charter; ...'

Enshrined in these provisions are the concepts of territorial integrity, political independence and domestic jurisdiction of a nation state. Article 2, paragraph 2 and 3 of the 1988 Convention seems to reflect these themes. While article 2, paragraph 2 of the 1988 Convention was couched in the language of article 2, paragraph 4 of the Charter of the United Nations,[11] paragraph 3 of the 1988 Convention reflects the essence of article 2, paragraph 7 of the Charter of the United Nations.[12] Article 2, paragraph 1 of the 1988 Convention emphasizes international cooperation and advocates

[9]Article 12 of the 1988 Convention. Table I and Table II mean the correspondingly numbered list of substances annexed to this Convention, as amended from time to time in accordance with Article 12 of the 1988 Convention.

[10]Article 12, paragraph 12 of the 1988 Convention.

[11]Article 2, paragraph 2 of the 1988 Convention provides: 'The Parties shall carry out their obligations under this Convention in a manner consistent with the principles of sovereign equality and territorial integrity of States and that of non-intervention in the domestic legislative systems.'

[12]Article 2, paragraph 3 of the 1988 Convention provides: 'A Party shall not undertake in the territory of another Party the exercise of jurisdiction and performance of functions which are exclusively reserved for the authorities of that other Party by domestic law.'

measures, in conformity with the fundamental provisions of their respective domestic legislative systems.[13]

Article 6 of the 1988 Convention provides for extradition. Unlike the 1961 convention, the 1988 Convention obligates parties to include narcotics offences listed in article 3 of the 1988 Convention in 'every extradition treaty to be concluded between them' and provides that these offences 'shall be deemed to be included as extraditable offences' in all extradition treaties previously concluded between the parties. However, treaties concluded between a party and a non-party are not covered by these provisions.

Despite the existence or non-existence of extradition treaties, there have been instances of kidnappings to bring the illicit drug traffickers before the national judicial tribunals. In 1989 the United States went to the extent of sending troops to the Republic of Panama and prosecuted General Noriega before the United States courts. When prominent drug smugglers are brought before the municipal courts, court rooms become war zones. Organized crime is a big problem, when one tries to halt illicit trafficking in narcotic drugs. As a result, on 23 November 1994, the Naples Political Declaration and Global Action Plan declared a global plan of action against the organized transactional crime.[14] The Declaration urges the states which have not yet become party to the 1988 Convention to join the Convention.

Treaty-Based Crimes

In the context of the United Nations, the existence of a treaty on a particular subject matter is significant when dealing with domestic jurisdiction as laid out in Article 2, paragraph 7 of the Charter of the United Nations. It has been contended that the United Nations may always act where treaty rights and duties are involved.[15] Applying this analogy, one could contend that a treaty-based crime is a matter of international concern. Since

[13]Article 2, paragraph 1 of the 1988 Convention provides: 'The purpose of this Convention is to promote co-operation among the Parties so that they may address more effectively the various aspects of illicit traffic in narcotic drugs and psychotropic substances having an international dimension. In carrying out their obligations under the Convention, the Parties shall take necessary measures, including legislative and administrative measures...

[14]See GA Res. 49/159; text in A/49/748.

[15]See Rosalyn Higgins, *The Development of International Law Through the Political Organs of the United Nations*, (Oxford, 1963), at 83-87. In the question of the treatment of Indians in South Africa a very early resolution referred quite explicitly to the international agreements concerned. In an advisory opinion of the

not every crime is included in a treaty, the treaty-based crime such as illicit drug trafficking crosses into the international domain. In fact, the 1988 Convention in its perambulatory part clearly recognizes that 'illicit traffic is an international criminal activity, the suppression of which demands urgent attention and the highest priority.' Moreover, the 1988 Convention expressed its deep concern that this illicit trade poses a serious threat to the health and welfares of human beings and adversely affect the economic, cultural and political foundations of society.[16] Given this recognition and serious threat of the illicit traffic in narcotic drugs and psychotropic substances all over the world, this treaty-based crime can no longer be confined to the domestic jurisdiction of a nation state.

Narco-Terrorism

Illicit traffic in narcotic drugs in the context of international terrorism poses a serious threat to peace and security. It was expressed that illicit drug trafficking was a scourge that affected the sovereignty of small states and many small states were unable to prosecute the perpetrators of such traffic when carried out on a large scale in their own territory. Some states were virtually helpless in the face of illicit drug trafficking. Narco-terrorism could have a destabilizing effect on some countries, notably those in the Caribbean. The international drug cartels could destroy small states and have a disastrous impact even on the larger states. Furthermore, illicit drug trafficking endangers the survival of man while providing funding for other forms of crime, such as terrorism and subversion. As a result, the International Law Commission ('ILC') at its 47th Session (1950) included illicit

Contd...

Permanent Court of International Justice, as early as 1923, in Nationality Decrees case observed: 'It may well happen that, in a matter which ... is not, in principle, regulated by international law, the right of a state to use its discretion is nevertheless restricted by obligations which it may have undertaken towards other states and the dispute as to the question whether a state has or has not the right to take certain measures becomes in the circumstances a dispute of an international character.' (PCIJ, B. 4, at 4). In the case of Interpretation of Peace Treaties, the International Court of Justice observed: 'The interpretation of the terms of a treaty ... could not be considered as a question essentially within the domestic jurisdiction of a state. It is a question of international law which, by its very nature, lies within the competence of the court.' (ICJ Rep. 1950, at 601).

[16]A similar determination under Article 39 of the Charter of the United Nations as to the existence of any threat to the peace, breach of the peace and acts of aggression will take the matter out of the purview of Article 2, paragraph 7.

traffic in narcotic drugs as a part of the Draft Code of Crimes Against The Peace and Security of Mankind. The Code which was provisionally adopted by the ILC after first reading provides:[17]

'1. An individual who commits or orders the commission of any of the following acts:

undertaking, organizing, facilitating, financing or encouraging illicit traffic in narcotic drugs on a large scale, whether within the confines of a state or in a transboundary context shall, on conviction thereof, be sentenced [to...].

2. For the purposes of paragraph 1, facilitating or encouraging illicit traffic in narcotic drugs includes the acquisition, holding, conversion or transfer of property by an individual who knows that such property is derived from the crime described in the article in order to conceal or disguise the illicit origin of the property.

3. Illicit traffic in narcotic drugs means any production, manufacture, extraction, preparation, offering, offering for sale, distribution, sale or delivery on any terms whatsoever, brokerage, dispatch, dispatch in transit, transport, importation or exportation of any narcotic drug or any psychotropic substance contrary to internal or international law.'

Given these concerns of the members of the International Law Commission as to illicit traffic in narcotic drugs and drafting the above Article 25 right after the provision on international terrorism is quite significant. The Special Rapporteur proposed to confine this crime of illicit traffic in narcotic drugs to 'a large scale or transboundary context.'

However, some members favoured the exclusion of Article 25 altogether. Whatever may be the differences, crime of illicit traffic in narcotic drugs

[17]See Report of the International Law Commission, 47th Session (1995). GAOR, 50th Session Supplement No. 10 (A/50/10), at paragraphs 112-118. Cf. The new text of draft Article 25 proposed by the Special Rapporteur reads as follows:

'1. An individual who commits or orders the commission of illicit traffic in narcotic drugs on a large scale or in transboundary context shall, on conviction thereof, be sentenced [to...]

'2. Illicit traffic in narcotic drugs means undertaking, organizing, facilitating, financing or encouraging any production, manufacture, extraction, preparation, offering, offering for sale, distribution, sale delivery on any terms whatsoever, brokerage, dispatch, dispatch in transit, transport, importation or exportation of any narcotic drug or any psychotropic substance contrary to internal or international law.

'3. For the purposes of paragraph 2, facilitating or encouraging illicit traffic in narcotic drugs includes the acquisition, holding, conversion or transfer of property by an individual who knows that such property is derived from the crime described in this article in order to conceal or disguise the illicit origin of the property.'

keeps haunting the world community and it is a matter of international concern as it knows no boundaries. Terrorism and its association with illicit drug trafficking is a serious threat and deserves the attention of the world community. However, inclusion of the crime of illicit drug trafficking in the Draft Code of Crimes Against Peace and Security of Mankind is significant.

The Proposed International Criminal Court

The 1994 ILC's Draft Statute for an International Criminal Court[18] has a provision for crimes within the jurisdiction of the court. The ILC's Draft was adopted by the Preparatory Committee on the establishment of International Criminal Court. Article 20 of this Draft Statute provides:

'The Court has jurisdiction in accordance with this Statute with respect to the following crimes:

(a) the crime of genocide;
(b) the crime of aggression;
(c) serious violations of the laws and customs applicable in armed conflict;
(d) crimes against humanity;
(e) crimes, established under or pursuant to the treaty provisions listed in the Annex, which, having regard to conduct alleged, constitute exceptionally serious crimes of international concern.'

Included under the Annex are crimes involving illicit traffic in narcotic drugs and psychotropic substances as envisaged by article 3(1) of the United Nations Convention against Illicit Traffic in Narcotic Drugs and Psychotropic Substances of 20 December 1988, which with regard to Article 2 of the Convention, are crimes of an international dimension.[19]

Two views emerged at the Preparatory Committee on the Establishment of an International Criminal Court. According to one view:

> 'Some delegations expressed the view that particularly serious drug trafficking offences which involved an international dimension should be included, that these offences had serious consequences on the world population and that there was no unified system for addressing these crimes because of divergences in national laws. Reference was made to the

[18]GAOR, 49th Session, Supplement No.10 (A/49/10), at 70.

[19]Report of the Preparatory Committee on the Establishment of an International Criminal Court, Vol.II, GAOR. 51st Session Supplement No.22A (A/51/22).

Convention listed in annex to the ILC draft statute as well as the new definition proposed by the ILC Special Rapporteur.'[20]

Another view was expressed:

'that drug trafficking should not be included because these crimes were not of the same nature as those listed in other paragraphs of Article 20 and were of such a quantity as to flood the court; the court would not have the necessary resources to conduct lengthy and complex investigations required to prosecute the crimes; the investigation of the crimes often involved highly sensitive information and confidential strategies; and the crimes could be more effectively investigated and prosecuted by national authorities under existing international cooperation arrangements.[21] However, illicit trafficking in narcotic drugs and psychotropic substances finds its place as a treaty-based crime for purposes of the proposed International Criminal Court.'

Prosecuting the Illicit Drug Traffickers

Prosecuting the illicit drug traffickers before the Permanent International Criminal Court—how far will the nation states go along with it? The situation is fluid. However, we are not concerned here, with bringing every heroin addict before the International Criminal Court. What we are concerned with are the large scale drug traffickers operating transnationally. We have Article 20(e) of the Draft Statute providing jurisdiction for the International Criminal Court to prosecute them. The 1988 Convention clearly recognizes this crime as an international crime and considers it as a serious threat. Moreover, it is a treaty-based crime. One could argue that prosecution by an international body is much preferable even if there will be similar problems of extradition and international cooperation. The existing adhoc international criminal tribunals, such as, the International Criminal Tribunal for the former Yugoslavia ('ICTY') and the International Criminal Tribunal for Rwanda ('ICTR'), would encourage the idea of a Permanent International Criminal Court. At the criminal trial a local court in a small state would be at the mercy of the powerful drug lords. Local threats, bribery and influences by the drug traffickers on the judges and justice system in municipal courts would have much stronger effect on the outcome. There may not even be a trial at all. Some of these factors may

[20]Summary of the Proceedings of the Preparatory Committee during the period 25 March - 12 April 1996. A/AC.249/1, 7 May 1996, at para 71.

[21]Id. at para 72.

have a lesser impact before an international tribunal. At an international trial, costs may be enormous but it is a small price to pay for the bigger justice to ensure safety and welfare of many human beings.

As to when the proposed International Criminal Court would come into being is a question yet to be answered. While there are ongoing efforts, the situation is still fluid. However, that will not go against the desirability of an International Criminal Court. Unlike the Nuremberg and Tokyo Tribunals, wherein the victorious powers prevailed on the world community to have those tribunals prosecute the vanquished, we have to await the political will of the 185 States. It is preferable for the nation states to allow the International Criminal Court to prosecute the illicit drug traffickers than for some other State to force its way in and take them to their country to prosecute. Given the existing international cooperation under the Conventions, bringing the illicit drug traffickers before the International Criminal Court would be a step further.

Conclusion

The above analysis shows that illicit traffic in narcotics and psychotropic substances does not have to be dealt with under the domestic jurisdiction alone. It is a matter of international concern. As a treaty-based crime under Article 20(e) of the draft Statue of the International Criminal Court, it gives jurisdiction to the proposed International Criminal Court to prosecute the illicit drug traffickers. This is a step further to secure peace and security to mankind.

PREVENTION AND CONTROL OF DRUG ABUSE AMONG CHILDREN

Hira Singh

The proliferation of drug abuse among children, in recent years, has universally been perceived as an unprecedented threat to the quality of life. With the globalization of and interdependence among national economies and the resultant breakdown of socio-cultural and economic barriers, the problem is increasingly assuming an international character. The trend is most ominous for developing countries which are struggling to overcome their basic problems of poverty, hunger and disease and trying hard to mobilize enough resources for development. Apart from the national interest at stake, the situation raises a more fundamental issue of the right of children to grow and flower as wholesome individuals and the responsibility of society to protect this right. In any case, the induction of children into drug abuse, who are neither fully aware of the implications thereof nor adequately prepared to advocate for themselves, is the most blatant form of child abuse that no civilized society can afford to condone.

Research the world over has amply established that children, because of their physical and mental tenderness, are particularly prone to being swayed into addiction and to their instrumental use in drug trafficking. A nationwide study conducted in 33 cities and areas in India during 1989-90 revealed that the age group of 15-35 is most vulnerable to drug abuse. While deprivation, destitution and neglect are among the major factors that expose children to an unhealthy social environment, their instinctual curiosity and urge for adventure render them easy prey to the racket in illicit drugs. Adverse circumstances within the family make children much more insecure, shaky and fragile than adults to withstand the pressures that precipitate drug abuse. The condition of children living in slums or squatter dwellings or on the street, who are devoid of an equitable sharing of socio-cultural and economic opportunities, is most precarious. A recent study undertaken by UNDCP on the problem of drug abuse among street children has brought to fore a close association of addiction with AIDS, STDs, delinquency and various other forms of social deviance. Case studies from counselling and deaddiction centres, run by various governmental and non-governmental organizations, invariably show how children are first introduced to dependence, turned into hard-core addicts and then manipulated as tools in the pushing and trafficking of prohibitted drugs by highly organized criminal syndicates.

Undeniably, law plays a pivotal role in the prevention and control of drug abuse. However, the legal approach towards children in drug abuse has to be protective, preventive and rehabilitative rather than being merely punitive, for several reasons. Drug abuse among children is an offshoot of the disorganization of society itself and there is no justification for punishing the child for an act which is not of his/her own making. Experience points out that when a child is involved in drug abuse he/she is more of a victim than a perpetrator. Even if he/she is found to have committed an act defined as crime, the child is not yet mature enough to be equated with an adult in terms of his/her culpability. Also, in the interest of society, the legal approach towards children in drug abuse needs to be differentiated. A child who is still in the process of learning and transition certainly offers a better chance for behavioural change, correctional treatment and social mainstreaming. Moreover, a higher priority being accorded to investment on children who are yet to assume a productive role in society would be much more profitable than a focus on adults, from the view point of social development. These aspects have been well recognized by the international community in various instruments, including the International Convention on the Right of the Child, the United Nations Standard Minimum Rules for the Administration of Juvenile Justice, the United Nations Guidelines for the Prevention of Juvenile Delinquency and United Nations Rules for the Protection of Juveniles Deprived of their Liberty.

Juvenile Justice Approach

The problem of drug abuse among children and their involvement in drug laws needs to be tackled in its full range. A comprehensive approach to this end can be conceived only within the framework of juvenile justice. Though there is no standard definition of juvenile justice to be applied uniformly in different social structures, it is deemed to be an integral part of the total effort towards the prevention and control of juvenile social maladjustment. It is generally responsible for most of the decision-making with regard to the care and protection of juveniles vulnerable to abuse and exploitation, as also in matters of adjudication, placement and rehabilitation when juveniles are in conflict with the law. The process is based on a delicate balance between the rights of the child involved in crime and the interest of society from the viewpoint of social defence.

Such a framework of juvenile justice would bring into focus a wide range of contributing factors and conditions before and after the onset of drug abuse among children. The preventive initiative against drug abuse among children may entail a two-pronged strategy to safeguard and promote the well-being and welfare of all children by assuring a healthy, harmonious and supportive environment on one hand, and to identify children with adjustment problems or in irregular situations and to provide correctional measures before they enter into confrontation with the law, on the other. Action after the involvement of children in drug abuse has to based on a fair, just and human handling of broadly three specific categories; those in need of care and protection, those who actually manifest deviant behaviour and are beyond control, and those who fail to respond positively to various protective and remedial measures and pose a threat to themselves and society. Thus, the juvenile justice intervention towards prevention and control of drug abuse among children has to be multi-dimensional.

At the operational level, the three internationally debated models are: (1) the due process model which aims at protecting the substantive and procedural rights of juveniles subject to legal processes; (2) the welfare or *parens patriae* model which tends to provide justice to juveniles primarily in terms of state interventions that promote their social and economic well-being as they come in contact with the legal system; and, (3) the participatory model which emphasizes active participation of the community in curbing disruptive behaviour of juveniles, the re-integration of marginalized juveniles into the social mainstream and the minimization of legal intervention in the lives of juveniles. However, no single model stands on its own and most of the juvenile justice systems seek to harmonize the essential elements of various models, in keeping with their historical, socio-cultural and economic compulsions. Accordingly, in relation to the children involved in the abuse of and trafficking in drugs, each country may have to evolve its own methodology to cater most effectively to the indigenous milieu.

At the same time, in dealing with children in drug abuse through the juvenile justice system, it has to be noted that no formal system by itself can undo the aberrations of the wider socio-economic structure that marginalize children from the social mainstream and push them into a deviant life-style. When a society itself is riddled with disparities and the benefits of development are not being equitably shared by the people at the grassroots level, a chunk of the child population remains in danger of drifting away from the accepted social norms. Even a temporary deprivation during childhood leaves a permanent impact on values, attitudes and behaviour in the life of an individual. As the child has only one chance to manifest his/her innate talents and potentialities, society has a duty to protect him/her against the workings of the adult world. Therefore, the problem of drug abuse among children has to be grappled with not only when it comes to the surface but also by forestalling and counteracting conditions and factors associated with their induction into it. Any indiscriminate recourse to the law in managing a child in drug abuse often becomes counter productive as it not only takes away or curtails freedom but also results in labelling and stigmatization.

Besides the processing of children in conflict with drug laws in a specialized manner through the formal system of juvenile justice, the strategy for the prevention of drug abuse amongst them has to centre around the basic institutions concerned with their care, nature and socialization. In this respect, the specific and complementary roles of the family, the school, the community and religion in sustaining the child are to be strenghtened. While reinforcing the functions of these institutions, adequate provision and accessibility of health, education and welfare for children, especially those in the lower strata, has to be fully ensured. For this purpose, the juvenile justice system must constantly interact with and draw upon the resources of various sectors of socio-economic development. As far as possible, the problems of children prone to drug abuse must be resolved within their immediate environment in a developmental context. Only such children in situations of drug abuse as are really in need of special care or legal support to be shielded from anti-social elements, or are found to have violated laws may be subjected to judicial proceedings. Even when the child passes through the formal system, every effort has to be made to bring him/her back into the open community and to restore his/her freedom. This aspect brings into focus the necessity of construction linkages between the juvenile justice system and non-statutory measures for the welfare of children, between state intervention and informal initiatives within the community, and between governmental and non-governmental organizations concerned with the recovery, re-education and rehabilitation of children in drug abuse.

Legal Issues

Significantly, the Convention on the Rights of the Child, adopted by the United Nations General Assembly on 20 November, 1989, contemplates a holistic approach to the welfare of children vulnerable to abuse and exploitation and to their eventual induction into crime. The Convention makes it obligatory for state parties to take all appropriate measures to protect the child from physical or mental injury or abuse, neglect, maltreatment or exploitation. Besides its general provisions relating to the family, education, employment, living standards, health, recreation, mass media, exploitation and abuse etc. the Convention calls for the establishment of juvenile justice administration which recognizes the right of the child accused of or found to have infringed upon the law to be treated in a manner to promote a sense of dignity, worth and respect for human rights and fundamental freedom. It provides, inter alia, that all children deprived of their liberty are to be treated with humanity and respect and in a manner that takes into account their special age-related needs. It stipulates that the deprivation of liberty of a child can only be employed as a matter of last resort and for the shortest possible period. It obliges state parties to take appropriate measures to promote physical and psychological recovery and social re-integration of the child victim of any form of neglect, exploitation or abuse, or of torture or any form of cruel, inhuman or degrading treatment or punishment.

Further, inviting the application of the United Nations Standard Minimum Rules for the Administration of Juvenile Justice, the Convention requires state parties to prompt the establishment of laws, procedures, authorities and institutions specifically applicable to children accused of or recognized as having infringed the penal law. Moreover, state parties are to establish a minimum age below which children shall be presumed not to have the capacity to infringe the penal law, to offer measures without resort to judicial proceedings, to provide that human rights and legal safeguards are fully respected, and to make available a range of dispositions, such as care, guidance and supervision orders, counselling, probation, foster care, education and vocational training programs and other alternatives to institutional care, so as to ensure that children are dealt with in a manner appropriate to their well-being and proportionate both to the circumstances and the offence.

In India, the Juvenile Justice Act, 1986, represents the blueprint for the enunciated action against drug abuse among children within the overall framework of the rights of the child. The Act envisages not only a specialized approach towards children in confrontation with the law but also provides a protective umbrella for those in situations of vulnerability to drug abuse. It also penalizes adults who are found to use children as an instrument in the abuse of and trafficking in drugs. The definition of *neglected juvenile* as covered by the Act, includes, inter alia, children who have a parent or guardian unfit or incapacitated to exercise control, who are found to associate with any person leading an immoral, drunken or depraved life or who are being or are likely to be abused or exploited for immoral or illegal purposes or unconscionable gain. Such children are to be processed though the Juvenile Welfare Board and taken care of in special institutions like Observation Homes, Juvenile Homes or After-care Homes, if their restoration to the family or placement with a fit-person or fit-institution is not deemed conducive to their mainstreaming. The Act also has salutary provision for the transfer of children addicted to narcotic drugs or psychotropic substances to specialized centres for treatment. More importantly, the Act lays down that whoever gives, or causes the giving to, a juvenile any intoxicating liquor in a public place or any narcotic drug or psychotropic substance, except upon the order of a duly qualified medical practitioner or in case of sickness, shall be punishable by imprisonment for a term which may extend to three years and shall also be liable to a fine.

Similarly, a child committing any drug-related offence would be treated as a delinquent under the Juvenile Justice Act and handled through specialized institutions like Juvenile Court, Observation Home, Special Home, After-care Home, etc. Apart from a liberal scope for release on bail, the Act may allow a delinquent juvenile to go home after releasing him/her on probation while being placed under the care of any parent, guardian or fit-person or fit-institution, or impose a fine if he/she is over 14 years of age and earns money, or make an order for the juvenile to be sent to a Special Home. When the children involved in the abuse of and trafficking in drugs are charged with an offence under the Narcotic Drugs and Psychotropic Substances Act, 1985, as amended in 1988, the penal provisions of this law have to be taken into account in providing for a specialized approach under the Juvenile Justice Act, 1986.

The Narcotic Drugs and Psychotropic Substances Act, 1985, as amended in 1988, prescribes stringent punishments for contravention in relation to poppy straw, coca plant and coca leaves, prepared opium, opium poppy and opium, cannabis, manufactured drugs and preparations and psychotropic substances; for embezzlement of opium by cultivators; for illegal import into India, export from India or trans-shipment of narcotic drugs and psychotropic substances; for allowing premises to be used for the commission of an offence, etc. The punishment in such cases ranges from 10 to 20 years of imprisonment with a fine from Rs. 1 to 2 lakhs which can be exceeded for reasons to be recorded. Such punishment could be enhanced for repeaters by way of 15 years to 30 years with fine from Rs. 1.5 to 3 lakhs which can be exceeded for reasons to be recorded. While the Act allows the application of probation in cases of persons below 18 years, an amendment made in 1988 prohibits any suspension, remission or commutation in any sentence awarded, irrespective of the age of the person involved.

The implications of such an amendment of the Narcotic Drugs and Psychotropic Substances Act, 1985 on the handling of children involved in the abuse and trafficking in drugs through the Juvenile Justice Act, 1986, needs to be carefully examined.

Indeed, the protective, preventive and rehabilitative aspect of the Juvenile Justice Act, 1986 is highly relevant to the safeguarding of children against their induction into and instrumental use in the abuse of and trafficking in drugs. The Act has definite provisions for the utilization of linkages with non-governmental organizations and community-based welfare agencies. The Juvenile Welfare Board is supposed to be constituted largely by non-official public spirited individuals. The Juvenile Court is to be assisted by a panel of two honorary social workers. Any non-governmental institution can be certified or recognized as Observation Home, Juvenile Home, Special Home or after-care organization. Any person or organization, authorized for the purpose, can bring a neglected juvenile before the Juvenile Welfare Board for suitable placement with any person or a voluntary institution for taking charge of a neglected or delinquent juvenile. Each Home established under this Act has to have non-official visitors up to three in number. Each state has to establish an Advisory Board including experts and representatives of voluntary organizations. The state government is required to create a fund for the welfare and rehabilitation of juveniles dealt with under this Act. Thus, the Juvenile Justice Act, 1986, offers ample scope for the mobilization of community resources in the care, treatment and social re-integration of children in drug abuse.

Suggestions

In view of these considerations, it is necessary that concerted steps are taken for the protection of children against and for weaning them away from drug abuse within the provisions of the Juvenile Justice Act, 1986. The Narcotic Drugs and Psychotropic Substances Act, 1985, as amended in 1988, may be reviewed to differentiate children from adults in keeping with the internationally accepted principles of Juvenile Justice. The counselling and deaddiction-cum-rehabilitation centres, run by non-governmental organizations under the scheme for prohibition and drug abuse prevention of the Ministry of Welfare may be selectively certified and recognized under the Juvenile Justice Act, 1986 in the best interest of the children involved in the abuse of and traffic in drugs. In order to ensure that, as far as possible, children affected by drug abuse are dealt with in their natural environment of the family and the community, high priority may be accorded to awareness building among and the orientation of parents, teachers and community leaders. Given the manner in which the problem is found to acquire alarming proportions and, in certain segments of the child population is seen to be closely associated with HIV/AIDS, on-going research and training of functionaries in the relevant disciplines may be undertaken as essential components of program development. Above all, the prevention and control of drug abuse among children may be pushed as an integral part of the planning for social development, both through sectoral and interesectoral interventions.

DRUGS-RELATED CRIME AND CRIMINAL JUSTICE SYSTEM—A GENDER ANALYSIS

Mala Kapur Shankardass

Despite international interest the relationship between women, crime and justice has not been documented in India in a systematic way. To address this problem information was obtained through intensive field work and by analysing arrest statistics and conviction rates. The Narcotic Drugs and Psychotropic substances Act and the Prevention of Illicit Traffic in Narcotic Drugs and Psychotropic Substances Act contain stringent provisions for the detention of persons clandestinely indulging in drug-related criminal activities. However, in many cities and more frequently in semi-urban slum areas, organized drug trade continues unabated.

With respect to the gender perspective, it is clear from available data that increasing numbers of females are economically, socially and/or psychologically compelled to participate in the drug trade, largely as couriers who transport substances by hiding them in their clothing. Crime reports reveal an increase in the number of women arrested who are traffickers, peddlers, street pushers or abusers. But statistics do not present the complete picture because they do not reflect the crimes for which no arrests/convictions are made. There are also some inherent loopholes in the compilation of the statistics which cause and reflect a gender bias. Women are particularly vulnerable to manipulation and exploitation (by the planting of evidence, for instance) because of their well recognized structural dependency in society and because their social roles provide excellent cover for the crimes they commit. Special procedures for arrest, search and seizure laid down in the NDPS Act are not always followed because law enforcement officers have discretionary powers either to arrest or not to arrest, under the same Act. These discretionary powers facilitate the trapping of innocent women who are often jailed for several years for offences they did not commit. Many women who are thus exploited turn into `hardened criminals' due to the stigmatization that follows such arrests. Experienced `victims' manipulate procedures for search. seizure and arrest to ensure that they are acquitted.

Thus, the NDPS Act appears inadequate on both counts--harsh and disproportionate on real victims and lenient on seasoned offenders.

In theory, legal rules are believed to be uniform in application and unproblematic. In practice however, gender and socio-economic biases and inequalities in the justice system loom large. It is very important, for this reason, to consider the gender variable in any exercise of reviewing or formulating global and national drug laws. Specifically in India it is necessary to stop illegal arrests, unlawful searches and illicit means of gathering evidence by delineating statutory guidelines regarding the procedure to be followed by concerned officials during the investigation of such criminal offences. It needs to be ensured that undue complexity and impracticality of procedures do not lead to non-compliance with procedures.

ADOLESCENTS AT RISK: LOW SOCIOECONOMIC STATUS AND EARLY ONSET DRUG USE IN THE U.S.

Geoffrey M Curran and *Helene R White*

Evidence of troubling trends in adolescent illicit drug use has been surfacing in the major household and school surveys of substance use in the United States. For example, the Monitoring the Future (MTF) study[1] of junior and senior high school students has documented increases in lifetime, annual, and thirty-day prevalence of illicit drug use every year since 1992 for each of the three school years studied (eighth- tenth- and twelfth-graders). Similarly, the PRIDE study[2] of grades 9-12 has shown yearly increases in illicit drug use since 1992. Perhaps the most troubling finding is that drug use among eighth-graders (ages 13 and 14) has risen the most sharply. For example, annual prevalence of marijuana use among eighth-graders doubled from 1991 to 1994. These figures indicate that claims of victory in the 'war on drugs' have been premature and that increased effort is needed in the areas of prevention, especially for the youngest adolescents.

In this paper we focus on the relationship between low socioeconomic status (SES) and the early onset of substance use among adolescents. Each has separately been identified as a risk factor[3], but little work has studied their relationship. One previous school-based study[4] found lower SES ado-

[1]Johnston, L.D., O'Malley, P.M., and Bachman, J.G. *National Survey Results on Drug Use*: *The Monitoring the Future Study*, 1975-1994, Rockville, MD: National Institute on Drug Abuse (1995).

[2]Hall, D. *Student Use of Most Drugs Reaches Highest Level in Nine Years* (Press Release), Atlanta, GA:PRIDE (1996).

[3]Hawkins, J., Catalano, R., and Miller, J. Risk and protective factors for alcohol and other drug problems in adolescence and early adulthood: Implications for substance abuse prevention, *Psych Bull*, 112, 64-105 (1992); Labouvie, E., Bates, M.E., and Pandina, R.A. Age of first use: Its reliability and predictive utility, *J Stud Alcohol*, in press.

[4]Johnston et al., *supra* note 1.

lescents at higher risk of early onset, and we investigate this relationship in a population based sample from one state in the United States. We begin with a review of the literature pertaining to SES and adolescent rates of psychopathology and substance use.

SES and Adolescent Mental Health and Substance Use

Research focussing on SES and substance use has grown out of the larger literature on class differences in adolescent psychopathology in general. In this body of research, numerous studies have demonstrated that poor children experience more psychological illness and antisocial behaviour than nonpoor children.[5] Importantly for the issue of causation, McLeod and Shanahan's[6] longitudinal study showed that children who lived in poverty at baseline were more likely to report depressive symptoms and antisocial behaviours in later years of childhood. These authors also showed that for antisocial behavior, children in persistent poverty, as opposed to episodic poverty, showed higher rates of disorder.

The research investigating SES/substance use relationships has also consistently found poverty and lower levels of parental/family SES to be related to higher levels of drug and alcohol abuse. In terms of alcohol use, Zucker and Hartford[7], Conger et al[8] and Smart et al[9], have each noted increased drinking and drinking problems in adolescents with low family/ parental SES. A smaller body of research has investigated the influence of neighborhood and/or census-tract-level characteristics on alcohol abuse. For

[5]McLeod, J.D., and Shanahan, M.J. Poverty, parenting, and children's mental health, *Am Sociol Rev*, 58, 351-366 (1993); Aneshensel, C.S. and Sucoff, C.A. The neighborhood context of adolescent mental health, *J Health Soc Behav*, 37, 293-310 (1996); Gore, S., Aseltine, R.H., and Colton, M.E. Social structure, life stress and depressive symptoms in a high-school-aged population, *J Health Soc Behav*, 33, 97-113 (1993); Harnish, J., Dodge, K., and Valente, E. Mother-child interaction quality as a partial mediator of the roles of maternal depressive symptomatology and socioeconomic status in the development of child behavior problems, *Child Dev* 66, 739-753 (1995).

[6]McLeod, J.D., and Shanahan, M.J. Poverty, parenting, and children's mental health, *Am Sociol Rev*, 58, 351-366 (1993).

[7]Zucker, R.A., and Hartford, T.C. National study of the demography of adolescent drinking practices in 1980, *J Stud Alcohol*, 44, 974-985 (1983).

[8]Conger, R.D., Lorenz, F.O., Elder, G.H., Melby, J.N., Simons, R.L., and Conger, K.J. A process model of family economic pressure and early adolescent alcohol use. *J Early Adol*, 11, 430-449 (1991).

[9]Smart, R.G., Adlaf, E.M., and Walsh, G.W. Neighbourhood socio-economic factors in relation to student drug use and programs. *J. Child Adol Sub Abuse*, 3, 37-46 (1994).

example, Pallas[10] found higher rates of family alcoholism within the lowest SES census tracks (of a large mid-western state), which usually were centrally located in the largest city in the region. Smart et al[11] also found large numbers of problem alcohol using adolescents in low SES areas with high rates of single parenthood and lower rates of income in Ontario, Canada.

Mirroring the alcohol use research, several studies have found lower SES adolescents to be heavier and more frequent users of drugs, including cigarettes, than their higher SES peers.[12] Further, research with an international perspective has identified SES and youth as risk factors associated with opiate, stimulant, cocaine, and inhalant use in Europe, Scandinavia, and Mexico.[13]

While the inverse relationship between SES and substance abuse is often found, little research has demonstrated a clear direction of causation. Two competing hypotheses have been offered to explain the relationship. The first, *social selection* or *drift* hypothesis, contends that substance abuse leads to downward social mobility. The work of Mullahy and Sindelar[14] demonstrating that job status and income are adversely affected by alcoholism supports this contention. The second hypothesis, *social causation*, contends that the lower SES existence, characterized by stress associated

[10]Pallas, D. The ecological distribution of alcoholic families; A community study in mid-Michigan. Unpublished Master's Thesis, University of Wisconsin, Oshkosh, WI: (1992).

[11]Smart et al., *supra* note 9.

[12]Johnston, L.D., O'Malley, P.M. and Bachman, J.G. *National Survey Results on Drug Use: The Monitoring the Future Study*, 1975-1994, Rockville, MD: National Institute on Drug Abuse (1995); Smart, R.G., Adlaf, E.M., and Walsh, G.W. Neighbourhood socio-economic factors in relation to student drug use and programs, *J Child Adol Sub Abuse*, 3, 37-46 (1994); Wills, T.A., McNamara, G, and Vaccaro, D. Parental education related to adolescent stress-coping and substance use: Development of a mediational model, *Health Psych*, 14, 464-478 (1995); Murray, D.M., Perry, C.L., O'Connell, C., and Schmid, L. Seventh-grade cigarette, alcohol, and marijuana use: Distribution in a north central U.S. metropolitan population, *Int J Addict*, 22, 357-376 (1987).

[13]Babor, T.F. Overview: Demography, epidemiology and psychopharmacology—making sense of the connections, *Addiction*, 89, 1391-1396 (1994); Pickering, H., and Stimson, G.V. Prevalence and demographic factors of stimulant use, *Addiction,* 89, 1385-1389 (1994); Hartnoll, R.L. Opiates: Prevalence and demographic factors, *Addiction*, 89, 1377-1383 (1994); Tapia-Conyer, R., Cravioto, P., De La Rosa, B., and Velez, C. Risk factors for inhalant abuse in juvenile offenders: The case of Mexico, *Addiction*, 90, 43-49 (1995).

[14]Mullahy, J., and Sindelar, J.L. Alcoholism, work, and income over the life cycle, Unpublished manuscript (1991).

with poverty and reduced opportunity, lack of social support, and increased exposure to drugs and alcohol, creates the higher levels of substance problems found among lower SES persons. At present, a greater number of studies report findings consistent with or supporting this latter perspective. For example, the research finding parental SES as predictive of substance use among adolescents[15] is consistent with this hypothesis (as childhood SES status exists and is *operating* before introduction to substance use). Relatedly, the research showing that lower status persons experience more frequent exposure to stressful life events (and may be more vulnerable to them) is also consistent with this perspective.[16] The most recent work investigating mediated relationships between SES and substance abuse also supports the social causation argument in that the inverse relationship has been found to be partially explained by SES differences in parental support, parental hostility, negative life events, marital discord, academic confidence, and friends' use patterns.[17] It is likely, however, that the relationships between SES and substance abuse are not strictly due to *cause* or *drift*, but a combination of the two over the life course and across generations.

SES and the Early Onset of Substance Use

One area of research which has received little attention in the literature is the relationship between SES and early onset of substance use/abuse. Both SES and early onset (as measured by 'age of first use') have been identified separately as risk factors for late adolescence and adult problem use

[15]Johnston, L.D., O'Malley, P.M. and Bachman, J.G. *National Survey Results on Drug Use: The Monitoring the Future Study*, 1975-1994, Rockville, MD: National Institute on Drug Abuse (1995); Smart, R.G., Adlaf, E.M., and Walsh, G.W. Neighbourhood socio-economic factors in relation to student drug use and programs, *J Child Adol Sub Abuse*, 3, 37-46 (1994).

[16]Gore, S., Aseltine, R.H., and Colton, M.E. Social Structure, life stress and depressive symptoms in a high-school-aged population, *J Health Soc Behav*, 33, 97-113 (1993); Liem, R., and Liem J. Social class and mental illness reconsidered: The role of economic stress and social support, *J Health Soc Behav*, 19, 136-156 (1978); McLeod, J.D., and Kessler, R.D. Socioeconomic status deferences in vulnerability to undesirable life events, *J Health Soc Behav*, 31, 162-172 (1990).

[17]Conger et al., *supra* note 8; Wills, T.A., McNamara, G, and Vaccaro, D. Parental education related to adolescent stress-coping and substance use: Development of a mediational model, *Health Psych*, 14, 464-478 (1995).

behaviors[18], but only one major study to our knowledge[19] has reported data on their relationship. The Monitoring the Future (MTF) study has consistently found a strong inverse (and largely linear) relationship between parental SES and (1) annual prevalence of marijuana, hallucinogen, LSD, cocaine, heroin, and tranquilizer use; (2) thirty-day prevalence of cigarette, smokeless tobacco, and alcohol use in general and drunkenness in particular; and (3) two-week prevalence of five or more drinks in a row for eighth-graders (note that onset is defined here as use/prevalence at a certain grade level). The strength of the relationship is reduced for tenth-graders, and is completely gone or reversed for twelfth-graders.

These findings indicate that low SES predicts early onset of illicit drug use and heavy drinking. Johnston et al.[20] did not speculate as to the causal pathways leading to the findings for the eighth-graders, but they reasoned that the tenth- and twelfth-grade findings could be explained by the higher status adolescents catching up with their more *precocious peers* from the lower SES, and/or that the early onset users dropped out of school at higher rates. Past research has indicated that early onset adolescent drug users and students of lower SES are more likely to drop out, be involved in crime, and experience higher rates of prolonged use.[21] As well, Moffitt[22] has shown that early onset juvenile delinquents are the most likely to persist in deviant behaviour into adulthood, while later onset delinquents tend to mature out faster. It is possible then that low SES is predictive of the early onset of drug use and problem drinking, which in turn may place these adolescents at higher risk for chronic substance and legal problems. Given the policy and prevention implications of being able to identify such an early risk group, we sought to investigate the relationship between SES and early onset substance use and to replicate the findings of Johnston et al.[23]

[18]Hawkins, J., Catalano, R., and Miller, J. Risk and protective factors for alcohol and other drug problems in adolescence and early adulthood: implications for substance abuse prevention, *Psych Bull*, 112, 64-105 (1992); Labouvie, E., Bates, M.E., and Pandina, R.A. Age of First Use: Its Reliability and Predictive Utility, *J Stud Alcohol*, in press (1996); Chou, S.P., and Pickering, R.P. Early onset of drinking as a risk factor for lifetime alcohol-related problems, *Br J Addict*, 87, 119-1204 (1992).

[19]Johnston et al., *supra* note 1.

[20]Johnston et al., *supra* note 1.

[21]Eggert, L., Seyl, C., and Nicholas, L. Effects of a school-based prevention program for potential high school dropouts and drug abusers, *Int J Addict*, 25, 773-801 (1990); Bentler, P. Etiologies and consequences of adolescent drug use: implications for prevention, *J Addict Diseases*, 11, 47-61. (1992).

[22]Moffitt, T.E. Adolescence-limited and life-course persistent antisocial behavior: A developmental taxonomy, *Psych Rev*, 100, 674-701 (1993).

[23]Johnston et al., *supra* note 1.

Method

The data to be used in this study were gathered for the Rutgers Health and Human Development Project (RHHDP), a prospective longitudinal study begun in 1979. The study began with a sample of 1380 New Jersey adolescents located through a random telephone survey, and has followed them into young adulthood. To date, three retests have been completed, with the subjects returning every three years for the first two retests, and after seven years for the third. The thirteen year follow-up rate was 91 per cent (N=1257). We used data largely from the two older age cohorts of Wave 1 (when the subjects were 15 and 18 years of age, N=933) to mirror the ages in the Monitoring the Future Study (eighth- and twelfth-graders), but some longitudinal analyses were performed using data from all four test times as well. As is discussed below, we also investigated use pattern among the youngest cohort at Wave 1 (twelve year olds) but the results are not included here because of the negligible substance use of this age group.

The original sample was largely white ((89 per cent), slightly higher than New Jersey's proportion (83 per cent), as measured by the 1981 U.S. Census, and closely mirrored the state's religious and economic make-up. The educational attainment of the subjects' parents was unusually high for a population-based sample, and the implications of this are discussed below.

Measures

The data used in this study were derived through self-reports. Self-report data is very popular in the social sciences, particularly in the study of deviant behaviour.[24] The potential validity problems due to deliberate falsification of information, error in recall, and measurement effects appear to be minimal with the use of professional interviewers, short recall times, and assurances of confidentiality.[25] The two major areas of self-report data used in this study are the measures of SES (parental education—reported by parents) and alcohol and drug use (reported by subjects).

[24]Kandel, D.B. Convergencies in prospective longitudinal surveys of drug use: Use in normal populations, in D.B. Kandel (Ed.) *Longitudinal Research on Drug Use : Empirical Findings and Methodological Issues*, 3-38, Hemisphere Press (1978); Elliott, D.S., Huizinga, D., and Menard, S. *Multiple Problem Youth: Delinquency, Substance Use, and Mental Health Problems*, New York: Springer-Verlag (1989).

[25]Elliott, D.S., Huizinga, D., and Menard, S. *Multiple Problem Youth: Delinquency, Substance Use, and Mental Health Problems*, New York: Springer-Verlag (1989)

SES: We used a parental education measure to best replicate the MTF's operationalization of SES (average of parental educational level). This measure is commonly used to assess a family's socioeconomic status.[26] To maximize the cases included in the analyses we used a 'maximum level' measure of educational attainment whereby the highest year of education reached by either the mother or the father was used as the proxy for SES. A four category operationalization was used: Group 1 = 'high school graduate or below', Group 2 = 'post high school and some college', Group 3 = 'college graduate', and Group 4 = 'post college'. These categories resemble the MTF operationalization, however we collapsed the high school graduates and below into one category (whereas MTF did not) because there were very few parents in the non-high school graduate range. The RHHDP sample exhibits unusually high educational attainment among parents (for example, 22 per cent of the male parents had post college education, 44 per cent were college graduates, and 65 per cent had post high school educational attainment), and the potential consequences of this are discussed later in the chapter.

Substance Use: The subjects were asked to report separately the frequency of use of numerous substances (marijuana, cocaine, heroin, PCP, inhalants, psychedelics, stimulants, sedatives, and non-medical analgesics) within the past year. A ten item scale was used with possible responses from 'I didn't use' to 'more than once a day'. Dichotomous (yes/no) past year, monthly, and weekly use variables were created by collapsing the responses to these questions by the time frame in question. We created an *any illicit drug use* measure by combining the responses from the individual drug questions (not including alcohol). We also used a measure of *number of times drunk* in the past year to create a *frequent drunkenness* measure (twenty or more times in the last year = yes) to replicate the MTF analyses relative to adolescent drunkenness (five or more drinks in one occasion in last two weeks). As found in the MTF study, *onset* was defined here as use/prevalence at a certain age point.

[26]Wills, T.A., McNamara, G, and Vaccaro, D. Parental education related to adolescent stress-coping and substance use: Development of a mediational model, *Health Psych,* 14, 464-478 (1995); Barr, K.M., Farrell, M.P., Barnes, G.M., and Welte, J.W. Race, class,and gender differences in substance abuse: Evidence of middle-class/underclass polarization among black males, *Soc Problem*, 40, 314-327 (1993); Herd, D. Predicting drinking problems among black and white men: Results from a national survey, *J Stud Alcohol*, 55, 61-71 (1994).

Analyses

In the main set of analyses, the composite drug use measure was used, along with the individual substance measures for marijuana, cocaine, and heavy alcohol use, in chi-square tests of group differences in age of onset by SES. The other drug use measures were not used because so few adolescents had begun using them by age fifteen (in fact, the same can be said for cocaine use in the sample, and this virtually guaranteed non-significant findings). Very little drug use was reported by the twelve-year-olds, and they were not used in the analyses (N for fifteen- and eighteen-year olds = 933). Further, the RHHDP fifteen-year-olds better matched up with the MTF eight-graders in age than the twelve-year-olds. The RHHDP eighteen-year-olds closely matched the MTF twelfth-graders in age. In a smaller set of preliminary analyses, logistic regression was used to test the ability of adolescent SES to predict adult frequent drug use patterns (in a model controlling for prior use, age, and gender).

Table 1
Percent Any Illicit Use, Fifteen-year-olds, N=418

Parental Education	*Weekly*	*Monthly*	*Past Year*
1	2.6*	5.0*	11.0
2	4.3	7.7	12.7
3	1.7	3.2	6.5
4	.5	2.9	9.1

Note: For parental education, 1 = 'high school graduate or below', 2 = 'post high school or some college', 3 = 'college graduate', 4 = 'post college',* $p < 0.05$ (for column)

Results

Table 1 presents the findings from the chi-square analyses of fifteen-year-olds concerning any illicit drug use. In terms of any illicit drug use, lower SES is significantly associated with weekly and monthly prevalence. For reported weekly use, 2.6 per cent and 4.3 per cent of the fifteen-year-olds in the lower two SES groups were users, while 1.7 per cent and 0.5 per cent of their higher SES peers (groups 3 and 4 respectively) reported weekly use. For monthly use, 5.0 per cent and 7.7 per cent of the respective lower SES fifteen-year-olds were users, while 3.2 per cent and 2.9 per cent of the higher SES fifteen-year-olds used. These group differences were significant at the $p < .05$ level. In a difference from the MTF study (for which only past-year prevalence rates of most illicit drugs were reported in their SES analyses), SES was not predictive of use within the past year in our sample. Further, while the MTF study found essentially linear relationships between SES and onset, we found the second group (subjects whose parents had completed high school but not college) to be at higher risk than the lowest SES group (group 1). In general the relationship is inverse, but with a sawtooth-like pattern emerging around the high school to college graduate range (as was found by Helzer et al.[27] in their analyses of prevalence rates of alcoholism and educational attainment).

Table 2 presents the findings of similar analyses with the eighteen-year-old subjects. The differences in the percentages are largely reduced, and more importantly, none of the differences is statistically significant. These findings mirror the data from MTF and suggest further that low SES is a risk factor for early onset of drug use, but not use in late adolescence (eighteen years of age). The findings relative to weekly and monthly use of illicit substances are an extension of the MTF study which did not investigate weekly (or heavier) use patterns, and suggest that low SES is a risk factor for early onset of heavier use patterns.

The findings from the marijuana use analyses were very similar to those from the previous analyses of 'any illicit use'. For weekly marijuana use, 2.6 per cent and 3.8 per cent of the fifteen-year-olds in the lower two SES groups were users, as opposed to 1.4 per cent and .5 per cent of the higher SES fifteen-year-olds (significant at $p < .05$; note that these rates are almost identical to the 'any illicit substance' weekly use rates—this is because virtually all of the weekly use of illicit drugs among fifteen-year-olds in this sample involved marijuana). For monthly use, 4.8 per cent and 7.2 per cent of the two lower SES groups used marijuana, while 3.1 per cent and 2.9 per cent of the two higher SES groups were users ($p=.07$). As was seen in the earlier drug analyses, the sawtooth-like pattern of risk was found. And also like above, there were no significant SES difference in use rates for eighteen-year-olds. These findings suggest that lower SES adolescents are at higher risk for early onset frequent marijuana use. The MTF study only looked at past year prevalence of marijuana use for eighth-graders, and their results were not replicated here. There were no significant differences across SES groups in past year prevalence of marijuana use for both age groups.

[27]Helzer, J.E., Burnam, A., and McEvoy, L.T., Alcohol abuse and dependence, in L.N. Robins and D.A. Regier (Eds.) *Psychiatric Disorders in America*, 81-113, New York: The Free Press (1991).

Table 2
Percent Any Illicit Use, Eighteen-year-olds, N=337

Parental Education	*Weekly*	*Monthly*	*Past Year*
1	5.0	9.5	15.4
2	7.7	13.1	19.9
3	5.6	8.0	12.5
4	6.5	9.8	17.2

Note : For parental education, 1 = 'high school graduate or below', 2 = 'post high school or some college', 3 = 'college graduate', 4 = 'post college'. None of the group differences was significant.

The drunkenness and cocaine analyses did not produce significant SES differences in onset rates among young adolescents (data not shown). It is likely that the make-up of the RHHDP sample contributed to the non-replication of some of the MTF findings in these areas. In large part, the suburban, middle class nature of the sample and the high parental educational attainment precluded the inclusion of significant numbers of heavy drug users among fifteen-year-olds. Hence, these null findings can be explained by the fact that a number of the cell sizes were too small to generate statistically significant differences. For example, only one fifteen year-old subject used cocaine weekly at Wave 1. In contrast, the MTF study's large sample contained many more students of lower SES backgrounds and larger numbers of heavy drug users. The RHHDP sample did contain larger numbers of younger 'binge' drinkers (here measured as the report of more than twenty episodes of drunkenness in the past year) and in our analyses SES was not related to early onset. For the eighteen-year-olds, however, we did find the second lower SES group (parents who had completed high school but not college) to have slightly elevated rates of drunkenness—10.7 per cent reporting twenty or more episodes of drunkenness in the last year, as opposed to an average of 7.5 per cent in the other three SES groups. In the MTF study the highest SES students reported more frequent binge drinking. Our findings here may be reflecting the fact that our study was based on a population sample, and therefore did not experience the 'dropout phenomenon' discussed earlier regarding the MTF school-based data. If this is the case, our data may be showing that SES can affect the rates of heavy drinking in older adolescents as well. Future research with non-school-based, nationwide, and representative samples is necessary to better inform our knowledge about drinking among older adolescents.

In the logistic regression analyses, we chose the 'any illicit use' category to maximize the number of heavy users, and tested parental SES as a predictor (in a model with prior use, age, and gender controlled) of weekly, monthly and past year use in each of the retests (results not shown). In the weekly analysis, the SES measure was a significant (inverse) predictor of the Time 2, Time 3, and Time 4 use categories (i.e. predictive of weekly use 3, 6 and 13 years later). For monthly and past year use, SES was not significantly predictive in any analyses. While preliminary in nature, these findings indicate that SES is a more likely longitutinal predictor of heavier use patterns. The models with significant SES predictors explain small amounts of variance (5-12 per cent), and did not include other known longitudinal predictors of drug use (e.g. personality traits such as disinhibition and experience seeking), so these results only indicate the possibility of longitudinal SES predictability. Future analyses with more complete models is warranted.

Discussion

The above analyses suggest that lower SES adolescents are at increased risk for the early onset of both moderate and heavy patterns of illicit drug use. These findings are consistent with patterns identified in the Monitoring the Future study[28], however, they are not a true replication. The MTF study found an inverse relationship between SES and past year prevalence of several categories of illicit drug use, whereas we found lower SES relating to the early onset of monthly and weekly use patterns only. It is possible that our sample's middle class over-representation precluded the finding of a more general SES/use relationship and that the influence of SES would be seen more in the heavier use categories (as compared to a more representative sample such as in the MTF study). This possibility, however, remains speculative, and taken together, the present study and MTF indicate that SES is a likely predictor of the age of onset of both heavier and more experimental use patterns. More specific analysis of the MTF data (using 'weekly' and 'monthly' use variables, for example) would help to greater flesh out this relationship. Our logistic regression analyses, while preliminary in nature, indicate that low SES in adolescence may be predicitive of heavy adult patterns of illicit drug use, and that longitudinal relationships should be explored in greater detail and specificity.

In general, our data and the MTF study, coupled with the general SES/adolescent etiological research, support the notion that lower SES adolescents should be considered at special risk for substance abuse. Data from

[28]Johnston et al., *supra* note 1.

the criminal justice system support this notion as well. The Drug Use Forecasting (DUF) network[29] reported data from male adult arrestees in San Diego, which showed that the median age of onset of marijuana use was twelve, and fourteen for cocaine, inhalants, PCP, Valium, LSD, and crystal methadrine. Further, data from the full twenty-city DUF study showed that over 50 per cent of male and female arrestees did not complete high school. These data indicate that the U.S. criminal justice system is largely occupied with persons of lower socio-economic standing who began drug use at an early age. Moffitt[30] and Kandel[31] report that early onset of drug use and other deviant behavior is predictive of persistent drug use and deviance, and taken in total, the data described here clearly place low SES adolescents at special risk for drug and criminal problems which span into adulthood.

Given this situation, public policy responses are needed with regard to prevention and treatment programs aimed at the special needs of low SES, high-risk adolescents. In terms of prevention, recent reviews[32] suggest that most of the drug prevention programs in the United States do not target high-risk groups, but rather focus on the general adolescent population. The most widely used prevention programs are school-based[33], and while evaluation of the most popular program, DARE (involving uniformed police as instructors in classrooms), have been mixed [34], outcome studies from a few new programs indicate progress is being made in preventing and/or delaying onset of drug use in the general school population. For example, evaluation of Project ALERT [35] and a program implemented by Botvin et

[29]Wish, E. Drug testing and criminal justice practices as regulators: What works, ethical issues, and which social burdens are affected. Paper presented to Interdisciplinary Proseminar on Substance Abuse, University of Michigan, January, (1997).

[30]Moffitt, *supra* note 22.

[31]Kandel, D.B. Epidemiological and psychosocial perspectives on adolescent drug use, *J Am Acad Psych*, 21, 328-347 (1982).

[32]Hawkins, et. al. *supra* note 3; Tobler, N. Drug prevention programs can work: research findings, *J. Addict Diseases*, 11, 1-28 (1992).

[33]Donaldson, S., Graham, J., and Hansen, W. Testing the generalizability of intervening mechanism theories: understanding the effects of adolescent drug use prevention interventions, *J Behav Med*, 17, 195-216 (1994).

[34]Rosenbaum, D.P., Flewelling, R.L., Bailey, S.L., Ringwalt, C.L. and Wilkinson, D.L. Cops in the classroom: A longitudinal evaluation of drug abuse resistance education (DARE), *J Res Crime Delinquency*, 31, 3-31 (1994); Ennett, S.T., Tobler, N.S., Ringwalt, C.L., and Flewelling, R.L. How effective is drug abuse resistance education? A meta-analysis of Project DARE outcome evaluations, *Am J Pub Health,* 84, 1394-1401 (1994).

[35]Ellickson, P., and Bell, R. Drug prevention in junior high: a multi-site longitudinal test, *Science,* 247, 4948, 1299-305(1990).

al.[36] have revealed that prevention efforts involving peer-pressure resistance training, normative education (i.e. anti-drug use socialization), 'life skills training' (i.e. assertiveness, stress management), and 'booster' sessions in later grades have the potential to produce reductions in drug use which last into young adulthood.

Clearly, however, low SES, high-risk adolescents need greater attention than the general population. These youths often come from single-parent homes in high-drug-availability neighbourhoods, and they are more prone to drop out of school. The issues of increased stress, low self-esteem, social isolation, and poor bonding with family, school, and community that are associated with poverty and living in low SES environments [37] present significant obstacles to drug prevention efforts, and most programs are not equipped to deal with them. One model program, Project SAFT[38], is attempting to address the needs of high-risk, African-American adolescents by employing broad interventions among fourth— sixth graders. The program combines individual skills training for the adolescent (impulse control, resistance training, school tutoring) with family/parenting education (household organization, child management) and a community activities component (sports, music) after school and in the summers. Longitudinal evaluation will tell if these measures prove effective in curbing substance use, but it appears that this type of 'early risk factor' programming is a step in the right direction. Hawkins et al.[39] also recommend the early risk factor approach to prevention among high risk groups and stress the importance of family involvement and a focus on early academic achievement. Other research indicates that community-based programs housed in youth organizations (e.g. Boys and Girls Clubs) may be effective alternatives/supplements to the more traditional school-based programs.[40]

[36]Botvin, G., Baker, E., Dusenbury, L., Botvin, E., and Diaz, T. Long term follow up results of a randomized drug abuse prevention trial in a white middle-class population, *JAMA*, 273, 1106-12 (19995).

[37]Wilson, W.J. *The Truly Disadvantaged*, Chicago: University of Chicago Press (1987); Van Hasselt, V.B., Herson, M., Null, J.A., Ammerman, R.T., Bukstien, O.G., McGillivray, J., and Hunter, A. Drug abuse prevention for high-risk African-American children and their families: A review and model program, *Addict Behav*, 18, 213-234 (1993).

[38]Van Hasselt, V.B., Herson, M., Null, J.A., Ammerman, R.T., Bukstien, O.G., McGillivray, J., and Hunter, A. Drug abuse prevention for high-risk African-American children and their families: A review and model program, *Addict Behav*, 18, 213-234 (1993).

[39]Hawkins et. al., *supra* note 3.

[40]Kaltreider, D., and St., P.T. Beyond the schools: Strategies for implementing successful drug prevention programs in community youth-serving organizations, *J Drug Ed,* 25, 223-237 (1995).

Along with prevention efforts, drug treatment must be available to adolescents who have progressed into substance abuse and other deviant behaviors. The juvenile criminal justice system needs to be most responsive in this area because a large proportion of juveniles who come in contact with the criminal justice system are drug users. Recent DUF data found that 43 per cent of the juvenile male arrestees/detainees tested positive for illicit drug use at time of arrest.[41] Unfortunately, a number of researchers have found treatment options to be lacking.[42] Ewing[43] maintains that: 'Juvenile offenders are likely to be drug and alcohol users. Second, they are likely to receive little or no evaluation, assessment, or diagnosis. Third, these youth are likely to have had no appropriate interventions or to have failed in a number of interventions that were not culturally, socially, psychologically, educationally, economically, or developmentally appropriate' (p 155). This grim picture is darkened by the challenges associated with rehabilitating low SES adolescents who, as described above, often live in high-crime and high-drug-availability neighborhoods, and face social and economic barriers to educational and occupational opportunity. As well, it has been shown that earlier onset drug users are less likely to complete treatment.[44]

A review of adolescent drug treatment programs of Catalano et al.[45] indicated that some treatment is better than no treatment, but no single treatment modality has shown itself to be superior. They did note, however, that adolescents with more severe drug histories (early onset) seem to benefit from

[41]Wish, *supra* note 29.

[42]Farrow, J.A. Service delivery strategies for treating high-risk youth: Delinquents, homeless, runaways, and sexual minorities, in E. Rahdert and D. Czechowicz (Eds.) *Adolescent Drug Abuse: Clinical Assessment and Therapeutic Interventions*, Rockville, MD: NIDA Research Monograph 156, National Institutes of Health (1995); Ewing, J. Substance abuse programs, in L.S. Thompson and J.A. Farrow (Eds.) *Hard Time, Healing Hands: Developing Primary Health Care Services for Incarcerated Youth*, Arlington,VA: National Centre for Education in Maternal and Child Health (1993).

[43]Ewing, J. Substance abuse programs, in L.S. Thompson and J.A. Farrow (Eds.), *Hard Time, Healing Hands: Developing Primary Health Care Services for Incarcerated Youth*, Arlington, VA: National Centre for Education in Maternal and Child Health (1993).

[44]Feigelman, W. Daycare treatment for multiple drug abusing drug adolescents: Social factor linked with completing treatment, *J Psych Drugs*, 19, 335-344 (1987).

[45]Catalano, R., Hawkins, J., Wells, E., Miller, J., and Brewer, D. Evaluation of the effectiveness of adolescent drug abuse treatment, assessment of risks for relapse and promising approaches for relapse prevention, *Int J Addict*, 25, 1085-140 (1990-91).

longer and more intense treatment (i.e. residential), and that criminal offender/addicts benefit from offence-specific treatment (e.g. violent offenders receiving drug and impulse control treatment). Evidence from adult population offenders indicates that therapeutic community-model and other intense treatment programs may be effective in reducing recidivism.[46] Other research indicates that some adolescents (especially inner-city youths) respond to treatment and rehabilitation which includes recreational learning activities, such as the 'Outward Bound' program which takes adolescents on rigorous hiking excursions.[47] Especially important is the evidence indicating that, for adolescents, treatment outcome is positively related to voluntary treatment entry, or the perception thereof.[48] Hence, merely mandating treatment does not guarantee successful completion.

Conclusion

Several limitations of the present study should be noted. First, the measures were gathered from self-reports, a practice with some well-known reliability and validity problems. Second, the RHHDP sample is mostly white, and the results are not generalizable to non-Caucasians. As well, the sample is mostly from suburban, middle-class backgrounds, which precluded a test of the relationship between low SES and early onset using a sample more representative of SES differences. Further, the sample was gathered from one U.S. state only (New Jersey), and does not reflect national, or for that matter international, differences. In general, this paper has dealt almost solely with research from the United States, and thus its reach is limited to more industrialized nations. Our purpose was not to review international drug treatment and prevention efforts for adolescents; rather, we sought to identify a group of adolescents in our country who are at increased risk of early onset drug use and subsequent problems with drugs and criminal activity, and to urge others to investigate the relationship between socioeconomic status and adolescent drug use. We hope our evidence is compelling enough to stimulate such work.

In light of the study's findings, we offer the following recommendations: (1) lower SES adolescents should be targets of increased drug pre-

[46]Field, G. The effects of intensive treatment on reducing the criminal recidivism of addicted offenders. *Fed Prob*, 53, 51-56 (1989); Wexler, H.K., Falkin, G.P., and Lipton, D.S. Outcome evaluation of a prison therapeutic community for substance abuse treatment, *Crim J. Behav*, 17, 71-92 (1990).

[47]Garrett, C.J. Effects of residential treatment on adjudicated delinquents: A meta analysis, *J Res Crime Delinquency*, 22, 287-308 (1985).

[48]Catalano et al., *supra* note 45.

vention efforts in their schools and neighborhoods; (2) once involved in the juvenile justice system, these youths need age-appropriate drug treatment; (3) drug treatment/criminal justice probationary action should be directed at creating positive, supervized activities for offenders, especially after school and on weekends because these youths are in special need of prosocial activities and the development of prosocial peer groups; and (4) the juvenile justice system also needs to focus on identifying and addressing the educational and occupational deficits faced by these children, because adolescents who see no future for themselves in the 'legitimate world' will be less responsive to drug treatment and rehabilitation.

PART V

NEW DELHI CHARTER ON GLOBAL DRUGS LAW

NEW DELHI CHARTER ON GLOBAL DRUGS LAW

PART I

Background

The Indian Law Institute (ILI)—an international centre for advanced socio-legal research in co-sponsorship with the United Nations International Drug Control Programme (UNDCP) and the International Law Association (India Regional Branch) organized an International Conference on Global Drugs Law. The Conference was inaugurated by the Hon'ble K.R. Narayanan, Vice President, Republic of India and presided over by the Hon'ble Justice A.M. Ahmadi, Chief Justice of India/President, ILI in order to evolve a global drugs law to make the world drug-free; and to carve out a strategy to achieve this objective, with qualitative inputs from experts specializing in various disciplines related to the problem of drug abuse and trafficking. The provisions of the New Delhi Charter on Global Drugs Law were read and accepted in the Closing Ceremony of the International Conference addressed by Hon'ble H.D. Deve Gowda, Prime Minister of India and presided over by Hon'ble Justice A.M. Ahmadi, Chief Justice of India.

The Global Drugs Law envisages the following objectives:

(i) Revamping criminal justice systems to meet the drug challenge. For instance, in systems where the law does not distinguish between the offenders and the victims seeking rehabilitation or treatment, grave injustice may be caused when equal punitive sentences are imposed on both;

(ii) Encouraging the use and effectiveness of mutual legal assistance and other forms of international cooperation; the establishment of national control authorities, trained to administer laws and procedures in a flexible and understandable way, will greatly facilitate effective cooperation; to overcome the obstacles to cooperation that arise from the differences between legal systems, flexible extradition and mutual assistance legislation and practices should be adopted and implemented;

(iii) Overcoming the obstacles to effective cooperation by ensuring that extradition laws facilitate speedy surrender of alleged criminals to face the charges against them in the countries where relevant crimes are committed. This may require the amendment of national laws which do not assist the courts to overcome the differences between legal systems and result in the creation of safe havens;

(iv) Establishing effective methods of depriving drug traffickers of the proceeds of their crimes, both through national laws and through international cooperation to enforce those laws;

(v) Ensuring that drug traffickers and other serious offenders are unable to launder the proceeds of their crimes, by adopting appropriate legal and financial controls and coordinating the efforts of those responsible for implementing them;

(vi) Having specially trained investigators/prosecutors with sufficient expertise, who are able to understand the specific nature of the operations of the drug trade and to successfully counter the ingenious methods adopted by the traffickers;

(vii) Generating universal consciousness of, and determination to battle, the drug problem in all its pervasive forms at the national, regional and international levels; and

(viii) Adopting a balanced approach to deal with this malaise affecting millions of people around the globe, and ensuring the prevention of abuse, treatment and rehabilitation of drug abuse victims, who should be accorded the same decency of life and importance in policy and action as is accorded to other citizens throughout the world.

The New Delhi Charter unanimously adopted by the International Conference reaffirms our faith in human dignity and the human rights of the victims of drug abuse. It is further committed to wage a war on an international scale against the drug menace, illicit trafficking and resultant criminal activities, like money laundering and illicit arms financing. The priority for action centers around the preventive role of nation states and the governments in developing appropriate national strategies to curtail the menace, and optimal measures to strengthen international cooperation.

The Charter recognizes the important role of UNDCP, WHO, the Crime Prevention and Criminal Justice Division and other United Nations entities within their respective mandates in efforts to battle drug abuse and illicit trafficking, and the significant role played by non-governmental organizations.

PART II

Preamble

(1) The Conference reiterates its faith in human dignity and the legitimate aspirations of humankind for a decent and advanced life with moral, humanitarian and spiritual values in a healthy, safe and decent environment, as well as a concern for human suffering, loss of human lives, and social conflicts, especially the impact of this malady on the youth of the world—the reservoir of energy and wealth of countries all over the world have to be viewed in serious perspective.

(2) The Conference, aware of the devastating impact of drugs on humankind and on countries' economic, social, political and cultural structures, and equally on their sovereignty and security, commit ourselves:

(a) to vigorous international actions against the illicit trafficking in drugs as a primary policy guideline;

(b) to strengthen action and achieve cooperation at national, regional and international levels to implement the pragmatic object of a drug free international community.

We unanimously agree on the following:

(1) We urge the governments the world over to accelerate the struggle against the scourge of drugs, and to adopt urgent measures to strengthen international cooperation as well as a balanced, comprehensive and multidisciplinary approach. We emphasize the pivotal role of governments in developing appropriate national strategies in which such objectives can be achieved.

(2) In formulating effective action against drug abuse, illicit production and trafficking, we emphasize the need for the international community to adopt uniform measures within the framework of policy guidelines in major international conventions.

We urge states to allocate appropriate resources for the elimination of illicit production, trafficking and drug abuse, at least to a level to match their publicly expressed political commitments.

(3) As an expression of our commitment, we also agree for the promotion of inter-regional and international cooperation in:

(a) *prevention and reduction of demand*: The initiative in this area must rest with the developed nations, as the bulk of illicit demand for drugs comes from these affluent nations;

(b) *control of supply*: The developing nations must play an important role in curbing the supplies as these nations are the primary production and supply areas;

(c) *suppression of illicit trafficking*;

(d) *treatment and rehabilitation*: Needs to be given more emphasis. The national laws must establish a clear difference between the rights available to an offender and the right of de-addiction and rehabilitation of the victims;

(e) *humane approach towards the victim of drug abuse*.

(4) The nodal agency in each country assigned to carry out the task should be guided by certain general and uniform principles, which may be concretized within the framework of the existing national legislation, with amendments where required, and other such principles drawing inspiration from policy guidelines recommended by the international conventions.

(5) There must exist a comprehensive system for the collection, evaluation and dissemination of data. Such a system may function under the umbrella of the above mentioned nodal agency.

(6) There must also be a comprehensive and effective education program for counteracting drug abuse worldwide. At the national level the appropriate authority should establish a multi-disciplinary unit with which teaching personnel who have received training in the subject of prevention of drug abuse must be associated. The unit should perform the functions of:

(a) prescribing or recommending, at all levels of educational institutions, the development of drug abuse prevention curricula and instructional material, taking into account cultural values, traditions and cultures—emphasizing the benefits of drug free and healthy lifestyles and the devastating effect that the abuse of drugs causes upon the physical, mental and psychological faculties of the individual;

(b) preparing training and educational materials for the unemployed and under educated, and for young people to assist them in developing vocational and self-employment opportunities.

(7) Prevention of drug abuse in the workplace should emphasize deterioration of productivity and performance, defective quality of products, loss of qualified employees, accidents, loss of culture and professional disqualification, all of which are costly to the individual, the employer and the community.

(8) The role of the media is very essential to reach the vast majority of people every day. The contribution of media to the campaign for preventing drug abuse is significant, however, publications and broadcasts can also be damaging and counter-productive and must be checked.

(9) There must be proper enforcement of a system for the international control of narcotic drugs which includes control of cultivation, production, manufacture, use, demand and supply of drugs for licit use and to prevent their diversion into illicit channels and to prevent the laundering of the proceeds from illegal transactions.

(10) The relevant ministries in every country and the national law enforcement agency should understand international treaties and bilateral agreements, to enable them to operate closely with a view to enhancing effectiveness of their law enforcement action to suppress illicit drug trafficking. To achieve this objective they should establish and maintain channels of communication between their respective law enforcement agencies so that information can be exchanged without interruption or delay. This is more important for countries which are not party to international conventions or bilateral treaties providing for extradition. These countries must be made to understand, by means of independent international agencies, the importance of charging drug offenders and extraditing them expeditiously.

(11) It is of utmost importance that there should be an absolute curtailment of the enormous funds generated from the drug trade by means of money laundering. Relevant amendments shall be made by States to their banking laws facilitating disclosure of accounts held by the traffickers and consequent seizures. Financial institutions and banks must develop mechanisms to prevent money laundering by means of scrutinizing large scale money transfers across countries through drafts, telex transfers, and electronic mail.

(12) There is also an emerging need to create a special task force of committed and honest personnel having the sanction of the relevant government agency to infiltrate the networks of drug trade operators and charge them in order to bring them to justice-without risk of prosecution for acts carried out in good faith in pursuit of those duties.

(13) States should determine the types of cases to be dealt within their formal criminal justice system and develop alternative disposal options to handle cases which are not appropriate to be dealt with through that system.

(14) States must also allocate sufficient funds and appoint requisite number of judicial officers to expedite trials of those arrested for drug-related offences. This is urgently required in order to reduce the growing number of prisoners awaiting trial, and to reduce the backlog of pending cases.

(15) Pharmaceutical and drug manufacturing companies across the world must work within the guidelines suggested by international agencies, such as WHO, to maintain uniformity in pharmaceutical manufacturing, and through an appropriate regulatory framework involving prescribing physicians and pharmacists, in order to minimize the misuse of drugs.

(16) The Global Drugs Law accepts the rational use of pharmaceuticals containing narcotic drugs or psychotropic substances for alleviation of severe pain.

(17) Illicit trafficking of drugs generates immense funds, and frequently these funds are used to finance arms trade and international terrorism posing a serious threat to peace and security. Hence narco-terrorism should be dealt with effectively at the international level, with national governments entering into specific agreements to prevent the transfer of funds and smuggling of arms across national boundaries.

(18) We recognize that the fight against serious drug related crime is undermined by corruption, that drug trafficking is facilitated by corruption, and that success in the fight against such crimes depends on success against corruption. We urge that States review the effectiveness of national laws and strategies against corruption and their implementation in relation to drug trafficking and other serious crimes.

Resolved

The participants of the International Conference on Global Drugs Law resolve, in the pious hope that the provisions of the New Delhi Charter will be widely circulated to every national and international organization and to the member states of the United Nations, to accept and implement the above provisions with a strong commitment to make a drug-free future for humankind.

PART VI

ANNEXURES

ANNEXURE 1

INTERNATIONAL ADVISORY COMMITTEE

Hon'ble Mr. Justice Michael Kirby
Judge, High Court of Australia, Canberra, Australia

Professor Lawrence Gostin
School of Law, Georgetown University, Washington D.C., U.S.A.

Professor Barry Rider
Director, Institute of Advanced Legal Studies,
University of London, London, U.K.

Professor Bernard Dickens
Professor of Law, University of Toronto, Toronto, Canada

Dr. Phillip Emafo
International Consultant, Pharmacy Law, Benin City - Benin, Nigeria

Mr. Rick McDonell
Head, Asia Secretariat, Financial Action Task Force, Sydney, Australia

Dr. Norbert Gilmore
Professor of Medicine
McGill Centre for Medicine, Ethics & Law, Montreal, Canada

Ms. Dianne Stafford
Assistant Director, Legal and Constitutional Affairs Division,
Commonwealth Secretariat, London, U.K.

Dr. Eric R. Ram
Director, International Health & International Relations
World Vision International, Geneva, Switzerland

Dr. Clarence J. Dias
President, International Center for Law in Development
New York, N.Y., U.S.A.

Mr. Harman F. Woltring
Director, United Nations Interregional Crime and Justice Research Institute, Rome, Italy

Ms. Vivienne Chin
Secretary General
Commonwealth Magistrates & Judges Association, London, U.K.

Prof. William Gillmore
Head, Department of Public International Law
University of Edinburgh, Edinburgh, U.K.

Mr. David R. Beale
Executive Secretary
Inter-American Drug Abuse Control Commission,
Organization of American States, Washington D.C., U.S.A.

Mr. Marius Stephan
Rechtsanwalt, Berlin, Germany

Dr. Christopher Williams
Global Security Programme, University of Cambridge, Cambridge, U.K.

ANNEXURE 2

ORGANIZING COMMITTEE

President

Hon'ble Mr. Justice A.M. Ahmadi
Chief Justice of India / President,
The Indian Law Institute.

Chairpersons

Hon'ble Mr. Justice J.S. Verma
Judge,
Supreme Court of India,
Treasurer, The Indian Law Institute.

Hon'ble Mr. Ramakant Khalap
Union Minister for Law & Justice.

Mr. Ashok H. Desai
Attorney General of India.

Mr. T.R. Andhyarujina
Solicitor General of India.

Executive Chairmen

Mr. R.K. Anand
Sr. Advocate / Vice President,
The Indian Law Institute.

Mr. P.R. Parekh
Advocate / Organizing Secretary,
International Law Association.
Regional Branch, India.

Vice Chairmen

Hon'ble Mr. Justice B.N. Kirpal
Judge,
Supreme Court of India.

Mr. F.S. Nariman
Senior Advocate,
Supreme Court of India.

Mr. B. Sen
Senior Advocate,
Supreme Court of India.

Mr. Soli J. Sorabjee
Senior Advocate,
Supreme Court of India.

Mr. K.K. Venugopal
Senior Advocate.
Supreme Court of India.

Secretary General

Professor R.K. Nayak

Treasurer

Mr. Rakesh Munjal
Advocate,
Supreme Court of India.

Members

Hon'ble Mr. Justice Ashok A. Desai
Judge,
Bombay High Court.

Hon'ble Mr. Justice Anil Dev Singh
Judge,
Delhi High Court.

Hon'ble Mr. Justice Swatanter Kumar
Judge,
Punjab & Haryana High Court.

Dr. V.K. Agarwal
Secretary,
Ministry of Law & Justice.

Mr. R.K.P. Shankardass
Senior Advocate,
Supreme Court of India.

Mr. A.K. Ganguly
Senior Advocate,
Supreme Court of India.

Mr. Harish Salve
Senior Advocate,
Supreme Court of India.

Dr. A.M. Singhvi
Senior Advocate,
Supreme Court of India.

Dr. S.P. Narang
Secretary,
Institute of Company Secretaries of India.

Mr. S.K. Tandon
Delhi Higher Judicial Service.

Mr. Andrew Wells
Senior Legal Adviser,
UNDCP Headquarters (Austria).

Mr. Koli Kouame
Director a.i.,
UNDCP (India).

Dr. D.C. Jayasuriya
Regional Project Coordinator,
UNDCP (India).

Mr. K.S. Bhati
Registrar,
The Indian Law Institute

ANNEXURE 3

AGENDA

DAY 1: Friday, February 28, 1997

REGISTRATION OF PARTICIPANTS
INAUGURATION AND OFFICIAL OPENING

DAY 2: Saturday, March 1, 1997

PLENARY 1: APPROACHING THE YEAR 2000: THE DRUG SCENE

End of millennium overview: recent developments, patterns and trends at global, regional and national levels
- * drug abuse
- * trafficking and related serious crimes, such as organized crime, money-laundering, corruption, terrorism, etc.

International legal and policy framework
- * the international drug control treaties (1961/72, 1971, 1988)
- * other multilateral instruments, such as United Nations Global Plan of Action, regional conventions (Council of Europe, Council of Arab Ministers, South Asia Association for Regional Cooperation, Economic Community for West African States, Organization of American States, etc.), Commonwealth Schemes, Financial Action Task Forces recommendations, United Nations International Drug Control Programme Memoranda of Understanding, etc.
- * bilateral treaties, arrangements and understandings

The justice system and drug problems: capacity, impact and needs

PLENARY 2: INTERNATIONAL LEGAL COOPERATION AGAINST SERIOUS CRIME

Inter-legal system issues impacting on international legal cooperation
- * extradition
- * mutual legal assistance, including assets forfeiture

* transfer of criminal proceedings
* transfer of prisoners to serve sentences

PANEL DISCUSSIONS: UPGRADING JUSTICE SYSTEM CAPACITY AND IMPROVING INTERNATIONAL LEGAL COOPERATION

Panel I:	Upgrading justice systems to meet the drug challenges beyond the year 2000
Panel II:	Overcoming inter-legal system obstacles to international legal cooperation
Panel III:	Simplifying and expediting extradition
Panel IV	Increasing the use and effectiveness of mutual legal assistance and other forms of international legal cooperation

PLENARY 3: PRESENTATION/DISCUSSION OF REPORTS OF PANEL DISCUSSIONS

PLENARY 4: NATIONAL EXPERIENCE IN IMPLEMENTING DRUG-RELATED LAWS

Strategic overview presentations by selected speakers
Panel discussion

DAY 3: Sunday, March 2, 1997

PLENARY 5: JUSTICE SYSTEM IMPACT ON DRUG PROBLEMS

Criminal justice system process issues

* investigation phase (eg. case selection/development priorities and management; evidence gathering and procedural processes (eg. investigatory powers, arrest, pretrial disposal of seized drugs))
* prosecution phase (eg. guidelines for the exercise of prosecutorial discretion, case priorities and management)
* judicial phase (eg. bail; impact of rules of evidence, including the admissibility of domestic and foreign evidence; pretrial and trial practice, procedure and case management; judicial review of administrative action/inaction); special drugs courts or special procedures for drug related cases; sentencing options, policies and practice; other disposal options (eg. treatment/ rehabilitation measures at any stage of the justice process).

Improving intra and interdisciplinary professionalism, teamwork, co-operation and coordination

* amongst key players in the criminal justice system
* amongst different disciplines/professions typically involved (eg. health care and criminal justice)
* between different legal systems (eg. common-law based and civil law based systems)

Other important problem issues for the justice system

* money laundering and asset forfeiture
* protection of witnesses, prosecutors, magistrates and judges
* cases involving drug users, abusers, addicts or specially vulnerable groups (eg. women, children).
* anti-corruption efforts

PANEL DISCUSSIONS - IMPROVING NATIONAL JUSTICE SYSTEM IMPACT

Panel I: Improving criminal justice system impact against major drug-related crime, reducing justice system process problems; improving intra/inter disciplinary/sectoral teamwork. co-operation and coordination.

Panel II: Making asset forfeiture work-ensuring effective restraint and eventual confiscation of criminally derived or laundered proceeds and instrumentalities.

Panel III: Better dealing with cases involving drug users, abusers, addicts and subgroups at special risk (eg. children, women, HIV-AIDS infected persons)

Panel IV: Reducing the scope, incidence and impact of corruption

DAY 4: Monday, March 3, 1997

PLENARY 6: PRESENTATION AND DISCUSSION OF PANEL DISCUSSION REPORTS

PLENARY 7: ADOPTION OF CONFERENCE RECOMMENDATIONS AND ACTION PLAN

PLENARY 8: CLOSE OF INTERNATIONAL CONFERENCE

ANNEXURE 4

LIST OF DELEGATES

Anthony, P.J.
Manager
The New York Times
56, Janpath
New Delhi 110001
India

Agarwal, Kamlesh
Executive Director
Nangal Devat. Opp.
Export Cargo Complex
IGI Airport, Tr-II
New Delhi 110037
India

Alengaden, Varghese
Director and National
Co-ordinator
Dharma Bharthi National Institute
35, Saket Nagar
Indore, 452 002
M.P., India

Arora, Shyam Lal
H.No. 40, Ward No. 9
Bhatwara
Faridabad Old 121 001
Haryana,
India

Araoz, Julio Cesar
Secretary of the Programme
For the Prevention of the
Drug-Addiction and Control
on Narco-Traffic of Argentina
Buenos Aires, Argentina

Arora, Davender K.
Student of LL.D.
Lucknow University
485/14, Mohan Meakin Road
Daliganj
Lucknow, 226003
U.P., India

Agarwal, Suresh Kumar
Indian Board of Medicine
80, Chowranghee Road
Calcutta, 700001
W.B., India

Allsop, Steve
National Centre for Education
and Training in Addiction
and Visiting Research Fellow
Edith Cowan University
Perth, W.A.
Australia

Agnihotri, Satish Mr.
Advocate & Member, ILI
119, Lawyers Chamber
Supreme Court
New Delhi 110001
India

Amoss, Chhgovanyika
Student [Economics]

Afzal, M
Reader, Faculty of Law
Aligarh Muslim University
Aligarh, 202002
U.P., India

Akhtar, Saleem Justice
Judge Supreme Court of Pakistan
Islamabad, Pakistan

Bardhan Harsh
Additional Director General
Investigation & Registration
Department of Co. Affairs
Government of India
New Delhi
DI/6, Satya Marg
Chanakyapuri
New Delhi 110021
India

Bala, Anandan
Deputy Public Prosecutor
BIK 98 # 15-1896 Bedok
North Ave. 4,
Singapore

Balwada, Praveen
Advocate
L-4, Krishna Marg
C. Scheme
Jaipur, 302015
Rajasthan
India

Bastagli, Francesco
Director, Division for Treaty
Implementation and Policy Development
UNDCP
Austria

Bentur, Nand Kumar
Lecturer
C/o R.V.Bhaangoudar
Venketesh Kripa
SBI Colony
Dharwad
Karnataka, India

Bhattacharya, Sailaja Nanda
6/6/1, T.N. Chatterjee Street
Baranagore, Calcutta 700090
W.B., India

Bolt, Annabelle E.
Head of Customs
International Criminal Division
H.M. Customs and Excise
New Kings Beam House
22 Upper Ground,
London SEI9PJ,
United Kingdom

Bhardwaj, R.N.
Advocate
275 Civil Side
Tis Hazari
Delhi 110054
India

Bhattacharya, Bishwajit
H-1559, Chitranjan Park
New Delhi 110 019
India

Benjamin, Ranjith Nihal
Senior Supdt. of Police
Director, Crime Division
Police Headquarters
Colombo-1
Sri Lanka

Banatwala, M.A.
Advocate, Solicitor & Notary
5th Floor, Reliance Bldg.
269, D.N. Road, Fort
Mumbai, 400020
India

Bauer S.
UNDCP Liaison Office
New York
USA

Brenny, Patrick
Country Programme Adviser
UNAIDS
Red Cross Road
New Delhi 110001
India

Broome, John
Co-Chairman
Asia Money Laundering Symposium
Financial Action Task Force
Asia Secretariat
201 Elizabeth Street
Sydney, NSW 2000
Australia

Biswas, Juthka
Visiting Professor
Bombay University
L-421, Sarita Vihar
New Delhi 110044
India

Boister, Neil
Student
University of Nottingham
Nottingham,
NG 72-RD
United Kingdom

Balakrishnan, K.G. Justice
Judge, High Court of Kerala
Ernakulam, Kochi 682011
Kerala
India

Chatterji, B.
C/o Justice S. Chaterjee
Judge, High Court of Orissa
Cuttack, 753002
Orissa, India

Chatterjee, I.
C/o Justice S. Chatterjee
High Court of Orissa
Cuttack 753002
Orissa, India

Choudhary, Arun Bhaurao
274, Central Bazar Road
Ramdas Peth
Nagpur 440 010
Maharashtra, India

Choutapalli, Raju Suvarna
Law Reader
Nagarjuna University
Plot No. 66A, Road No. 4
Srikanakadurga
Vijaywada, 520004
A.P., India

Choutapalli, Sahu
Ramakumari
Lecturer
M.M. College of Law
Plot No. 66A, Road No. 4
Srikanakadurga
Vijaywada, 520004
A.P., India

Chitnis, Vijay S.
Prof. & Head Dept. of Law
Mumbai University
International Student House
45, C-Rd., Churchgate
Mumbai 400 020
India

Chogle, Shubha Anand
Head of Bio-Chemistry Dept.
Breach Candy Hospital
Mumbai 400026
India

Chingale, Sadanand Narayan
Professor
Plot No.4, Ranjeet Towers
Shaniwar
Karad 415110,
Distt. Satara
Maharastra, India

Conzalez, Edurardo Luis
Director of the Secretariat
of the International Affairs of the
Programme for the Prevention
of the Drug Addiction and Control on
Narco Traffic Argentina
Buenos Aires, Argentina

Chatterji, S. Justice
High Court
Cuttack, 753002
Orissa, India

Curran, Geoffrey M.
University of Michigan
Substance Abuse Research Centre
475 Market Place
Suite D, Box 1649
Ann Arbor, Michigan 48108-1649
USA

Chakrabarty, C.
Member, INCB
A-604, Purvasha Apartment
Anandlok Housing Society
Mayur Vihar Phase-1
Delhi 110091
India

Chappell, Duncan
Former Director of the
Australian Institute of Criminology and
currently Deputy President of the
Administrative Appeals Tribunal
Federal Court Building
Philip Street,
Sydney, Australia

Choudhary, Anoop George
Former Advocate General
"Madhyavart" 7, S.P. Marg
Chanakyapuri, New Delhi 110021
India

Chogle, Mrudula A.
Department of Law
University of Mumbai, Fort
Mumbai 400020
India

Dash, K.C.
Sr. Lecturer in Law
at Kafla Chhak
Cuttak 753002
Orissa, India

Dhawan, Seema
24, Panchsheel, 5th Floor
Veera Desai Road
Andheri
Mumbai 400049
India

Dandu, Gopal
Principal
Sri RKM Law College
Nr. Govt. Hospital
Chittoor 517001
A.P.
India

Dave, Rekha Kanayalal
3, Jagnath Plot "Ritraj"
Nr. Jagnath Aptp.
Rajkot 360001
Gujarat, India

Dutta, Kumar Deo
SDJM Civil Court
East Champaran
Motihari 845401
Bihar, India

Dimri, K.N.
70-7, Chander Nagar
Dehradun 248001
U.P., India

Dayal, Keshav
Sr. Advocate
C-98, Saket, DDA Flats
New Delhi 110 017
India

Dastagir, C.K.M.
Director
Karnataka Welfare Society
Kwality Estate
P.B. No. 28
Chikiballapur 562 101
Karnataka
India

Davis C.
Team Leader
UNAIDS
1, Red Cross Building
Red Cross Road
New Delhi 110001
India

d'Oliveira, J.A.V.S.
Attorney General, Transvaal
Private Bag X300
Pretoria 001
Republic of South Africa

de Speville, B.
de Speville & Associates
55 The Avenue
Richmond, Surrey TW9 ZAL
United Kingdom

Elbe, Frank
German Ambassador to India
Embassy of Germany
Shantipath
New Delhi 110021
India

Farrer, Robin
Asst. Chief Investigation Officer
National Investigation Service
HM Customs and Excise
United Kingdom

Fredericks, Michael E.
U.S. Drug Enforcement Administration
American Embassy
Shantipath
New Delhi 110021
India

Farooqi, M.A.
Additional Registrar
Supreme Court of Pakistan
Islamabad
Pakistan

Fernando, Palitha
Senior State Counsel
Attorney-General's Department
Colombo-12
Sri Lanka

Gupta, C.J.
Advocate
224, Ajmeri Gate
Delhi 110006
India

Gupta, Mohanlal
Executive, Managing Committee
FICCI & FAPCCI
Hyderabad 500027
A.P.
India

Gandhi, Pankaj
Law Teacher
Rangdoot Apartment
IInd Floor, NR. Law College
Surat 395007
Gujarat
India

Ghoshal, Subhra
Student, P.G. Deptt. of Law
Berhampur 760 007
Orissa
India

Gugnani, Anjila
Lecturer and Counsellor
31, Uday Park
New Delhi 110049
India

Ghormade, Vijay N.
Principal, New Law College
Ahmad Nagar, 414001
Maharashtra
India

Gupta, Rajender
6/79, W.E.A. Gurdwara Road
Karol Bagh
New Delhi 110005
India

Ghodse, Hamid
President, INCB and
Professor, University of London
St. George's Hospital
London SW 17 ORE
United Kingdom

Gopal, D.
Principal
Sri R.K.M. Law College
Chittoor 571001
A.P.
India

Gilmore, Norbert
Professor
McGill University
Centre for Medicine, Ethics and Law
Montreal, Quebec
Canada

Hadi, A. Abdul Justice
Judge, High Court of Madras
36-A, Greenways Road
R.A. Puram
Madras 600028
India

Imhasly, Bernard
Bureau Chief
Handles Glatt [German Daily]
C-74, Defence Colony
New Delhi 110024
India

Islamovich, Mamadiyar
Justice
Isabaev
Chairman,
Supreme Court of Kyrgyz Republic
Bishek, Kyrgyz Republic

Jain, Kamla
Professor & H.O.D. [Law]
F-94/23, 1250, Tulsi Nagar
Bhopal, 462003
M.P., India

Jain, Sampat Raj
Professor
78, Nehru Park
Jodhpur, 342001
Rajasthan, India

Jethmalani, Rani Advocate
Chairperson & Trustee
Warlaw Express Building
9-10, Bahadur Shah Zafar Marg
New Delhi 110002
India

Jain, S.K.
Principal, Law College
Ujjain 456 001
M.P., India

Jayasuriya, D.C.
Regional Project Coordinator
Precursor Control Project
UNDCP Regional Office
40 Max Mueller Marg
New Delhi 110003
India

Jost, Patrick
Senior Financial Enforcement Officer,
Strategic & International Programs US
Department of the Treasury Financial
Crimes Enforcement Network
2070 Chain Bridge Road, 2nd Floor
Vienna, VA 22182
USA

Jauhar, D.N.
Reader in Law
Punjab University
Chandigarh 160 014
India

Jayasinghe, Nihal
Deputy Solicitor General
Attorney-General's Department,
Colombo 12
Sri Lanka

Jaramillo, Carmenza
Ambassador of Colombia
Embassy of Colombia
82-D, Malcha Marg
New Delhi 110021
India

Kapur, Swadesh Kumar
Managing Director
510, Swastik Chambers, CST
Road Chembur
Mumbai 400 071
India

Kaushik, V.N.
Professor, Vashaney College
Agra University
Aligarh 202001
U.P., India

Kishore, Kaushal
Lecturer in Law
S.V. College
Aligarh 202002
U.P., India

Kolluru, Rama Brahmam
Lecturer
9-10-15A, Guddikeedhi,
Srikakulam 532001
Karnataka
India

Khan, Bashir Ahmad Justice
Judge, High Court of J&K
Jammu
J & K
India

Karinthayil, Fr. Chacko
Director, Shalom Rehabilitation
Centre Shalom
Chumukedima
Nagaland 797103
India

Ketty, Kumar Manglam
Advocate
30-A R Complex, R.K. Puram
Sector 13
New Delhi 110022
India

Kodagoda, Yasantha
State Counsel
Attorney-General's Department
Colombo 12
Sri Lanka

Kokje, V.S. Justice
Judge, Rajasthan High Court
C-3, P.W.D. Road
Jodhpur 342001
Rajasthan
India

Kumar, Ranjit
Advocate
16, Todarmal Road
New Delhi 110001
India

Kumar, Jayant
Singjami Mathak
Chongtham Leitei
Imphal 795001
India

Kumar, Vineet
Director [Narcotics Control]
Ministry of Finance
Government of India
Dept. of Revenue
Room No. 48-C, North Block
New Delhi 110001
India

Kohli, Chandrika
Student, LL.M
Delhi University
S-301, Greater Kailash
New Delhi 110048
India

Kouame, Koli
Director a.i.
UNDCP Regional Office
40 Max Mueller Marg
New Delhi 110003
India

Kochhar, N.C. Justice
Judge, Rajasthan High Court
A-11, Gandhi Nagar
Jaipur 302015
Rajasthan
India

Kanakaraj, J. Justice
Judge, High Court of Madras
3, Justice Ramanujam Road
Thiruvanmiyur
Madras 600041
India

Kishore, R.R.
Chief Medical Officer
Ministry of Health and
Family Welfare
Government of India
D-11/198, Kidwai Nagar [West]
New Delhi 110049
India

Kunduru, Pavan Kumar Indu
Student LL.M.
Nagarjuna University
5-50-26/1, Brodipet-6/14
Guntur 522001
A.P.
India

Kumar, Krishan
Block-B, 50/2, DDa Flats
Naraina
New Delhi 110028
India

Khan, Fazal Ilahi Justice
Judge
Supreme Court of Pakistan
Islamabad, Pakistan

Maqbool, Ejaz
C-13, Sector 20
Noida 201301
U.P., India

Malhotra, I.J.
Professor of Law
Lal Bahadur Shastri
National Academy of
Administration
Mussorie 248179
U.P., India

Mohile, Girish Nilkanth
Department of Law
Mumbai University
502, Akar Park,
Cooperative Housing Society Ltd.
G.B. Road Charai,
Mumbai Thane 400 601
India

Mohammed, Nashar ABU
Student
P.G. Deptt. of Law
Berhampur University
Berhampur 760 007
Orissa, India

Mohapatra, A.K.
Student LL.M.-II
P.G. Dept. of Law
Berhampur University
Berhampur 760007
Orissa, India

Massaba, K.S.
Director of Public
Prosecutions
Dar es Salaam
Tanzania

Mollen, Milton Justice
Graubard, Mollen & Miller
600 Third Avenue
New York, N.Y. 10016
USA

McDonnel Rick
Head
Asia Secretariat
Financial Action Task Force
201 Elizabeth Street
Sydney, NSW 2000
Australia

Mishra, O.N.
Lecturer, Faculty of Law
J.N. P.G. College,
Lucknow 226003
U.P., India

Mishra, Prafulla
Reader, P.G. Dept. of Law
Utkal University
Bhubaneshwar 760004
Orissa, India

Morje, Mahabaleshwar N.
Advocate & Member of Forum
Against Drugs, Sona Mahal
Marine Drive
Mumbai 400020
India

Malpe, Sudhakar
Advisor
Forum Against Drugs
2, Sona Mahal
143, Marine Drive
Mumbai 400 020
India

Mishra, P.S. Justice
Chief Justice
High Court of A.P.
Ashok Vihar
Road No. 7
Banjara Hills
Hyderabad 500 034
A.P., India

Masilamani, G.
Addl. Solicitor General of India
42-(Y) Block, Anna Nagar
Madras 600040
India

Mehra, L.K.
292 [SFS} Phase IV
Ashok Vihar
New Delhi 110052
India

Michael Patrick
Student, Nottingham
United Kingdom

Mittal, Sunil
S.G., Caring Foundation &
Director, Delhi Psychiatry Centre
B-46, Swastha Vihar
New Delhi 110092
India

Narasimhachari, T.V.S.
Advocate
133, Lawyers Chamber
Supreme Court of India
New Delhi 110001
India

Narayanan, Vijaya L.
D.I.G. Prison
Office of I.G. of Prison
807, Annasalai
Madras 600001
India

Nadagoudar, Suresh
C/o Rajanagoudar Compound
Raddy Colony
Dhanbad 580002
W.B., India

Naik, P.C. Justice
Judge, Orissa High Court
Cuttack, Orissa
India

Nath, Anil
"ADHIKAR"
J-167 Saket
New Delhi 110017
India

Nicholas, Roger
National Centre for Education and Training on Addiction and Visiting Research Fellow
Edith Cowan University
Perth, W.A.
Australia

N.M. De. Wing Commander
Harikuti 444, Sector 9
Faridabad 121006
India

O'Keefe, S.J. Barry
Commissioner,
Independent Commission Against Corruption
191, Cleveland Street,
Redfern
Sydney, NSW 2016
Australia

OTU, EE
Research Scholar
Faculty of Law
Delhi University
A-2/107/1, Safdarjung Enclave
New Delhi 110029
India

Parameshwaran, Subramanyan Lawyer & Consultants
P.B. No. 2477 "Rajarajeswary"
KSN Menon Road, Ernakulam
Kochi 682016
Kerala,
India

Panda, Bhavani Prasad
Reader, P.G. Dept. of Law
Berhampur University
Berhampur 760 007
Orissa
India

Prabhu, Gitanjali Pundlik
Dept. of Law, Mumbai University
General Insurance Bldg.
Ist Floor
232, Dr. D.N. Road
Mumbai 400 001
India

Patnaik, Raghunath
Reader, P.G. Dept. of Law
Utkal University
BBS 751004
Bhubaneswar,
Orissa
India

Panigrahy, P.K.
Student LL.M. II
P.G. Dept. of Law
Berhampur University
Berhampur 202 322
Orissa
India

Pattanaik, S.K.
Student LL.M. II,
P.G. Dept. of Law
Berhampur University
Berhampur 760007
Orissa
India

Plumbly, Derek
International Drugs Coordinator
Foreign and Commonwealth Office
United Kingdom

Prost, Kimberly
Sr. Counsel, Director
International Assistance Group
Department of Justice
239 Wellington St.
Ottawa, Ontario
D1A OH8
Canada

Pati, P.C.
Reader, M.S. Law College
Cuttack 753001
Orissa
India

Patra, R.K. Justice
Judge
Orissa High Court
Cuttack 753001
Orissa
India

Pant, Lokeshwar Singh Justice
Judge
Himachal Pradesh High Court
Shimla 17102
H.P., India

Pereira, J.H.
Managing Trustee
Mt. Carmel's Church
81/A, Chapel Road,
Bandra,
Mumbai, India

Prisquilas, F.R.
Programme Coordinator
CMAI, A-3, Plot No. 2
Janakpuri
New Delhi 110058
India

Pol, Nanette Hulshoff
Concerned Women
20, Amrita Shergill Marg
New Delhi 110003
India

Pati, Bina Pani
Lecturer
Jagat Law College
Jagatsinghpuri
Bhubaneswar 751001
Orissa, India

Panda, Ram Prasad
Principal
Veerjalli Law College
Rajamundry 533103
A.P., India

Raghupathy, Venkataraman
D.G.M. [Excise & Custom]
Indian Oil
Room No. 711, Core-Z
Scope Complex
Lodi Road
New Delhi 110003
India

Rahman, Mahmood
Vice Chancellor,
Aligarh Muslim University
Aligarh 202002
U.P., India

Rao Meena H.
Reader
Dept. of Law
University of Mumbai and
G.C. Member, ILI
14, Sai Amar, Evershine Nagar
Malad [West]
Mumbai 400 064
India

Rao, R.V.
Professor of Law
Andhra University
Vishakhapatnam 530 003
A.P., India

Rao N.S.J.
Profesor & Head
P.G. Deptt. of Law
Berhampur University
Berhampur 760007
Orissa, India

Rothe, V.P.
Deputy Registrar &
Additional District Judge
High Court of Bombay
Nagpur Bench
Nagpur 440002
Maharastra
India

Rao, M.N. Justice
Judge, High Court of A.P.
Hyderabad
A.P., India

Rajgopalchari, K.
Director
Asian Paints [India] Ltd.
Nirmal Tower, 5th Floor
Nariman Point
Mumbai 400021
India

Raheja, Devinder
Head & Prof. Law Faculty
Kurukshetra University
C-547, Ist Floor
Chitranjan Park
New Delhi 110 019
India

Ratnayake C.L.
S.S.P.
Director, Police Narcotics
Bureau
Police Headquarter,
Colombo 1
Sri Lanka

Rath, P.C.
Advisor, Action Group for
Empowerment of the Poor
P.O. Satashankha
Puri 752046
Orissa
India

Rao, R. Venkata
Professor
Faculty of Law & Course
Coordinator
Dr. B.R. Ambedkar College of Law
Andhra University
Vishakhapatnam 530 003
A.P., India

Reynolds, D.D. Graham
Assistant Deputy Attorney General
720 Bay Street
Toronto ONM5G 2KI
Canada

Rodd Robin,
Historian
22 Salamandea St.
Dianella
Western Australia 6059
Australia

Ramakrishna, M. Justice
Chief Justice of J&K High Court
Jammu Wing, Jammu
J & K
India

Srivastava, Mohan Kumar
Reader [P.G. Law Deptt.]
T.H. 9. University Campus
Barkatullah University
Bhopal 462026
M.P.
India

Saxena, Dhani Ram
Professor
Head of Department [Law]
Barkatullah University
Bhopal 462026
M.P., India

Saxena, Hari Sharan
Teacher (PT) UTD [Law]
Barkatullah University
Bhopal 462026
M.P., India

Sharma, Narendra Dutta
Asso. Prof. of Law
University of Rajasthan
48/110, Rajat Patty
Mansarovar
Jaipur 302004
Rajasthan, India

Shankardass, Mala Kapur
Lecturer,
D-79, Defence Colony
New Delhi 110024
India

Saikia, A.H.
Ex-Principal
J.B. Law College
Hedayetpur
Guwahati 781003
Assam, India

Singh, Daljit
Professor & Head,
Department of Law
GNDU, Regional Campus
Jalandhar 144008
Punjab, India

Singh, Gurjeet
Reader in Law
Guru Nanak Dev University
Amritsar 143001
Punjab, India

Saxena, Shobha
Assistant Professor
B-13, Arvind Nagar
Jodhpur 342001
Rajasthan, India

Shah, Ramesh
Joint Secretary,
Ministry of Home
Kathmandu
Nepal

Singh, Niranjan
Divisional Accounts Officer
Water Resources Division
Satna 485001
M.P., India

Sinha, S.K.
A.D.J.
Nalanda at Biharsharif 803111
Bihar
India

Sharma, Navin
Reader of Dept. of Law
Punjabi University
Patiala 147001
Punjab, India

Sankaran, M.V.
Legal Advisor,
Dept. of Atomic Energy
Mumbai 400 039
India

Sharma, B.L.
Reader, Saurashtra University
H-32, Kalkaji
New Delhi 110019
India

Siddiqi, M. Zakaria
Professor
Faculty of Law
Aligarh Muslim University

Aligarh 2022002
U.P.
India

Sebastian, P.D.
Professor in Law
SDM Law College
Mangalore 575001
Karnataka, India

Scott, Michael D. Justice
Fiji High Court Judge
FLRC, P.O. Box 2194
Govt. Buildings
Suva, Fiji

Shastri, Satish C.
Associate Prof. of Law
University of Rajasthan
L-2A, University Campus
Jaipur 302 004
Rajasthan, India

Stafford, Dianne
Commercial Crime Unit
Commonwealth Secretariat
Malborough House
Pall Mall
London SWIY 5HX
United Kingdom

Sharma, S.K.
Professor, Dept. of Sociology
14/3, Chaturvedi Nagar
Bhind, M.P.
India

Shrotriya, V.K.
Head, Dept. of Law
Government M-J.S.
P.G. College
Serothiya Lane, Kila Road
Bhind, M.P.
India

Sircar, V.K.
District Judge
51 Cantt.
Kanpur 208004
U.P., India

Sukumaran, K., Justice
Judge, High Court of Kerala
29, Supreme Enclave
Mayur Vihar-I
New Delhi 110092
India

Sharibu, Z.O., Col
Student
D-321, Defence Colony
New Delhi 110024
India

Sahgal, Mamta
Patiala House Court
F-46, Green Park (Main)
New Delhi 110016
India

Saxena, Yogendra, K.
General Secretary
"AWARE-N-AIDS"
D-16, Delhi Admn. Flats
Timarpur
Delhi 110054
India

Skelemani, P.T.C.
Attorney General
Attorney General's Chambers
Private Bag 009
Gaborone, Botswana

Singhvi, A.M.
Additional Solicitor General
of India
B-8, South Extn. Part II
New Delhi 110049
India

Swami, K.A. Justice
Chief Justice
High Court of Madras
23, Greenways Road
R.A. Puram
Madras 28
India

Srinivasan, M. Justice
Chief Justice, Himachal Pradesh
High Court
Shimla, H.P.
India

Singh, U.P. Justice
Chief Justice
High Court of Kerala
President, Kerala Unit
of ILI
Ernakulam 682011
Kerala, India

Singh, Hira
National Institute of Social Defence
West Block No. I
Wing No. 7
R.K. Puram
New Delhi 110022
India

Sharma, Subhash
Reader
Dept. of Law
GND University
Jalandhar 144001
Punjab, India

Singh, Daljeet
Professor & Head Dept. of Law
GND University
Jalandhar 144001
Punjab, India

Shah, Giriraj
Dy. Commandant General
Home Guards
Jail Road,
Lucknow, U.P.
India

Srinivasan, Nara
Dept. of Justice Studies
Edith Cowan University
Perth, W.A., Australia

Singh, K.K.
Professor Dept. of Physical Medicine
and Rehabilitation
All India Institute of Medical Sciences
Ansari Nagar
New Delhi 110021
India

Singh, Manjit
Concerned Women
D-148, Defence Colony
New Delhi 110024
India

Sahu, P.K.
Chairman, Centre for Youth
and Social Development
A-70 Sahidnagar
Bubneshwar 751001
Orissa, India

Shah, Jayant
President, "CAIM" Society
T-10, Green Park Extn.
New Delhi 110016
India

Sudhir, I.C.
Advocate
Kali Bari Marg
New Delhi 110001
India

Singh, Uma Nath
Advocate, Supreme Court of India
A-27, Gulmohar Park
New Delhi 110049
India

Sinha, R.N.
Narcotics Specialist
U.S. Embassy
Shantipath
New Delhi 110021
India

Shuaibu, Z.O. Colonel
Student
Defence College
D-321, Defence Colony
New Delhi 110024
India

Saxena, R.P. Justice
Judge, High Court of Rajasthan
Jaipur Bench
1/1284, Malviya Nagar
Jaipur 302005
Rajasthan, India

Sarup, Surinder Justice
Judge, High Court of H.P.
Shimla 171002
H.P., India

Shah, Sajjad Ali Justice
Chief Justice of Pakistan
Islamabad, Pakistan

Tiwari, Yogendra Kumar
Asso. Professor of Law
JNU University
Behind Marwah Khadi Sangh
Jodhpur 342001
Rajasthan, India

Tauber, Jeffrey Justice
President
National Association of Drug Court Professionals
901 North Pitt Street
Suite 300, Alexandria
Virgina 22314
USA

Talbot, Kennedy
Barrister
Furnival Chambers
32 Furnival Street
London EC4A 1JQ
United Kingdom

Thapa, Rabi Raj
Director
Drug Advisory Programme
Colombo Plan Secretariat
12 Melbourne Avenue
P.O. Box 596
Colombo 4
Sri Lanka

Taluja, Pradeep Kumar
Management Consultant & Teacher All India Management Association Centre for Management Education
170 Anand Vihar, Pitam Pura
Delhi 110034
India

Tirupati, Annam Rao
Advocate
D/1/176, Lajpat Nagar
New Delhi 110024
India

Verma Sushil Kumar
Professor
Law School, BHU
11, Brahmanand Nagar Extn.
Durgakhand
Varanasi, U.P.
India

Vadodaria, R.R.
Principal
Shri N.S. Patel Law College
Modasa 383315
Gujarat
India

Verma, Anand Kishore
Student Corporate Law, ILI
M.B. 133, Street No. 5
Shakurpur, Delhi 110092
India

Vallance, Peter
Head
Confiscation, Money Laundering
and War Crimes Section
Home Office
United Kingdom

Varshini, D.P. Justice
District & Sessions Judge
Pratapgarh
U.P.
India

Wojcik, Mark E.
Asst, Professor of Law
The John Marshall Law School
315 S. Plymouth Court
Chicago, IL 60604
USA

Wehrli, A.
Chief, Regulatory Support Unit
World Health Organization
1211 Geneva 27
Switzerland

Wells, Andrew
Sr. Legal Adviser
Legal Advisory Group
UNDCP, Vienna International Centre
P.O. Box 500
A-1400 Vienna
Austria

Wildash, James Richard
First Secretary, British High Commission
Chanakyapuri
New Delhi 110021
India

Yadav, Ramchandra D.
Student
Raja Cottage,
Koldongri, Sahar Road
Andheri [E]
Mumbai 69
India

Yoshida, Tokuo
Chief
Regulatory Control Unit
Programme on Substance Abuse
World Health Organization
1211 Geneva 27
Switzerland

Yadav, Shiv Lal
Dept. of PM & R,
All India Institute of Medical Sciences
Ansari Nagar,
New Delhi 110021
India

Zaglio, Angelo
Institute of Hygeine
School of Hygiene and
Preventive Medicine
Policlinico B. Go Rona
Verona City
Italy

INDEX

AIDS 23, 24, 31, 34, 51, 71, 232, 351, 354
Adolescents 162, 414-429
Assets, forfeiture of 308
Attorney General 198, 199, 203

Bribery, evidence of 340

Cannabis 117, 385, 390-394
Child, Convention on the Rights of the 407
Children, drug abuse among 404-411
Civil
    law countries 89, 106
    rights violations 219
Cocaine 117-118
Compensation to victims of violent crimes 60
Confiscation 180-190
Consumerism, rise in 47
Consumption of drugs 47
Co-operation
    forms of 288
    in combating transnational crimes 99-113
    in customs matters 96
    international 99-113, 317
    to combat crimes 89
Controlled delivery 326-328
Corruption 20, 31, 438
    and crime 31
    durg trade and police 329-344
    Independent Commission against 329-337
    Prevention of 334
Council of Europe 59, 90
Crime
    action plan against 29
    against humanity 401
    and corruption 31
    compensation to victims 60
    confiscation of proceeds 108-109
    co-operation to combat 89
    draft code of 400-401
    drug-related 80
    of aggression 401
    of genocide 401
    organised 29, 46, 62, 346, 412-413, 438
    other forms of 399
    prevention 140
    proceeds of 96, 108-109, 125, 190-204
    transnational 29, 99-113
Criminal 60
    exploitation 47
    international court 395-403
    jurisprudence 146
    justice procedures 350
    justice system 28, 137-141, 180, 229-234, 365, 367, 412-413, 425, 427
    legislation 85
    offences 326
    operations 46
    sanctions 245
Cultivation
    of narcotic plants 166
    recent trends and development in illicit 47
Cyberpayments 257-260

Death penalty 18
Deforestation 32
Detention 148, 350
Detoxification 230

Disclosure 182
Discrimination 354

Education, health 226, 351, 371
Employment 351
Epidomiology 209-210
European
 Convention on extradition 59
 Convention on human rights 94, 349
 Council 90
Evidence 100-108, 111, 124, 151
Extradition 59, 63, 91-93, 111-113, 121, 166, 288, 320

Financial Action Task Force 59, 248-250, 281-290, 293-304
Forfeiture 110, 200-201
 assets 308
 fine in lieu of 310
 of property 149, 319
 procedure of 309
 relief of 201-202

Gender analysis 412-413
Gold
 demand for 266
 smuggling in 267
Golden
 Crescent 17, 48, 156
 Triangle 17, 48, 156

HIV 24, 51, 71, 215-216, 218, 232
Harm minimization 370-379, 380-394
Hashish 117-131
Hawala 19, 252, 261-280
Health 35, 69, 78, 370-371
 care 233, 236, 351
 danger to 31
 education 226
 legislation, programme on 349
 mental 415-429
 public 364-366
 right to 240
Herbicides 32
Heroin 118-119
 consumption of 50
 illicit traffic in 152

Human Rights 35, 92, 220, 226, 348-369

Illicit
 cultivation of 48
 drugs 382, 383, 394-395
 drugs demand for 50
 drugs trade 80, 82-87
 drug traffickers prosecution of 395-403
 drug trafficking, victims of 205
 laboratories, detection of 49
 traffic in heroin 152
 traffic, prevention of 148
International Law Commission 399-402
Interpol 85

Jails 168, 178
Judges 169-179, 220, 329

Law
 civil 318
 domestic 318
 enforcement 72, 326, 328
 reform, about drugs 380-394
 to prohibit, the cultivation of narcotic plants 166

Methaqualone 116, 119-121
Money Laundering 20, 29, 46, 63, 110, 180-190, 245-260, 269, 281-290, 291-304, 305-320, 321-325
Multilateral treaties 55
Mutual legal assistance, international 63, 100-105, 114-130, 203

NGOs 24, 410
Narco-terrorism 399-401
Narcotic drugs 21, 32, 40, 53, 131-135, 196, 199, 305
Nationals, non-extradition of 112
New Delhi Charter on Global Drugs Law 433-438

Operation Noah 371
Opiates, medical use of 235-240
Opium 18, 30, 45, 145, 157, 160, 306
Organised Crimes 29, 46, 62, 304

Pain killers, accessibility to 235-240
Prisons 168, 178
Private behaviour 359-364
Prohibition 386
Proof burden of 310
Public
 agreement 367
 health and harm reduction 364-366
 interest 352
 international law 77
 menace 359-364
Prosecutions 333
Punishment 173-174

Receivership 182
Rehabilitation 233, 234, 429
Rights and duties 220
 civil 220
 cultural 220
 Declaration on 220
 International Covenant on 220
 of the child, 407
 social 220

SAARC 40, 165
Search and seizure 101
Smuggling 267, 301
Soil degradation 32
Sustainable development 32

Terrorism 60, 80, 226
Transnational crimes 29, 99-113
Treatment 230-244
Treaty
 based crimes 398-399
 international drug control 45, 235-240
 regime 395

United Nations
 Charter of 397-398
 Commission on Narcotics 35, 240
 Conventions 27, 41, 70, 78, 79, 125, 126, 128, 129, 130, 308, 311, 395-396
 against illicit traffic 246-247, 326
 drug trafficking 70
 progress with accession to 129
 conventions 53-55, 70, 78, 79, 125, 126, 128, 129, 130
 control, legal effect of 57-58
 General Assembly 28, 58, 226
 instruments 165
 model treaty 104
 trusteeship system 222
 1998 Special Session 28, 87

UNDCP 18, 24, 27, 29, 35, 47, 48, 50, 84, 85, 86, 87, 105, 127, 384, 434

WHO 22, 69, 78, 235, 236, 237, 243-244, 349, 434
Water pollution 32
Women 412-413
World Bank 31, 238